QUEER IN AZTLÁN

Chicano Male Recollections of Consciousness and Coming Out

Edited by
Adelaida R. Del Castillo and Gibrán Güido
San Diego State University
University of California, San Diego

academic publishing

Bassim Hamadeh, CEO and Publisher

Michael Simpson, Vice President of Acquisitions

Jamie Giganti, Managing Editor

Jess Busch, Senior Graphic Designer

Seidy Cruz, Acquisitions Editor

Gem Rabanera, Project Editor

Alexa Lucido, Licensing Coordinator

Printed in the United States of America

ISBN: 978-1-62131-807-1(pbk)

Contents

I. Presence

II. Recollections

III. Embodied Self

IV. Coatlicue State

V. Men of Heart

VI. Marifesto: The Black and the Red of Jotería Studies

VII. International Print Sources

*To John Rechy and to the youth, butterfly
warriors, who seek a reflection of self.*

Preface

Adelaida R. Del Castillo and Gibrán Güido

The editors of this anthology first met as participants (professor and graduate student) in the master's program of the Department of Chicana and Chicano Studies at San Diego State University. It was there that we began work on *Queer in Aztlán: Chicano Male Recollections of Consciousness and Coming Out* in the hope of sharing with a general readership a growing consciousness among a largely younger generation of queer Chicanos absent from the plans, political agendas, and literature of Aztlán, the ironic metaphorical homeland of a people in sociopolitical struggle. Even so, dystopia—source of our social justice commitment to a more expansive liberation ethos—allowed us to envision the queer Chicano/Mexicano male as citizen subject and human rights holder among local communities and cultures in US society. It led us to the crafting of a book representing a greater complexity of queer youth identity, sexuality, masculinities, and political activism yet not forgetting the effects of HIV/AIDS, homophobia, sexism, and violence in Mexican and American culture, which still threaten after having already ended innocent lives. The book resists silence, erasure, innuendo, and practices linked to patriarchy, heterosexuality, and homophobia as definitive of Chicano male subjectivity at the turn of the twenty-first century.

Specifically, our intent for *Queer in Aztlán* was to put together a collection of mainly original work by queer Chicanos/Mexicanos that would lend expression to youthful discoveries of sexuality, coming out, and critical moments of identity formation. Capturing the complex and varied experiences of young men coming of age and going on to young adulthood in activist, artistic, literary, and academic fields encouraged us to remain open to the different ways our authors chose to communicate their lived experiences. This lends the collection a candid—and at times, unorthodox—raw quality that may be provocative but crucial to conveying a certain sensibility about queer male sexuality. In addition, the framing of experience through varied and hybrid language use (Standard Spanish, Mexican Spanish, Chicano Spanish, Standard English, slang English, Spanglish, etc.) stresses the significance of cultural identity as part of sexual identity and partly explains our use of the term Chicano/Mexicano (see the Introduction). Our contributors make use of autobiography, essays, recipes, poems, plays, and prayer to evoke new possibilities for being and belonging to more inclusive communities of friends, families, and political allies. Later still, some authors withdrew from the project after they found having to recollect and describe disturbing moments in their lives far too difficult to endure as memories gave way to pain, fear, and anxiety.

To date there is no comparable anthology such as *Queer in Aztlán*, which brings to light notions of diversity and lived experience directly related to class, ethnicity, gender, sexuality, and male queer identity within the context of family and Chicano/Mexicano culture, one of the largest sectors of the Latino population in the United States. The work and personal narratives of a collection such as this on queer male subjectivity and gay consciousness are meant to be accessible to a wide audience to better convey what it means to be a queer male of color in a dominant heterosexual and homophobic society and culture. Lastly, we hope the book encourages current scholarship in Chicana and Chicano studies to expand its conceptualization of the discipline beyond traditional confines of male sexuality and masculinities by including male queer content in course curricula and discourse.

Acknowledgments

We would like to thank the many individuals who helped shepherd this project to its completion. We specially thank our contributors—we are grateful for the trust, compassion, patience, and love that shows in your work and *palabras*, enriching the inspiration for the collection. Your willingness to share your most vulnerable moments with our readers and us serves as a guide for envisioning new possibilities and new beginnings. Omar O. González and Pablo Alvarez kindly took time from their busy writing and teaching schedules to serve as part of our advisory board and meet with us in San Diego and Los Angeles. Thanks also to Rigoberto González, Walter O. Koenig, Rosaura Sanchez, Susan Cayleff, Rodolfo Acuña, and Rosalinda Solorzano for patent, contract, and editorial advice. Walter O. Koenig also took the photographs used in the book. Michael Nava boosted our spirits with his exceptional generosity by allowing us to use material from his unpublished memoirs. Pablo Alvarez made it possible for us to consider the inclusion of works by the late Gil Cuadros and we are indebted to him, Kevin Martin, Terry Wolverton, Robert Blake, and the Gil Cuadros estate for making his unpublished work accessible to us—in particular, the selections "Coming Out" and "Last Supper." We also thank Robert Drake and Terry Wolverton for permission to reprint the poem "Birth" by Gil Cuadros, which appeared in *His 2: Brilliant New Fiction by Gay Writers*. Yosimar Reyes allowed us to reprint *For colored boys who speak softly*. Thanks also to Carlos Manuel for permission to reprint *La Vida Loca*. At Cognella Publishing senior editor Seidy Cruz found our work worthy, shared tea and coffee with us, and marshaled the publication of the book; project editor Sarah Wheeler's great sense of humor made working with the press a pleasure, as did the beautiful work of graphic designer Miguel Macias.

Thanks also to all those who provided counsel, guidance, hope, love, and nurturing, including family members Nazaría Rosa Duarte, Maria Lozano, Omar Guido, Jose Lozano, Elizabeth Lozano, Gina Lozano, Cindy

Lozano, Rosean Moreno, Rosemary Moreno, Adrian Moreno, David-Alexander Moreno Ramirez, Christian Andrew Ramirez, Castiel Samuel Ramirez, Oscar Christopher Eckroad, and Logan Gabriel Amezcua; and to friends who *are* family—Jonathan Lowe, Sergio Sanchez, Vincent Arreguin, Brandy Garcia, Pablo Alvarez, Omar O. González, Inés Hernández-Ávila, Yvette Flores, Adela de la Torre, Sergio de la Mora, Angie Chabram-Dernesesian, Ernesto Martinez, Daniel Enrique Pérez, Michael Nava, Michael Hames-Garcia, Carolina Ramos, Larry Baza, Rosiangela Escamilla, Wendy Aguirre, Alicia Chavez, Francisco Carlos Mendoza, Alicia Valle, Oscar Guerra-Vera, Juan Carlos Espinoza-Cuellar, Yosimar Reyes, Alicia Nunez, Mariela Nunez, Monica Delgadillo, Sara Solaimani, Sherman Lee, Xaime Aceves Equihua, Monica De La Torre, and Roberto Daniel Rodriguez. Thank you also to the Department of Chicana and Chicano Studies at San Diego State University, Latina/o Services at The Center-San Diego LGBT Community, National Association for Chicana and Chicano Studies Joto Caucus, and the Association for Jotería Arts, Activism and Scholarship.

Editors' note: The use of accents on an author's name has been decided by the author's personal preference or previous use in print. Therefore, similar names for different authors may or may not have accents.

Birth

Gil Cuadros

I conjure you, Armisael, angel who governs the womb, that you help this woman and the child in her body.
— Rf. Trachtenberg, *Jewish Magic and Superstition*

I feel it well up inside of me. It grows with every pass of the sun, steals what little energy is left in my beleaguered body. The lesions that spread daily across my testicles and legs now cease to multiply. I sense the formation of an umbilical cord connecting me to another. I am nervous of what it will become and how it will decimate the remnants of my strength. I tell my lover I am carrying a child inside me, demonlike, it drags embryonic nails slowly down my internal organs. Marcus looks skeptical, eyes squint as if thinking, what next, commit me to a home, send me to a spiritual healer. He smolders sage and copal, washes me in their cleansing smoke. He strikes bells to startle me out of my stupefaction but realizes the presence inside me, glides his hand across my stomach, enjoys electricity. With a fit of anger he yells, "How selfish can you be? What if you die before the child is raised?" The neighbors bring sprigs of baby's breath, castor-bean stems, and nail them to our door. The air smells rancid and cloying.

I will name the creature Armisael. The growing fetus confines me on my balcony all hours reciting Psalms. I burn news articles one at a time on the hibachi: the volcanic eruption on modern Pompeii, a killer virus emerging from the rain forest, the increase of rabid coyotes filtering into the hillside communities, feasting on small children.

The strips of newsprint writhe in my hand as they approach the fire like Swedish fortune fish curling inside a palm's heat. I see an indigo gleam radiating from my fingertips; it garners tear-shaped flames, encapsulating the ardor like the many pills I take. They float away into the atmosphere the way soap bubbles defy gravity, lyrical as Ptolemy's music of spheres.

Walking down the boulevards near my home, I expect the community to revere me, to step aside out of deference. Rather, lips snarl, hands move to strike, filthy looks, the kind I imagine Jesus encountered on his trek to Calvary. The women are the harshest, spitting before me, hacking their phlegm deeply and loudly from inside their corpulent bodies. They turn in disgust as if to deny my existence and my child's potential. It is hard to ignore my aspect, my withered limbs seem to negate any fruitfulness. Still the jacaranda trees blanket the sidewalks with their purple flowers for me; the elms canopy the sun's glare, limbs low enough to grab and even cradle me when I tire.

Returning home, I must lie down. Nausea overwhelms me throughout the day. The only thing that helps is placing ice packs underneath my arms and on the back of my neck. My head swims with sounds: the buzz of EMF high-tension lines. Marcus hangs crystal prisms in the bedroom windows and lights cinnamon candles around our bed. He touches me too gently, nuzzling my side. He licks the well of my ear, says I taste bitter. He wants to gather me up tighter, his arm a vice around my waist. He is afraid he will hurt me, cause some deformation to the child.

The child becomes apparent through translucent skin, jade eyes seem conscious, pierce the iridescence of the amniotic sac. My lover thinks he is a lowly Joseph, not important in the scheme of this miracle. I watch him stare off into the horizon, the sunset nearly blinding. In his hand a cigarette burns, smoke coils from his fingers. He worries what kind of parent would he be and sees all his flaws magnified, especially his lack of patience. I desire to comfort him, go down on my knees and press my face next to his crotch. Strongly, he pulls me up, tells me it's a piece of immortality, a part of us will survive after we're gone. I warn him not to become too attached, that there might be a chance the child will catch my disease and die early too. Marcus refuses to hear, says he can already see the changes in the world: the sky becoming gentian, the foliage smaragdine, the land ginger. From where I stand, I see darkness drain the landscape's hue, leave somber details, an industrial fog, thick and noxious.

In my dream, I place the child in a basket and float it down a mighty river. Marcus rages at heaven for what I have done, curses me till the day of his death. The child shall never know his real fathers, or have comfort with the toys we would have made, our faces appearing god-like over his crib. How can an infected man like me be worthy of this blessing?

I do not know if the little one will appear launched from my head, or emerge from the muscles of my legs. But when the moment happens it will be as if a part of me dies. When I release him to the river I will surely crumble to the ground, crying out for Marcus, my body disintegrating into the stuff of protons, neutrons, quarks, shattering back into the dark matter of an unforgiving universe.

Introduction

Queer Chicano Sexuality, Culture, and Consciousness

Adelaida R. Del Castillo and Gibrán Güido

"At the end of 1987, AIDS totally devastated my life; my lover died suddenly, I was diagnosed with the fatal disease and all my 25-year-old aspirations were killed. Out of this hell I found two things: I wanted to write, and I was a survivor. My new life is built on this simple but strong foundation."
Gil Cuadros, *Blood Whispers*, Vol. 1

This book took us on a journey to things past we had not expected. Who knew? We followed an unfamiliar path and were dazzled by a new beauty, life-risking deeds, and piercing ways; a sexual sensibility unknown to many readers—a male one, queer and ethnic, of ancient intensity, direction south to the blue Region of Uncertainty.[1] There ... humming ... lay the Land of Aztlán! Place of arrival and departure, origin and destination, of civil rights promise for a brown people whose ancestors in the Time of Myth traveled south, south of the southwest. For had not the ancients told of Anahuac as the "navel of the earth," green site of equilibrium, portal of change and movement? So we too followed and descended far south as if on a shaman's quest for the life force in all things—leveler of human hubris—that rocks, plants, animals, humans are! Just are. We arrived but found no beginnings or

---

1   According to classic Aztec cosmology of the universe, color, aspect, symbol, and direction are used to represent place and metaphysical significance. See Alfredo López Austin, *Cuerpo humano e ideología: Las concepciones de los antiguos nahuas,* Tomo I (México, D.F.: UNAM, 1990).

origins; somewhere there we came across the printed word on desire already in flux.

Why Queer?

How should we identify Chicano/Mexicano same-sex desire, identity, and culture? Chicana/o political awareness has taught us that terminology matters and that identity categories may communicate much about an aesthetic, awareness, and political consciousness. North of the US-Mexico border same-sex-identified Latinos are embracing terms such as *jotería, joto, jota,* and *mariposa* as well as "poz" (for HIV/AIDS positive status). The English-language terms "gay" and "queer" [2] as in "gay Latino men" or "queer Latino men" are also used by *jotería* in the United States as monikers of identification.

The author John Rechy, to whom the anthology is dedicated, does not easily welcome labels, sexual or otherwise. In the past, he preferred the term "homosexual" for its stress on sexual orientation, but gives the impression he no longer uses it. He also doubts whether "queer" will ever be acceptable to him as descriptive of self, community, or theory; for a person of his generation the word is too closely connected with "hatred and violence." There was also a time when he refused to use the term "gay" for what seemed sheer silliness, possible nineteenth-century association with actresses stigmatized as whores, or its application to cross-dressers.[3] Presently, "gay" is the term he most frequently uses for male same-sex sexuality, possibly due to its popular use in the media of literary criticism.

---

2   For a brief discussion of differences between "gay" and "queer" see David William Foster's Introduction to *El Ambiente Nuestro: Chicano/Latino Homoerotic Writing* (Tempe, AZ: Bilingual Press/Editorial Bilingüe, 2006).
3   Debra Castillo and John Rechy, "Interview: John Rechy," *Diacritics* 25.1 (1995): 113–25, 114.

Today *gay* is often used to refer to a sexual identity, lifestyle, and same-sex erotic preference whereas *queer* can be used as a theoretically charged concept critical of 1) modern fixed and essential notions of sexuality and identity, and 2) a tool for exposing white privilege, middle-class status, and heterosexuality as normalizing agents.[4] In this way **gay** captures a lived experience and **queer** offers a theoretical tool for making sense of that experience. Queer can also be used as a verb as in **"to queer"** a reading, which may involve the interrogation of narrative and textual strategies that hide the crafting of what is represented as normal. Or **"to queer"** can mean to violate the limits of normativity by reassigning it queer values and aesthetics.[5] Some Latinos embrace the term "gay" but not "queer." Others prefer "queer" for the radical and theoretical play it allows, and still others use the terms interchangeably. We prefer **queer** for its *inclination* toward the uncommon, open, political, and unpredictable possibilities.

But labels are troublesome, and David William Foster has warned us about imposing Eurocentric gay perspectives on Latin American same-sex cultural practices, beliefs, and values.[6] His concerns may apply to queer Chicanos in the United States who seem to be embracing terms that resonate cultural aesthetics. Foster, for example, finds the use of foreign terms and sensibilities inapplicable to homoerotic relations in Latin America due to the latter's great cultural, regional, and linguistic diversity as well as differences of class, ethnicity, and race. He is concerned that European and North American cultures of

---

4   Ibid. These notions also can be seen as constructed by specific compromised knowledges linked to regimes of power that help to sustain patriarchy and heteronormativity. Nonetheless, for a critique of queer theory see Michael Hames-García, "Queer Theory Revisited," *Gay Latino Studies: A Critical Reader*, ed. Hames-García and Martínez (Durham, NC: Duke UP, 2011) 19–45.

5   For the use of "queer" as a verb and as a theoretical approach see Sandra K. Soto, *Reading Chican@ Like a Queer: The De-Mastery of Desire* (Austin: U of Texas P, 2010). It is also understood that "queer" applies to LGBTQ sensibilities.

6   David William Foster, "Latin American Literature," *GLBTQ: An Encyclopedia of Gay, Lesbian, Bisexual, Transgender, and Queer Culture* (2002) 9 Jan. 2013 http://www.glbtq.com/literature/latin1_am_lit.html>

a predominantly white, middle-class, and male sort are influencing the gay heritage of Latin America and erasing its differences. Many queer Chicanos and Latin Americans[7] find the label "homosexual" offensive as do *Mexicanos* not only because of its past derogatory use but because it stresses the sexual act over affective relations.[8] Foster also finds that Latin Americans associate the English word "gay" with a foreign ideology and Latin American middle-class privilege, economic status, and consumption of international influences. Undeniably, Latin America's middle classes, through travel, have had greater exposure to international trends of same-sex European and North American sociopolitical and cultural influences. This appears to be the case for Mexico, especially for Mexico City where its same-sex liberation movement began in the early 1970s. Its activists prefer use of the term "gay," fly rainbow flags originating in the United States, celebrate gay pride parades annually, and campaign for and have legalized same-sex marriage in the Federal District. The matter of identity is emergent for queer Latinos in the United States and the making of Jotería studies as an area of gay/queer Latino scholarship seems to be on the horizon, to which this anthology is a contribution.

Over One Hundred Years of Published Work

In an effort to familiarize ourselves with queer Chicano/Mexicano literature we searched through American and Mexican sources and publications to gather a bibliography on queer Chicano and Mexicano sexuality that grew increasingly to some fifty pages.[9] The bibliography can be found in **Section VII** of the anthology.

---

7   Ibid.
8   León Guillermo Gutiérrez, "Sesenta años del cuento mexicano de temática gay," *Anales de Literatura Hispanoamericana* 41 (2012): 277–96.
9   See Section VII of this book.

To our surprise we discovered that publications on homoerotic desire and same-sex sexuality for Mexico alone span more than one hundred years[10] and, except for the decade of 1910, is continuous throughout the decades of the twentieth century, with growing output toward the end of the century and the turn of the twenty-first century. This literature stands in contrast to what we found for same-sex desire and identity for Chicano or Mexican-origin groups in the United States. Although the latter is in need of much research, it is our impression that sources for the United States go back at least sixty years. But Pablo Alvarez is right to call attention to the need for the documentation of a queer Chicano presence through a literary heritage. In "Gil Cuadros' Azt-Land: Documenting a Queer Chicano Literary Heritage," Alvarez relates how at age sixteen he experienced the importance of the published text to cultural self-affirmation and sexuality. Tired of browsing through bookstores, he asks himself, "Will I ever find a queer Chicano writer?" Then something looks promising. "I slid the book out of its slot," he writes, "read the title *City of God* and felt a familiarity with the front cover of the book design ... [candles with the image of] the Sacred Heart of Jesus, like the kind of candles my mother always brought home from the local *carnecería* and kept lit every evening on the kitchen table ... Cuadros' short stories and poetry reflected a reality that I understood." There is no doubt, nonetheless, that the untimely deaths to AIDS of queer Chicano authors such as Arturo Islas, Gil Cuadros, Lionel Cantú, Jr., and others have influenced scholarship and publications to some extent. Even so, there are seroconverted "poz" authors that continue to write, including several who contributed to *Queer in Aztlán*, and we have left to their discretion whether they identify as such.

Both the Mexican and Chicano sources present a variety of approaches linked to narrative fiction, poetry, literary criticism, biography, autobiography, history, journalism, sociology, anthropology, political

---

10   A more exact figure would be 142 years if we agree with Carlos Monsiváis that Mexico's first gay novel was published in the late nineteenth century.

science, demography, psychology, criminal studies, medicine, and theater with much of it listed in the bibliography presented in **Section VII** of the anthology. The wealth of this material as a source for future research and the writing of master theses and doctoral dissertations is promising. For reasons of time and space, we did not segregate the Mexican from the Chicano sources nor did we identify the entries according to disciplinary perspective.

The existence of both the Mexicano and Chicano literature questions traditional cultural impressions and biases, literary myopia, and ignorance that represent queer men of Mexican origin as if deficient of will, identity, voice, or oeuvre for this is clearly not the case.

Queer in Aztlán[11]

The anthology *Queer in Aztlán: Chicano Male Recollections of Consciousness and Coming Out* is about the lived experience of queer desire and identity in culture. It's about youthful discoveries of sexuality, coming out, and the making of identity *en un pueblo sin fronteras*. Who knew that Chicanos and Mexicanos could be queer? These accounts are open and honest, but they can be blunt, and perhaps even offensive, but they won't lie to you. In the work "In Search of My Queer Aztlán" Luis H. Román Garcia relates how home, school, and the patriarchal nationalist movement of the land of Aztlán have treated him and brown queer men; his disgust with matters at hand furiously culminates in "A Big Fuck You!" But he also writes of love and loyalty in a terribly private letter—a child's longing—for his dear mother, now prematurely old, overworked, and dangerously ill.

---

11   This phrase was inspired by Cherríe Moraga's "Queer Aztlán: The Re-formation of the Chicano Tribe," *The Last Generation: Poems and Essays* (Boston: South End, 1993) 145–74.

The authors in this collection speak to the reader about deeply personal and sexual awareness in the context of culture through autobiography, essays, manifestos, recipes, poems, plays, and sacred offerings to ancient aspects of the universe. Their writings depart from a land that once honored other ways of knowing self, of seers and shamans, grandparents who still watch over us. Now Aztlán is a place of varied cultures and language use—Standard Spanish, Mexican Spanish, Chicano Spanish, Rarámuri, Zapotec, Mixtec, Standard English, slang English, Spanglish, and others—whose authors write of being, belonging, and staying alive in a more inclusive community of lovers, friends, family, and political allies. For these reasons queer identity is cultural identity is class identity is sexual identity.

The anthology does not intend to simplify what it means to be a queer or Chicano; some of our authors are of mixed heritage and/or Latinos raised in Mexican barrios. Through the use of different voices, practices, and priorities many of the selections touch on diverse themes such as being the child of immigrant parents; family relationships; grade school experiences; body shape and attractiveness; first awareness of same-sex attraction and first-love interest; making love and having sex; betrayal of trust; physical, emotional, and sexual abuse; fear of family and *raza* (one's people); attempted suicide; sexual identity in the context of cultural identity and/or its denial; religion and spirituality in relation to queer identity formation; contracting and living with HIV/AIDS; poetic expression of pride, pain, and disappointment; and queer political insights, alliances, and activism. We are also aware that an indigenous aesthetic and spiritual insights may frame new ways of being alive and staying alive in twenty-first century Aztlán.

Several of the contributors to the anthology remind us to keep an open mind regarding identity and its fluidity or lack of fixity as does Gibrán Güido in "My Shadow Beast," which evokes an Anzalduan Coatlicue state and nepantla sensibility in the process of becoming self, not quite set or identifiable. Güido discourages misconceptions about the end result of "coming out" as necessarily leading to a gay or queer identity; rather, he presents us with the disruption of a previous sexual identity and the possibility of a new unfolding sexualities. Similarly, Aarón Aguilar-Ramírez in "Maybe Ever Changing" reminds us to be careful in our attempts to essentialize identity: "There are many who can untangle their identities and proclaim a single one ... My identity is still under construction." In the essay "Being Frank," Raul Martin Serrano is aware of the power of fixity in language and of the power of naming to fix and demean the other: "Cocksucker. A lifestyle, a romantic attraction, and intimate sexual acts are reduced to just one word ... because power is built into our language." In Luis Alberto Salazar's "The Gypsy, the Best Friend, and the Mother," the discovery of a queer identity is allowed to emerge layer by layer through the eyes of a gypsy seer, a friend, and a son coming out to his mother.

The anthology is divided into seven sections: **Section I. Presence** affirms queer Chicano identity and celebrates it by presenting the reader with a non-apologetic, entitled stance by authors who have come to know and accept themselves for who they are, and who refuse to ask forgiveness for being true to self as does Luis Alberto Salazar in "The Gypsy, the Best Friend, and the Mother" when he writes "Every fucking morning I wake up ALIVE AND GAY! ... I'm not going to change, not now, not EVER!!!" Even so, the importance of culture remains vital to many of these authors, of which Ernest Doring in "Growing Up Gay and Latino" is very clear: "Being gay is only part of who I am. Just like being Latino, or a man." Rigoberto González, author of the award-winning memoir *Butterfly Boy: Memories of a Chicano Mariposa*, goes so far as to affirm in "The Gay Brown Beret Suite" that " ... it's my ethnic identity that comes first, my sex and sexual orientation follow, though not very far behind." Identity may also emerge through a consciousness-raising epiphany as shared by Carlos Manuel, who comes to the United States while still an inquisitive and precocious youth. In "Immigrant, Maricón, and Mexican, Any Questions?" he uses humor to reveal his failed and cosmetic attempts at heterosexual assimilation and mainstream identity: "I got rid of the color contact lenses, the fake blond hair, and the idea that I needed to be white in order to be perfect. I accepted myself as a brown man, as an immigrant with an accent, as a descendent of the Aztecs, and as a member of the campesinos' force. By the time I graduated college I was a new person, full of life and ready to take on any challenge, gay, straight, and foreign."

In **Section II. Recollections** family relationships emerge as key for many of our authors, especially relationships with mothers, which can be troubled and/or supportive as parents adjust to the lives of their sons. In "Coming Out," published for the first time in this anthology, the late Gil Cuadros shares a mother's vehement reluctance to accept her son's queer sexuality. Cuadros compares the mother's attempts to control her son's sexuality with the stilted control over one's driving by a Driver's Ed instructor. In the end, the son placates and distracts the mother by showing her his newly acquired driver's license—a simulacra of normalcy and laminated self-representation. Roberto Rodriguez's "Chile Relleno" uses a recipe for the Mexican dish of the same name to frame his coming out plans to his friends and mother. It is telling that culture, food, and the reaction and role of mothers during a son's revelation of sexuality are closely associated. In the poem "To our mothers" Xuan Carlos Espinoza-Cuellar and Emmanuelle Neza Leal-Santillan celebrate their mothers' defiance against class oppression, patriarchy, and homophobia; these small brown women of uncommon strength "that not even sickness can fuck with." But when their sons come out to them, they break down "because they knew what we would face." This does not diminish, it only increases their love of their sons …"y luego fuimos a comer pozole together" ("and then we all went for pozole"). Here again food and a son's coming out are closely associated as if to allay emotional strain with culturally familiar sensations.

Another dimension of identity concerns body image and our society's privileging of thin and beautiful over fat and flawed skin as the desired body aesthetic. **Section III. Embodied Self** addresses these and related issues. In "Opulence" Xuan Carlos Espinoza-Cuellar writes of one who hurts himself, pummels, cuts, and scratches his body because it is fat; he speaks to his body as if it were an entity apart, preventing the giving and receiving of love. In "Crevices and Cicatrices" Eddy F. Alvarez reflects on the self as marred by the burden of weight, severe cystic acne, and the emotional and physical scars left on the body. But after encountering much disappointment as an adolescent and young adult, Alvarez brings to light an alternative queer aesthetics of beauty and self-worth rooted in a new body consciousness. The poem "Rain Dance" by Edgar-Arturo Camacho-Gonzalez also visits the body as the metaphorical and physical place of a vital life-giving ritual made possible by same-sex love and consummation between men, but something has gone wrong in Lorenzo Herrera y Lozano's "children of wilted suns" where once life-giving brilliance comes to an end "in pale green hallways."

In her book *Borderlands/La Frontera*, Gloria Anzaldúa constructs the notion of the "Coatlicue State" (derived from the name of an Aztec earth goddess) to convey Aztec notions of the underworld, dissent into the abyss, and emotional stasis from which, she tells us, one can and should try to emerge. In an ancient past, the Aztec underworld was the realm of the dead, but it was also the domain where shamans descended to recuperate the spirits of the lost or afflicted. For Anzaldúa the Coatlicue state represents a realm to which she dangerously descends, hopefully to emerge transcendently creative with the knowledge of the seer. We have titled **Section IV. Coatlicue State** to allow expression of profoundly vulnerable and troubled states. Some provide vivid testimonies of childhood and coming-of-age experiences that are shared here for the first time. A foster child's longing for family and home as the path to love, identity, and support begins Mario Martinez's "Personal Resilience" and follows a trail of unspeakable adversity including childhood sexual abuse, HIV/AIDS infection, and attempted suicide by the time he celebrates his twenty-second birthday. Here also is presented a selection among the unpublished memoirs of Michael Nava, renowned author of the Henry Rios mystery novels, regarding his own preadolescent discovery of homoerotic desire in a homophobic family and school environment that lead the boy Michael to try to end his life. Several of the accounts in this section are framed by Chicano/Mexicano cultural identity amid a homophobic home culture and society that give rise to different forms of violence. The Christian pastoral upbringing of the author of "Still Flaming" has Vincent D. Cervantes "attempting to pray away the gay" and when this fails he submits to a ritual of exorcism, which also proves ineffective. In time Cervantes conceptualizes a new masculinity inspired by Anzaldúa's new mestiza consciousness that integrates his Christian faith, queer sexuality, and Chicano identity.

Section V. Men of Heart is not unlike the selections in section four except that these may be more attentive to interrogating and reconfiguring homoerotic desire and masculinity through verse and prose. Carlos Manuel's play *La Vida Loca* is reproduced in its entirety in this section. He subtitles it "An apolitical in-your-face odyssey of a Mexican immigrant," but it is also a social commentary on both American and Mexican culture by a keen observer with a great sense of humor. Raúl al-qaraz Ochoa in the hybrid text "New Man" (from which we borrowed text for the title of this section) is faced with a situation not many young men must face when he writes: "I don't neatly fit into the meaning of manhood. I feel powerless, suffocating, experiencing things beyond my control. How can I question the expectations of manhood

I have been taught all my life? How many people will I disappoint?" In "On Reclaiming Machismo" Xuan Carlos Espinoza-Cuellar writes of the need to end machismo's cultural privilege to batter women and gay men, the power of a husband to abuse his wife, or the right of a brother to assault his gay sibling: "Brothers need to cry too / Let their anguish out through their eyes / Instead of living skin / Instead of wounded flesh." And, lastly, the selection "Coming Out" by poet Yosimar Reyes points to the cultural and political differences of "coming out" for Mexican youth when he writes: "Brown boys don't come out of a closet like other boys do ... We jump borders, break chains, break systems; we escape jails, we run, we hide. We don't come of closets."

For several of our authors, coming-out experiences have shaped their commitment to queer identity and issues that have helped to transform their work as Chicano scholars and community activists. In "Out in the Field: Mariposas and Chicana/o Studies" Daniel Enrique Pérez tells how his university undergraduate experience resulted in self-affirmation and validation as a queer of color: "Chicana and Chicano authors taught me how to love myself and how to accept every aspect of my identity." Pérez delights in the discipline's subject matter and describes how he "devoured all the books I could get my hands on that confirmed that there were others who shared a history and an identity with me. The experience was so transformative that I decided to dedicate the rest of my life to the field." Importantly, he and other queer Chicanos acknowledge the work of Chicana lesbian feminists Gloria Anzaldúa and Cherríe Moraga as invaluable to their sexual and cultural self-awareness and acceptance.

Queer Chicanos have also learned to make their way through social, cultural, and political structures and sexual borderlands even as they express loyalty to a civil rights movement that doesn't embrace them, families that abandon or are ashamed of them, and an LGBTQ community that exploits and marginalizes them. In addition, as the media begin to address the issue of teen suicides we must ask how many of our queer Chicano youth have faced the decision to take their lives? How many of their stories will never be told, shared, or welcomed by their families, friends, and community because of homophobia, patriarchy, sexism, and self harm? If the deaths of queer youth tell us anything, they tell us of the need to embrace our youth, share their stories, and begin to create a space where queer Chicano men can heal by breaking the silence of their lived experiences. We hope the anthology may serve to inform and encourage dialogue about Chicano queer sexuality and aesthetics within diverse communities. Challenges and contradictions such as the above represent important steps toward the development of a queer oppositional consciousness expressed in **Section VI. Marifesto: The Red and the Black of Jotería Studies**. Gibrán coins the Spanglish term "marifesto" from the English "manifesto" by inserting the first two syllables of the word "mariposa," which is Mexican Standard Spanish for "butterfly" or Mexican Spanish slang for "queer." Also, the section's subtitle brings to mind an Aztec writing method known as *difrasismo* where two nouns linked by a conjunction are used to create a novel concept.[12] In this way the phrase "the red and the black" tells of a *jota/joto* aesthetics unfolding through "wisdom and writing." This section reaffirms the unrepentant stance of the first section of the anthology but goes a step further by framing a political program for queer Chicano activism. In "Mapping New Directions for a Radical Jotería Agenda" Omar O. González gives expression to a *jota/joto* ethos for queer Xicana/o[13] subjectivity, identifies topics and issues

---

12   Miguel León-Portilla, *Aztec Thought and Culture* (Norman, OK: U of Oklahoma P, 1963).
13   González uses the "X" instead of the "Ch" in the word "Chicana/o" to signify a decolonial status.

of concern for Jotería studies, and articulates a political agenda for queer Xicana/o identity, culture, and activism.[14]

Many of the selections in the anthology evoke an indigenous past that honors the mystical and shamanic worldviews of past ancestors. Poet Yosimar Reyes reminds us that life and the dual nature of sexuality are sacred. In "For colored boys who speak softly" (recalling Ntozake Shange's poem), he writes: "That / Centuries ago / We were / Shamans and Healers / Gifted Warriors / Two-Spirited People / Highly respected by villagers." In "Shihuahua" poet Lorenzo Herrera y Lozano embodies indigeneity: "I am a child of the corn / I come from valleys far / from the land where people were / created from clay." Omar O. González too begins his life history by honoring his *antepasados* (ancestors) in "Constructing an Ofrenda of My Memory": "I am drawn toward the sacred site. The ocean's rhythmic hum is a comforting yet insufficient replacement for the haunting desert of the Southwest. I search for the antepasados and humbly request direction."

Lastly, we draw attention to the lived experience of HIV/AIDS among Latino gay men, of which the statistics suggest a state of urgency.[15] Our authors tell us their families fear for their sons when they learn of their same-sex attraction. Parents dread their sons will be hurt physically for being gay and/or will contract HIV/AIDS and die. Several of the anthology's authors are HIV/AIDS positive and some openly address the impact of the disease on their bodies and its significance in their lives. Omar O. González writes: "As I offer my communion of ingesting my own regimen in memory of those like Kramer who forced our government into action, I offer the memory of my own life to those who have recently seroconverted, to hope and dream of a cure and for a world without HIV."

---

14   First presented in October 2010 at the 3rd National Association for Chicana and Chicano Studies (NACCS) Jotería Conference held in Eugene, Oregon.

15   See Kurt C. Organista, ed., *HIV Prevention with Latinos: Theory, Research, and Practice* (New York: Oxford UP, 2012).

Others such as Gil Cuadros have left us moving accounts of their experiences with the disease. His poem "Last Supper" (also first published here) evokes a biblical punishment, surely an end to life, due to homoerotic pleasure and the lovers' mistaken belief that "the body [was] safe in nature." The beauty and power of this poet's work led us to open the anthology with a piece by him titled "Birth" because of its of sexual duality and astonishing creative force in the face of the author's impending death. Cuadros begins by presenting the reader with a troubled procreational project: a pregnant male who is infected with a deadly disease is nearing gestation. This is at once strange and dangerous and yet hopeful and promising of new possibilities despite, or perhaps because of, what appears to be a suspension of male/female human biology and the finality of death. In the end we are left to anticipate that something extraordinary but long awaited is at hand.

Section I

Presence

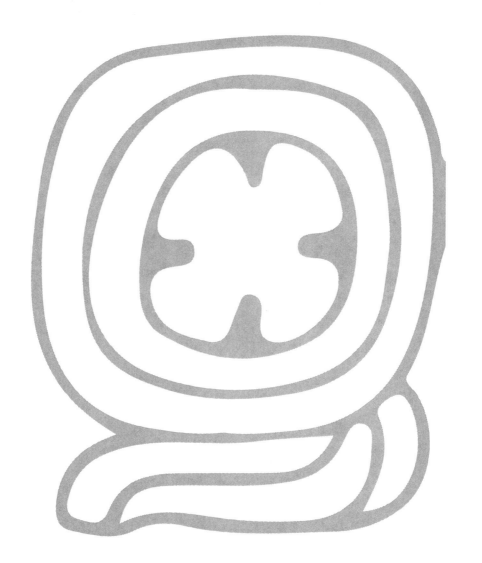

For colored boys who speak softly

Yosimar Reyes

For colored boys who speak softly,
I would build a stage on top of the world
Give them a microphone and let them free flow
Because they too have something to say
And this is more than rainbows coloring our face

This is broken spirits speaking for a better day
So in the tenderness of our words we carry blades
To cut ourselves free from gender roles
Build a life free from social norms
Redefine humanity and sexuality through our own terms ...

For colored boys who speak softly
I would sacrifice my tongue
Make an offering to the Gods
Pray to them to wash my mouth clean
'Cause boys like us
Should never taste cum
And men should never lie with men
Because this is a crime punishable by death
And it is in this very same dark silence that many of us rest
Left bruised and dead

For those who speak softly
I would crucify myself like Christ
Let my blood purify and sanctify these words
Create a doctrine and go knocking door to door
Letting the people know
That the messiahs are here
That we are all messengers
Although, we embody the word queer

That we are a reminder
Of how colonization has destroyed *NUESTRA CULTURA*
They Burned our Villages, *NUESTROS PUEBLOS*

Implemented Homophobia, Sexism, and Machismo
En las cabezas de nuestros abuelos
Brainwashed our ancestors into believing
That boys like us are a manifestation of the devil

For colored boys who speak softly
I will remind the world
That
Centuries ago
We were
Shamans and Healers
Gifted warriors
Two-Spirited People
Highly respected by villagers

And now we've become
Nothing more than FAGS and QUEERS
Making ourselves believe
That capitalism will solve our issues

For colored boys
I will clothe and Cover
Every naked body
Used to represent our community
Because not all of us were taken into consideration
When they developed our identity
Telling us we should act like this
Exploit our sexuality
Rather than embrace our divinity

For those who speak softly
I will recognize
That there is more than one wound to heal
More than one struggle that we feel
But this ignorance
Blocks us from seeing the bigger picture
The greater evil

And these same issues
Transcend Borders
Because
Brothers and sisters
In Oaxaca
In Chiapas
In the Philippines
In Iraq
Are resisting
This very same system

For those who speak softly
I would slit my throat
Let this truth be proof
Of my loyalty

Make human dignity a priority
Because all of us are part of a deeper history

We are NOT what you call "immigrants"
We are People who live in poverty
We fail to assimilate
And continue
To fight racist policies

For colored boys
I will remind my people
Que somos diferente
Que Somos gente
Con cultura
Con orgullo
Con poder

We are people and with the people we stand
Breaking borders and stereotypes
Fighting
Systems
Like the one that exploited our hands

For colored boys who speak softly

I will die in silence knowing
That the beauty in our color
Stands defiant to a racist, sexist, and homophobic GOVERNMENT!

Shihuahua, the place from which I write

Lorenzo Herrera y Lozano

I am a child of the corn
I come from valleys far
from the land where people were
created from clay

Yo soy fruto del desierto, a drop of sweat from the branch of a mesquite, a son of sierra miners and of desert farmers. Birthed in the once-orchard filled valley of San José, California, trained in the hot pecan groves of Eastern Aztlán, known also as Tejas.

I am a trampled seed
pedacito de elote
stepped on and stabbed by the sons of my white fathers
inevitably sprung and cast aside by the crushing
of my mother's womb

My father has always said we do not belong in California; we belong in Shihuahua. Sí, in Shihuahua. A place where, as layers of caliche, decades upon decades contain piles of structural, cultural, financial, educational, and, of course, religious practices carving in stone that Tarahumara's do not belong. A place where not even the chastising whip of the white tongue que es el español, can strip our lips from the Rarámuri etched onto the woven cords of our throats.

There is nothing mythical about Shihuahua, about the tree with a sign saying "Aquí murió Pancho Villa." There is no mythology in the voices of children running up and down the overcrowded streets of Parral, extending their hands and whispering in a coy and angry voice: "Kórima." Children who will never see the inside of a classroom, whose parents will never be employed by the white-only industry of the region; children who will pee on the tree crippled by the wreckage of a car carrying the dying body of Pancho Villa. Shihuahua is not a land of a past that those of us carrying the foreign scar of lighter skin are trying to forget.

I am the manifestation of an occupied land
the rivers of my veins
invaded
by a plague as dangerous
as men determining the reproductive rights of
my sisters
as harmful
as the four religions that raped
my soul

I am a Xicano, sí, with an X. This indigenously birthed brown body is the land on which I build bonitas fincas de adobe. Casitas that house the memory of stampedes of mining companies drilling and exploding all that stood in their way, leaving behind ruble, vestiges of a land who will not forget. My body is not separate from the arid terrain of Shihuahua. The topographic maps of mi tierra mark the high mountaintops of my curves, rising violently from the fluctuating valley of my back. My body is not separate from Shihuahua. On me, brown men go in search for berries, buscando liebres, building fires, building home.

I am a queer Xicano, sí, un joto. This indigenously birthed brown body carries the rivers that rip and roar through the arid valleys of farmland, of communities of hope, of kindergarten playgrounds. My veins, too, carry the plague of disease, of toxic waste, of bodies that will never be named, of bodies that will never be missed. My body is not separate from Shihuahua. My veins are extensions of el Río Parral, growing angry and large as it is fed by the sudden storms of August. As this river I swam in naked as a child, my veins will never be cleansed. Even as the still-ness of clear water spring currents welcomes you, even as the dormant undetectable viral loads of my desire call to you, we are not clean.

I am of a rising people
gente con piel de nixtamal
lengua de huisache
manos de surco
y ojos de lechuza

I am Antonia's grandson, waking at 4:00 a.m. to grind the corn of the one inch-thick tortillas that will feed us during winter, the poorest months of the year. I rise at 4:00 a.m. to grind a keyboard with the memories that will fill the quarter-inch books you might read during the poorest months of your solitude. I am Antonia's grandson, feeding wood into the fire of a stove of steel tight enough to hide the smoke, strong enough to hold the flames. I am the steel stove whose lips are no longer tight enough to hide the smoke of racism, of misogyny, of hope for a world where children run free; I am not strong enough to hold the flames. I am Antonia's grandson, sinking her raw fingers into the steaming hot masa of tortillas to lather them with chunks of year-old butter. I sink my raw fingers into the steaming hot masa of men to lather them with chunks of thirty-one-year-old love.

I am my mother's son
fed by her brown breasts
carried in her dark arms
protected by her black eyes
I am her only son

Como siembra de temporal, my parents were unsure if they were to birth children. As farmers who pray to the heavens in hopes that rain might descend with the coming season, and make way for the frail sprouts of a bean pod, mis padres prayed to San Lorenzo that, after two miscarriages, a child might be born. Yo soy frijol de temporal. I am the frail sprout that the April rain made way for. My body is not separate from Shihuahua. As the omnipresent god of the Christians, where I am, Shihuahua is.

In the pale and unwelcoming hallways of the academy, I am a minero. In the oxymoronic board rooms of nonprofit organizations, yo soy campesino. On the beating dance floors of the Castro, I am a matachín. Yo soy un poeta.

> *I am what the white picket fence*
> *meant to keep out*
> *I am in*

While my Rarámuri brother continues to fiercely run through the never-ending canyons of la Sierra Tarahumara, this Rarámuri walks quietly through the never-ending desert of blank pages. As the veredas, the trails, we followed on our way into las labores, the farmland, I continue to follow the pathways forged by my ancestors. Shihuahua is a place of bones, of untold burial grounds left by la Revolución. A place of bones, where my ancestors lay buried under all-telling pecan trees that once gave shade to enslaving landowners, and today give shade to tired farmers. My body is not separate from Shihuahua, the place from which I write. My body is a place of bones, the land on which I write.

The Gypsy, the Best Friend and the Mother

Luis Alberto Salazar

 The fortune teller, in her late twenties, had full round cheeks and flowing red hair and was wearing dangly gold earrings along with a dark blue bandana sprinkled with yellow crescent moons and assorted stars. She looked like an extra out of a Lon Chaney Jr. movie, and she was about to tell me about my future. The Gypsy asked for my palm; she examined it briefly before promptly declaring, "You're gay."

Distracted by the clinking of her earrings I stupidly asked, "What?"

"You're gay," she repeated, plainly and clearly.

Refusing reality as though it were a drunken whore flinging herself at me, I questioned again, "What?"

"You're gay?" Now doubting her own gift.

"Excuse me, I don't think I heard you." Hoping she was using flapper terminology from the roaring twenties.

"You ARE gay, right?" Now, even she was unsure if she'd just insulted a straight man. I sat up, "I'm sorry, what did you say?" reeling from the psychic blow she'd just delivered. Doubt crept into her voice and showed up on her face. "Are you gay?" She asked point blank. An anemic "Uh, yeah" was all I could produce, not sure what I'd just admitted to, but images of shirtless men on the dance floor, writhing to the latest screeching diva over an insistent bass line, un sinh, un sinh, un sinh, un sinh, un sinh, dominated my mind's eye.

Having received confirmation of her initial psychic impression she happily continued while I stared off into nothingness, my face frozen in a visible question mark. I wondered how she could've known something I'd hidden so well, for so long, from so many. Yet there I was, on a stifling summer night, sitting inside a tent at the county fair, the smell of hay, corndogs, and cowshit wafting in, reminding me of where I was and how I needed to come back to reality. The Gypsy spouted other things concerning my future, but they paled in comparison to what had just occurred. And then the panic set in!

I was terrified. I'd just admitted my most potentially damaging secret, to a woman dressed as a movie extra! WHAT THE FUCK?!!! What's worse was that she so easily identified my sexual orientation and presented it to me, as though it were a cancerous tumor and she was some sort of surgeon who had recognized my condition instantly and excised it quickly without my permission in order to save my life. Could others tell so readily? I won't lie, I felt violated and at the same time relieved. The burden I'd carried with me all these years was suddenly being shared. Now what? The rest of my adventure at the county fair that year is a bit of a blur, but I do remember walking out of the tent and being greeted by my friend Boo. I'd completely forgotten he had been waiting for me outside.

Boo was an unassuming soul, good looking, well-natured and intentioned, and that sometimes left people with the impression that he was dumber than a box of rocks, but what he lacked in academic acumen, he more than made up in how he related to people and how he cared for them. Boo inquired about my palm reading session and I scrambled for a plausible answer, "Uh ... just stuff, you know, stuff."

Boo pressed for details, noting that "stuff" wasn't really worth a ten-dollar palm reading session.

"I don't know dude, she just said I was gonna be a dad with like three kids and I'd be famous and some shit and that I was good at working with my hands." I wondered if in that last part she was referring to me giving excellent hand-jobs in the back seats of cars. Of course I omitted the salient part about my being gay and how she was the first person I'd ever admitted it to.

Boo seemed satiated with the bits of information I fed him, but even he could tell something wasn't quite right.

I glossed over further questions posed by Boo, and he eventually gave up. We proceeded to wander around the fair, checking out the animals, snacking on corndogs, and laughing the day away. We covered the fair grounds at least twice, and the entire time I wondered if anyone could tell I'd been outed earlier. It didn't matter; my secret had been spoken aloud and there wasn't any turning back, at least in my mind. The question was, who would be the next person I'd speak to about this, and how would they react?

Being a sixteen-year-old living in a rural, mostly Latino, socially conservative but agriculturally rich desert valley, I had developed an ardent reputation for outrageousness and saying socially inappropriate things, or voicing thoughts many were thinking but were reluctant to say. I guess every town needs one, and I was more than happy to oblige. At the time, I relished my role as the town's Greek chorus, rather than that of the village idiot. I was constantly linked to friends and acquaintances via rumor and innuendo, and it didn't matter if it concerned a woman, a man, or a friend from school. If I was seen out and about with them, then people were talking, and for whatever reason, there was always an undertone of sex and sexuality embellishing the gossip. I was amused by the talk—hell, even flattered—but surprised because I thought my life was boring. I really wasn't having much sex, I hadn't had alcohol at the time, and I wasn't smoking or doing any drugs, and yet people thought I was some out-of-control party animal. My antics, real or imagined, kept the locals entertained in our sleepy little town.

One week later: I was hanging out with my best friend, David, in his front yard. David was the kind of guy who, when he walked into a room, made people sit up and take notice. He was highly intelligent, funny, dynamic, and excelled at every sport, seemingly effortlessly. He had one of the most beautiful singing voices I had ever heard, and everyone would marvel at the ability of his gift to induce goose bumps and convey such depth of emotion. As if God hadn't granted nearly enough to this individual, David happened to be blessed with a handsome face and a body borne out of rigorous workouts and striving for excellence. Well, it didn't go unnoticed by the many girls who swooned every day as he'd pass them in the halls at school, or by the insecure straight guys who were envious of his six-pack abs and general social and genetic standing. There was no denying that the guy had it all, and yet for the most part, he was a nice guy and not just a nice guy to everyone, but a nice guy to me—to me! Man, I felt like the luckiest sonofabitch in my hometown. It was as though I had an opportunity to hang out with a rockstar behind the scenes, but I could also sincerely call him my friend.

We had just returned from grabbing a bite to eat, or watching a movie, or something when the subject of George Michael came up. We stood there in his front lawn, the sun going down as David wondered aloud as to why George Michael would choose to be gay; since he was so good looking and famous that he could have any girl he wanted, it didn't make sense!

I laughed and said something to the effect that it clearly was not a choice, since no one in their right mind would ever choose to be ostracized, hated, and ridiculed. David continued, stating that it WAS a choice, and argued his case. I stood there, in disbelief, examining his face, searching for compassion, but finding other things I'd never known from him: anger, some fear, perhaps disgust. I could feel the anger welling up inside me as he unknowingly wounded me; it didn't help that I was being eaten alive by mosquitoes, yet their bites weren't nearly as painful as the unintentional barbs being slung my way by my best friend. I was psychically bleeding out right in front of him, and he was completely and thoroughly unaware.

Should I say something now, I wondered. This would be a perfect opportunity to show him how ignorant he truly is, something out of a movie. To disclose or not to disclose—the dilemma weighed me down like a loaded backpack as I attempted to navigate this philosophical divide. In the end we agreed to disagree, but for me this was a milestone in our friendship; I had decided it was a turning point in my life. I chose not to disclose, and I was disappointed in myself. Here, the outspoken guy all of a sudden couldn't find it within him to confront bigotry or ignorance when it mattered most. I decided to go home, tail between my legs and anger in tow.

I lived close enough to David's house that it took a short five-minute walk to travel from his house to mine. In the time it took me to get home, the small sparks of anger that had begun during my conversation with David had become a raging, seething inferno. I decided I would confront ignorance from now on, whether it meant the cost of my friendship or something more. I was hoping my mom would be home, because I would let her have it. I would present her with the truth and maybe an ultimatum.

Now, keep in my mind, I was an only child, living in a single-parent home. My mother was born in Arizona, and at the age of three her mother died. Her father was unable to care for her and her five older siblings (two sisters and three brothers), and they were shipped off to Mexico to be raised by aunts. By all accounts the time spent with these aunts was harrowing at best; it would be an understatement to say the children were abused and harangued, and they were eventually sent off to a Catholic orphanage. In her twenties, my mother moved to California and worked as a migrant worker in the fields; she did so until she became pregnant with me at the tender age of thirty-nine. So my mom knew of pain and loss, and yet she always had such a positive, optimistic disposition. I always wondered how she did it.

At any rate, once I arrived at my place, I flung the door open and found my mom sitting down, relaxed and sewing. She looked up from her project and smiled, and then I let loose.

"Listen here lady! I'm sick and tired of people in this goddamn world thinking people who are gay have chosen to be this way. I didn't ask to be born this way; in fact, ever since I realized in fourth grade that I was gay and discovered there was a name for it, I have prayed to God on a nightly basis to either turn me straight or kill me in my sleep, and guess what? Every fucking morning I wake up ALIVE AND GAY! I didn't want this. I DIDN'T CHOOSE THIS! I don't want to be hated by the people I love, for something I had no control over! And I would love for you to be a part of my life for the rest of my life, but if you don't want to, that's fine too. I just need to know what you're going to do and what you're going to choose, because I'm not going to change, not now, not EVER!!! But I need to know if you're going to be a part of my life, or not, so I can plan accordingly! But you gotta tell me and you gotta tell me now!"

My mother remained silent for what seemed like an eternity, put her sewing project down, and said, "Luis, you're my only son. I love you. Nothing's going to change."

And with those few words of love and kindness, she quelled the raging storm inside me. She effectively took all the wind out of my sails. Now what battle did I have to fight?

"Well, good! Thank you. I'm going to my room."

Not much else was said about that particular subject for about a year and a half. I'd moved out of my little hometown and into San Diego, to begin my year-long stint in AmeriCorps*National Civilian Community Corps, or NCCC, revitalizing communities and working on education and environmental projects. The years spent at AmeriCorps*NCCC were some of the best years of my life. I had an opportunity to come out to many people there and be accepted. Then, in my first year away, I received a card from my mother, a few days before my birthday. In part, it read, "Son, it's been difficult to find the exact words to express how proud I am of you and who you've become, but this card is exactly what I'd been searching for! You're my hero and I will always love you, just the way you are. Your mom who loves you very much, Sara."

In the years since her passing, I've come to realize how remarkable a woman she truly was and that she showed me the blueprint for how to deal with others, especially when they're hurting and raging against the world.

Thank you, mami.

Growing Up Gay and Latino

Ernest Doring

Although fate presents the circumstances, how you react depends on your character.

Anonymous

Introduction

From the onset, let me say that I never fought my fate. I did not challenge my culture or my sexual identity; I worked with and embraced them. I never expressed guilt or felt remorse over who I was, partly because of what my parents taught me. From my father, I learned how to work with the system (society): work hard and obey. From my mother, I learned what to do when society failed you: fight to protect yourself and be proud of who you are. Combined, these lessons help make me what I am today—that is my fate. By the way, my excessive use of "fate" doesn't imply defeat or compromise; rather, what it means to me focuses more on the "Anonymous" quote above—my fate rests with how I react.

You may agree or disagree with the contents of this paper. This may not be your experience, but it is mine. If there is something to gain from my experience, embrace it; if not, walk away. We all have choices. As gay brothers and sisters, we are enjoying the fruits of the battles fought so valiantly by those of years past. Let us pass it on to the next generations.

Background

I was ten years old when Cesar Chavez pronounced "¡Sí se puede!" in Phoenix, Arizona. But words are meaningless if action is not taken. Obviously, at age ten I had no clue what taking action was or meant. I relied on observing my parents' actions and hearing their viewpoints. As both were immigrants, I was fortunate to have three cultures to guide my formative years: my mother's culture from El Salvador, my father's from Germany, and the one I learned in school and on the streets—American (US).

My parents married young, and I wonder today whether they had the choice of learning who they were first before marrying and having children. Both were twenty-one when they married and twenty-two when they had my sister. I wonder aloud how good their English was at the time. Who knows what those first awkward moments were for them. My mother had somewhat of an advantage to address these awkward moments—three siblings and several aunts lived close when she moved to San Francisco. My father had no one in his immediate family nearby—no one to share fears, anxiety, joys, or successes. Unfortunately, his parents died shortly after he moved to the United States. But it was the late fifties, and regardless of whether you had fears or not, no one gave a damn. It was survival of the fittest. There was no assistance or aid. You made it or you didn't. Resilience, self-determination, and work were the mantra of the day!

I recall my father telling me that when he first arrived in the United States, he fought with the ignorant who believed that because he was a German, he was therefore a Nazi. But there is something more significant about what my father shared with me. When I was young, he asked me whether I had ever smelled people burning. This was a common experience for him when he was growing up in Berlin, Germany. He was seven when WWII was over, and living in the capital of the Third Reich prior to the war ending meant daily bombings, rape, starvation, death, and carnage. After responding that I had never smelled people burning, he said, "that no matter what you do in life, make sure that it never happens again!" Through no fault of his own, this was my father's early experience. Just recently he shared with me that his mother used to put him to bed early when he was a boy, telling him that sleeping makes you forget about being hungry. To this day, I believe, my father struggles with his early experience. This shaped his outlook on life. But it also shaped mine—he taught me not to be afraid and to be a survivor. These traits, I believe, are extremely necessary today when so many are willing to treat us like second-class citizens, treat us as if we don't exist, as if we have a choice as to whether we are gay or not, or worse!

My mother, on the other hand, lived well as a child. Not excessively so but not in need of life's basic necessities. Servants, private school, summers playing basketball, weekends at the beach. This shaped her outlook and mine, too—to enjoy life, to be social. In addition, her family was intact when she came to the United States. This shaped her outlook on life.

What both parents offered was love of family, respect for their parents, and pride in their respective cultures. They passed those characteristics unselfishly to me.

Factors Which Shaped my Childhood

The first few paragraphs of this paper were to set the stage—to provide you with my experience at home. In addition to what my home life was, several factors contributed to who I am and how I cope with my culture and my sexual identity. It is difficult to say if one was more important than the other, or which one came first. What I know is the combination of these factors shaped who I am today. I am pretty proud of that.

Born in 1962 in San Francisco and seven years before Stonewall, I was exposed to gay culture early. In the late sixties, my parents drove through the Castro to see "those people". Although I didn't know what gay, or homosexual, or queer was, I did know that I "kinda and sorta" liked what I was seeing. I recall driving down South of Market with my folks, which was a lot seedier then, to see the guys in leather. I don't think my parents were hip. I don't think my father cared to go; my mother pushed him. She "suggested," he followed—you know how it goes. In addition to driving to the Castro, we would drive through the Haight Ashbury district. Unfortunately, I also liked what I saw there—illegal substances. But that discussion will be left to another paper. This early experience made me realize later, as I came out to my parents, that at least they had limited exposure to gay culture.

I heard from many of my friends how the church affected their coming out. Church is very big in the Latino culture. Not so much in mine. My father always worked weekends to provide for his family. He was Lutheran, and I don't recall ever going to a Lutheran service. My mother was Catholic, and we went to Church more because of an obligation. Her siblings were not very religious except her older brother, but I believe his wife had a significant influence on their family going to Church. One thing I was never subjected to growing up was the threat of "if you do so-and so, God is going to punish you." Fear was not tattooed on my forehead.

Family influence, I believe, also played a big part. There are several key points to make here. First, my sister. My parents focused on her while I growing up. She had behavioral issues that my parents had to deal with. I, on the other hand, did well in school, never got into fights, got scholarships—you name it. In other words, I was left to my own devices. Second, my mother's older brother has always been a role model for her. I think they talk more to each other than to their respective spouses. His oldest daughter came out shortly after I did. The simultaneous coming out helped my mother and her brother with whatever guilt and pain they initially suffered. Again, my mother had someone to share her fears with. I say "fears" because I remember my mother being scared with my coming out. Although we now lived in the "burbs" right outside San Francisco, she had heard enough of the Anita Bryants, Jerry Falwells, and all those other dumb asses. Finally, my mother's younger sister was VERY liberal and would always confront my mother or her older brother when they got out of line on ANY issue. My mother was afraid that others might know I was gay and that they would hurt me. She was concerned that I did not have an inalienable right to be gay. My response to her was that I didn't care. I told her that until half the population of the world (WOMEN!) received their unconditional rights, how could I reasonably expect my rights?

Neighbors and co-workers also had an influence on my coming out. When I was about six, we lived two houses down from two guys with a white poodle. I never heard my parents say anything disparaging about them, at least not in front of me. Also, my mother had a co-worker who was gay, and I remember how sad she felt when he died well before AIDS ever hit.

So What—What Does All This Mean? My Coming Out

Although I never had a girlfriend or got caught screwing around, my parents were, I believe, more pleased with how well I did in school and shared this with their friends and family. I was self-sufficient. From an early age, I was very independent. I landed my first job at twelve. They were also very proud to tell their friends that I never got in trouble at school or with the cops. Truthfully, though, I never got caught. My parents never put limits or controls on what I could do. They wanted me to have the freedom that they may not have had when they first got here. I believe this to be true even more so with my father. Also, I did well in school, both academically and athletically. My parents never asked me whether I wanted to go to college; I told them that I was going.

I came out to my parents and friends when I was twenty-one. I have always been pretty blunt, so I had no hesitation telling my parents. I did not have to follow the ACT-UP method. It was time to tell them, and I loved them. I never believed or was afraid that I would be abandoned. Why should they abandon me now? They had never done it before.

Besides, I have to live with myself and, therefore, had to be truthful to myself. If was going to be a good son, I had to be an honest son. I had to be sensitive, proud, and fight if needed—the same traits my parents bestowed on me as discussed early in this paper.

At first after I came out, there was initial shock and pain. They thought they had done something wrong. They were embarrassed. What would they tell their family and friends? This was to be expected. But a surprise? Please! How can someone not know you are gay when you are a red-blooded male who does not have girlfriends, a poster of Farrah Fawcett with her nipple so pronounced on his wall, and no hidden Playboys? But the pain lasted only a few weeks. It was my responsibility to walk them through their fears. There were some rough spots where the shit hit the fan, but love always prevailed. There was one bad moment when my father verbally attacked me for being gay, but I drew the line in the sand—if he wanted respect, then he needed to be respectful. That and not talking to him for a couple of months after the incident proved my point.

Regarding my friends, it was not difficult. Although my friends were straight and mostly males, they already knew. I told them one by one. No one shunned me. We were buddies; we drank beer together and a few other things. Some would join me at gay bars on the condition I would go to straight bars. Oh, the sacrifices I had to make. Undergraduate school was pretty simple, too. San Francisco State was very gay.

Several months ago, my sister, my only sibling, died at fifty-one years of age. I will never forget that when I came out to her prior to telling my parents, her response was "tell me something I didn't know." I am so grateful to God that the relationship between my parents has always been solid because now, more than ever, I need my parents, as they need me, in this time of grieving. Without them, who knows where I would be.

Conclusion

I began by talking about fate. Fate—that which is inevitably predetermined. Being gay is only part of who I am. Just like being Latino, or a man. My familial heritage and my job are also only parts of who I am. My point is that I need to look at my whole self. As I don't like segregation in any form, why should I segregate myself into smaller definable terms? Don't our foes do that for us? So let them!

I believe my understanding and acceptance of who I am is based on my experiences and my relationship with my family and my community coupled with my willingness to learn. This attitude greatly influenced how I approach my life. This attitude helped significantly when coming out.

But I know that others are not so lucky. I remember Matthew Shepard. I remember meeting those one-night stands in San Francisco who were so happy to be there because they were finally free. It was difficult to empathize because I was not in their shoes. I remember the words of hate with Proposition 8. I remember what Jesse Helms said about gays and AIDS and how we deserved it.

So in closing, I say we can fight homophobia by sharing our stories and our mutual love and respect for each other. Yes, we can! Let us be compassionate, tolerant, and understanding, especially to those who fear us or condemn us.

Let us not be afraid of who we are. We were made exactly the way we were meant to be.

Together we can and will fight the discrimination at school, on the job, and in our own lives. Peace to you my brothers and sisters.

Being Frank

Raul Martin Serrano

Dario was the first boy I looked at with reckless abandon. I was fifteen, and every Monday afternoon I sat across from him for an hour and a half as we prepared for our confirmation. While the priest taught us about the sacraments and how our bodies were instruments of the lord, but our natural impulses the work of the devil, Dario would catch me looking at him. Awkwardly, I would look away and remind myself to be vigilant. I didn't believe that nonsense that Jesus was watching me masturbate in the shower, but I knew that I had to be careful with my mannerisms, the inflection I gave my words, and my wandering gaze because, with no role models and a deafening silence surrounding homosexual desire, what I felt had no name.

The body knows truths that our minds can't sense. I sort of always knew I was different and chose to keep that fact to myself. It was easy for me; I have always kept to myself. I wasn't one to show my emotions or talk about anything very personal. I learned that my natural inclination to withhold would serve me well in this secret I irrationally felt I needed to keep. Frankly, I lacked the boldness of many teenagers. Unsure of myself, I choose to keep this fact, along with many other things, namely feelings, to myself.

Knowing the boy I was, I still don't know why I walked into the family room one night and came out of the closet to my parents. I peeked out: I told my parents I *thought* I was *bisexual*.

"Have you told anyone?!"

"*Noh!*" I said.

We have always been a private family. We don't deny our facts, we discuss issues and problems as a family and work them out together, but we believe that no one else need know.

"I think it's best to keep this to yourself," my father told me, smiling. "At least for now. We can figure out what this is and how we can help you."

"Don't tell your cousins," my mother said, the fear and dread in her voice. "We can work this out."

Life has taught me that others will look to you in order to figure out how to treat you. As my mother was intimately aware, the world is cruel and strewn with violence, malice, and aggression. I was a confused (bisexual) seventeen year-old boy, sitting as small as possible on our couch. Could her baby boy shoulder gossip, ignorance, or skinheads wielding aluminum bats?

We only talked about that night once more. Months later my mother asked in passing about my "confusion." I had logged an inordinate amount of hours on the Internet watching naked men kiss when I told them I was bisexual, and as soon as I uttered the words to my parents I knew the truth—I was gay. I wasn't technically lying when I told her I was no longer confused.

At eighteen I flew to New Hampshire to begin my freshman year at Dartmouth College. While I made some good friends and generally had a good time, the school and its students initially intimidated me. A gifted student all my life, I grew up going to awards ceremonies where well meaning organizers met my parents and me at the door, told us how "so very, very happy" they were to see us, and to "sit there." In these circumstances I adopted a strategy of inoffensiveness.

One night I was sitting in the aisle at a theater screening of a documentary about the Weather Underground, a homegrown terrorist group made up of radical college students in the 1960s. The professor introduced the feature: "One of the reasons I like this film is because it's about students like you: privileged, upper-middle class, and white."

My reaction should have been, "Fuck her. Lets see what this movie is about."

Instead I held my breath.

I had been bold enough to apply to Dartmouth and not think twice of its distance or its winter, but my presence on the elite campus, I felt, was tentative. Feeling out of place, I fell back on my habit of with-holding, keeping my emotions to myself. Considering the anxiety I was feeling, I didn't think I was ready to open up about my homosexuality except to a small group of friends.

At the end of my freshman year I heard about a girl who was on suicide watch. It turned out her father was a criminal, not a lawyer, and her mother was a phlebotomist, not a doctor. A lot was said about this girl, none of it very nice, but in my heart I sympathized with someone who was so humiliated by the simple facts of her life.

The real fear is standing at the edge of the diving board; once you will yourself to jump, you take to swimming instinctively. I knew that I just had to start living my life. Besides, I was well aware of the fact that I was missing out on some prime hooking-up years. This was college.

Taking the first steps to living my life openly was easier for me because most people didn't immediately assume I was gay. I was quiet and dressed in boring earth tones, none of which screamed "fierce" or "fabulous." I was able to ease into my life as a gay young man. I could gauge a group, usually find the kindest girl in the room, and control what people knew and when.

While I never had that irrational fear of standing in a room and hav-ing people point and laugh at the *homosexual*, I still feared the reality that people, especially privileged, young people (myself included) can be assholes. I still could do a pretty convincing "straight dude," but this particular crutch makes you vulnerable to "spot the fag."

I would mention a boyfriend in passing or someone might overhear me talking about an event sponsored by the "Gay-Straight Alliance," and suddenly I would find myself under a brutal scrutiny until an intonation in my voice, a movement of my hand, or an appreciation of Madonna elicited a knowing smile: there is the *fagginess*.

I had a propensity to withhold, draw back, and found great comfort in that strategy, but the year before had taught me that one cannot change the facts of one's life. More importantly, we cannot control the reactions of others or exist in their gaze.

I was home after my sophomore year, working with special needs students at a local high school. The students mostly had developmental disabilities such as autism and Down syndrome. Once a month we took the students to the mall to teach them how to take the bus, interact in public, and buy things at a store.

I was assigned a student in a wheel chair and two girls who had plans of starting a girl group in order to perform for Michael Jackson and the Pope. We were discussing their clothes. I thought cheetah prints would be too much for the Pope and had suggested a sensible pants suit, when we turned a corner and ran into a former high-school classmate, Miguel.

When you're young, gifted, and privileged, you think you've got it made and it's your responsibility to make sure no one forgets it. I was cruel to Miguel because he couldn't just learn calculus while doodling in his book; he had to work at it.

He approached with a smirk.

"Thought you went to Dartmouth."

Dartmouth has a "Sophomore Summer" when students get a chance to bond as a class while taking a full course-load. Most students take the following winter off. I didn't know if he'd believe me when I explained why I was home in February.

He looked at the student in the wheel chair.

"Don't you have to diaper the kids? I was gonna do that, but I make more money at the Verizon Kiosk. That's my girl over there. She works at Cinnabon."

I froze, had nothing to say. I couldn't produce positive proof that I was still enrolled at Dartmouth and doing well.

He snorted and walked away.

I couldn't prove my enrollment at Dartmouth, express the joy these students brought to my life, or make him see the dignity of my work.

At Dartmouth I met a young man who was pretty, mean, and conceited. "Cunty" is what he was called because he didn't give men the time of day. We had a few mutual friends, so I spent my junior year making myself a familiar presence in his life. The summer between my junior and senior years was spent racing home after work so that I, who was working with special needs students in San Diego, could talk to him, who was home in New Jersey. We began dating exclusively our senior year.

All those previous fears simply evaporated as I fell deeply in love with this boy and watched him fall in love with me. He was gorgeous, and I lived for Friday nights when I could take him to a party or dinner with friends and be seen with my hand on his lower back. The message was clear—he is coming home with me!

You can't have self-esteem without having something to esteem, and having this boy made me feel tall. This consuming love came at a time when I started to carve a place for myself at Dartmouth. I was leading clubs on campus, volunteering my opinion in class, and I knew I had a knack for writing.

We graduated, and he moved to San Diego, where I found out that living an honest life has nothing on living authentically. While he and I were both private people who didn't feel the need to make out in public and hold hands through the library, if you saw us together it was clear we were a couple. I couldn't do that in San Diego. Each trip to the movie theater or a restaurant contained the risk of being seen by a cousin, a neighbor, or a friend from church.

When I spoke to my parents, I talked to them about work, new stories I was writing, movies I had seen. I didn't mention finding out that five vodka gimlets were too much to drink in one night, that one can stare at a lava-lamp for hours with the help of pot-brownies, or the time I spent with my boyfriend. This young man whose pajama tops I would steal so I could have his scent the nights I couldn't spend with him was in the category of the illicit, the things that can't be named.

At family gatherings aunts would tease me, "When are you getting married and having kids?"

Gay men, or people with secrets, know how to insinuate and how to edit facts. I would tell my aunts, "When you wife a woman, she stops doing what she's told ... respectfully."

The married men who scour craigslist for "Down-low men" are never without a good reason to withhold or deny that one small fact. While the details are always different, it always comes down to fear. There was no way I could keep my secret living in the same city as my parents. After two years, my boyfriend and I packed up and moved to New York City. As it happened at Dartmouth, having the entire continental United States between my family and me allowed me to live an honest life without fear. An honest life that was by no means authentic.

A friend had recently come to his senses and divorced his wife and, making up for lost time, jumped head first into the circuit, a series of days-long, drug-fueled parties held in cities all over the world. When the circuit hit New York, I joined him. Andy Warhol said, "Time is and time was." These men live fast lives; the present moment is constantly slipping into the past. They are materialistic; they believe only what they see and morality, right and wrong, judges the execution of a gesture. These are men who have been abandoned by their families and live fractured lives: two sets of friends, two sets of clothes, two sets of mannerisms, two different personalities. When they get together at these parties, there are no limits and there is no tomorrow. In other words, their lives are exhilarating.

The steady stream of EMTs spoke to the recklessness of a constant present. A woman sat on stage weeping while a muscular young man pumped his fists with angry joy; his face read, "I hate you, dad!" I needed to take a break. I stepped outside to smoke a cigarette and ran across a man who had mixed GHB, aka liquid Ecstasy, and alcohol and was holding on to a pole, shouting nonsense and trying his hardest to stay on his feet. These drugs should never be mixed, and those who mix them can get violent, so I kept my distance. A blond young man from the party, a better man than me, walked over to offer assistance. Someone shouted *Faggot,* and the blond young man grabbed him by the collar and started screaming, *do you think this is funny?* The jerk, an aging frat boy in a buttoned down blue shirt, tried to reason with him, talking the young blond man down from his anger. Finally his *bros* showed up and pulled the young blond man off. Suddenly the jerk grew a pair of balls and had to be held back. He screamed "cocksucker" as he was "forced" away.

Cocksucker. A lifestyle, a romantic attraction, and intimate sexual acts are reduced to just one word. Cocksucker. Its like slut, nigger, wetback, and slant-eye cunt—there is no comeback, nothing you can call a heterosexual white man that would even come close because power is built into our language, the very way we organize our thoughts. In this framework/structure the term "gay man" is an explosive oxymoron, the clusters of meaning around the two words fly apart, but since the coin has got two sides, you can chose to be torn apart by the shrapnel or you can weave the wreckage into a custom-fit armor.

After I broke up with my boyfriend I decided to map out the kind of man I wanted to be. I looked upon my father, for whom "man" was defined by actions—the way you do a job and how you treat your family—and not sex, because sex was kept, ironically, in the closet. That would be my starting point, and I would define myself, and my manhood, on my own terms.

Taking to the jungle with a machete, no map, and a vague idea of what you are trying to discover is dangerous; you can get lost. I had met a boy and confused his happiness with my desires. I regained my bearings and decided it was time to finally affirm to my parents that my homosexual desires were not a phase, but the way I needed to and chose to live my life.

My father said nothing; he just smiled. "You're still my son" was the message. My father is stoic; he believes in action and has no time for gestures. He plays the hand he's dealt. My mother, who dedicated her life to keeping me from harm, even from stubbing my toe, said, "live your life, but people don't need to know your business."

It is said that the past is another country. To our parents the past is literally another country. My mother remembers having to whisper to salesladies when she needed to buy "unmentionables" and then being lead to a small, private room. Years later, in America, her son was telling her he liked being intimate with men.

"There was a young man," she said. "He lived in my neighborhood and … the awful things people would say."

"I'm not going to worry about what people say," I told her. I can't be obedient to everything.

"So you don't care," she asked, defiantly. "You don't care what people think?"

"I know men who are crazy because they can't keep up the lie, and I don't want to have to have that steel."

"What about those who would deny you a job? Those who will hurt you?"

I refused to go back into the closet; that doorframe was shattered, the hinges cracked.

"There are people, members of our family, who think it's funny that I spent $120,000 to go to school and now work two jobs and have dreams of being a writer."

"Those people are fools."

"But where do we draw the line?"

"You must give us time."

My mother came to the United States alone at twenty-two. With no English and limited formal education, compromise and discretion were strategies for survival. For me, compromise and discretion were strategies for defensive navigation.

"I am telling you now in order to give you time. I just broke up, and it takes time for me to catch feelings. It will be years before I meet another man, before I decide to pursue a relationship, and before we start spending holidays together, but make no mistake, your son will have a husband, and I will not leave that man alone because he is not welcomed in this house or because you don't want people to know.

"In my heart I know you will come around. You will always be part of my life, but now you have to decide to what extent. I realize the position I am putting you in, but these are the facts of my life."

Immigrant, Maricón and Mexican, Any Questions?

Carlos Manuel

 I was born in Mexico City around the time the country was getting ready to welcome the world to an international summer games celebration. Government officials were working hard at bringing a positive image of my country to the whole world. Any signs of disobedience were to be taken seriously, and so one evening military soldiers surrounded hundreds of high school and university students in Tlatelolco Plaza and proceeded to quiet them down forever. If you don't know what I'm talking about, it is time for a history lesson because I'm referring to the 1968 Summer Olympics and to the Tlatelolco Massacre, both events happening ten days apart from each other. At the time, these two events meant nothing to me, mainly because I was no more than a babe, but twenty-five years later, these two events would shock me.

I suppose my life as a child was ordinary and extraordinary like every other child's life. I went to school; I learned to read and write, and I grew up. Nothing seemed to be out of the ordinary. Except for the fact that my family were poor campesinos, struggling to make ends meet on a daily basis, and for the fact that at an early age, I felt I was different.

If I compare my attraction to boys to Juan Gabriel's song, "A mis Dieciseis," a song where he declares how everyone started to fall in love but not him because he was "not born to love anyone," I have to say that I was a very early bloomer. That's right, boys and girls; I first realized I was attracted to boys at the age of nine. I knew it because there was an "American" TV show I religiously watched every time it was on. I only watched it because Donny made my heart jump every time he sang. I didn't care about Marie at all, and I only paid attention to her because I had no choice. She was always next to Donny. Most of the time I watched the TV show on my own, and I remember getting closer to the TV screen so I could "touch him." Yes, I'm referring to the "Donny and Marie" variety show.

But it wasn't until I was twelve years old that I discovered how my body responded to the unintentional touch from other boys. There was something about the way their skin felt against mine and something about the way the hair on my body stood on end every time I saw their young sweaty bodies glisten under the sun. At that time I had two best friends, Carlos and Manuel (not their real names), and they served as the vehicles for "exploratory" experimentation. Carlos was the first boy who pressed his crotch against me as we both tried to learn Bible verses for our Catholic morning class or as we both sang in the choir. Manuel was the first boy that showed me and let me touch his "pajarito."

Fast forward: It is now the mid-1980s, and I have arrived in the United States of America. At first, I was simply another Mexican kid who had arrived with the entire family. We were, like many before us and after us, searching for a better life in El Norte. We were a Mexican family joining thousands more. In our eyes, and in my own eyes, we were here as part of life and nothing else. I was too young to understand what it meant to move not from one house to another, or one small town to another, but from one country to another. Moving from Mexico to California was something that even today, after more than twenty years, still affects me.

At first I didn't think anything about our migration. As I stated before, it was just "part of life." But within weeks of settling in Stockton, CA, reality started to sink in. First, everything around us was in a foreign language: English. And even though I had studied at school, one thing is learning a language sitting down and another is to actually try it out in the real world. I quickly found out I knew nothing. As if the language barrier wasn't enough, there were the cultural differences that clashed against each other, complicating matters among family members, friends, and neighbors.

Our new house was located two blocks away from a small local convenience store. My hermanos and I liked going there because we could buy candy with the few coins we had; we would walk to the store several times a day. We were there so often that soon the clerk knew who we were, and even though we couldn't communicate with words, we managed via finger pointing. I remember one time how my sister and I were in the mood for some marshmallows. Happily she and I headed to the convenience store. Once we arrived, we couldn't find them, so I asked. Mejor dicho, I tried to ask because even though I knew what I wanted, I had no idea how to ask for it. And it wasn't that I couldn't ask where the marshmallows were—I didn't even know what the word for those soft, white, pink, and fluffy semi-round things, commonly known to me as "bombones" was. I had heard the word, at school and on TV, but I wasn't sure of its exact pronunciation. So, when asking for them, I said, "marmallashoes." The clerk had a confused expression on because he had no idea what I meant. He and I went back and forth, yet after about five minutes, nothing got accomplished. I was getting very frustrated because I couldn't explain myself and because my sister couldn't stop laughing, either because she thought it was amusing or because she was embarrassed and laughter was her way to cope with the situation.

Soon a stranger walked into the store; the clerk told him something, then instructed me to say what I was looking for and I said, "Marmallashoes." The stranger said, "Marshmallows?" and I happily said, "Sì." Once the clerk found out what I wanted, he proceeded to bring a bag; my sister and I paid for it, and before we exited the store the clerk said, "Remember for next time, marsh-mal-lows." I assure you, I haven't forgotten the lesson.

On another occasion, later than the marshmallows incident, y de esto sí estoy seguro because I was already on my second year of high school, I was hanging around with my high school friends. I was still learning to communicate, but unlike before, I was a little better at formulating thoughts and sentences. Still, I had speech problems and my fastest way of communication was through writing. (I had an incredible ESL teacher who very clearly taught me to understand the English language structure.) I was already a senior, and for the most part I hung around with the theatre club students and my two best friends, Carlos and Manuel (not their real names.) I remember rushing out of class to meet my two best friends at the parking lot. As seniors, we had the privilege of leaving campus for lunch. I didn't have a car but Carlos did, so every lunch period was spent away from the school grounds. That particular time Manuel and I reached the car at the same time, and since we both wanted to be in the front seat we pushed each other trying to get in first. Once inside, (Manuel won) I was so excited that I exclaimed, "Oh, my gooseness!"

I remember my two friends looking at each and bursting into laughter. I had no idea what was going on, so I also laughed. But then, as we drove down the street to our eating destination, Carlos started saying "Oh, my gooseness" for no apparent reason. It was then I realized I had not used the correct phrasing and neither Manuel nor Carlos corrected me on it. Instead, Manuel and Carlos used the incorrect phrasing every time an opportunity presented itself. In fact, many years later (about twenty), Manuel was able to reconnect with me via email. When I communicated with him and he let Carlos know about our recent cyberspace reunion, he wrote back: "Oh, my gooseness!" When I read that phrase my body shivered; I realized that even though Carlos and Manuel were just "joking and having fun" and there was no harm intended behind their actions, I had been negatively affected by the way they imitated me.

The experiences of learning English were mostly positive for me. Yes, I was teased in school for not being able to speak the language; yes, people laughed at me when they heard me uttering words that many times had no meaning; yes, many used my inability to speak or the fact that I have an accent to attack me physically, mentally, and emotionally. Pero como dice el refrán, "what doesn't kill you makes you stronger" ¿qué no? Yet to become stronger, one must first realize one is weak. And I did, in more ways than one, by denying my heritage, my culture, and my roots. By refusing to speak my own native language and by trying to get rid of my accent. Yet, at the end, I learned my lessons and grew stronger. It took me many years to learn my lesson and grow stronger, but I prevailed.

Today, if people make a comment about my accent, I let them know that the only reason I have one is because English is my third language. If someone tries to bring me down because of the way I speak, by referring to me as someone inferior or stupid, I quickly tell them that my accent is a sign of my ability to not only communicate in English, but also in Spanish and Italian. And if they still don't get it, well, there's nothing I can do because after all these years, I still am not able to speak Ignorant.

But let us leave behind the language arguments and move forward to a much more pleasant subject: my sexuality. Here are a few things I have learned throughout my life. If, like me, you are male and like males, there's nothing you can do about it. You were born with such desires and attractions and not even God (whoever that is) can change that. You can make the effort to hide such attractions—I did—but I warn you, the consequences of such actions are not very pleasant. If you decide to accept your homosexuality, y con mucho orgullo declare to the world that you are a JOTO, congratulations, be ready to defend yourself every day of your life because once you decide to be out, you will have to come out every time you meet someone new. Y como si eso fuera poco, there are a lot of pendejos out there who will refuse to accept you or will refuse to welcome you. But don't worry. You are not alone. You are not the only one and you will not be the last to experience such things. Yes, there are a lot of pendejos out there, but let me tell you, we, los vivos, outnumber them, and como todo un miembro de la famila, "We are here para darte una mano." You know, a hand.

I mentioned earlier that I knew I was different at the age of nine years old—thank Donny Osmond for that. Who would have thought that a Mormon man would wake up my sexual desires? Pero de que chingaos hablo? Many Mormon men have awoken my sexual desires; some of them have even taken part in them, and I don't mean in my mind.

I also mentioned that I was twelve years old when my friend Carlos (not his real name) rubbed his crotch against me. It was also at that age when I saw and touched the first "pajarito,"—"Manuel's pajarito" to be exact (also for both, not their real names either.) It didn't take long after that for me to engage in some forbidden sexual activities with boys my own age. I went through middle and high school experiencing a few sexual things. There weren't many, but those encounters that came to be were enough to excite and scare me.

But even though I was willingly participating in these activities, I did not consider myself a gay man. No male in my school who participated in such activities considered himself gay. Because gay, maricón, mariposa, joto, o puto were not something we were just because we engaged in a sexual encounter with someone of the same sex. No! In my country, in Mexico, the definition of "gay/fag" only applied (and still does) to those men who were overtly flamboyant and who, at the time of the sexual act, were the "passive partners"—the ones who allowed themselves to be penetrated. If you were not one of them, you were simply having some fun. Yes, I know. There is a lot to say about such a mentality. Trust me, such a philosophy has always been in my mind, and it has bothered me so much that I dedicated a year of my life to trying to understand it. I read many books, consulted many oracles, and even interviewed different people in order to understand such a way of thinking. The results: an ethnodrama, una obra de teatro titled

Vaqueeros where I pose the question of male sexual behavior and where I compare what it means to be gay in the USA vs. what it means to be gay in Mexico.

Living life as young man who was having sexual encounters with other young men was exciting and dangerous at the same time. Even though I was always keeping myself to myself and trying to not be "obvious" or let my guard down, there were a few times when the guys in the soccer team caught me staring at them a little too long, or times where I suddenly let out an "out of the ordinary" expression, or times where my speech patterns were a little too high or a little to feminine. So even though I am not and have not been a "very flamboyant" person, there have been times when I have been "obvious enough" to be teased by others, or to find myself in the middle of taunting situations and worse, in the middle of embarrassing, emotionally and physically abusive situations.

I am not the kind of person who likes to let others know what I've gone through in order to be where I am. However, someone once told me that I need to tell my story so others may know that they are not the only ones experiencing discrimination, racism, and homophobia. Still, I don't feel very comfortable talking about abuse (physical or emotional). The best way for me to share such experiences is through my plays. Yet, not one or two but more than four people had tried to make me write about my experiences, so here I am, attempting to express myself the best way I can. (Once again, I digress.)

Once my family immigrated to Stockton, CA, my so called "joto life" changed. As mentioned earlier, once I started going to school, I dedicated myself to learning English and to becoming part of the gringo people; thus, I was not really interested in my sexuality as much as I was interested in "assimilating." Soon, I left my culture, traditions, and roots behind because at the time I believe that was the only way to be part of the "American people." When I felt I had "accomplished" this goal, I once again started paying attention to my sexual feelings. This time, however, things were different. I was growing up, and I was not only fighting to fit in as an immigrant but I was also questioning my existence as a person, as a human, as a male who felt attracted to other males, and as a young man who was trying to figure out what "I wanted to be when I grew up." All these issues became a burden in my life. Soon I found myself fighting against myself, against my own feelings and desires, against my own thoughts, against my family and friends, and against everything Catholicism had taught me. I became a confused individual, ashamed of being brown, of having an accent, black hair and brown eyes, of being short, of my nose, my eyes, my lips. The worst, however, were my homosexual feelings.

I started to blame God for allowing me to experience such attraction to other men. I believed he was testing me, setting up temptations for me to see if I was really worth being his child. I tried to resist the temptations and blamed myself for being weak whenever I couldn't resist. I prayed to la Virgen de Guadalupe (Really, is there any other saint Mexican Catholics pray to?) asking her for strength, for love, for understanding, asking her to advocate for me and to tell God that I had already been through enough. Yet, no answers, no relief, no apparitions, and no peace came my way. Tired of trying to be "normal," tired of praying without any results, and tired of so much pain, I decided, in a moment of desperation, that the best way to have peace and calmness in my life was by ending it all. And I tried, but obviously I wasn't successful. And it wasn't because I didn't try hard enough; it was because at the time I was living with a good friend and her husband, and this friend somehow suspected my tribulations and without getting in my way, kept an eye on me, recognizing my intentions. At the appropriate moment, she intervened, and with her help, I accepted that having homosexual feelings wasn't a sin, or a disease, or something I had acquired through the water.

Yet, even after accepting my own homosexuality and feeling somehow liberated, unafraid and ready to be myself, I felt some sort of fear whenever I visited my family. Around them and around my raza, I felt tremendously shameful and fearful for being who I was—no, not a vendido but a homosexual. This was due to a conversation I once heard among some of my family members. They were discussing how Mexican people weren't gay but once many of them came to the USA, they would turn gay because they were either brainwashed by white men or were encouraged to engage in homosexual acts for money. And with time, those people who "did things for money" would end up liking such sexual encounters, becoming used to them, so they would simply continue having them, even without getting paid. I was too young when I first heard such a conversation. And even though it didn't make much sense to me at the time, it did have a lasting impression on my young mind.

Nowadays I understand that many of the Mexican male immigrants that come to the USA feel more at ease in this country, letting their guards down and feeling comfortable enough to explore their sexuality. Whatever feelings and sexual practices they kept to themselves back in their homeland continued to be felt and practiced in this country. Many of those immigrants, like me, accept who they are and feel more at ease about themselves and their feelings while living in the United States, but once around their own families or once back in their countries, many of them bury their feelings once again. Those who don't are chastised, made fun of, and pushed away; they are labeled "maricones" and become outsiders within their own communities. Because I had heard about such situations and had witnessed a few, while I had sexual encounters with other males my age, when being around my own family, I kept such activities secretly hidden not only for fear of being rejected and made fun of but also because I was afraid of becoming the "shame of the family." I strongly believed that in the eyes of many of my relatives, especially the men, I was going to be chastised for allowing the gringo to "corrupt my mind."

In my play "La Vida Loca," I claim that the best years of my life were my college years. Despite the fact I was severely beaten for being gay, this is still true. And it is because not only did I come out to the college community, but I also came out to my mother, and once I came out to her, I no longer cared who knew. I was lucky enough to be accepted by my mother and my brothers and sisters, as well as by the majority of my friends. They gave me the support I needed, so my life as a young openly gay man went on. It was in college where I left behind the ridiculous goal of trying to fit into "American" society. By an act of revelation (and an encounter with Mr. Chicano himself—actor Edward James Olmos), I got rid of my color contact lenses, the fake blond hair, and the idea that I needed to be white in order to be perfect. I accepted myself as a brown man, as an immigrant with an accent, as a descendent of the Aztecs and as a member of the campesinos' force. By the time I graduated college I was a new person, full of life and ready to take on any challenge, gay, straight, and foreign.

Today I'm happily married to my partner of twelve years. We have two dogs and we all enjoy life to the fullest. Of course I still fight against ignorant people. Every now and then I'm reminded that I'm not an "American," that I'm not welcome in this country because of the color of my skin or my sexuality. Every now and then I get into arguments with people who tell me I should go back to my country because this is America and I don't belong here. Every now and then I argue with politicians, right-wing extremists, religious fanatics, and moralistic individuals because I don't hide the fact that I'm gay and I have a husband. But even though every now and then I have to deal with those issues, every day I smile because no matter how hard those people try, how hard those people shout, and how hard those people try to push me away, I and many thousands more like me continue to be here, fighting for equality and for our survival. I know many of us will continue the fight until the end. I know I will continue the conversation until all of us are equally accepted. We may never be welcome, but we will be equally accepted—that I know for sure. And no matter where I am, no matter how old I get, and no matter how many times people try to shut me down, I will always be standing strong, proudly and flamboyantly shouting: I'm an immigrant, a maricón, and Mexican. Any questions?

The Gay Brown Beret Suite

Rigoberto González

 E veryone deserves to channel their inner drama queen. Here is my effort. The story of my life: moving through different landscapes; speaking different languages; comfortable here, there, and everywhere; yet frequently contending with miscommunication and cultural mistranslation.

Over the years I have learned to weather these moments of disconnect with humor, though this can also lead to more frustration or offense. Like the many years I've had to deal with the response to my name. Once people hear it is "Rigoberto," a few well-meaning types will inevitably ask, "Does it mean something in Spanish?"

When I was younger I'd say, "No, it doesn't mean anything." Which, of course, is false, since it means I'm Mexican, that I've inherited my father's connection to his Purépecha roots, and that my parents made the wise decision not to Anglicize my name even though I had been born in the United States all those many years ago.

As I got older and sassier, I'd answer: "It means shit-kicker." Which is true to a certain extent since I've been fighting my way through college and life, adapting and adopting, assimilating and acculturating, pressing my thumb and forefinger around the rosary bead as firmly as I press my thumb and forefinger around the stem of the martini glass.

And if I'm feeling really naughty I answer: "It means cocksucker." Does that require further explanation?

In any case, it's my ethnic identity that comes first; my sex and sexual orientation follow, though not very far behind. It's like my female African American colleague says: "When I enter the room, the first thing people notice is that I'm black. The second thing they notice is that I'm a woman." What she doesn't say is that these two parts of her identity reveal themselves only milliseconds apart, and yet the political movements that these two parts of her being can espouse couldn't seem farther away from each other. Though notable efforts have been made—and usually by black women themselves—to build bridges between the groups that struggle for racial and gender equality, I can certainly relate to belonging to two groups whose philosophies and histories come across as mutually exclusive.

I turn the mirror on myself and see: a Chicano and a gay man. Both are politicized identities. One was shaped by the need for community, a communal voice to speak out against the institutional discrimination against Mexican-born citizens and their American-born children. A need for visibility and space, for safety and dignity, and we will take to the damn streets if we have to! The other was shaped by the need for community, a communal voice to speak out against the institutional discrimination against American-born citizens. A need for visibility and space, for safety and dignity, and we will take to the damn streets if we have to! The overlap is obvious, isn't it? And, yet—

If I walk as gay man into my Chicano community, its shortcomings become apparent—our Catholic roots and history of machismo give way to a discriminatory practice within it. Oh, let me not start on the gay jokes, which are the first jokes we learn as young men to distinguish the healthy lifestyle from the unhealthy one, between normal and desirable masculine behavior from the not-normal, not-masculine, and certainly not-desirable. In our jokes, we not only learn about the effeminate and grotesque gay man, but about gay dogs and gay cars and gay clothes and gay predators who lurk inside our fears, just waiting for a window to open, an opportunity to take advantage, to seduce and corrupt. The gay man is the devil incarnate, except that he doesn't want to enter our hearts; no, he wants to enter a more forbidden place—our pants.

And so I enter the rally and screech, swiveling my head, "Chicano power, people!" How well that goes over—how the presence of a mariposa, a joto, a maricón among straight men, Chicanos, is an invasion, an encroachment, a threat. What is it about straight men anyway that they flatter themselves with the ability to attract men of the same sex? Seriously, vato, some of us queens have standards, or at the very least, eyesight.

Now let me enter the queer space, where we already know what we do and brag about how often and, really, girl, it ain't all about that, because we've got plenty of fight in the rainbow arena—it's all about gay rights and the cure for AIDS, no matter where on the spectrum you set your queer self. But, seriously, the movement has been dominated by gay white men, and white men who are gay don't like to be reminded of white privilege or male privilege because they're gay, and gay means subject to ridicule, violence, and oppression, and isn't that en par with other types of discrimination? Perhaps, but I also recognize the Othered position of gay men of color within white gay space—how we are exoticized and eroticized: the black stud, the Latin lover, the dark chocolate, the café con leche, the big black dick, the "fuck me in Spanish, papi chulo." I also know that growing up gay means worshipping the white male body—the dominant flesh on pornography, the dominant character in fiction and film, that dominant face on gay magazine covers. White is beautiful, white is beautiful. And you, little Mexican boy, are not white. You are not white. You are gay. And you already know what your people think about that.

And yet these two troubled spaces are my spaces, my troubled, complicated, cherished homes. Imperfect, dysfunctional, and sometimes a little intimidating given that the focus is on the repulsion or appeal of one's sexual prowess: one place won't let me in, the other one won't let me out.

I once gave a presentation in a LGBT literature class whose students had read my memoir *Butterfly Boy*, which is my coming of age, coming out, and coming to America story. Once the class was dismissed, a young white man rushed up to me and asked: "There's just one thing I don't understand: if it was so difficult to grow up gay in your community, why would you want to go back?"

I gave a quick, impulsive answer: "Because I love my people."

I have had to answer similar curiosities when I make appearances in Chicano Studies classes: "Why do you call yourself a gay Chicano writer? Why can't you just call yourself a Chicano writer? Or better yet, why can't you just call yourself a writer and let the work speak for itself?"

Because I love my people, and I celebrate my people, and I claim both my ethnicity and my sexuality in the literary landscape where "just a writer" means universal, and if I were to draw a picture of "just a writer" he would be a male, he would be white, he would be straight. Just like it happens in books—the universal male character is white, unless the author points out he's black or Latino or Asian. And he is straight, unless the author points out that he's not.

If I feel like being flippant or dismissive I simply say: "I call myself a gay Chicano writer because I love accessories!" But if I had the time to pronounce not only my criticisms but also my appreciation for the positive elements of my two communities, I'd say:

When I enter Chicano space I swell with pride—the history and culture of a people who work and play and make love beneath the universe with the pre-Columbian tongues—Coatlicue, Huitzilopochtli, Quetzalcoatl—who listen for the guidance of the living and the dead, whose fury and activism is fueled by the fires of Spanish, of familial loyalty, of Mexica nationhood, of a spirituality whose ceremonies are both secular and sacred, biblical and mythological. The legend says that we are brown because we are the children of the sun; heat simmers and boils in our blood depending on our emotions—and we are capable of many, from passion to rage.

We are also the children of the earth, laborers and nurturers, the people who express grief and praise in song, poetry, and prayer—give us a guitar and we will strum you a music that's a combination of all three. Lend us your ear and we will break your heart.

We are the storytellers and the travelers, the healers and the magicians, the bordercrossers who can move through walls, fences, and international lines, with or without permission. This extraordinary legacy inspires my work and pushes me into action when choices like apathy and inaction seem simpler and easier to achieve.

When I enter queer space I swell with pride at the ultimate expression of visibility and fierceness—the forbidden language of intimacy and same-sex touch, affection, and attraction made public and beautiful. The dark rooms where we have been taught to place our desires and fantasies have earned the hard-won light of the queer pioneers: the writers, the librarians, the teachers, the administrators, the politicians and the lawyers, but also the postal workers, the mechanics, the barbers, the nurses, the factory workers and the window washers. You can't turn to any profession without one of our faces showing through.

It is in this space where I learned to lose my shame and to welcome the moment of recognition—"ah, so you are as well, how wonderful for the two us."

It is in this space where I learned not to feel asexual or abnormal—those convenient closets that explain us to and dismiss us from the heteronormative world. What a lovely act is the act of love when it's not shrouded in secrecy or whispered. And how empowering to enter the room that flowers with the necessary symbols—from the rainbow flag to the pink triangle, the beacons of a safe zone.

I suppose that in an ideal world I wouldn't have to remind Chicanos that issues of sexuality are now part of the concerns to be engaged by the our Brown Beret movement in the new millennium; and I wouldn't have to remind gay men that issues of race are now part of the concerns to be engaged by the "pink beret" movement in the new millennium—and indeed, bridges are being built, but the burden usually falls on the queer Chicano, queer men of color in general. And then there are those greater obstacles, bigger than any one person or movement.

Indeed, this is not, despite Barack Obama in the White House, an ideal world—not yet. And the reminders of the long rocky roads to harmony sadden me.

The Latino vote and its participation in the anti-gay marriage campaign reminded me of shame, not mine but my community's — how immigrants bring with them the marvels of the kitchen and the cruelty of religious values, how the families that I love choose not to love me back. This homophobia took a personal turn for me when I wrote the children's book *Antonio's Card,* a picture book about a young Latino with two mommies. The book was subsequently banned from various schools and libraries, and my email was (and continues to be) sullied by death threats and insults: You are garbage! You're disgusting! You make me sick! Very unimaginative put-downs, I might add. People need to read more.

There I was, offering a gift to the same-sex couples who parented and blessed our broken world with kindness, and suddenly, the unkindness came from people who were also parents and who couldn't see themselves in the illustrations depicting love and understanding.

I hope that my young adult novel, *The Mariposa Club,* will fare better as it runs along to the school of hard knocks, though I suspect this book about four gay high school seniors will alarm more than amuse. I wrote that book inspired by the tragedy of Lawrence King, the young gay student from Oxnard, California, who was shot to death by another young man who felt threatened after Lawrence King revealed his crush on him. In 2008, twenty years after I graduated from high school, we're still frightened by the gay kid. If I could wave a magic wand and make this dangerous condition go away, I would, but all I've got is a sharp pencil and a muscle on the forefinger that's ready to flex. And I flex.

My contributions to the cause have been literary because I'm a writer; that's my chosen path. So it hurts me when my labor is chastised and denied. When I was first starting out, writing and publishing my early poems and stories, I heard a veteran writer say to another, "That Rigoberto, he's a promising young man, but too bad he's gay." That "too bad he's gay" has haunted me ever since, and at night I can hear it beating like a pulse in the dark, and sometimes it keeps me awake at night because it reminds me of the times when I tried to hide my gay skin beneath my brown one, and how that deception during my fragile adolescence nearly pushed me to suicide. Yes, suicide, the ultimate "I'm sorry I was born this way."

And though I find more tolerance and acceptance as a Chicano writer in the queer community, the dismal representation of gay Latino or Chicano writers in queer-themed anthologies and conference panels makes it difficult for me not to feel like a token when I'm often the only one or one of a few. And if I express my discontent I get this answer: "But we try to reach out and we get very little response from Latinos." Oh, sister! It's what white heterosexuals have been saying all along as excuses and explanations for the dearth of Latino representation in publishing. Now I have to hear it from my girlfriends in struggle too?

And, yet, I continue doing what I set out to do, perform activism with ink—writing it down so that my words remain in print long after my voice falls silent. With my poetry, my stories, my essays, and even my children's books and books for young adults, I am not going away so easily, and with each book I'm making it harder and harder to be ignored. I am brown, I am queer, here I write, here I am.

All I have to do to give myself some sunlight during the dark times is to look south of the border—if the anxieties in Latin America can be assuaged, then anxieties can be assuaged anywhere. A bit overdue, but more than gestures of equality all the same: In 1998, Ecuador's new constitution introduced protections against discrimination based on sexual orientation. In 1999, Chile decriminalized same-sex intercourse. In 2000, Rio de Janeiro's state legislature banned sexual orientation discrimination in public and private establishments. In 2002, Buenos Aires guaranteed all couples, regardless of gender, the right to register civil unions. In 2003, Mexico passed a federal anti-discrimination law that included sexual orientation. In 2004, the government of Brazil initiated a program with non-governmental organizations to change social attitudes toward sexuality. In 2006, Mexico City approved the Societal Cohabitation Law, granting same-sex couples marital rights identical to those for common-law relationships between a man and a woman. In 2007, Uruguay passed a law granting access to health benefits, inheritance, parenting, and pension rights to all couples who have cohabited for at least five years. In 2008, Nicaragua reformed its penal code to decriminalize same-sex relations. And as of July 22, 2010, same-sex marriage is legal in Argentina. Now I'm holding my breath for my own home, the United States of America.

Funny, isn't it, how a country that flaunts its freedoms and its democratic process can be so selective about whom those freedoms and that process serves? In our beloved country, the two groups that seem to be constantly under governmental siege are my two communities: my Mexican family and my queer family. Sometimes I wonder why I haven't been deported and gay bashed at the same time—me, the queer son of "illegal immigrants."

I suppose this is the part where I should own up to my self-designated label as a Gay Brown Beret and call into tough cookie question this hatred for the Mexican, this hatred for the queer, and sadly, I have plenty of personal experience to draw from—from being called a wetback when I was a professor in Illinois to being called a faggot when I was a visiting writer in Arizona, from watching my mother afraid to go to work when the INS (now ICE) started raiding the packinghouses to shaking hands with my lover when we said our good-byes at the airport, from freaking out that I would lose my student loan with the approval of California's Proposition 187 (an anti-immigrant law) to being picketed at one of my readings of Antonio's Card, from getting pulled over by the immigration officer as I was driving back to college to getting denied service at a Mexican restaurant on the border because "they didn't serve people like me."

If anything, these victimizations have taught me not to surrender to the role of victim, but to rise to the call to action—to protest and speak out. In the beginning the fire was similar to the one that politicizes many young people, and so I signed up for the rallies, the sit-ins, the marches, the petitioning and the vote-getting. Oh, sure, the body was more resilient and energetic during the college years, and I could stay up all night making protest signs and stand on my feet for hours the following day on no sleep. But those hardcore days are limited, and when I knew I could reach larger numbers through my writing, the decision to stay behind and sit in front of the computer was a logical one.

What many people don't know is how solitary this form of activism is. In fact, I would say that it's lonely, the sitting down and sipping on cold coffee when the only other voice in the office is that little beep on AOL that lets you know you just received a new message in your inbox—and then what a heartbreak when it turns out it's a spam announcement letting you know your email address just won the Irish lottery. But it's a necessary effort. How else will the idea of a better world survive?

Survival; is that what I call this key-stroking—interesting word, that one—in the early hours of the morning, in the later hours of the night? I must; I have no other method of dealing with the shitty news that comes my way: just recently I was informed that my column in the El Paso Times is going to shut down after ten years of reviewing exclusively books by Latino writers; just recently my best friend in Albuquerque called me, distraught that the Senate in New Mexico rejected a bill that would allow domestic partnerships because it was "marriage in disguise"; just recently I heard back from my young cousins who have been in hiding in Texas for months after their parents, my aunt and my uncle, were deported.

The human in me, the advocate, the friend, the cousin in me, sat down and cried because I'm entitled to the visceral grief that can overwhelm even an iron butterfly like me. It feels like I get it from all sides, and not in a good way. I always thought that having two communities doubled my chances of a date on a Saturday night, that being in the middle was akin to playing the role of the Lucky Pierre in a ménage a trois, but in reality, getting fucked by both sides is not a pleasant experience at all. (I guess I should have listened a little more closely to my bisexual friends who complain that they get alienated by both the queer and the straight communities.)

But then, when the tears evaporate, when the crumpled tissue papers look more like daisies than knots of Kleenex stiffened by dried mucus, when the screen tires of deaf blankness and thirsts for interaction, I turn on the computer and open the files that run on the double-fight, not the double-fuck that is my birthright.

Indeed, I am hopeful. A few Novembers ago I was crossing the border and getting detained for carrying a Day of the Dead skull into the country. The border patrol guard lost his cool when I expressed surprise that he had never seen one of these sugary confections before. How could that be, I thought to myself, given the time of the year that it was, given the color of his skin? "Aren't your parents Mexican, [I read his name tag] Rodrigo?" I asked in all earnestness. And he barked, "I ask the questions around here, sir!" Anyway, despite that particular cultural mistranslation, I knew that I was stepping back into a different country than the one I had stepped out of just that morning because the gay-hating, Mexican-hating administration was not going to remain in office. Now we have a not-so-gay-hating, not-so-Mexican-hating administration in office. Will it ever become love? I doubt it, but one thing I do know: we brown folk, we queer folk, were here long before President Obama, and we will still be here long after. And that's where my hope lies, in the perseverance of my communities that have yet to march in step but that are marching forward nonetheless. I'd like to believe that people like me, representatives of the double identity, double indemnity, are up front raising the baton, but I'm much too modest for such a proclamation. I'd rather say I'm part of the band, fourth or fifth row, just another vato, just another girl, sticking her neck out trying to make the group shot for the yearbook. Isn't that what matters in the end? Not what you do, but what you did? And with whom?

Is that a gay Brown Beret? It is.

It sounds odd speaking of myself and my experiences as if I were reaching the end of a life or an era—after all, I am only in my early forties and still going strong—relatively healthy, relatively happy with a tenured appointment at a state university and—as of this year—a boyfriend (yes, mami, the candles and daily prayers to San Antonio do work!), but one thing I've learned is not to let the comforts trick me into complacency, because it's not about me but about something bigger than me.

Last year I was engaged in a teleconference with the board members of a prestigious poetry organization. I pointed out—yet again—that this organization's efforts at addressing diversity were uninspired at best, that white liberal guilt becomes so easily soothed with the inclusion of one or two African American poets into their season's programming. What about Latino poets? Our population is only fifty million or so. What about Chicanos? We are only two-thirds of that US Latino population.

I was met with silence, and then one of the head honchos said to me: "I don't understand, Rigoberto. The poetry world has been so good to you, publishing you and giving you awards. Why do you keep complaining? Why don't you just let it go and enjoy the fruits of your labor?"

That comment reminded me of the earnest young man I spoke about earlier, the one who came up to me when I visited the LGBT literature class: such ignorance disguised as innocence, such refusal to recognize the activist who doesn't carry the picket sign or chant the protest songs but who acts out of communal duty nonetheless. I do it because I love my people. I speak up, I act up, I stand up, because I love my people. I write because I love my people.

I am not embarrassed by the sentimentality of these proclamations, I am empowered by them. Therefore my politics cannot be a costume; certainly I couldn't sustain such a theater, especially during these times of economic hardship in which the arts and literature are under assault and simply dismissed as luxuries. This is probably the time we need it the most—we are suffering such terrible losses already, let us not lose the right to imagine, to express and to address.

My name is Rigoberto González, and I am a gay Brown Beret—I've got a mouth, an attitude, and many languages. I've got much work yet to do and plenty left to say.

Section II

Recollections

Coming Out

Gil Cuadros

(10/11/91 National Coming Out Day. My boyfriend is in Sacramento protesting the veto of AB101, after the California Governor campaigned saying he'd sign a bill to protect Lesbians and Gays from job discrimination.)

When my mother said, "Why are you trying to drive me to death?"
I remembered the kind of car we had in Driver's Ed,
two large wheels on the dash, two speedometers,
two sets of brakes. The homely instructor
smelled of body odor, polyester, a low-paid academic, hairy.
He led me to believe I was the one in control,
maneuvering through traffic, city-born to drive.
When I went too fast, the needle at 35, he'd slow me down,
grab the steering as I made a corner, yell "Left on Garfield,
not Albright." He'd ask me to pull over,
use the example of other students' abilities to yield,
to merge smoothly behind the car in front of them,
as if speed or talent to find alternative routes weren't necessary.
The instructor would say, "Driving is a privilege, not a right."

I knew I'd get my temporary permit anyway,
had always done well on written exams, could quote the ratio

of acceleration and stopping, how many deaths per year
were caused by driving under stress. All my mother could do
was crush her heel into the carpet like she was trying to stop
the world, she didn't want her son to be queer.
I tried to calm her, as if to say, "See, mom, here's what I look like,
name, address, weight, color of hair,
laminated, all perfectly normal,
the word "license" emblazoned on the top,
the state seal golden, a grizzly, an Amazon,
the motto "Eureka."

To our mothers

Xuan Carlos Espinoza-Cuellar
and Emmanuelle Neza Leal-Santillan

to our mothers:
> queer advocates

their activism:
> raising fierce jotas
> teaching us comadrismo

to our mothers:
> who cried the day we came out because they knew what we would face
> but looked us "straight" onto our queer eyes and said: "tu eres mi hijo y te quiero mas ..."
> y luego fuimos a comer pozole together

to our madres:
> who taught us the art of making tamales
> whose different shades melt together
> whose hearts are so strong that not even sickness can fuck with them

to our mothers:
> whose manos shake of coraje/anger at the sound of injustice
> to our mothers whose hands harvested both:
> los frutos de la tierra
> y nosotras los frutos de sus vientres

to our mothers:
>> whose mouths grew tired of silence
>> whose voices are heard across borders
>> whose dyed hair shows gray/brown roots—just as they show on our palabra

to our mothers:
>> who gave us more than nourishment but una herencia genetica of a defiant sense of rebeldía

to our madres:
>> who refused to carry the cross of patriarchy and liberated us from the viacrucis of shame

to our mothers:
>> whose short brown body runs and walks for miles ... and miles
>> ...

to our mothers:
>> whose broken english sounds like the most beautiful poetry ever spoken

to their activism:
>> not always present in/on the form of signs, chants of press releases

to their struggle:
>> not always written, not always filmed, seldom mentioned

to their flesh:
>> who taught us how to love in our queer existence
>> in the way we caress and kiss
>> for they allowed us to live in it for nine moons

to their sweat

    salty rivers of change

    pain and hope

    their greatest form of love

to their labor

    who built our cities

    the structures where they'll never set foot

    the rooms where they'll never stay

    the food that will never touch their lips

to their future ...

Chile Relleno

Roberto Rodriguez

Se ponen a dorar los chiles pasilla

I planned out my coming out carefully. I was in my second year of college and felt overwhelmingly frustrated living a closeted life. I gained a great group of friends from the previous year, and we did absolutely everything together. Having lived in the dorms the previous year together brought us all extremely close, and what we enjoyed the most was the *chisme,* the gossip we could share with each other. That *chisme* was what ultimately built up the curiosity in my friends. Our love lives, or lack of, was no exclusion to our gossip. Although none of us were in any kind of relationship, my girls would tell me about all of the boys that they were interested in, but when it came to my turn to share, I had nothing to contribute. I remember being eager to agree about all the boys they talked about, but at the same time I felt this heavy lump in my throat that would keep me from speaking about my own hidden desires. I was leading a life that I thought I was supposed to be leading, but it wasn't my life.

Remover las semillas de los chiles

Walking through campus I would notice a sign with rainbow colors. I would usually shy away from the sign because every time I passed by it I felt like all eyes were on me, watching, judging. My cowardice and irrationality brought me to look up the fraternities on campus through the school's website, and I discovered Delta Lambda Phi, a national social fraternity for gay, bisexual, and progressive men. I decided that this was my chance to finally step into the queer world with a group of support from men who identified, for the most part, like I did. What I was looking to gain was a group of brothers who would support me, even if everyone else rejected me for who I was and who I loved. The three-month process to brotherhood did not go unnoticed by my friends, and they began to question why I suddenly had less time to spend with them. Having found a new group of support, I decided to take my plan into action: I would come out to my friends. I felt that an intimate experience would make it easier for me, and it would reveal how they truly felt about me, so I chose to talk to them one by one. I got a range of reactions from shock to "oh I had a feeling," which I thought was hilarious because I was so sure that I was great at covering up my sexuality. Once I came out to my closest friends our *chisme* time became much more entertaining. It felt great to finally be able to join in on the "boy talk" and argue with them over who would eventually date Carlos, our dorm's senior resident advisor from the previous year. Once I came out to all of my friends, it was time to move on to my family.

Crack about two eggs and remove the yolk, beat the egg whites until they become foamy

I had set up a strategic plan for myself. First, I joined a brotherhood that would not reject me because of my sexuality. With that support in line I was ready to face my friends, who then gave me the courage to face the people I cared about the most and whose reactions I was terrified to confront. I come from a really small immediate family; it's just my mom, older sister, niece, nephew, and myself. Right after the first quarter of school ended I went home for winter vacation. I figured that Christmas would be the perfect time to come out to my sister. She and I are really close because we basically only had each other growing up, so I knew she would be supportive, but I was nonetheless extremely nervous. I got choked up every time I thought about talking to her, so I decided to write her a letter. I was emotional the entire time I wrote out my truth on paper because I was feeling liberated as I was writing but I was also nervous about the whole situation.

Stuff the chiles with queso fresco and seal the chile back up with a toothpick

The letter began with: "This year my gift to you is my honesty and trust." I revealed to her that I was a gay man who had known of his sexuality from the time he was about six years old. There were mixed emotions expressed on her face as she read the letter. I saw tears rolling down her eyes as she read it, but I also saw a smile on her face. I felt good, accomplished, and when she came up to me, she told me, "I've known just about as long as you have. I was just waiting for you to tell me." With both of our confessions out in the open, we laughed; I breathed a huge sigh of relief and was filled with encouragement because of such an amazingly strong support system ranging from my fraternity brothers to my friends and family. The last person I needed to come out to was the other woman who mattered the most to me, my mami.

*Sprinkle flour over the chiles **and** dip the chiles in the battered egg whites*

Sitting at the Memorial Union on my campus, my girls and I wasted countless hours. The hours spent talking about boys were ridiculous, but I enjoyed every minute of them! It was around this same time that my friends pointed out a student to me as the "bi guy." I thought it was hilarious that this guy had gained this reputation on campus and was also a little annoyed with the fact that my friends thought that I would be interested in every guy that happened to be queer. I brushed off the comment and tried to ignore it, but curiosity got the best of me. I contacted this "bi guy," and we hit it off really well; it eventually blossomed into my first real relationship with another man. This was all too perfect, and I couldn't have asked for a better coming out experience, but there was still the small detail of coming out to my mom. Now that I was out to everyone, had joined a gay fraternity, and had been dating a guy for several months, I felt that the relationship between my mom and me was growing even more distant. Not only was I withholding my sexual identity from her, but I was also keeping my whole life from her. I had been with my boyfriend and the fraternity for half a year now, and it was on a July afternoon that I decided that I had to tell her.

Fry the Chiles until the outer covering becomes a golden brown and the chile becomes tender

My mom was preparing some chiles pasilla to make chiles rellenos. My mom spends most of her time in the kitchen, cooking, reading, watching television. The Kitchen is her space; she is the most comfortable there. So I went over, washed my hands, and started helping her take out the seeds from the chiles. It was quiet at first; we made small talk about how to correctly de-seed the chiles so that they don't fall apart when you stuff them. Then it was quiet again. So I just came out and said, "Mamá, quiero hablarle de mi." That's how the conversation started, and I finally got the courage to tell her about what I had been up to for the past half year and how for the first time in a long time I was actually happy and I was actually living the life I wanted to live. She blamed herself at first for never giving me a father figure, believing one would have made all the difference. I did all I could to explain to her that it was not a matter of blame and that I was actually really happy with the way she raised me and with my current life. I know that the support I got from my brothers, friends, sister, and my loving boyfriend gave me the strength I needed to get to this point. At last after a long, emotional, exhausting, and liberating conversation she said the words I was hoping to hear, "Mijo, yo te quiero seas lo que seas." I have to say, my coming out experience was unique because it was a positive experience. I know I am fortunate and blessed to have had this experience because of the difficult experiences that men like me go through when coming out.

Maybe Ever Changing

Aarón Aguilar-Ramírez

This is not the first time I have delved inside my archive of thoughts and experiences in an attempt to define myself. Trying to define myself ... what a daunting task! It is not the first time I have tried, and I am no longer surprised that I fail each time, without exception. I admire those who can loudly exclaim, *Yes, I am gay, or bisexual, or queer! Yes, I am Chicano, or Mexican, or Latino!* Whatever it is they are, they know. There are many who can untangle their identities and proclaim a single one—a complex one, to be sure—but a single, solid one nevertheless. Sometimes I wish I could do just that. I know I am Chicano, and I know I am queer, and I am certainly proud to be both at once. But I can't be fair to myself—nor to you, nameless reader—to say that in this ever-growing archive inside my head I have found the clarity to define, in just a few words, what I am. My identity is still under construction. Instead of brooding longer over these sentiments, I will begin with my story:

I was born and raised in a small Mexican town near Guadalajara and lived there for almost ten years. I formed part of a traditionally Catholic family and attended a small, Catholic school where all the teachers were either nuns or unmarried women (men were not allowed to teach there). When I was a young boy I was very religious, although, I must confess, I always hated attending mass. On most Fridays, the entire school congregated in the small chapel that stood, cramped and crumbling, in the center of the school. My best friend and I snuck out of line on several occasions and hid behind a pillar, sniggering as our classmates filed into the chapel for mass. I would feel guilty later, but it was worth it then. He and I explored our small town together in the afternoons after school. Every day we sought his grandfather in the town plaza and badgered him for a few *pesos* that we would later use at a local arcade. We graffitied our names on the walls of our local church (and got caught and spanked by an aggravated old man). We talked about the girls we had crushes on—he liked a girl named Marisol all through elementary school. I liked Teresa.

My family moved to Los Angeles just a few months before my tenth birthday, a place where most people were of Mexican descent but where I stood out from all of my classmates. I could not speak English. I was made fun of because I raised my index finger to ask a question instead of my open palm. I couldn't grow out of the habit. Everyone looked like me with my brown skin and my dark hair and eyes, and yet we *were* so different. I didn't fit their mold: how they treated their friends with what to me smelled so badly of indifference; how they treated their teachers (in my eyes very rudely), and how their relationships with their parents seemed hard as plastic. It was not a fair evaluation, but to me they seemed that way. They were what my parents called *pochos*. I was not. I was a boy who could not speak English.

Growing up in the United States, I was not a *pocho* like my classmates but I was, at least until I was eighteen years old, a boy without a sexuality. I had been dimly "aware" that I was attracted to other boys since I was twelve years old, but it was a truth hidden somewhere deep in my mind, in a tenuous hiding place that sometimes gave way and exposed the sexuality I always attempted to conceal. But most days, I merely stumbled (or mumbled) my way through a heterosexual adolescence.

"What do you think of that girl?" This was a typical question all through middle and high school.

"Which one?"

"That one, the one with long hair and the *tiny* shorts. Damn, her legs look real good, huh?"

"Hm ... think she's in my English class."

"Do you think she has a cute face, though?"

"Yeah, I guess."

"Fuck, she's so hot."

And the conversations would trail off. I was heterosexual by default—merely because I did not deny being so—but I never spoke about sexuality to anyone. They thought I was timid (which I was, to some degree); they thought I was just shy or too respectful to approach a girl. Sometimes I believed them.

When I was seventeen I started to go out with a girl I had met through one of my middle school friends. She was from Guadalajara, she was very funny, and she was a big *chivas* fan just like me. Naturally, we got along really well. We had started talking on the Internet and met personally just a few days before I started my senior year of high school. I could easily talk to her, and we had quite a few things in common: music, food, and a distaste for terribly dubbed films—you name it. We were both distinctly "Mexican" in a way that my classmates and her friends were not. On our third date, we were walking down a badly lit street in San Fernando, sustaining a scattered conversation I can no longer remember. We had been walking a while when she slipped her hand into mine, almost by accident. I was very nervous. A long silence followed in which I could hear my breath and a heavy thumping in my chest. In truth, I actually felt quite terrified.

"Are you going to ask me out?" She said.

No, I thought to myself. *You can't.* There was a moment when I knew what I had to do, but then ...

"Would you like to be my girlfriend?"

We were together for thirteen months.

When I began my undergraduate career at Whitman College I embraced my *mexicanidad* in a way I had not before. In truth, the "transformation"—if it can be called that—began before I moved into my dorm in a somewhat ironic fashion. My high school friends often reminded me that I would be going to White Man College in the fall. They asked, jokingly, if I was tired of the Mexicans, if I could make friends with white rich kids, if I would miss the beans and *carne asada.* That last point was the only one that made me truly nervous. I was ready to move out. I was anxious to leave. I was not "tired of the Mexicans," but I was searching for someplace completely different. I wanted out.

Rather than abandoning "the Mexicans" when I moved in for my first year of college, I found a place where my brown skin and dark hair and eyes were a minority. I had expected it but had never previously experienced it. I had prepared myself to find racism—the kind my mother had warned me about as we flew into the United States nine years previously.

"They may call you 'beaner' or 'wetback.' If they make fun of you because you don't speak English, don't worry because you can speak Spanish better than all of them. They may ask you if you're illegal. *Pero no te preocupes, tu diles que no y que chinguen a su"*—my mother has always been valiantly vulgar.

Instead, I found people who were very cautious about calling me Latino or Mexican. I may have been the only non-Caucasian student in the building, also known as "the one with glasses," or "the one with the ripped vans," or "the one with a cool style" (though my sisters would greatly disagree on this point), or "the one who kind of looks like a jerk" (I was genuinely shocked by *this* comment). I much preferred to encounter this attitude to my mom's grim predictions, but I sometimes felt the need to assert, *yes, I am Mexican—and it's all right to use that adjective.*

At Whitman I also allowed myself the possibility of being queer, although this is a term I've only very recently begun to use. In November of my first year, I finally told two of my closest friends that I was not attracted to women. It was an emotional moment for me—a moment when I allowed something to surface that had never done so before, at least not with my consent. And yet I had not really "come out." I had *told* someone, which was certainly important for me, but it was not a coming out experience. It did not mean I was comfortable with myself or that I was ready to define myself as gay, or queer, or questioning. I was not ready to be romantically or sexually involved with a man. So what did I come out as, if I could not yet proclaim an identity? I had revealed a truth about myself, not embraced it.

I have systematically made people aware of my sexuality since I started my undergraduate experience. Friends, siblings, parents. You could even say that the time I sat my mother down on the living room couch and nervously explained to her that I was gay was a very "traditional" coming-out experience. But it wasn't. Telling my mother I was gay (gay, because that is a word she could more easily digest, and because I did not know what other word I could use) was a difficult thing to do, but that was not a defining moment in consolidating my identity, either. Coming out is an experience typically guised as the climax to a mystery story—as that poignant jump-in-your-seat moment when the secret is finally revealed, and after which the characters slowly work towards a resolution. Instead, telling my mother was to initiate a conflict in an otherwise boring plot. Telling my mom did not help me assert my identity—it merely confused her. But despite her confusion my mother was, and is, supportive. She did not kick me out of the house or disown me; she did not ask me how I had turned gay or why I chose that "lifestyle." She held me close and wondered aloud why I remained quiet for so long.

"*¿Por qué?*," she asked. "¿Por qué no me dijiste antes? ¿Por qué no te ahorraste tanto dolor?"

It may have saved me a great deal of pain, but I had not spoken because I did not have the space to. As a teenager I was terrified of my family's reaction, I was afraid my friends would no longer be my friends, I was afraid of my own response when that secret burrowed deep in my mind finally surfaced. It was God, it was the *macho* family men, and it was the very word "Mexican" (a word that on its own right is incompatible with "gay"). It was Los Angeles and its congested highways; it was the pressure of "liking" girls, of courtship, of having sex; and it was tradition—whatever that meant. It was a myriad of reasons I cannot adequately explain or enumerate. Remaining silent meant sustaining and retaining everything that then "defined" me, while speaking meant throwing it all away—manhood, my Mexican identity, my family. Starting college was a symbolic rupture of that silence, and to me a rejection of everything that came before. It was a fresh start.

My "coming out" story, if it deserves that name, was not a time when I confessed what I was, but a series of events that blurred and questioned my identity. When once upon a time I was sure I was Mexican, now I am not so sure. When I visited my family in Mexico they criticized my Spanish ("¡que acento tan feo tienes!"). While once I was a heterosexual teenager because I never bothered to state otherwise, I now know for certain only that I am not this term. So what am I? Am I a queer Chicano, constantly evaluating and reevaluating his identity with every new experience? Maybe. If I am, I do not see this as a bad thing, or as a possible liability or weakness in my character. Rather, it is the possibility to continue to grow and to evolve, to learn something new with every step. It is this characteristic, perhaps, that may most closely resemble the queer Chicano I may or may not be. Perhaps not volatile, but maybe ever-changing.

Section III

Embodied Self

children of wilted suns

Lorenzo Herrera y Lozano

at the dawn of becoming a man
tests dressed me in the red
thorny laced gown that once
wrapped the necks of men
who loved as I love

children of sarape covered couches
children of atole raised abuelas
children of velvet Jesus churches
died alone
died in shame
in pale green hallways

children owed another day
waiting long, waiting still
golondrinas will paint our sky

at the dawn of becoming a man
I donned drapes of their destiny
I became home
home to men
who loved as I love

I am home
home to men who broke as I break
men who wait, wait in me
for the flight of golondrinas

I am the couch to their sarape
they are the atole that raises me
the velvet Jesus hanging over my bed
I am the orphan to their souls
the carrier of pillaged dreams
the son of men who died for love
love airbrushed on the walls inside of me

spirits dance every time
I kiss a man in offered sacrifice
to the memory of wilted suns
I am home
home to men
who kissed as I kiss

Crevices y Cicatrizes

Finding Liberation Through My Body

Eddy F. Alvarez

A few years ago I embarked on a relationship that moved a bit too fast, and although the signs were there that I probably shouldn't have been in it, I thought it was something "special" and I allowed myself to be vulnerable, to feel. I was falling hard for this guy who I shall call Tony. After only a few months our relationship ended. The details and cumulative nuances of why that happened can be left for another time. What I will focus on here was a major problem in our relationship (for him) and something I was unaware of or blind to until the end. A few days before breaking up, Tony and I were returning from a trip to Las Vegas. We had gone to a lecture by queer Chicana feminist playwright Cherríe Moraga at the University of Nevada, Las Vegas. Her talk was powerful and poignant, and I believe it opened us up (mostly me) to be honest once and for all. In the car, already back in Los Angeles and on our way to a concert, Tony shared with me that throughout our relationship he had "struggled" with my "skin condition," with my acne scars. He told me he was someone who took care of himself and expected the same of his partners. He also expressed that the only reason he had begun dating me was because I told him I went to the gym. He was attracted to me, he said, for many other reasons, but he usually dated "athletic guys." His words were piercing and hurtful, and all I could wonder was how after all the soul searching, all the liberatory work I had been doing through writing and graduate work, after all the heavenly guidance from Gloria Anzaldúa, how I ended up dating this guy. I asked myself how after all of the repair work I had done given previous relationships and my bouts with low self-esteem, all the body loving and reclaiming of desire, how was it that I was dating this guy? Needless to say, we only lasted a few more days.

I tell this story because it marks a crucial point in my life and in the journey through my body consciousness acceptance. Also, because I feel many may relate to it in some way. This experience with my ex-boyfriend made me once again look at my body, my chichis and lonjas, my pimples and my scars and remember how bodies like mine are read in US society. The cystic acne and scars that mark my body had become invisible to me for a long time, but Tony reminded me that they were there, that they were uncomfortable to look at, repulsive in some way. His words, while painful at first, eventually reminded me of my own strength. His words pushed me towards another level of consciousness. Interestingly, I now thank Tony for that experience and for the reminder not to forget the meanings inscribed upon my body. This essay is, to borrow from Puerto Rican author Judith Ortiz Cofer, "the story of my body."[1] I bring together my corporeal testimonio, poetic analysis, and some theoretical insights to map out my journey from adolescence to the present. In this mapping, every lonja and every scar, small and big, are points in the cartography of my body consciousness, of my process, an everlasting work in progress. This essay is also a call to find liberation through our bodies and to rethink the role of our bodies in our struggle for social justice.

My body has gone through several stages. Around the age of fourteen or fifteen I began to break out and used every topical acne medication imaginable. I used over the counter Oxy, witch hazel recommended to me by a friend in junior high, and *capsulas de vivora de cascabel*,[2] a remedy my cousin in Ensenada used to get rid of his acne.

---

1   Judith Ortiz Cofer, *The Latin Deli: Prose and Poetry* (Athens: U of Georgia P, 1993).
2   Rattlesnake pills

I used astringents, hot towels, toothpaste. You name it, I tried it. It was even suggested to me that I use cum or sperm and rub it on my face. That remedy I never tried, although it would have been fun! With the antibiotics I could access through my Medi-Cal I was able to improve my skin somewhat, but it always came back. In high school my acne got worse, developing into what I would later find out was cystic acne caused by overproducing sebaceous glands. I had large red cyst-like pimples on my face, neck, back, and chest, even my legs. Although it wasn't as bad on my face as on other people I had seen, it was still painful and embarrassing and affected my self-esteem.

Loney, Standage, and Lewis argue that how one perceives their skin to be evaluated by others has implications for self perceptions and may act as a barrier to sport/exercise participation.[3] This barrier to participation, I would argue, extends to other social activities like pool parties and beach outings, but also involve intimate activities like sex and lovemaking. The physical activity domain, they remind us, "affords many social opportunities for the skin to be observed and evaluated by others and thus causing social anxiety."[4] This, they argue, affects people's "dermatological quality of life."[5] For years I felt embarrassed by my body, refusing to take off my shirt in public, avoiding pool and beach parties, experiencing much of this social anxiety and living a poor dermatological quality of life.

In "Story of My Body," Ortiz Cofer tells of the trauma she experienced after the school nurse told her that for peeling chicken pox pustules she would end up with permanent scars. "I was nearly devastated by what the chicken pox episode had done to my self-image," she says. "But I looked in the mirror less often after I was told that I would always have scars on my face, and I hid behind my long black hair and

---

3   Tom Loney, Martyn Standage, and Stephen Lewis, "Not Just 'Skin Deep': Psychosocial Effects of Dermatological-related Social Anxiety in a Sample of Acne Patients," *Journal of Health Psychology* 13.1 (2008), 47.

4   Ibid, 48.
5   Ibid, 47.

my books."[6] Cofer's words resonate with me because hiding my acne and my fat became part of my adolescence. As I constantly tried to hide my body, it was not fun to constantly be asked if I had a hickey on my neck, and although I often wished I could say I did, it wasn't true. The marks on my neck were actually red cysts. To avoid that shame I often wore skin-colored Band-Aids on my neck or turtlenecks in the heat to cover my ugliness.

It wasn't until my undergraduate days at California State University, Northridge when I began to see a great dermatologist at the health center. He quickly put me on Accutane, a very strong medication that required I have my blood drawn every month. Although the side effects were extremely challenging on my body, my skin improved for a year, and according to me I looked better than ever. Despite my heightened "dermatological quality of life," I was still struggling with my weight even though I was at the "skinniest" I had ever been. This was, of course, because I was self-medicating with all kinds of drugs. In my head I thought I was fine, especially because my skin looked great. My blackheads even disappeared. I was finally attractive, and I possessed what Anita Revilla Tijerina would call "socially constructed beauty." A year later, however, my cystic acne resurfaced and I went back on Accutane. That also only lasted a while. Over the last few years I have taken other less severe antibiotics for acne, and I refused to take Accutane until recently. My acne has gotten better, and people I haven't seen in a while will undoubtedly tell me, "Your skin looks so good." "Thanks," I usually respond with a smile. Despite the temporary results from Accutane or any other medication, I have accepted that I live with adult acne, and I take care of it accordingly. It is a part of my life, but it does not have the effect it once had on me.

There are reminders of my battle with acne, however. After all those years of acne, many scars have accumulated across the geography of my body. In his analysis of the meaning of scars in the works of Jorge Luis Borges, Daniel Balderston writes that scars have a "rich and

---

6   Cofer, 143.

far-reaching iconographic history, from ancient times through Dante and Hawthorne to Stevenson, Borges, and beyond." He argues that it is important to note that facial scars (significant because they are visible) have functioned as signs with various meanings. The physical scar, for example, may be an indicator of past heroism or villainy; scars have also been imposed by divine intervention, as in the mark of Cain. His scar protects him from the violence of others, and at the same time it serves to remind them of his crime. Furthermore, Balderston writes, "Societies have marked or mutilated transgressors as a punishment and as a means to assure their identity."[7] Balderston's observations inform my own inquiries about the significance of scars in real life, upon physical bodies. I ask, then, how has society signified acne and acne scars, and punished those who are marked that way? I argue that only through a disruption in language, that is, a different way to talk about things, and through challenging discourses on beauty, can we make that change. We must dismantle binaries and find definitions through difference and through resignification. How does a body deemed monstrous by society become beautiful? How is the "monstrous" resignified as "beautiful"? The following analysis may help.

In his poem "The Beautiful Scars" by queer Bay area Afro-Chicano poet Robert Quintana Hopkins, he addresses his lover's scars and the love he feels for him and the scars that mark him.

> When we make love/I intentionally love his scars/I kiss them/I feel them/Impact with the car behind/threw them from the motorcycle/The divider in the middle of the freeway killed his friend/My partner lives/With mangled legs and hips/Huge textured scars cross his right hip and both knees/I strive to demonstrate that I find everything about

---

7   Daniel Balderston, "The Mark of the Knife: Scars as Signs in Borges," *The Modern Language Review* 83.1 (1988), 68.

him beautiful/I love his scars/I kiss them/I feel them/When
we make love.[8]

Through his poem, Quintana Hopkins resignifies scars as something
to be loved, as something beautiful. He finds everything about his lover
beautiful, and the scars are integral to the whole person he loves. He
even kisses the scars. Quintana Hopkins provides us with a language
to resist and redefine scars in contrast to what they typically have been
defined as—repulsive but also fascinating. There is nothing fascinating
or repulsive here; the scars are simply part of his lover's body, his skin
with different texture, worthy of love and desire. This poem reminds
me of the first time I took my shirt off in front of one of my lovers. I
made sure to make a disclaimer about my acne scars as I peeled off
my t-shirt, and he proceeded to tell me that my body was beautiful.
He kissed my shoulder, then my chest, and hugged me. This moment,
like Quintana Hopkins's poem, served to recalibrate my understanding
and perception of my own body, and through desire and the touch of
another man I was able to work through what Loney, Standage, and
Lewis refer to as "dermatological social anxiety."

With this lover I visited for the first time a nude beach in Santa
Barbara, California. My lover (still a friend of mine) is a white man who
identifies as a bear. He taught me a lot about desire and about loving
my body. Of course, his body, as a white man's, has not been marked the
way mine has; despite my lighter skin privilege, mine has been marked
as a man of color's. I dare to assume he's never been followed around
a store because his head was shaved and he was assumed to be a
gangster. "But your skin is whiter than mine," he always reminded me
jokingly, reflecting his inability to deal at some levels with his white
privilege. Although he is an amazing person, some things he'll never
get. With him, I learned to take my shirt off in the pool at barbeques
where his neighbors were present and at a nude beach, for goodness

---

8   Robert Quintana Hopkins, *The Glass Closet* (Oakland: AfroChicano Press, 2009),
     25

sake, where my lonjas and huevos hung freely. In his bed, where my nakedness found freedom and my bodily shame was suspended, he put his tongue and his hands in places no one had before, touched my body in ways I'd never felt, as he worshipped my penis *and* my panza.

When I found out how pleasurable being naked was and how liberating taking my shirt off was, I gained a new understanding of myself, of desire, and of my own sexuality. As I stripped away the clothes, I literally stripped away many narratives and discourses that had me confined. I came closer to understanding Jaime Cortez's words when he said "one liberation at a time."[9] I found in my own nakedness answers to many things, places in my psyche I had never visited, ways of knowing once unknown to me. Part of this liberation has come from the influence of women of color feminists and queers of color like Gloria Anzaldúa, Chela Sandoval, Audre Lorde, Cherríe Moraga, and of course Jaime Cortez, with his lyrically liberating *Virgins, Guerrillas and Locas*. Their writings have inspired me to find theory in my own flesh and love radically and intensely.[10] Through these liberationist writers, I have learned to find strength in my body and negotiate daily with the shame, fear, and loathing that may still exist within me. In this process I have liberated myself of the baggage that once confined me and taught me to hate my own body.

While this essay has been about the "story of my body," it may very well be the story of other people's bodies as well. It is important to remember that the "personal is political,"[11] and that as queer people of color our bodies are at the center of our sexual lives and our politics; our bodies and our desires have been racialized, policed, demonized, and branded historically. Unfortunately, we have internalized much of this and police ourselves and each other, treating bodies different

---

9   Jaime Cortez, "Sun to Sun" in *Virgins, Guerrillas and Locas: Gay Latino Men Writing about Love* (San Francisco: Cleis Press, 1999), 181.
10 Cherríe Moraga and Gloria Anzaldúa, *This Bridge Called My Back: Writing By Radical Women of Color* (New York: Kitchen Table Press, 1981), 23.
11 A key concept of the Women's Movement and feminist theory.

than our own with suspicion or making them invisible. Originally, this essay was going to be solely about weight, fatfobia, and my struggles with being a gay Chicano coming of age in the mid-1990s amidst skinny, white West Hollywood. In essence it still is, but as I revisited my memories, I realized that my struggles with cystic acne and with the scars it left upon my body, physical and emotional, cannot be separated from other body image issues I've endured. This essay is a reflection on finding liberation through and in the same body, my own, which I so despised years before. I have drawn from personal experiences and been influenced by women of color feminists and queer of color scholars and performers who have helped me to understand my own reality and how my body is intricately linked to the politics I engage as a queer poet and academic on a day-to-day basis.

Opulence

Xuan Carlos Espinoza-Cuellar

Confession
I can't love
No puedo amar con todo mi potencial
My insides hurt
My body has been terrorized
Trespassed, attacked, targeted
My mind esta dolida,
My body hurts
I want to sleep forever
Igual como aquel viaje de hace 10 years, sin retorno

I stood before the mirror and began beating myself
Scratching my lonjas until I made them bleed
I wanted them to cry
I wanted them to beg me for mercy
I wanted them to learn what it is to live in pain
Bleeding from the soul
It was all their fault

Each morning I would punch my stomach
Maldita gordura
Le daba palmazos a mis piernas
Hoping the fat would come out
Solo moretones

Solo marcas, cicatrizes, poemas tristes
Solo dolor

I couldn't see him loving me
I rejected him, and him and her
How can someone love a monster
Monster me?
Voluptuous me?

One time he said that I was beautiful "inside"
Yet, inside-beauty didn't cause arousal of a certain member of the
male body
Therefore I could be only his friend
So that he could exploit my mind whenever possible

She said, cover your body in shame
Wear black, she said
It hides your opulence
It makes you disappear
I got dark clothes
Dark clothes that hurt my spirit
My nana told me

Every time the desire to love awakens in me
The pain of not belonging strikes otra vez
Y I stay in shock
Una vez mas
Veo mi cuerpo con ganas de desgarrarlo
Slice my legs, my stomach, my arms
Hurt myself, proper punishment for not fitting in
Not fit
Fat
Not beautiful
Inadequate
Lazy

I can't be loved,

Fatties are to remain in the margins
On the sidelines
Awaiting a "chub chaser" to come to the rescue
So he can fill his penis into our opulence
And make us feel loved/desired for a few minutes
As we thankfully praise his willingness to trespass our bodies

Our bodies are broken
Our bodies are raped
And I can't, can't, can't
Can't love
Myself
Or anybody else.

Rain Dance

Edgar-Arturo Camacho-González

As I prepare for the ceremony, I cry.
It has been a long time since I have seen the
rain.
It is necessary for life.
I paint my face with the soft foundation brush,
bronze my cheek bones
what will be left on my pillow.

My garments are equipped to handle the rain when it comes.
Essential straps of Polyurethane for the rain dance.
A ritual practiced by my ancestors.
The beating of the drums in my head have traveled north,
from my chest and heart.
The sound is louder.
The rain is coming.

It has traveled as well.
Traveled far from a land that need not be watered.
You have traveled to see me, specifically.
You have brought me the water in a locked container.
I am the key.

To unlock you, we must rain dance together.
This ritual is vital to prosperity among the land.

As we dance the key is transferred,
From my tongue to yours it jumps.
Avoiding the twists and turns in our mouth.
Our muscles attacking each other in resistance.

As we dance our bodies touch.
The friction and our movements are subtle but strong.
We are naked.
You taste the salt in the soil that has preserved me.
I dance carefully.

The key has traveled southward toward the lock.
It has arrived.

The brown that covers my body is healthier.
This season's cosecha will be prosperous.
You have prepared me for it.

We will swim in our lake.
Our cum that fills it will dry soon,
The ancient land before the lake will be more fertile.

Section IV

Coatlicue State

chimera

Lorenzo Herrera y Lozano

and because I straddle
I am desert-risen *culebra*
I am McDonald's-fed Nintendo
player
concrete stuck under the fingernails
of memory
I am the hole in my teenage shoe
the first public erection

I was never free, not once
harnessed as *el Río Bravo*
I run just as dry

I eat dirt from adobe walls
drink hope from strangers' mouths
there is no logic to follow me
only shriveled reveries
and yet I straddle

I am a medley of unanswered *plegarias*
a *novena* for AIDS-related deaths
novena for my own
for the generation who shared my bed
I recite *Hail Papis*, for us

I am my only danger
a lover of many lovers
chuparrosa in a sea of *buganvilias*
abeja de seis panales
I am an altar of nameless sugar skulls

a concoction of mismatched dreams
until you kiss me
making sense of my fabrications
I become theory, stuck on your tongue
I become tongue, stuck on conclusions

and because I straddle
I am the decay of *alamedas*
the haunting of low-rider days
a rebel creeping through no-cruise zones

I loiter
beg for memories of those who could not leave
my soul, the echo of canyon walls

I am becoming ever beautiful
gray, thick and carved by the knife of time
I am the mirror of men I have always chased

older, not wiser, only older
I have become my father
the man I have always chased

of the lines carved out by time
I guard them all, all
are love and pain and loss,
are greedy lovers

scratching, marking my bed
I obey their tantrums; concede
offer candy from other lips
flavored lube, condoms that feel nonexistent
absent as the one bent before me

I break bread with so few
make bread of nearly all
I expand inside them
they are PCP to my dilated eyes

they cum, I go
I fuck as stone-butch dykes do
no, not as masculine
yes, as untouched

My Shadow Beast

Gibrán Güido

I am not the same person this very moment I was five minutes ago, five days ago, not even five years ago. Who am I? I'm a twenty-four-year-old queer Chicano. Now for some, my queer identity and my Chicano identity are abstract notions that may be taken for granted by those who have asked me how I identify and who may feel uncomfortable with my identity. Even so, I think to myself, good, because it will take a little more work for them to get to know who I am and what I've gone through.

So let me begin with Chicano, a word with a historical context and significance. My identification with the word began when I came to accept myself as part of my culture and traditions, because you see, I never claimed to be Chicano before going to college. Prior to this I was ashamed of even claiming that I was Mexican. Ashamed, you may ask? Well, let me explain. When I entered college I knew I was Mexican, but I took no pride in it because of all the cultural norms and traditions that subjugated Mexican women, especially the women who raised me. They were often subjected to domestic abuse and left to fend for themselves and their children, and I witnessed how much these women suffered, and I wanted no part of a culture where men were thought superior to women. These feelings may have been my first moments of gender consciousness; nevertheless, I denied being associated with a culture whose men abused the women I cared about. Ironically, I remember the very first lesson I was taught by the women who raised me, which was how to behave like a man; I am the boy that grew into a man because of the guidance of women. The Chicano part came much later, and to avoid any impulse to fall back on theory, my Chicano identity was inspired by my acceptance of my cultural heritage, my background, and the struggles of my people as well as the rejection of its negative gender and sexual stereotypes and patriarchal notions of masculinity. Funny though, wouldn't you think, that when I reflect back I realize that maybe this is the first time that I have Queered up my Chicano identity. So I embraced Chicanismo with a sense of pride and accomplishment. I knew who I was, culturally, and felt comfortable with my newfound identity. However, as I began to embrace this critically conscious cultural identity, it began to transform. I embraced a queer identity over time, not all at once or from night to day but with a gradual understanding of who I am in relation to the world(s) that I occupy, as a queer Chicano.

As I write this to you, a person I probably won't ever meet, I get a little nervous. So I take time and prepare myself. I get up, wash my face, and try to prepare myself to tell you about me, my sexual identity, and the experiences that happened that have led me to write this account, not just for me but also for you. Why, you may ask? It's because I want you to have something that I never had when I came out. What I needed I can only hope that this testimony will be for the reader, who may look for a reflection of their experiences that may complement and give strength to their own lives. While I was coming out I wanted to find a reflection of myself in someone else's testimony—a coming out story from a Gay/Queer and Chicano/Latino/Mexican. Something that I could read and re-read to understand what that writer had gone through because, you see, had it not been for some connection between my cultural and sexual identity through literature then I wouldn't be writing this today. So let me begin.

When I came out it was around the time that I was finishing a relationship with my ex-girlfriend after what was at the time my longest relationship. At this point we remained together but only casually, and it seemed that our relationship was nearing an end and we were prolonging the inevitable. Curiously enough, she would be the only one to really see my initial encounter with the questioning of my sexual identity, and I don't blame her for wanting distance between us after that. Because, you see, I didn't always know I was attracted to men at an early age, like some people have told me. No, instead I later came to that realization in my early twenties. Well, I remember the exact day: November 1, 2004. There are a few reasons that help me to remember this day. The first is because November 1 is the day before *dia de los muertos*. The second is because of the way I came to question my own sexual identity. It wasn't as though I came to the realization on my own, but it was my mother who helped me to realize that I might not be straight. My mother and I shared this really great relationship, and so I usually spoke to her over the phone while I was away at school. So one afternoon when my ex was with me, I called my mom. We spoke for a while about how things were going for her at home and how my brother was doing. She had asked how things were going at school, and I couldn't lie and say they were great because when you are an undergrad, there's all that work of going to class and working on papers. In our conversation I must have brought something up that made my mom respond and ask what she did. Even today I still can't remember what it was, but my mother asked, "G, are you trying to tell me something?" I really had no idea what she was talking about, and I said, "No, mom, what do you mean?" She said that I was always talking about gay issues and she thought that I was trying to insinuate and tell her something. This moment became the defining moment and, I suppose, the question that really made me who I am today. It was this point, with my mom questioning my sexuality, which seemed to impact me more at that time. To this day, I don't really know what at that moment, at the age of twenty-one, I questioned – an aspect of identity that I never had—but I trusted my mom to know me better than anyone else. My best guess would be that maybe being away from home, the unstable relationship with my ex and, finally, my mom's questioning put everything into place. All these factors may have been the reason why I had questions long ago, but I had no idea or was not prepared for what I would go through.

After that initial conversation and the parting of ways with my ex-girlfriend, I became a recluse. All I did at the time was keep to myself, in my room, in my apartment. I didn't go to class or communicate with my family back in San Diego. During this time I questioned everything about myself. Nothing really was now certain for me because I really questioned if I was attracted to men. I thought that I never had been before and why would I be now? I hadn't even considered the possibility. Would or should I try and see if I was attracted to men?

I believe now that I was deconstructing for myself twenty or so years of socialization and the reinforcement of what it "meant" for me to be a "man." This was the hardest week of my life because I worried so much about what my family and friends would think. Would my friends reject me or would my family disown me if I were gay? How was I repressing my sexual identity? One important event that I never really mentioned to very many people was how I felt I would disappoint all those who believed in me and loved me. I felt at the time that I would not be the person who they thought I was and that they would feel a sense of betrayal if I were gay. At this point I really contemplated the idea of suicide. I wondered to myself, would they really miss me or should I even put my family though all of this? I had also planned out how I would go about committing this self-inflicted violence, but fortunately I'm here writing this and putting into words my experiences. Nearing the end of this week and having come to terms with at least knowing that I needed to continue on, I did what came naturally to me whenever I felt alone or afraid—I read. My visit to the university library was by far the most distressing event ever because I felt afraid should anyone find out what books I was getting or find them anywhere in my belongings;

there would be no way of explaining or justifying why I had a book on being "gay" or "coming out." Simply put, I would be guilty by association. The literature that I checked out from the library consisted of an array of different topics: coming out, depression, adolescents and being gay, and teen suicides. I learned that the earlier one comes out the more likely they are to commit suicide. I also learned a very important lesson. I should prepare myself for the possibility of being disowned by my family and find some way to live independently on my own. Needless to say, I was scared of being disowned and kicked out of my house. I didn't know how to really understand this, especially because I was a Mexican male who was raised and supported by my family. One important cultural understanding in being Mexican is that one's family is everything. Without my family, what would I have? I also questioned if my pursuit of an individual sexual identity was worth the price of losing my family. More importantly, the more I read, the less I could identify with being Mexican and "coming out" and being male. Where was all that literature?! The pursuit of this topic would incite in me the motivation to continue looking. I found pieces here and there that spoke of a Latino male's experiences, but nothing providing me with any encouragement. One such piece that comes to mind is Reinaldo Arenas's *Before Night Falls*, an autobiography of his life growing up gay, Cuban, and an exile and the effects of HIV. He stated that gay men are prone to infidelity and that there was no such thing as monogamy in the gay world. At this point in time I was a sponge and actually believed such things. I had nothing to counter or question what literature I had read. Overwhelmingly, I began to notice that most of what I read was written by gay white men. This I would silently keep in mind and later critique for its assumptions and projected expectations, but just then any and all information about gay culture I took in and internalized.

The very first intimate contact I had with a boy was really supposed to be my "way of knowing" if I liked guys or not. Since "coming out," how could I really be sure that I was attracted to men? So during this week-long process, most of my initial information about gay culture was found online. It goes without saying that there wasn't much on being Mexican and gay, but there was plenty on being gay. So I got tons of my initial information online. As nerdy as it may seem, I studied and still feel as though I study gay culture because it fascinates me. So what I did was stumble across gay chat rooms. The one I used the most was "downelink." I obsessively signed on to chat rooms to see what guys were on and see what encounters I would have. In order to chat, one needed to set up a profile. So I set one up in minutes and began to explore what the website had to offer. Fortunately, I didn't have to put up all my information and I could still chat with people. Well, I really didn't chat at first, but when I grew comfortable I found myself chatting. Now, you wanna know how I really decided for myself that I might not be straight? Well, I let biology do its magic. I thought to myself, if I liked guys then I would make out with one, and if I was sexually aroused, then, hey, there was no denying it, right? So I used the website to see if anyone was interested. Don't think that I just went looking to hook-up, but I definitely decided that this was what I could do. So after some random conversations online, I came across a boy who was interested in me. So, not really knowing what I was supposed to do, I invited him to hang out in Davis, the small town where I went for my undergraduate studies. We hung out and spent the day together, and after feeling a little more comfortable, I invited him over to watch a movie. Now here's where I got really awkward and I didn't know what to do. He invited me over to lie next to him, and I did. As nervous as I was, I think he could sense that I was, and so he made the first move; I just responded. I closed my eyes, and for the first time ever, at the age of 21, I made out with a guy. Before kissing a man I had all sorts of thoughts running through my head about what this experience would be like. As soon as we started to make out and we were both into it, I became sexually aroused. This was really a defining moment for me because it justified for me that I had some attraction to men, because I was sexually aroused, but I was still a little timid about what could and would happen as a result of this. I guess he could tell, too, that I was into it because not long after we started to make out he wanted me to go down on him. Now, that I wasn't ready for, and especially for someone who I had thought was really only into just hooking up. I'm sure he was disappointed because I almost instantly told him "no" and that I wasn't ready for that, and I really didn't care what his reaction would be.

So after the initial make-out session, we met up a couple of times, but we really didn't hit it off. So it was because of a random guy, who I met online, that I discovered that I was sexually aroused by men. It was not a romance or "that special one" whom I gave my first kiss to, but this experience was what I needed to know if I would even be interested in men.

One thing that I did learn about the gay community early on was the concept of "hooking up." I learned that when you chat with someone online and they ask you if you want to "meet up," "hook up," or just get together, there's a pretty good chance that there's going to be some messing around. At the time when I was just coming out, I thought hooking up was literally just getting together kind of like a date. So when I was asked by another guy if I wanted to hook-up, I went along and made plans to meet at a Denny's about halfway between where he lived and where I lived. We met up and had coffee and a really casual conversation. I remember that I thought we were just getting together to hang out and talk, but maybe it was naïveté on my part because when he asked if I wanted to come over and watch a movie, at midnight, I should have gotten the big hint. Although I thought it was a little strange, I went along with it and took his invitation. We drove separately and went back to his apartment. What I didn't know prior to meeting up, or driving over to his apartment, or even right before I walked into his apartment door was that I would have my first sexual experience with a man.

Even before I put into words and on paper this really intimate and defining moment for me, I want to say that I really did appreciate this person's response and how he dealt with my reaction to what happened.

So, I walked in the front door and he invited me in and told me to make myself at home and to relax. After doing some last minute cleaning up, he asked what movie I wanted to see. We chose some random movie that he had been watching, and we sat down on opposite ends of the couch. After about ten minutes or so, he got closer and leaned forward to give me what was my second kiss from a man.

I don't know what it was, but I think that maybe it was how comfortable I felt around him. We kept making out, and it wasn't long before it got really intense between us two. The difference between this guy and the one that I had met before was I felt that this guy was genuine and that even though he was a complete stranger, there was something special about him. We made out, and he guided me over to his bed. As nervous as I was, things progressed from there. Now, since I had no sexual experience with a man I really didn't know what I was doing and really let him take the lead, and he did. He went down on me, and an array of emotions and pleasures captivated me. I enjoyed this experience but was afraid for the act I was doing. That's really why I think that when I was finished, I was completely overwhelmed with all my anxieties, fears, and excitement over what was true, because I began to cry. At the time I felt that it was really happening that I was gay/bi and that there was no turning back. I still remember thinking to myself that my life would never be the same anymore. I knew that things would change for me and I could never go back to the comforts and pleasures that I had when I had straight privilege because things would be much harder. Simple pleasures like public displays of affection and introducing my partner to my family would be different, and my biggest fear at the time was that I was no longer safe because I could be physically attacked or gay bashed at any moment if I "outed" myself in spaces that were not friendly to Queer individuals. When I mentioned earlier that I appreciated everything that this individual did, I mean that at the most awkward of moments when we were having sex and I began to cry, he did what I never expected. I think he recognized what I may have been going through because he held me. He held me and whispered in my ear, "Everything is going to be all right. It's all right. It's all right." I felt embarrassed for displaying these emotions, especially after having received oral sex. When I tried to apologize for my tears, he told me I didn't have to worry and apologize because there was nothing wrong with what I did. I felt ashamed for ruining the moment, but at that point in my life I had so much pent up aggression and tension over everything that had happened that I felt lost in it all. One of the sweetest and most intimate moments I had in my coming out experiences was with this special person who did everything he could to put me at ease. He held and comforted me.

As I was going through my own experiences, back at home I had no idea what my family had been going through. From what my brother and my mother told me later, my sexuality was a topic that wasn't discussed or brought up. They tried to understand what I was going through and how I felt. One day I called my mother and asked her if it was all right to come home for Thanksgiving. She later told me that this was one of the most hurtful things I could ask her. To her I was her son and I always had a home to go back to. So I believe that this was one of the first times that the literature I read would not apply, because I believe my ethnic/cultural background contradicted the usual gay white male experience of coming out.

So when I went back home for the holidays I prepared myself the best I could. Looking back now, I didn't do very much. I had information that I equipped myself with about who was Gay/Bi/Queer and Latino. When I searched online I came across a random website that had a list claiming Frida Kahlo, Emiliano Zapata, Ché, and Pedro Infante were Gay/Bi/Queer Latinos. I don't know how true this is for some of these individuals, but I wanted to believe it. I thought at the time, if these figures were Gay/Bi/Queer and they made a positive impact within Latino culture, then there wasn't anything to be ashamed of! It made me who I was, a unique individual capable of producing anything that would change the world. That holiday year was by far the hardest one I had to face since I came out.

While I was at home it was very awkward because neither my mom, my brother, nor I knew how to really communicate after I told them over the phone that I might be "bi." See, my parents got divorced when I was still in high school, and so there were only the three of us, as it always had been before and after the divorce. At times we would talk, but really most of the time we never really spoke about what I had told my mom. It seemed as though my coming out first began with the traditional Mexican norm where "everyone knows, except no one speaks about it." But I was never the person to just let things go unsaid. Our relationship, my mother's, brother's, and mine, was always very close, and so we never kept things from each other. We always spoke about what was bothering us, but this was a new challenge for all of us. I just didn't know how to tell my family how difficult it was for me—my feelings and thoughts, coming out on my own, how I searched for something or someone to connect to who would provide me with the answers I wanted, and someone or something who could tell me that I could be Mexican and Gay/Bi/Queer. At this point I still considered myself to be Bi/Questioning because I knew that I had liked women before in the past, but I didn't know if I still did or whatever that would mean for me. As uncertain as I was and as difficult as it was for me, I secretly wanted my mom to be there and tell me everything was going to be all right, that we were going to get through all of this. Eventually, she would placate my doubts. We didn't know how to go about with one another, but I was with my family; hey, they were going to get through this with me, but we would need time to do so. What eventually happened I believe made me stronger than I had ever been before and, luckily, I was able to handle and deal with what I needed to do.

When I went back to school and tried to continue my studies I found out over a period of time that I was "outed" by one of the very few people that I had told when I first questioned my sexuality. I was so upset and distraught at the time and felt betrayed because there was nothing I could do after this. I still believe I know who it was because there were very few people that I had told at the time. Over time, though, I've learned that to feel resentment and bitterness towards those I once trusted gives them the power and attention they may have been seeking. At the time I had outed myself to two people whom I believe outed me to mutual friends. I began to notice that some of my friends began to avoid me or stopped talking to me all together. I still feel that one of those individuals did exploit my coming out experience for their own gain. At the time this individual served as a mentor and counselor in the LGBT community but really took the opportunity to try and sleep with me. Although I won't claim to be naïve, I do think that it was irresponsible, and it is unfair to have that sort of experience when one is confused about their sexual identity and has no one to turn but a sexual predator in the guise of a counselor. Over time I figured out this individual's intentions and stopped any further relationship with him. So I dropped from the groups and organizations I was in while all this was happening and took the time I needed for myself to make decisions for myself in regards to what I wanted to do with what had already happened on campus and also to confront some of the rumors that were going around. To give an example of one, a rumor had spread by some individuals involved in one of the organizations of which I was a member that my leadership skills were not what they once were because I was "out clubbing all night and not coming back home and sleeping throughout the day," implying that I wasn't as responsible and reliable because I wasn't the same person that I once was. So, as usual with what happens when one confronts those who spread rumors, they either take responsibility and apologize or just feign and claim that they had no idea. Well, unfortunately, the latter was claimed and so I just let it go. Interestingly enough, though, the rumors stopped, and so I suppose I may have challenged the right person at the time. Luckily, at this point I also had made new friendships and reinforced old ones with friends that I never expected to come through for me. It really was because of them that I was able to get through all this drama at school, and to them I will always be appreciative for what they did for me.

I continued to struggle with my identity, but I was much more secure about certain things. I still held onto my Chicano identity throughout all this, but it really didn't quite fit with my newly identified sexuality. I found it difficult to mesh the Chicano and Gay/Bi identity. See, at the time I still considered myself bi because I had an attraction to women, but I wasn't sure if it was sexually, physically, or emotionally. So I really couldn't claim a gay identity, could I? I also found that claiming bisexuality made certain people uncomfortable because I believe they wanted to know if I was straight or gay; nothing else really fit. Bisexuality never really fit into their binary, gay or straight mind. Even now when the conversation comes up, bisexuality, unfortunately, still isn't considered an acceptable sexual identity when I try to claim it. As for a Gay identity, I found it still too much for me to handle because I had my past encounters with women, and I felt as though to claim a gay identity wouldn't be appropriate. It wouldn't be acceptable for me because I hadn't had the experience of growing up knowing that I desired men, or even the perspective of having gone through that. I grew up thinking and believing I was straight. So for most of my life I had what's called "straight privilege." This meant that I was socially accepted by society for my "sexual preference" in the opposite sex. Along with this privilege comes the socially and culturally expected assumptions of meeting the "right girl," getting married, having kids, making a family, and living in a home where I would be able to support and raise my family as a father and husband. Looking back on the formation of my sexual identity, I would say that during that week that was the most difficult for me, it was partially because I believe I was deconstructing all these socialized norms that were expected of me as a Mexican male by society, my culture, and my family's upbringing. Deconstructing these mechanisms and finding where I belonged in claiming a sexual identity meant for me what Anzaldúa refers to as "facing my Shadow-Beast." Facing that "Shadow-Beast" would be more than I imagined because of the events that would occur later.

After dealing with the issues I had gone through at school, I still had to face my sexual identity at home. Most of the time when my family and I would try and talk about it, it still remained an issue. I remember my brother telling my mother (later he confided in me) that when my mother asked him what she should do, he told her that I was still the same person and that I was no different from before. I think my brother's advice to tell my mother to try and talk to me about what I was experiencing helped to actually have her open up and connect with me. After many attempts, we began to re-establish our relationship. Over a considerable amount of time and with the support of my mother and brother, I planned to come out to my father.

This had to be one of my most difficult "outing" experiences because I couldn't anticipate how he would react. I remember preparing myself the evening that I asked him if we could meet up, just he and I without my brother. So we did the usual for whenever we met; we went to dinner, and instead of going out to a movie I asked him if I could speak to him. We parked in the parking lot of a supermarket close to his home. Nothing could prepare me to face him, but I knew that I wanted to tell him. So when we were in his car, in the parking lot, I said to him, "Dad, I think I may be gay." I don't think I will ever forget the expression on his face when I told him. For a moment there was a silence, with what seemed like the longest pause ever; I tried to fill the void by telling him about all those examples: Emiliano Zapata, Ché, Frida, Pedro Infante, but none of it mattered. His response to me was that it didn't matter that they were [gay/bi/queer] because they were not his son. What did I mean that I was gay!? I told him that it was something that I believed I was. He responded with, "I can't believe what you're telling me! Not even animals do that shit. How embarrassing would it be that whenever someone came over my house that my house would smell like shit and my sheets would smell like shit." What could I say in response to this? There really wasn't anything I could say. He filled in the uncomfortable void with a question, "Who else have you told?" I told him that I had told my mom and my brother. He asked what she had said. I told him that we spoke about it and we were getting through it. My father said that no one else needed to know and so I should not go around telling anyone else, especially my family. Reflecting back now, I don't suppose I could have expected any other response, but at the time I thought to myself, after he had dropped me back off at home, "Who the hell is he to tell me what I can and can't say to my family? I can out myself to anyone I damn well please without his approval. This is my decision to make and no one else's." My mother and brother helped me get through that experience because it was traumatizing then and something that I had to work through for a very long time after.

Even today I still remember vividly what that was like and the same feelings of anxiety, anger, and resistance still come up. After that I felt as though I possessed the right to tell whomever I wanted and no one could take that away from me. So I began to tell a very few select individuals in my extended family. I told two cousins who were like a brother and sister to me, an aunt who always took care of me, and one of my uncles. When I told my uncle, my tío Joe, it meant more to me because he was like a father figure to me, so it was important to me that he know. His reaction was to be expected; he asked me questions and I tried to answer them the best I could. I told him that it meant a lot for me that he know because of how I felt and how I saw him as a proxy for the father who was never really there for me. I told him that I was a little worried over his reaction and how he would take what I had told him. He said that what I told him wouldn't change anything between us. He asked if my mom knew, and I told him she did, and he asked about my dad's reaction, and I told him. My tío tried to explain what my dad was feeling and as always, my tío tried to make sure that I still understood that my father was still my father. For that I respect my uncle, and especially for what he told me next. He said that I was always welcome in his home and should I ever be in need there was a place to stay in his home. If I ever wanted anyone over, a "friend" [boyfriend] then I could bring them over without any worry. He also said, which really meant so much to me, if I had any problems, or if anyone ever said anything disparaging to me or made comments about my friend, he would handle them. Because to my uncle I was still his nephew and whatever anyone told me in his home would be disrespecting him, and he wouldn't stand it and neither should I. His home would and still has been a safe place to bring over whomever I want. There are moments in our lives that challenge us and help define who we are, and the events surrounding my coming out have made me realize the truth about friends, family, and myself. I quickly learned valuable lessons that I still haven't forgotten. As I began to think that the worst had already passed, I was entirely mistaken.

I went back to school and began to do my own research on sexuality and looked for ways or literature that combined both an ethnic/ cultural perspective and a queer/gay/bi sexual identity. I remember coming across authors like Gloria Anzaldúa and Cherríe Moraga, and I felt a sense of place in a culture that ignored or condemned who we are. I had found a new sense of strength in their work in cultural and literary resistance in creating a queer space where there once wasn't one—in Chicano/a Studies and Ethnic Studies. At this point in time I also changed my goals for my career. When I began my undergraduate career I knew that I wanted to pursue law and become an attorney. I nearly invested three years in preparing myself for the application process and building a network of students and information that would prepare me as well as the friends who also wanted to do the same and go to law school. After coming out, and as a result of my experiences, I reconsidered what I wanted for myself, personally and professionally. I felt motivated now in the pursuit of finding something that I could identify with, something that I knew made me feel a connection to or a passion for what I did. I felt a personal connection to my research and finding or attempting to find a relationship between my Mexican/ Chicano side and my queer identity because I felt there was a gap or lack of information on these issues. So it was at this point in time, and with an uncertainty of what I was going to do with all the work I had done, I changed my goals for my career and decided to consider the possibility of a M.A. instead of the three years of preparation for law school. So I began to focus on my Chican@ Studies major, and over time I double majored in Women and Gender Studies (with an emphasis in same-sex sexuality in Latin America), and later, when it became available, I minored in Sexuality Studies. Before I could complete these majors and while I was making the decision to potentially pursue graduate school, I found out, during my first summer of being out and my first pride, that I had been outed back home to my family.

It was around the time of my first gay pride parade in San Diego. I remember that I was looking forward to this. Although I was a little scared and nervous, I was thrilled at what pride might be. I went with my brother, who wanted to go and be there with me to lend his support. See, since I had come out, and as my family and I communicated and became closer again, my brother had become very protective of me and was proud of his gay brother. During pride my brother and I hung out and watched the parade and later met up with one of my cousins who was also there to support her friend(s). We decided to go and grab something to eat afterward, and that's when she told me the news. My cousin was one of the first that I had come out to, that sister that I described, and she told me over lunch that most of my family knew about me because of another family member who had found out about me. How could this person possibly know? Later I realized how it all happened. At that point I was so pissed. Rather than come and talk to me, this person felt the need to go and tell their mom, who in turn told her sister, and as gossip goes, soon most of my family knew about me. At the time I was completely caught off guard. I didn't know how to react or respond, and so I asked my cousin how she knew. She told me that it was because her sister had told her, whose mom had told her. I asked my cousin what the general response was and how my tíos and tías [uncles and aunts] reacted. She told me that my family was more concerned for my mom. They wondered how she would react when she found out; *y que pobre de ella* when she does find out about me. I couldn't believe that their concern was more for her than it was for me, but at the moment I couldn't and didn't want to believe what had happened.

To this day I can't forget who outed me to my family. I felt powerless since there was nothing I could do about it and there were so many family members and individuals who I considered friends who stopped speaking to me or acted differently toward me when they learned of my sexuality. Some openly showed their disapproval towards me while others covertly did so. Now even though some family members have begun to speak to me again, I still remember who those individuals were. Fortunately, although I was terrified to do so, I revealed my sexuality to select members of the family who I loved the most before I was forcibly outed. So in a way, that family member who outed me and hurt me more than I think she can possibly understand, only helped to make me the individual I am today. It was through this experience I began to appreciate what I had gone through and the challenges that I had overcome. Without these experiences, I would not be able to provide my own perspective and an alternative coming out story. By alternative I mean different than a narrative of a coming of age where I initially had an attraction to men, but instead an account entirely separate from anything I came across in the literature.

Five years later ...

So where am I now with all that I have had to confront? Well, let me first say that love has come and gone in my life with the men that have taken my heart. I've even come to realize that love is love, regardless of any societal restrictions or gendered boundaries. Maybe I'll one day write not about the hardships of being accepted and accepting myself but of falling in and out of love with the men that have come into my life. One truly definitive notion I've learned is that my Queer Chicano identity is as Anzaldúa describes, "The home I carry on my back," meaning that I am part of a culture that will reject, reprimand, and deny my existence but yet I am here to defend who I am and those others who, like myself, have endured their own hardships. This struggle is not one that I've chosen but one that I've assumed by the pursuit of my own desires and happiness because, like her, I choose to identify as queer; "It's not me that rejects my culture, but it me" (Anzaldúa). This, in part, is what radicalizes my sexual identity. I use my gay/bi identity and produce this queer identity as an act of resistance; what I do in my own sheets I radicalize and take with me to the streets. I know that I occupy a space not sanctioned by both the gay community, which accepts and normalizes specific racial, body, age, and gender percep-tions, which by default I already fall out of, and my Mexican identity, which looks at me as perverse, not a man, a maricon, jot@. And yet I'm proof of this reality that you may not be willing to admit yourself. This Queer Chicano identity gives me the opportunity to give insight, strength, and inspiration to others who may, too, look for a reflection of themselves. Here is a text and a body of literature through which you may find yourself, which you may identify with and hold onto as proof to legitimize who you are. In this body of work you have friends, allies, and colleagues, and if anything a collective voice that resists everyday, so that the hardships we've endured may somehow in our own individual and collective efforts be lessened for you. In my own mind I write to that young, questioning Chicano male who looks for exactly what we've attempted to produce, a Queer Chicano presence through which you can find comfort from a world who tells you who or what you need to be. At this point I wish to queer a figure well known to many and recontextualize his words for the sake of this paper: "Let me say, at the risk of seeming ridiculous, that the true revolutionary is guided by great feelings of love." (Che)

1966

(Excerpt from an unpublished memoir)

Michael Nava

One of the scariest things about starting junior high school was gym because you had to change clothes before class and then shower afterwards. That meant being naked in the presence of strangers, including eighth and even ninth graders who were practically grown-ups in the eyes of a twelve-year-old boy. When the big day came, I paused for a moment from my frantic attempts to get out of my street clothes and into my gym uniform as quickly as possible and saw a ninth-grade boy standing in the aisle. He was completely nude, talking to one of his friends. He was, I later learned, a farmer's son, his body conditioned by hard work to adult musculature, and so physically mature that by the end of the day dark hair stubbled his face. The same black hair dusted his chest, covered his legs, and grew thick around his genitals. I knew enough not to stare, but I couldn't look away. It was as if a switch had been flicked on inside of me; I was electrified by his maleness.

Winter arrived with a frost that whitened the grass. I walked up Potomac Street to Northgate to catch the bus for school. The trees were bare, their leaves turning black in the gutters, and I could see my breath in front of me. Out of nowhere, I heard someone say, "I'm a queer."

I stopped and looked around for who had spoken, but there was no one else on the street and it came to me that the voice I had heard could only have been my own. "I'm a queer," I said. As the word died in the air, I not only knew that the first voice I had heard was mine, but also that it was true. I *was* a queer. "I'm a queer," I said, a third time, as if the words were an incantation that could roll away the stone that blocked the entrance into a cave where something was hidden in the darkness. But what was it?

My classmates were beginning to enact the rituals of boy and girl, and if they were uncertain of how, exactly, to proceed they needed to look no further than the adult world of man and woman. I had my secret to preserve, and this was easier without friends to whom I might have to account for my complete lack of romantic interest in girls. Fortunately, I was also at my least prepossessing, a fat boy with a patch of acne across his forehead, not the kind of boy to whom girls passed elaborately folded notes with the tell-tale SWAK (Sealed With A Kiss) scrawled in red ink across them. Now and then, for the sake of appearances, I showed up for one of the Friday afternoon dances in the cafeteria where I danced with any girl who would have me. When Kathy Hamilton rested her head against my shoulder while we shuffled our feet beneath us to a slow song, she could have been a mannequin for all my body cared. It was Denny Jacobs, dancing with his girlfriend on the other side of the room, who raced my pulse.

I launched into a campaign of desissification, attempting to rid myself of any affect that might give me away as a queer. I began to carry books against my side rather than pressed against my chest and learned to swear and to smoke. Yet even this was not enough because the sine qua non of teenage masculinity was an interest in and ap- titude for sports. I had neither. I had held my own in the free-form games of childhood where what mattered most was energy, but I was a wash-out at organized sports. I was too fat to run very far or very fast, too uncoordinated to throw a ball, and too myopic to catch one, and because I didn't play them well, football, basketball and baseball held no interest for me even as a spectator. I cast around for a model of masculinity that didn't involve field goals and batting averages and discovered my grandfather, the grim Indian from the Arizona desert.

Now in his early sixties, he was still the scowling presence who had frightened and mesmerized me when I was a child searching through his lunch pail for scraps of food as if, by eating his leftovers, I could also absorb his mystery. My grandfather's interest in sports was limited to the occasional baseball game on TV, and he never talked about women. Indeed, he rarely spoke at all. A loner, his only male acquaintances were his sons and sons-in-law and the strangers with whom he drank on weekends nights at a downtown bar. He never had a single visitor to his house to whom he was not related by blood or marriage. Though he was the antithesis of the sports-addicted, girl-crazy, gregarious teen-age boys who surrounded me, my grandfather was unquestionably a man. In his example, a man was someone who worked hard, fulfilled his obligations, and kept to himself. It was just the example I was looking for, and it could not have been more destructive to my basic temperament, which was almost the polar opposite of his.

My grandfather was stoic, I was emotional; he was silent while I was filled with words; he was governed by a sense of duty to his family while I was guided by an internal sense of self; he genuinely disliked other people while I was isolated by circumstance. He was someone who, when he was in his twenties, the family legend went, had killed another boy while, when I was in my twenties, I would be in love with one. Still, I gratefully wrapped myself in his gloomy maleness because it protected my secret, not realizing the prison I had let myself into or how hard it would be to emerge from it.

I was glad to get back to school, to have somewhere to go during the day. When the last bell rang, I was reluctant to return home and, if I couldn't corral one of my teachers to talk to, I headed out to the athletic field behind the school and sat in the bleachers where I read until the light faded. Various school teams would come out to practice—the football team, the baseball team, and the track and field boys. I would look up from whatever ponderous book I was reading and watch the sprinters and the high jumpers, the shot put throwers and the distance runners. I remembered what it had been like, before I imprisoned myself in fat, to run for the sheer joy of it, and what I felt when I looked at their lean, fit bodies was as much envy as lust.

One of the runners was a classmate named David. He was a quiet boy, slender, fair, green-eyed, making his unobtrusive way through adolescence. We had several classes together. His ambition was to become a forest ranger, and he often talked about the camping trips he had taken with his father and brother. These were not conversations I had with him, but ones I overheard between him and his best friend, a Chinese boy named Sam. I never talked to David about anything more personal than how he'd done on a test or if he'd watched a particular TV show the night before. So it came as a shock to me when I began to have feelings for David which, if Shakespeare and Edna St. Vincent Millay could be trusted, had to be love.

My first response was shame. Although I was resigned to being a queer, I was determined to conceal it, for the rest of my life if necessary. It was easy enough to avoid behaving like the homosexuals described in books like *The Sixth Man*. I had already developed the facility for constantly monitoring my behavior for manliness in the way I walked, talked, and carried myself, where I looked, what I noticed. But I had no defense against my feelings. Despite the belief of eminent psychologists and my fourteen-year-old classmates that homosexuality was a matter of behavior and appearances ("Queers were green on Thursday" was the schoolboy equivalent of the psychologists' dictum, "All homosexuals are sexually promiscuous"), it was on the inside where this trouble originated. If I could have changed the way I felt, I would not have needed to worry about how I acted, but when those feelings announced themselves—"I'm a queer"—it was not as a question but a statement of fact.

I was also confused by these feelings for David. They were different than the lust with which I regarded other boys. I could accept my sexual attraction to them and still believe I was basically normal because, as weird as it was to want sex with another boy, it was not, to judge from my classmate's joking comments, unimaginable to them. The jockiest among them were the loudest on the subjects of cocksucking and cornholing. The mere fact that they could use the words meant they had thought about the acts and, even if they never performed them, they were at least among the universe of sexual possibilities. This made me think it might be possible to have sex with other guys and still be accepted by them as long as it was just sex.

But just sex was not what I wanted from David. I found myself, to my horror, daydreaming about walking with him between classes, my hand in his, pulling him out to the dance floor on a Friday afternoon for a slow dance, kissing him good-night as I boarded the bus for home. I could, and sometimes did, imagine that he might allow me to have sex with him someday. It was remotely possible that, with the right amount of coaxing, he might let me put my mouth on his penis, but the notion that he would permit me to touch my lips to his was beyond belief. The very image was ridiculous, absurd. But at night, in bed, it was holding him that I fantasized about, nothing else.

My fear that love would make me unmanly was confirmed by my observations of my family. There, it was the women who loved, but their love was commingled with their powerlessness, making it pitiable, a consolation prize that failed to console. It appeared to me that weak people, like my mother, offered love because they had nothing else to give, whereas a powerful person like my grandfather, who provided the actual necessities of life, didn't bother about love. Men, I concluded, did not love. If I loved David, what did this make me?

Naturally, then, I resisted my feelings for him. Since we were not really friends, it was easy enough to avoid him, to sit on the other side of the classroom or the cafeteria. When I began, however, to plan in ever greater detail how I would avoid him, I stumbled into obsession, and it was not long before I thought of nothing else but how to attract his attention. I was humiliated but unable to prevent myself from discovering where he lived and taking long walks that inevitably led me past his house. At school, I sought him out between classes, at lunch, and after school, and I tried to keep a conversation going from the few threads of our common interests. He was obliviously friendly, a well-behaved, ordinary boy who, I quickly determined, had not as yet developed an interest in girls and so had no idea of what drove me into his company.

David was so transparently a normal boy that I could never delude myself that it was possible for him to return my feelings. Yet I persisted in my surreptitious courtship of him because I began to experience the cauterizing power of love. There were moments when we were together, or even, sometimes, just thinking about him when I felt something so completely unexpected that at first I didn't know what it was. It was hope. I had rarely felt hope before in relation to my own life; ambition, restlessness, and desire, yes, but not hope. This hope, moreover, was not for a specific thing but was pervasive and softening. I, who lived so often in anxiety, began to relax. At home, I was kinder to my mother and my siblings. At school, I didn't have to drive myself so relentlessly, as if, should I let up for even a second, I would fail. Love, I discovered, was not a form of weakness but the thing that made all other things possible. I saw in a different light my grandmother's devotion to her little Jesus, her diosito, my mother's devotion to her children. I was on the brink of the great discovery about love, that love heals its bearer and its object alike.

This revelation, however, required, finally, some reciprocity. Even love which is returned is difficult to sustain; love which is not returned is impossible. In time, unrequited love becomes either obsession or nostalgia. If my love for David brought me hope for happiness, it also made me excruciatingly aware of the many obstacles to that happiness, not the least of which was my inability to say the words to him that might make the rest possible. I could not say them because I knew this love was impossible. Men did not love, and certainly not each other. I really was queer, in every sense of the word—a freak, an outcast. My feeling of hopefulness faded, replaced by a self-loathing so vicious that I began to physically mutilate myself, tear out clumps of hair, drive staples into my arms, slam my head against trees and walls, trying to kill this hapless, humiliating love. My longing and sadness tortured me. My courage failed me. One morning, I arrived on campus, as usual, an hour before the first bell rang and went out to the athletic field. It was a chilly spring morning; the field was the fresh green of new grass. My shoes left watery prints in the dew as I lumbered toward the bleachers that overlooked the running track and climbed to the top row. I was carrying a paper bag that contained a carton of chocolate milk. In my pocket was the bottle of Phenobarbital. I sat with my back to the school. Beyond the fenced in athletic field, across the road, were the skeletons of houses where a new subdivision was going up in a tomato field. The workers had not yet arrived to start their day. I opened the milk carton and dug into my pocket for my bottle of pills and uncapped it. Then I took them, one by one, alternating with sips of chocolate. There weren't enough pills in the bottle to kill me as I had planned, only enough to intoxicate me. When the first bell rang and I discovered I was not dead, I staggered toward the school and collapsed outside of Mr. Braun's room. He came out and asked me what was wrong. From my slurred speech and incomprehensible response, he concluded that I was on something. The next stop was Balducci's office, where I tearfully admitted what I had done. He called home and a few minutes later my mother and Butch arrived.

Balducci showed them the empty bottle. "Mike said he took all his pills. You better get him to an emergency room."

I was passing in and out of consciousness by the time we reached the county hospital emergency room. A doctor heard my story, shone a light into my eyes, took my pulse and yelled at me, "How many pills did you take?"

"I don't know," I mumbled.

"Was the bottle full? Half full? How many?"

"Less than half," I said. "Less than half full."

I closed my eyes and heard him consulting with my mother. "Well," he said, "we could pump his stomach, but I think he'll be okay if he just goes home and sleeps it off." The next morning I woke up, still groggy, and went into the kitchen. I took one look at my mother's swollen, wept-out eyes and it all came back to me.

"I'm not going to school today," I announced, and I went back to my room, where I remained for the rest of the day. In fact, it was a week before I had the courage to go back to school, but I needn't have worried. No one said anything to me about what had happened; while at home the only mention it merited was when Butch pulled me aside and said, "Don't ever worry your mother like that." And so, my secret was safe.

Still Flaming

Vincent D. Cervantes

 rowing up I always knew that I was a little "different" than the other boys; however, my ability to understand my queerness was limited and crippled by my family's traditional understandings of homosexuality in Mexicano and Chicano culture. In México, and most of Latin America, homosexuality is matter of gender difference that is expressed by both sexual behavior and deviant gender practices. As a result, homo-sexuals are not categorized as men or women, but instead are pushed to the margins of society and occupy an ambiguous space outside the gender binary because they do not conform to the tropes of what is a man and what is a woman. Through my family's understanding of gender and sexuality, the language to understand my queerness did not exist. However, I was raised to and expected to conform to the tropes of what defines a Chicano man.

My family's teachings on Chicano manliness set the precedent for me to suppress and reject my own queerness. That suppression and rejection was only amplified by Christian pastoral teachings that also defined what a man was supposed to be. Unlike at home, I developed a language to describe homosexuality within my church: sinful, immoral, abomination, etc. As I grew older, I became fully aware of my same-sex attractions and the ability to suppress it anymore was lost. However, once I admitted to myself that I was queer, I went into an identity coma, paralyzed by a spiritual and cultural crisis. I did all that I could to repackage myself into the mold that was presented to me by my family and church of what a Chicano Christian man is supposed to be. After years of attempting to pray away the gay, and even going through exorcism, I failed to become the man that I was told I needed to be. Instead, I have began to seek a way to construct an empowering *identidad* that challenges institutions of heterosexism and homophobia, but that doesn't isolate me from my Chicano and Christian identities.

In this essay, I reflect on my experiences of reconciling three seemingly incompatible identities and the way in which I now blend elements from all of them to forge a new *identidad*. I focus on the painful and violent experience of finally reaching the door of the "closet" I came out of. I explore first my early childhood and adolescence of growing up "different" in my family and among the other boys at school. I then examine my attempt to reject and "correct" my queerness through "ex-gay" therapy. Finally, I discuss my process of accepting myself and trace my attempts to create an *identidad* that blends being queer, Chicano, and Christian, all in hope of not only liberating myself, but also of transforming understandings of homosexuality for Chicanos and Christians alike.

The Chicano Macho

At surface level, my childhood experiences seemed to be nothing more than full of the same mundane routines as any other brown boy growing up in California's Central Valley. In other words, I was raised essentially the same as all the other boys, with the traditional Mexicano/Chicano values and cultural forms our parents and grandparents had been raised with. Despite being raised similar to the other boys my age, I always knew that I was "different" from them. In comparison to my cousins and my fellow classmates, I never shared the same interests or wanted to do the same things, and I rarely acted the same way.

Growing up I was always comparing myself to those around me. I would look at them and wonder, "What are they thinking about me?" I was afraid of what it would mean to be "different" or to challenge the status quo. As a result, I was never very honest with myself about who I was. My effeminate mannerisms developed at an early age, and they were difficult to hide. My male cousins and classmates quickly picked up on the realization that I was not like them, nor was I like what a man "should" be. They began to taunt me, calling me names like "gay lord" and "maricón" and spreading rumors that I had AIDS - - at the age of eight. In comparison to the boys that tormented me, I knew that I was different, but I did not know that I was gay. For them to call me such names went beyond my level of comprehension. That word was not a part of my vocabulary. I was fully unaware of the fact that I was queer; I only knew that I was not like the other boys.

Home was a space of confusion and imbalance. Patriarchy was the foundation on which my parents attempted to build our family. My father worked an excessive amount of hours as an upholsterer in a factory to support my family, while my mother remained unemployed to tend to the household chores and children. Due to his heinous work schedule, it was very common for us to go a week or two without seeing my father once. As a result of his regular absences, my mother began to assume the role as the actual "head" of our household, developing into the "active" role of our family structure. This created an imbalance in the patriarchal structure that was in place, thus resulting in many fights in our home over who really "wore the pants." In a sense, my mother's emergence into her new role posed a threat to my father's masculinity. In other words, by taking on an active role in our family structure, she not only demoted my father from his role as the head of the household but emasculated him altogether. These gendered struggles over power and dominance set the stage for the emergence of my queerness in my family.

As is the case for many queer boys, I was very attached to my mother growing up. My mother was not just a parent, but my role model and hero. The bond between us was one of sameness; in my mind I was just like her. It was convenient for my mother to raise me just like my younger sisters (I was the only boy). I was always her "special" boy. Given the close affinity between my mother and me, I somehow became involved in their fights. I would stand by her side, ready to defend her from my father. It never mattered to me what they were fighting about or who was right or wrong, but just the mere fact that my mother was threatened.

On many occasions the fights between my parents were about the bond of affinity between my mother and me. My father accused her of always favoring me and being overbearing, which in our Mexicano/Chicano working-class home had strong undertones of feminization and emasculation. What my father was actually saying was that she was turning me into a non-boy. As I got older, these arguments continued and became more frequent. Eventually it was my father and me doing the arguing.

Despite my closeness with my mother, I still sought my father's approval. Like most other boys, I wanted to make my father proud of his son. In an attempt to foster a relationship with my father I tried spending more time with him when his availability changed. I was receptive to letting him teach and mold me into the man he wanted me to be. Through my interaction with my father I developed the language to describe how a "real" Chicano man should be—at least according to my Mexicano father, and his father, and his father's father, and so on.

My father's teachings on Mexicano/Chicano masculinity created a hyper-masculine archetype that I call "the Chicano macho." The Chicano macho is the complete opposite of all that is feminine and passive, because a "real" Chicano man is forceful, responsible, and is willing to display a strong sense of authority when it is necessary. He is expected to learn to control those around him (especially women) and his emotions because this exercise of male authority is the epitome of a being a "real" Chicano. My father never treated me or referred to me as just a boy, but instead as an *hombrecito*. To be a boy meant to be a quasi-woman, through physicality and responsibility; therefore, if I was to be a man (a real Chicano macho), I was to be treated as one. And finally, the Chicano macho is expected to be heterosexual; to be a sissy, joto, or maricón was out of the question. My father laid it on me to embody each one of these macho tropes of hegemonic Chicano masculinity.

In my determination to fit in with the other boys and to make my father proud, I began to change all sorts of things about myself, externally at least: the way I walked and talked, the way I dressed and combed my hair; I even joined the soccer and wrestling teams. But nothing ever seemed to work. I didn't feel good about myself, and no one treated me better, not even my father. The name-calling unfortunately continued. I transferred to several different schools in my district, hoping to find a fresh start somewhere, but the same pattern of gendered bullying followed me. I continued throughout middle and high school trying to be accepted as nothing more than just a "normal" Chicano man. It took a lot of convincing. However, I was still unaware of my same-sex attractions. It wasn't until later that I began to realize that I had feelings for my best friend. Feelings that I could not explain. I thought to myself, "I'm liking him as much as I should be liking a girl right now." I thought I was just being a really good friend by always caring about him and his emotions and wanting to be around him 24/7. Alas, I had discovered my queerness.

The queerness that I was now aware of only complicated my life. As much as I knew that I couldn't become the Chicano macho my father wanted me to be, I still wanted to try. By the mere fact that I knew I was homosexual, I began to feel culturally out of place. There was no way to define myself within the binary system I knew: man or woman. To be a man would mean to be heterosexual. Because of my gendered struggle to understand my homosexuality, I entered into a cultural identity crisis. However, not wanting to threaten the system my father worked so hard to create for me, I suppressed all my queer emotions. So long as my homosexuality was not explicitly named, there was still hope that I could become the Chicano man I was expected to be. I would continue to endure the mistreatment and deny any accusations of being queer, all in hopes of one day "fixing" what I believed to be a mistake. It was at that point that I began to seek drastic measures.

Deliverance

In the summer of 2008 I was awakened in the middle of the night by a disturbing and frightening dream I had never dreamt before. I quickly sat up in my bed, completely drenched in sweat and shaking. As I began recalling the images of my dream, tears began streaming down my face and my heart began to race. The dream was replaying over and over again in my head. I couldn't breathe.

Hands feeling all over my body, pressing against my chest and stomach. I sat firmly in the chair while the four men surrounded me. I could hear them yelling, but I couldn't make out what they were saying. It was a language I could not understand. They kept grabbing me. The room was getting hot. I could hear the sound of metal being kicked from underneath the chair. The men were getting louder, still feeling my entire body. Bam! I was forced out of my chair and hit the floor face down.

"I command you, Satan, in the name of Jesus, to let this young man free from your grip! Holy Spirit, heal him from this evil homosexual demon!"

The images rushing through my mind as I was sitting up in bed were anything but imagined; instead, they recounted memories of a traumatic and violent experience. Replaying through my mind was the exorcism, or deliverance rather, I had undergone two years earlier in my pastor's candlelit office. A deliverance that promised to "heal me" from my homosexuality. More scars were left than healing.

In hopes of finding a solution to my gendered cultural identity crisis, I knew that I needed to change the very thing that made me not a man. When I reached college my emotions became too much to handle. Being gay not only conflicted with the image of being a Chicano man, it also did not fit into the image of being a Christian. The hegemonic tropes of Chicano manliness that I understood were only amplified by my Christian identity. The myth of the Chicano macho was complemented by the Muscular Christian narrative that dominated evangelical Christian understandings of masculinity and sexuality.[1] Although traditionally most Latin Americans are Catholic, and still remain so, my family had converted to Pentecostalism by extension of the Evangelicalization of Latin America (including Latina/o communities in the United States) that began in the 1980s. The ideologies of Muscular Christianity, which originated among White Evangelicals, resonated well with the machismo culture already in place in the Chicano culture. As a result of the both masculinist narratives combining, heterosexuality was not only reemphasized as a trope of manliness, but homosexuality was regarded as sinful and a one-way ticket to hell. To save myself from eternal damnation and to reclaim my Chicano masculinity, I sought out help from my pastor to help me overcome my homosexuality.

I spent years praying to God, begging for change. The more I tried and wanted to be freed from my sinful same-sex attraction, the more I began to hate myself. Again, nothing seemed to work. I began to hit rock-bottom. I was alone in my dorm room one night and I couldn't bear the feelings of self-hate and guilt anymore. I fell to my knees and yelled out to God in desperation:

"Señor, por favor, en el nombre de Cristo, ¡Ayúdame! Cámbiame en el nombre del Espíritu Santo! Satan, te reprendo en el nombre de

---

1   Muscular Christianity was introduced through the novels of Charles Kingsley and Thomas Hughes, which fused hardy, physical manliness with the ideals of Christianity as a response to an "effeminized" form of Christianity. Muscular Christianity taught men to exert strength and control through their actions, just as they believed that Christ did; see Michael Kimmel, *Manhood in America: A Cultural History* (New York: Free Press, 1996), pp. 175–181.

Dios. Señor, cúrame de la homosexualidad. Cura mi alma. POR FAVOR, SEÑOR ¡SÁLVAME!"

Pero sin éxito. I laid there on my bed feeling helpless. Feeling empty. Feeling naked, with no one to clothe me.

After years of trying to pray away my homosexuality, spending over a year in pastoral counseling, and changing as much as I could externally, I finally consented to the one act that would change my life forever: a deliverance—a spiritual cleansing that would wipe out the evil spirits that were allegedly manipulating my spirit and body to have attractions towards other men. On a warm summer evening in June 2006, I gathered with my pastor and three other men from my church in my pastor's office. After reminding ourselves why we were there—to cleanse my soul of the evil homosexual demons—we began to pray. Hours passed with them anointing me with oil and crying out to God to deliver me from my evil and sinful homosexual attractions. They had their hands all over me, pressing on my chest, my stomach, my head. They were hoping that this demon would be expelled out of my body and into the metal bucket I kept kicking beneath my chair. Suddenly something came over me and I began to shout. The words coming out of my mouth were not my own. It was a language I could not understand. Then out of nowhere, I thrusted out of my chair and onto the ground. When I hit the floor after lunging out of the cold metal chair, I blacked out. I could still hear their voices and I could still feel their hands, but I no longer felt in control of my own body in that moment.

I left that night feeling like I had truly been delivered. Delivered from fiery pits of hell and delivered from the gendered cultural struggle I wanted to overcome. However, that feeling didn't last long. Almost one month later I realized that my same-sex attractions had not gone away. I was still very much queer. At that moment, I finally accepted the reality that I could not change. I accepted that I would always be queer. But I was not happy. I felt that I had not only failed my family, but I had also failed God. I knew that it would be impossible for me to embody the Chicano macho based on the fact that I could never be straight. I also knew that I still loved God and wanted to retain my Christian faith. I then asked myself how it would be possible for me to exist within both spaces as a queer individual. The asking of this question was my true deliverance. Not from the fiery pits of hell, but from the self-hatred and guilt I inflicted upon myself.

El Otro Mestiza/o

After years of trials and tribulations, I finally came to a place where I understood who I was and I accepted myself as a queer man. The process of self-discovery is a long and difficult journey, but very important in forging a person's *identidad*. After coming out, I was forced to understand my identity at the intersection of two forms of violence: cultural and spiritual. The marginalization of homosexuals in Latin America through homogenizing what is and isn't Chicano manliness is a form of cultural violence. Homosexual men are pushed to the margins of society to occupy an ambiguous space that strips away their identity as Chicano men by force—this is abuse. Additionally, I use the term "spiritual violence" to describe my experience with "ex-gay" therapy and my stint with an exorcism. The term "spiritual violence" denotes the act of using religion to persecute a particular person or group of people, which deems that person or group morally and spiritually inferior and "less than."

I had to rethink and redefine my own ideas of what it means to be a "real" Chicano man. I also had to question how it would be possible to reconcile my Christian faith with my sexuality. I came to a place of understanding that allowed me to do so. I held onto my Christian identity while still being able to celebrate and be proud to be Chicano as a queer man. Through the blending of these three identities, I became el otro mestiza/o. In the face of violence and oppression, I chose to stop trying to change myself in order to assimilate. Instead, I elected to confront the systems that marginalized me in order to find a space of balance and reconciliation.

I came out to my family as openly gay during the fall of 2006. My decision to name my queerness to them was an attempt to begin a process of healing for the scars that were left by the hegemonic Chicano masculinist ideologies my family was forced to grow up with. My family did not have any knowledge of my "ex-gay" experience or exorcism—I shared that part of my life with them in 2007. Not to my surprise, my mother's only reply to my coming out was that she loved me. Because of our strong affinity, I believe that part of her always knew, and it never mattered. When I told her about the deliverance that took place in our pastor's office, however, her response was far more dramatic. She couldn't believe that I would even consider such a drastic attempt at changing myself. As tears began streaming down her face, she looked at me and said, "Mijo, I'm not crying because you're gay. I'm crying because I must have failed as a mother for you to ever think that you would have to change in order to make me love you." In that moment I realized that "ex-gay" therapy had done more harm than good, not only to me, but even to the person that I believe to be the most important person in my life. My relationship with my mother has only strengthened since my coming out. She has become a strong advocate for the equal treatment of LGBTQ people, and now she has my back when I am the one that's threatened.

Being open about my queerness in my family allowed me to begin a new relationship with my father, one that didn't involve me trying to be somebody that I'm not. I know that I'm not the man that my father dreamed that I would be. But I am the man I want to be. I am all the man that I can be. And I pray that that is enough for him to be proud of his son. I do not hide my homosexuality from him at all. I discuss with my family the issues I face as a queer individual, while I share my critiques of heterosexism and homophobia. Sharing my queerness with my family allows me to engage in dialogue with them about race, gender, and sexuality, and to disrupt the hegemonic masculinist system that has been in place for far too long in Chicano families.

Through disrupting the Chicano hegemonic masculinist system, I am also able to unsettle the Muscular Christian narrative by exposing its oppressive nature. My understanding of Christianity is love. Jesus Christ taught his followers to love God and to love one another as they would love themselves—all the laws and teachings of the prophets were to hang on these two commandments.[2] My queerness does not compromise the love I have always had for God. Furthermore, being gay does not affect my ability to still love those around me. It took me a while to reach this level of understanding, but I'm glad I did. Since coming out I have worked relentlessly at examining the use of the Bible in discourses on gender and sexuality, in order to generate conversations in the Church that need to happen around LGBTQ-related issues. My prayer is that all people struggling in the closet accept themselves because they were told that they are sinful and going to hell; they should know that God loves them and affirms them without reservation.

Through labeling myself as el otro mestiza/o, I attempt to honor all the different components that have gone into making me the person I am today. I acknowledge the potential pitfalls of engaging in the selective extraction and blending of elements from diverse cultures, but I believe that the need for new forms of understanding on race, religion, gender, and sexuality justifies taking those risks. Mestizaje politics move beyond just the individual and focus on how individuals relate to one another in the pursuit of a common cause. In this case, the common cause is love, pride, and justice—I believe that all three communities can relate to these. And through love, pride, and justice, we can fight oppressive forces together as el otro mestiza/o.

---

2   Matthew 22:37–40

References

Kimmel, Michael. *Manhood in America: A Cultural History.* New York: Free Press, 1996.

Personal Resilience

Mario Martinez

As you sit down with this story between your hands, you will discover a truth no one ever knew about me. You will find answers to questions that I avoided and that I never got a chance to clarify. Right now what I can say is that my life was always lost in poetry, music, reading, writing, and running. I have run away because of fear and sometimes just because I wanted privacy, but not here. Here I take on a new face with no restrictions.

Every time someone knocked on the door I experienced a fever and a head rush, for I never knew who it would be. This time it was my social worker, Letty. She came for her weekly visits with me. She told me she was my friend and that I could trust her with anything; however, I couldn't really believe her because she never believed me. I kept a secret from her. It all started on a night about three weeks before the new kid, Kenny, moved in with us. At the age of four, I was not your ordinary child. Unlike most children, who spent their time watching television and playing with their toys, I was fighting for my life and finding ways to survive.

You would think that as a child I had everything in life. I didn't. All I ever had were two boys and a girl who I could count on: Kenny, Charles, and Amanda. I didn't want Olivia, my foster mother. Hate is such a powerful and strong word to use against another person, but

I hated Olivia. I was ever aware of her, observing the way she walked, talked, ate and just about every move she made because I was afraid of her and needed to be on my guard. She resembled a monster. Heavy, dark skin, long wavy black hair and dark brown eyes with a pace like a cat. Although that's how she looked to me, she was a beautiful monster: Long blond straight hair with light brown eyes that shined like the sparkling stars at night. She looked like a model even when just standing, her body and her curves were unforgettable. No matter how beautiful she was to the world, I saw her true colors. She was a monster.

I still ask myself if she is as perverted as she was back then. Maybe she still is because people like her don't change from one day to another. I can never forget those nights that she took from me. Those particular nights haunted me until one day I blanked them out of my memory.

Prisoner

As the night devoured my heart
You crept in through the dark
While I looked out the window into the sky
You crept my way

The cold wind burned my skin
As I cried for help with my mouth shut high
You slowly slithered inappropriately next to me
With your arms grasping my body

Filling your life with my silent woe
I can't stand the pain I'm going through
Knowing that I just died in your arms
And seeing your distasteful hunger fluster me

Gradually you feed your lips with my innocence
Taking every chance you get in this unlighted room
Lifting my pain up higher and higher
And I'm left here with more than I can take

Resting on this wee bed
Your breaths inadequately place me in a trance
While you enjoy that sparkle in your eyes
And butterflies in your stomach
This little boy dies giving unwanted passion

This feeling and temptation is so wrong
But how can you go wrong when everything is so right?
There's nothing that you could ever do
For you have stolen my precious virtue

I'm tired of this dream
Confused of what might go wrong
Not knowing whether I'll get a fever tonight from your damp skin
Or get cold when I'm left here bare with nothing to hold

I wonder sometimes what I enjoy the most
If it's the heat from your hands running up and down my physique
Or the pain and suffering of being isolated in a grotesque room

I just know that it's me in your eyes that pleases your form
And you in control makes you bleed
Never stopping that humming melancholy sound
Driving me insane so I won't move

Laughing as you shut your eyes thinking of heaven
I stay still as I see a prison in my mind
And fire burns my vein
Living a melancholy life

When you call my name I am by your side
Just to avoid the abuse of being thrown
Because whether I listen or not
My punishment is in the palm of your hands

I'm a prisoner in your world
With no escape
An error with no correction
A motionless body
Just fulfilling your adult desires ...

For almost a year of isolation and living in an empty world, I never lost hope. I always had a feeling that I didn't belong with this family, which later I learned was known as a dysfunctional family.

One day I experienced a strange feeling inside my tiny body. I don't know when this started or why it began at all. I just knew the first time Rosalba and Alfonso walked through the front door, they were the ones to take me away—my angels. Amanda had told me that I would find them one day and I would be taken to a better place and a better home.

One glance at them and I felt happiness and I felt alive inside my heart. I thought I was going to get sick because of the heat running through my veins. When I was introduced, I couldn't smile and I couldn't look into their eyes or tell them this feeling I had inside me while they spoke to the monster. I felt sad and wished I had never met them at all. Rosalba was rude. She didn't have to say anything. She was disappointed with this boy who she first laid eyes on. Her eyes alone said much to me. That's when I lost the little hope of ever escaping this dark world I lived in. Not wanting to spend another night here pleasing that woman's desires, I finally said, "Hello."

A few days passed before I saw them again. I spent my time with Charles or Amanda every time I had the chance to escape from my room. I would talk to them so I could feel some comfort from their loving words. Each moment unspent with them I was with Kenny, protecting him from the hideous creature lurking in the house. A couple of days later, Rosalba and Alfonso came back and began taking me out to places I didn't know or was scared of. I was used to being in the house all day, everyday, so being out in public with them was an unforgettable experience, yet I was terrified on occasions for I did not know what to expect.

You could say I was a naive child who was not well adjusted, especially in that household. I do thank Amanda and Charles for teaching me the little they could behind their mother's back. Eventually I got in the habit of learning something new on Sundays because that's when Rosalba and Alfonso came for their weekly visits with me. Sunday was my favorite day. The three of us named it Family Day even though we were not family, but to me it didn't matter because I felt like being part of a family with them. We would go anywhere so the three of us could spend time together and talk: parks, beaches, amusement parks, sometimes restaurants and the movies as well.

After much time being together and getting to know each other, I was finally adopted and accepted into Rosalba and Alfonso's home as their son. It made my heart warm and it brought a huge smile to my face. I was four years old at the time. It was said that when a foster child turns five years old adoption gets more complicated. They barely made the deadline because my birthday was around the corner from the day I was adopted. I remember the process, being in front of a judge and being honest about my wanting to live with them. He also asked if I was treated right and with respect, especially if I was feeling love from them and, of course, I said the truth and responded, "Yes."

My name changed from Mario Aguilar to Mario Martinez. We arrived at Olivia's house one last time to pick up the few things I had. It was the best day of my life, but at the same time it was the worst because I feared leaving Kenny unprotected. However, as much as I cried, kicked, and screamed, Charles and Amanda promised me that they would take care of him and protect him for me. I always kept my promises, so I took the chance and believed them from my heart. I talked to Kenny and I told him that I was not letting him down ever, but that I would return one day for him.

Waiting patiently with open doors, open arms, and open hearts, Rosalba and Alfonso took me to my new home, where I knew right away I was accepted and welcomed. With this family I learned the meaning of love and the meaning of family. As time passed I met all my immediate family members from both my parents' sides. I got the opportunity to travel to Michoacán, Guadalajara, Colima, Tijuana, and Sinaloa, Mexico. I learned where the Martinez family came from. I learned the Mexican culture and some Mexican history as well. I may be an American citizen born in Los Angeles, but I have no knowledge of where I come from. The little that I was told and that I always keep in my heart, though it hurts too much, is that my biological mother passed away after giving birth to me. She died of internal bleeding which the doctors couldn't stop in time. My biological father was nowhere to be found when I was born, so that's how I ended up as a foster child. Eventually, in time, I did find out that he was an alcoholic and that he probably died of drinking.

They say that a baby can remember special moments, especially when inside the mother's womb. There are times that a rhythm pops into my head and I sometimes hum it. I have tried looking for the title of the song, but then I realize that maybe, just maybe, it was a song my biological mother made up and sang to me during my dreams as an infant in her womb.

Both of my adopted parents worked hard every day to give me the life that they couldn't have when they were children. Even though their jobs kept them busy, my mother always found time to spend with me. She would help me with my homework and she would educate me. She taught me the best she could.

When I started high school, back in 2001, I had an easy life. I kept myself busy with Track and Field, Cross Country, Tennis, the Future Educators of America Club and, of course, keeping my grades up. I had a couple of girlfriends, but during my senior year I realized I was attracted to men. I hated myself for it. I thought something was happening to me, a change that I was not supposed to experience. To avoid conflict with my parents or have them dislike me or say I had the devil in me, since I was raised Catholic, I kept it to myself and found a way to put that feeling to the side.

It was troublesome to be in the boy's locker room and to know that I had small crushes on some of the boys. So what did I do? I would wait until everyone had changed and then I would get into my Physical Education clothes or simply change in the bathroom. It was even harder when I had my girlfriend in the same class; funny, yet very uncomfortable. It took me about a month to suppress feelings about men. I kept repeating to myself that it was wrong to be attracted to the same sex and that I would go to hell.

Towards the last few weeks of my senior year, without a girlfriend, my feelings towards men were coming back. I started to have wet dreams. I called them nightmares. Music has always been my passion. It has helped me go through difficult times. One song in particular, "Antología," helped me deal with my attraction to men. It was written and sung by the famous Colombian singer Shakira. It reminded me of my ex-girlfriend, Jahiry, who I once loved.

When I started college in fall of 2004, I was overwhelmed by the stress over hiding my feelings towards men. My feelings grew stronger each time I spent time with the first guy I ever met who was gay. His name was Miguel. I had the feeling he was gay because of his good looks and because there were times I caught him staring at me.

I never paid attention to the fact that we both took the same bus home at the same time and the same days of the week. I was reading a book minding my own business when suddenly I noticed someone sit next to me. To my surprise, it was Miguel. We rode on the bus for about fifteen minutes when I looked at what he was reading, and I recognized the book, so I had to ask him if he was learning Chinese. He responded, "Yes." That's how the conversation started between the two of us.

We exchanged cell numbers that same day and decided to hang out at the mall on the weekends and just spend time together to get to know each other. My first kiss at eighteen was with Miguel. Up to this date I still remember the song that was playing in the background in my car, "Ahora Quien" by salsa singer Marc Anthony. Every time I hear this song I remember our first kiss. I know I had the biggest crush on Miguel, but maybe I was in love with him. Our relationship as friends was not what you call "friends with benefits" because we never had sexual intercourse.

We were good friends for about five months before I moved to Denver. We kept in touch by writing emails to each other and via phone calls. When I first arrived at my cousin Claudia's house, I was ecstatic because it had been over three years since I had seen her and her family. While there, I came to the realization that I really liked Miguel because I missed him so much. I wrote him poems and letters that I never sent him because I was afraid. Little did I know, he did the same. We both liked each other very much but we both agreed it was never love; I don't know how we came to that conclusion. Maybe we were both in denial.

After two months of living with my cousin, Miguel and I lost touch. I was upset about it, but I moved on. When I got hired at Sam's Club, I met a girl who I later found out was lesbian. We became great friends. Finally, one day during lunch, I told her something I never expected to say about myself. I said, "Rachel, I'm gay." Her reaction and response flattered me. "Yes, Mario, I know that." Apparently there was so much for me to learn, yet for some it comes naturally. I'm referring to "Gaydar." She always told me that at some point I would be able to tell if a guy or a girl was gay/lesbian. However, to this day, I still cannot tell whether a person is gay or not. I believe it is because I don't really like judging people and to me "gaydar" is judging someone on their behavior and looks.

At first, though, before realizing that it was all judgment on my part, I did try my best to see if I could tell someone's sexual orientation. There was one particular guy named Freddie who also worked at Sam's Club. Every day I asked myself if he was gay or not. The way he spoke, dressed, and moved seemed to suggest he was gay. I asked Rachel if she thought Freddie was gay, and her response was always no. I did wish for him to be gay because I wanted to be understood, accepted, and not be the only gay guy at Sam's Club. I felt like an outsider, and I felt rejected even though I wasn't, but it was always on my mind. I accepted myself as gay but I was afraid of what my family and friends would think. I was frightened about being rejected and disliked for who I am.

On the fourth month of living in Colorado, I started to search for gay clubs, hoping I could meet someone. Someone who was out of the closet because I was only out to Rachel and myself. I mean, if they were out of the closet I would have someone to talk to and ask their advice. I wanted someone to be there for me just like I have always been there for my family and friends; of course, this situation was different.

I was able to find a park, Cheesman Park, where the gays would hang-out and meet up. However, as naive as I was, I got myself into trouble. The first time I showed up was probably around four o'clock in the afternoon. It was a beautiful afternoon during fall of mid October. I drove and drove around the park for about ten minutes until I decided to take a brisk walk around the park.

I got my iPod and started walking. I figured I would eventually run into someone, or at least I hoped someone would notice I was new to this area and start talking to me. Unexpectedly, I was overrun by a dog, a Doberman to be exact. You're probably asking yourself, how in the world would I lose my balance to a dog? Well, his owner and the dog were playing fetch and due to my distractedness, the dog and I collided. I lost my balance and fell and Michael, the dog's owner, came by to check if I was all right.

He was about twenty-nine years old, whereas I was only nineteen. He was a nice person, and we got together and talked for a while in the park. I had to ask him if he was gay and he responded that he was. Not only was he gay, he was single, recently out of the closet, and new in town. "He is perfect for me," is what I kept telling myself.

After the incident, Michael and I traded cell numbers and texted almost every day. I was really happy to have met him because he helped me through some dilemmas such as loving myself and not regretting being born different. My quaint sense of humor seemed to amuse him, especially since some of my questions didn't make sense half the time. Unfortunately, after I had known him for almost three weeks, he had to move out of town. I missed him as a friend and nothing else.

After Michael moved away I met Gabriel. He, not unlike myself, was a gay individual who was barely accepting of himself and not able to share that he was gay with his family because of the threat of rejection. He was around my age and also raised Catholic. According to Catholicism, a man is born to love and be with a woman forever. We both believed that just because we were sexually attracted to men instead of women didn't mean we were going to hell.

Gabriel was a very special friend to me. He was there for me as I was there for him. He introduced me to Mypace, and through it I met a guy who I started to talk to before I moved back to California due to a family emergency.

Two nights before I moved back to San Diego, my cousin Claudia sat down to talk to me. The topic of the night was "Are You Gay?" She didn't force me to tell her that I was gay, but the way she broached the subject was, quite frankly, hilarious: she told me people at work were questioning her about my sexuality, she had caught me once or twice gazing at soap-opera leading men, and then there was Gabriel. I denied it several times. As much as I denied it to myself and to her, I knew that the truth would eventually be revealed. So after a moment of silence I looked into her eyes and told her, "Yes, I am gay, and I'm sorry." As tears fell from my eyes and onto my cheeks, she looked at me and said that I didn't need to apologize for anything. However, after explaining to her how I feared rejection from both of my adopted parents, she explained to me that a mother's love for a child is unconditional, that of all people my mother would understand me and support my decisions.

The next morning, I packed my things and said my goodbyes to my cousin, her children, and her husband. As I got on the freeway I made a quick detour to Chessman Park one last time. Memories from spending time there by myself and other times when Michael was still around lingered in my thoughts and I cried a little; it hurt a lot to leave Colorado.

While on the highway, I decided to make a phone call to another cousin, Samuel, who I considered an older brother. When I got a hold of him, we talked for about an hour, and he didn't care that I was gay. He assured me that I was still the same person, and then he thanked me for calling him and letting him know my secret. He wished me luck.

My trip didn't seem to take as long as I thought it would. The sign read, "Welcome to San Diego." When I got a chance to log into Myspace, there was an unread message. I opened it and all it said was, "When you get to San Diego, call me at my cell phone." I didn't want to seem desperate, so I waited a week before I called Marco, who was in the United States Navy. He was originally from El Paso, Texas, but was stationed there in San Diego. We spoke on the phone for over three hours when he was supposed to be on duty. Though we still hadn't met in person, we arranged for that to happen soon. Honestly, for me it was love at first sight; for him it was not. It took him a little longer to fall in love with me. I still remember the first day we met, the first time I laid eyes on him. He was patiently waiting for me at the bus stop when I went to pick him up. I felt awkward knowing that I had fallen in love with a man as I had previously loved a woman. After dating for a while, we became boyfriends.

The best quality about Marco was that he was always there to listen to any of my concerns or problems. He was a great listener and knew when to give advice even when I didn't ask for it. In the first two weeks of being boyfriends, I continued school and had a part time job at Target as a cashier.

Our days consisted of going to movies for the night to cuddle, going to the beach a lot, and taking walks in the mall. I was in love with him and I dedicated a song called "Amor Real" by Sin Bandera. I also would get inspired and write poems to him. In just two weeks, we became very close and both of us were able to say, "I love you."

Eventually, it was time to tell my parents about myself. No matter what my parents thought, I decided to let them know the truth. It was time to unmask the Mario they didn't know. It was time to reveal the truth to them about the type of love I wanted to share for the rest of my life and to let them know that I was different but still the same child they had adopted.

Before I was able to gather both of them and talk to them, my mother beat me to it and called me to the living room wanting to talk to me. She went on and on about the topic of love and how beautiful it is to have a family and to be able to adopt a child if for any reason my "wife" couldn't conceive. I knew exactly where this was heading, so I saved her the trouble of asking about my sexuality. I told her, "Mom, I totally understand where you're coming from; however, I simply can't. At least, not yet. Maybe in the future I will adopt a child of my own and raise this child as mine. Mom, dad, I need to let you know that I'm gay."

As soon as the word gay came out of my mouth, my mom started crying and my dad stood up quickly, very upset, and almost turned abusive. He came to a halt, and I could tell he was holding back tears. His hands turned into fists so I quickly started to step backwards; he frightened me.

His exact words were, "What did I do wrong as a father? I can't have a homosexual child in my family. This is a burden; no, wait, maybe you're confused and this is a temporary 'phase' for you." I shook my head, "No," to every excuse he found. I could see his perplexed expression revealing his way of thinking. Eventually, his face froze as if he were looking at a ghost.

I assured my parents that I was the same person they had adopted. The same person they saw light in and believed in, and the same warm heart they taught to always carry a smile. I also told my dad that just because I chose a man instead of a woman to love I should not be treated any differently.

However, he told me that I needed to gather my things and leave the house immediately with no excuses before his shift from work ended, that if I were still here by the time he returned home he would not kick me out, but beat me out of the house. I stared at him while he told me all this, and I could feel his hate, fear, and disgust.

I quickly gathered my things and left, heartbroken, with non-stop tears and no clue as to where I was going. The only place that I could call home, where I once felt safe and secure, became my torture chamber. I became a failure and a disappointment to my father. This home which I thought would accept me for who I was became my worst enemy.

You're probably asking yourself where Marco was when all this happened. Well, he was at work; it was one of those days when he was on duty. He had no idea that I was about to tell my parents that I was gay. He was against it from the beginning because although he hadn't met my parents he said, "Your family is very old-fashioned, especially your dad. The way he was raised and his mentality is that a man is to be with a woman forever not with another man. He probably thinks you're the devil or that you're going to go to hell. He may even think he did something wrong." I denied that answer for a while because I was raised to believe that you never turn your back on your family. That love is love and no one deserves to be treated this way. I guess I was wrong. My dad hated the fact that I was gay, or maybe he hated me. My mother, who I mistakenly thought would support me, let me down. So now I was on the streets with nowhere to go. I called Joshua, one of my gay friends, and he introduced me to Ticin, who is also gay.

Ticin, who was thirty-two, helped me out and let me crash on the couch in his bedroom. His boyfriend, Anthony, was out to sea during the two months Marco and I crashed at his place. Ticin understood what I was going through. He kept reminding me that I didn't choose to be gay, but that I was born that way, that sooner or later my parents would apologize for what they did.

For six months the only family member I had contact with was my mother. It took her about two months to realize that just because I was gay didn't mean that I couldn't still be treated with the same love she always gave me. As hard as it was for me, it was hard for her as well. She felt like, "La espada en la pared," because she was trying to help me and make me happy without my father's consent while keeping him happy by not letting me near the house when he was there. Those visits to my mother's house were harsh. There were times when I had to sneak into the house just to receive money for food and gas. I was a part-time worker at Target, not earning enough to support myself. Marco helped Ticin by giving him money for the light bill; he also paid my cell phone and gave me gas for the car. I never had enough money to pay for everything.

For about four months we ate and slept in my car. I would drive around the city of San Diego just to find a spot where the police wouldn't drive by and spot us. Normally, I parked more than three times a week in residential areas where I knew people wouldn't notice an unfamiliar car in their neighborhood. I didn't let the fact that I was living in my car get in the way of attending school. Taking a shower was the least of my problems since Ticin never really locked his house, so we both knew around what time to show up and just use the bathroom and avoid him.

As time passed, I couldn't take it anymore—worrying about whether I was going to have food to eat or gas for the car. So in a split second I made the biggest mistake ever in my life. Still working at Target as a cashier, I stole money for about three weeks. I took $20 the first day; sometimes I would take $40; other days I took a bigger amount and I would take up to $80. After three weeks, I finally got caught by the manager. He was spotting the camera and came across me and noticed that I was acting suspiciously. So he called me into his office and sat me down. He had only to ask me one question and I knew what he was referring to: "Mario, why?" As I sat there I did my best not to shed a tear.

I confessed and spoke only the truth. "I stole money from the cash register because I wasn't making enough money from the hours I'm scheduled to work. I used the money to buy uniforms for work, pillows, a blanket, food, gas and sometimes a hotel because I was getting tired of sleeping in my car." After hearing what I had to say the manager sat there and was sympathetic, but at the same time I broke the law and he had to abide by the law. Two policemen came in and arrested me for petty theft. Marco and my parents were notified about what I had done. My mother felt horrible that I was sent to jail and my father was upset.

I blamed both of them for letting me down and giving me no support. After I was released, Marco and I decided that the only place where we both would have a better future than we would have in San Diego was his hometown, El Paso, Texas. In November of 2006, we drove to El Paso and arrived at his parents' house. Marco's parents didn't know he was gay, but he decided to tell them in person as soon as we got there. He sat with his mother and stepfather and told them that he was gay. Surprisingly, both of his parents knew this about him and were waiting for the time he came to realize it himself. Marco told me that whether I knew it or not, I was an inspiration to him. He thanked me for being there for him when he told his parents that he was gay.

His mother and father were different from my parents even though both families were old-fashioned and Catholic. I liked his parents a lot, and as much as I wished for mine to be that way, I was patient because patience is a virtue. Time passed and I learned that things happen for a reason. During the two years that I lived in El Paso, I received an unexpected call. Caller ID read, "Unavailable." It was my father's voice on the other end. The reason for his call was so he could apologize to me. It took him two years to come around. I stayed quiet and let him apologize. He said he had an epiphany that he was not embarrassed to have a gay son as part of his family, that he was not afraid or disgusted because I was his son, and that I deserved the same respect and love I had before.

From that moment on I've felt unconditional love from him. I thanked God for providing me with plenty of patience. I quickly went up to Marco and told him the great news I had received from my father. However, he didn't seem to care at all. Ever since we moved to Texas he had become a different person. He turned abusive, and I caught him cheating more then once, but because I didn't want to "believe" it I continued to stay with him.

After dealing with two years of humiliation, deceptions, and being either physically or mentally abused, I left Marco. I caught him cheating on me once and emailing other guys and texting guys about sleeping with them. There was one friend who I never lost touch with that I met through Ticin. His name was Phil. I called him after catching Marco cheating on me with a mutual friend of ours. I asked his opinion as to whether I should move back to San Diego or just move to a different location in El Paso. He suggested I come back home. I took his advice, and I walked away from my relationship with Marco and never looked back. I felt I had wasted two years and six months of my life living a total lie. I asked myself many times if Marco ever really loved me. On my way back home I called my parents and told them that I needed a place to stay. My parents let me stay with them, and I found a job at a retail store and at a hotel as a night clerk.

One day I decided to join the US Navy. The process was pretty easy. First, I had to enroll, then take the Armed Services Vocational Aptitude Battery (ASVAB), which I passed with a great score. After taking the test I had to get a physical, which is a little harder to do because you have to pass every single test. I passed, but I was having difficulty finishing the process. At first I thought it was due to my misdemeanor offense, but after completing two years and showing proof to the judge that I had stayed out of trouble, avoided citations of any kind, and because I was trying to join the Navy, he terminated my probation.

After presenting the requisite paperwork to my recruiter, I spoke to the Captain of the Ship over the phone and explained why I wanted to join the US Navy. I wanted to better my education, travel the world, and help people, so he approved me and signed a document stating that I was allowed to join the Navy after I pledged the oath. I was ecstatic; I was finally in the Navy. However, on August 19, two weeks after joining the military, I received a letter stating that there was a slight problem with my test. A result came in and I needed to make an appointment with the Head Chief and my recruiter. For three days straight, I literally went crazy trying to think what could be the problem.

I called Phil and read the letter to him to see if he knew what needed to be discussed with me. As soon as I was finished reading the letter, there was an awkward moment of silence. Right there and then I realized that I knew what he was about to say. I had a flashback to when I got sick in January of 2008. I had a fever and a headache for a week. I ended up going to the hospital to see a doctor. They never took a blood test to check what was wrong, but I did get a shot so my headache would go away.

The day to finally meet up with my recruiter and the Head Chief arrived. I was asked if I had any idea why I was called in. I said that there were many reasons I could think of, but honestly, I'd rather not make assumptions. One of them handed me a letter that explained why I couldn't be in the US Navy. According to this letter, tests revealed the Human Immunodeficiency Virus (HIV) in my blood. The letter said that I was HIV positive, though it didn't say that I had Acquired Immunodeficiency Syndrome (AIDS). I was advised by the Head Chief to take a second set of blood work to verify if these tests were correct. So I did, and the results were the same. What was I to do now?

The first thing I did was call my ex-boyfriend Marco and let him know that I was HIV positive. His response shocked me. He said that I was the one who probably gave it to him and that this was proof of my cheating on him. I hung up the phone and cried perhaps as much out of anger as out of sadness.

After crying for about an hour, I thought to myself that I had to take action and take care of myself. So I went to the Gay and Lesbian Center in Hillcrest and started to do some research by looking for support groups, a therapist, a doctor, and even a nutritionist. I found the perfect program for me after searching for almost two days.

I took a course in Positive Living for recently diagnosed HIV-positive persons. I learned about how sleep and exercising have a big impact on increasing T-cells. I took this course for about four months, and I took it twice because I wanted to make sure I knew enough about living with HIV. I considered the founder of the course, Rick, my mentor. I'm very grateful I met him because through him I was able to find a good place for getting a doctor and a dentist. I was able to settle down. I found a therapist who I visited once a week every week and a nutritionist who taught me how to eat in a healthy way.

My life seemed to be at a good point; there was no stressing about school and I had two stable jobs. I could say that I was content with how my life was going. However, I did still cry at nights because I was lonely and wanted someone to be there for me. I had support from my friends: Leroy, Phil, Alma, Cruz, and Francisco. I had the love of my family so far, even though they didn't know about my illness. That wasn't enough for my heart. I wanted to meet a great guy with whom I could share my love and life.

As if being gay wasn't enough trouble in this world, now I had to worry about disclosure. Having HIV is something you can't simply hide from someone, especially if you're considering a relationship. Nonetheless, even if you are just looking for sex, you need to disclose your status because of the risks you may be posing for the other person. Whether you're HIV positive or not, disclosure should always come across in your conversation. Better safe than sorry.

I handled my status in various ways. There were days when I was strong and didn't let it affect my day, and there were other days when I was depressed. Physically, I was well, but mentally and emotionally, I was not doing so well. The therapist made me focus on myself and what made me happy—for example, writing and poetry. She had me focus on writing my thoughts and feelings down. So I got a pencil and paper and started writing. At first it was just pure random thoughts. Then I started to write about love. My surroundings can affect my writing. I went to the bus stop and rode the bus for the entire route, not really wanting to think. I was blank after riding the bus and making it back home safely, after which I was inspired and grabbed a new blank sheet of paper and started writing. This is what came to me.

Bus

As I sit on the bus looking out the window
The city looking sleepy and hollow
I fall into a deep confusion
That takes my body instantly into pain

As I ride the bus through the dimly lit city
I see different people getting on and off
Reminding me of the grief I have caused myself

The different expressions they carry on their faces
Each one unique
Each one different
In their eyes I recognize—hope

I keep a smile, hoping to pretend that I'm okay
Never losing my mind

A loud scream in my head yells, "Help me!"
My heart starts pounding faster by the minute
It gets harder to breathe

Can't move …
Can't blink …
Can't live …

Slowly the sorrow swells inside me more and more
As people stare at me with the strangest glimpse
Not helping nor saying a word

I consume each and every single peek
Taking them to a land full of confusion
Leading them in such a wrongful manner

Suddenly, I am alone except for another with its brilliant shine
I look around and I'm still in the bus

As I grasp what's going on
I notice the angel or shadow dancing its way towards me
With a crooked smile
Sensitive yet lustrous eyes

It arrives to where I sit
Apathetically, I look at it …
This Aura …
This Shadow …
This Spirit …
Maybe even an Angel …

Confusing my world even more
I can't manage to take my eyes off of it

The more I look
The more clear it becomes
Like a fog clearing from the streets

I can slowly start to see his face
And I suddenly have an epiphany

This light that I see
Is me ...

Reminding me not to fall
To stand tall and firm
That I'm strong enough and not alone
That If I feel alone
To calm down and see that I have myself
Myself to help me
To find the light
A path with great power
The power of hope ...

Suddenly a rush movement distracts me
And I see that as I rode this bus
All this was a sudden realization of desire

As I'm still continuously on the bus
I understand my dream
That I'm the only one to cause myself pain

I'm the one who chooses to be happy
Chooses to be sad

Then a voice calls out my name
And as I open my eyes
I see the one I love standing next to me

I release a big sigh and comprehend
That I was dreaming in my own dream

So then all that I desire
All that I hope is love

Not just love from someone
But to love myself
Just me ...

When I finished writing this poem for my therapist, she made me read it out loud. As I read it to her, I started to see what she was doing. I understood her method, and I'm glad she did this for me because it helped me a lot. Any time that I felt sad I would read it.

The day that my parents found out I was HIV positive could have been the worst time ever, worse than when they found out I was gay. I didn't get the opportunity to sit with them and just talk calmly. I was in the kitchen crying because I didn't know if it was time for my parents to know. When my mother walked into the kitchen, she asked me if I was crying because she had drank my soda. I told her it wasn't that. Then she just sort of made fun of me because I was crying for no reason. So instead of walking to my room, I walked towards the living room and blurted out, "I'm sick and there is nothing you or my father can do. I can't fix it with Tylenol nor can I go back in time and fix this." As confused as my mother was, she asked me what I was talking about. I told her to sit on the couch but she refused to sit, and so I yelled, "I'm HIV positive, sorry."

Silence is golden. We learn to appreciate silence and that a quiet room is good for us time to time. I was hoping to hear a comforting sound. At least a small sigh or just the sound of her heartbeat would've been fine, but nothing. I sought silence, but she hurt me in the worst way possible: she said, "That's what happens when you're gay, you get AIDS and die." After hearing those words from her, all I could do was walk away. I went for a small walk down to the park that was near the house. I just couldn't fathom why she would say that. I wondered if she even loved me now that she knew I was gay. My thoughts ran wild all night until I came back home.

I walked back inside the house, and she and my father were locked in her room discussing what had just happened. So I went to my room, finally getting the silence I wanted. Oddly, I was inspired to write a poem, and I wrote two. One for my mother and one for myself. As days passed, my mother treated me as if I were a hideous monster.

She gave me my own dishes and cooking utensils and told me to keep them separate from theirs because I had HIV. I had to teach her the truth about how HIV is contracted and passed on. I told her many times that it's not airborn and that sharing utensils is not going to give her the disease. Any time that I tried talking to her, it always turned out to be a battle. Hateful words were thrown around like a game of ping-pong, back and forth, back and forth, never missing one shot.

After two months of tiring arguments and pitiful words, I did the unimaginable. It was one of the worst things I could have done to my mother, but it got the message across just fine. One day before she arrived home from work, I put all the dishes into the sink and got the bottle of Clorox on the counter and waited for her to arrive. When she got home she saw what was going on and questioned what I was doing. I responded, "I was washing the dishes when the phone rang, so I went to answer it. As I was talking on the phone I accidentally mixed up your dishes with mine. So I went to the bathroom and got the bottle of Clorox to disinfect the dishes; that way you don't get AIDS and die. Don't worry, I didn't miss a spot." Right when I said "spot," a gush of wind blew on my face and I realized she had slapped me. I looked at her and told her that unless there was blood-to-blood contact or we had sexual intercourse, there was no possible way for her to contract the disease and walked away.

She kicked me out of the house after throwing more repulsive words at me. "I regret adopting you." That one hurt me the most. I never gave up hope though. I left the house, not shedding a tear this time because it wouldn't do any good, especially since my T-cells were increasing and my viral load was decreasing. I moved to Hillcrest, the gayborhood, as I like to call it. I had to call Phil in order to have him help me move; he is the big brother I never had.

I only have one sibling, and his name is Kenny. He knows that I'm gay and he knows that I'm positive. I never told him this information, but considering the family I come from, we never keep secrets from each other. Kenny is fifteen now, and he is supportive in many ways I never expected from him. He is one of the few young adults I hear and see that has such an open mind. I know he looks up to me, so I do my best to prove to him that the world is not such a bad place as some people make it seem.

When I moved into Vincent's place, I felt peace and love like no other. Vincent has helped me in many ways. Twice, I experienced public humiliation because of being HIV positive. The first time, I was dating a guy who knew my status. He was still adjusting to the idea of dating someone who was HIV positive. One day, however, I went to his work to visit and have lunch together. When I left and we had both said our goodbyes, I went to the bus stop and had put on my earphones when an unexpected visitor from his work started yelling—not talking, but yelling—that I was a liar. He said I was a cheater and that I had AIDS and wanted to infect anyone I pleased. People stared at me the same way my mother did. I was so confused, and I had no idea what was going on, so instead of waiting for the bus I walked all the way home.

The second time I experienced public humiliation was about six months later, and this happened at a local gay club. I wasn't dating anybody at the time, but there was a guy, Luis, who was interested in dating me. I was with Vincent, having one of our "boys nights out." The club was getting ready to close up when Luis approached me, drunk, and asked me why I wouldn't date him. I tried telling him that I wasn't ready to date anybody at the moment and to leave me alone, especially since he was drunk. Finally, when the music got cut off by the DJ, Luis literally yelled as loud as he could, "Well, I don't date people with AIDS like you." People turned around to look at who he was talking to. Vincent and I played along and turned our heads and acted like we didn't know him. He kept saying, "You have AIDS." I pushed him hard into the crowd of people and walked away.

A year later, I was very content with my life, especially after all the challenges life had placed in my path. I still didn't speak to my mother, and the only communication I kept with my family was through my brother, Kenny, and my father. I was still working at the same job and still had my friends. When my twenty-second birthday came along, I spent it with friends even though I wished my family could've been there. Thanksgiving came, and it was the same situation. When Christmas came around, however, it was different.

I was in the deepest depression ever. I saw families gather together. Couples loving each other and being happy. I only had Phil, Vincent, and myself. My father and brother were in Mexico for Christmas, so I couldn't call them. I was being a little selfish, but all I wanted was to have a boyfriend, or at least not a broken family.

I started thinking about all the problems that I had overcome, and I broke down. I overdosed on my HIV medication by taking exactly thirteen pills. I went to the kitchen and got a knife to kill myself with. If I was going to be alone in this world, I thought, I might as well end my life there and then. I couldn't though. I was afraid to cut myself, and I couldn't do it. I called the paramedics and notified them that someone in the household overdosed on HIV medication, never saying it was me.

Vincent was out buying breakfast for both of us when I did all of this. When he came back I told him what I had done, and as upset as he was, he pinned me down to the floor until the ambulance came and took me to the hospital. On the way to the hospital, I was to drink charcoal so I could vomit. I was supposed to work that day, but Vincent called my co-workers and manager to inform them that I was in the hospital.

Jesse, Anthony, and Steve came by to visit and were upset with what I had done. They had every right to be disappointed because I was realizing little by little that my friends are my family. Jesse once told me that I can make my own family. That if I can't fix what is going to take a while, then why not just build my own family. That I had friends who were always there for me no matter what and that they were my family.

He was right. I didn't realize that my friends are my family—never giving up on me and always being by my side just like a family should be. I got really close to my co-workers, and I know that if I need advice on anything they are there to listen and give me advice. To build my self-esteem again, I did what my therapist had taught me a year earlier. I wrote all my emotions down; I wrote poetry about loving oneself and never giving up. I wrote about love, and I meditated for a while.

I reclaimed my life. I started volunteering again and continued working. I volunteer for a young gay men's community program called "In The Mix." It's a social group for gay and bisexual men of color ages eighteen to twenty-four. This group helps the community by giving you a space. It educates men and woman on same-sex relationships and sex and HIV prevention. Because I was a volunteer, they gave me the opportunity to be a spokesperson on World AIDS Day (December 1st), to speak about what it is like being a young gay male and living with HIV. Through my volunteering I've made great friends.

2010 is coming to an end; problems always arise no matter what. Whether you're positive, negative, short, tall, skinny, or obese, that doesn't mean that it should be the end of the world. In the past two years, I have learned so much. I learned that by helping people, I help myself. It makes me feel like a better person. I enjoy educating people about HIV and AIDS. I do my best to stay involved with the community and show my support. I know that no matter what happens in my life, I have my best friends who are always going to be there for me, and I'm always going to be there for them.

As I've said before, patience is a virtue. As someone once told me, "Be the better person and seek her (my mother) out yourself and try it again." So I did, and both of us now talk, but we never mention the past. We only apologized to each other.

I am no longer alone. I have my friends, and my family is slowly coming around. I've also been involved in a serodiscordant relationship, meaning my partner is HIV negative. I never thought I would end up with someone who would accept me the way that I am, especially after having gone through such harsh times with being positive. Charles, who I consider my other half, is very supportive of what I do. He has gone with me to my doctor's appointments and makes sure that I am physically, emotionally, and psychologically stable. We have been together for four months now, and our connection is only getting stronger. When you have that communication and that trust, it takes a lot to break something like that apart.

Charles and I have faced quite a few problems for being in a relationship like ours. It doesn't mean that it's not going to work, but we have to be extra cautious because of our health differences. We have to be careful when it comes to sexual intercourse because anything can go wrong, and in a split second without us knowing, I might pass the virus to him. You can't tell you have it in a day or so, but getting tested on a regular basis helps. Not only do we need to be careful with HIV, there are also Chlamydia, Syphilis, Gonorrhea, and other different types of Sexually Transmitted Diseases (STDs). We are two people who love each other and make the best of our relationship. Not only does a relationship have to be sexually happy, but also mentally stable. If I stay mentally well and he is too, there shouldn't be a reason for sadness or depression. Charles has not only taught me, but has demonstrated that anyone can be loved. Whether I am short, Mexican, positive or different, I still deserve love.

So here I am now, very happy with my life in my own hands. I have my friends, my family, and my other half, Charles, who supports me. I may still struggle with everyday life problems, but I know that at the end of the day, I have love surrounding me. This is my story so far. I have slowly put my life together again. I have managed to keep my best friend, Phil, regain the love of my family, and find a new love in Charles.

As long as I get to breathe and wake up the next day, I should be happy with life. Why morn for something that cannot be undone? It's like they say: "What doesn't kill you makes you stronger." So instead of getting depressed about me being positive, I look at my status as striving for survival. How far will I go to survive? There is no limit. I don't let this virus control my body, nor should you. I thank God for who I am now and for giving me this day to live and enjoy.

Last Supper

Gil Cuadros

Phillip and Matthew's tongues are
locked.
They spread themselves over plates
and knives,
the dinner table shakes,
and the wine spills over.

I am the one tearing the bread
while my sweet Judas is across
peeling back the petals
till he reaches the heart.
There is butter in his smile.

Later among the olive trees,
the river's bend, the shepherd's crook
we meet secretly.
I can still taste his soft wool,
legs wrapped in linen
and the hill bedded with ripe fruit
that oiled the skin.

Alone we thought that nothing could break
our world of bushes and night,
the body safe in nature.
Our shadows grew bold

as the Pharisees approached
with lanterns and clubs.
They carried the temple's footstones,
tested the rocks' weight, solid in hand
like a ball game, or how children
corner a small animal, ready to pelt.

Constructing an Ofrenda of My Memory

A Queer Poz Indo-Xicano Maps His Way Home

Omar O. González

Prologue/Ofrenda of Origination

The sacred drum beats its lament of defeat on the journey south, towards a seemingly barren land, its people held captive as prisoners, spoils of war. This band of Pueblos will have to construct a new home, a new identity, a new destiny. Nearly three hundred years later, a group of Tigua Indians, the descendants of the banished Pueblo tribe, dance in front of the San Antonio de Padua mission in Ysleta, Texas, simultaneously celebrating the life/mourning the death of my maternal grandfather, Simon Carrasco Villanueva as they bid him farewell on his journey home. Although I was not yet imagined, out of my grandmother's grief was borne a sorrowful rage, one that would later save my life and foreshadow my destiny.

Ofrenda of Consciousness/Quinceañera

I am drawn toward the sacred site. The ocean's rhythmic hum is a comforting yet insufficient replacement for the haunting desert of the Southwest. I search for the antepasados and humbly request direction.

Eduardo Galeano opens *The Book of Embraces* with the definition of the Spanish word for remember—"*Recordar*: To remember; from the Latin *re-cordis*, to pass back through the heart" (11). To return memories through one's heart can be a painfully difficult, sometimes impossible, process when recalling traumatic events and feelings. The memories I recall in this work are the thorns of a maguey tearing, scarring, scraping, and cutting the flesh of my heart. The heart of an aged maguey is eventually broken, its liquid harvested to produce the sweet and gastrointestinally healthy drink known as pulque.[1] This alcoholic drink is simultaneously intoxicating and nourishing, an alternate form of sustenance.

Recollections continue to seep through the cracks of my own irreparably damaged heart. The fragmentation of my corazon parallels the jagged, nonlinear flow of my memory. I continue to bleed my offering to the gods for granting me the opportunity, the *privilege*, of remembering. I willingly rip open every ventricle, every chamber to offer my flesh and blood, allowing all who wish to partake of my sacrifice. The liquid of my

---

1   According to Francisco Clavijero's history of Mexico, published in 1807, pulque was a staple of the ancient Mexican diet and compensated for the lack of legumes in impoverished diets. The indigenous peoples of Mesoamerica treated gastrointestinal conditions, particularly diarrhea, with the administration of pulque. Additionally, the Rodale Institute, a nonprofit organization dedicated to the implementation of organic farming as a way to mitigate the effects of global warming, cites an analysis performed on pulque and concludes that it contains the following nutrients: thiamine, riboflavin, niacin, pantothenic acid, and a host of bacteria essential for a healthy gastrointestinal tract. Finally, Rodolfo F. Acuña in *Occupied America* reiterates the healthful aspects of pulque. Thus, pulque nourishes our bodies as it soothes our souls.

memories—the tears of utter joy, crushing loss, mind-blowing ecstasy, and unconditional love—concurrently nourish and torment my soul.

In his controversial book, *Hunger of Memory*, Richard Rodriguez states, "But I write of one life only. My own. If my story is true, I trust it will resonate with significance for other lives. Finally, my history deserves public notice as no more than this: a parable for the life of its reader" (7). Rodriguez's words are powerful and belong to the book's readers as much, if not more, as to the author, evidenced by the decontextualized manner in which political conservatives have manipulated his ideas into shaping public policy. Conservative political forces championed his words at the height of the debate surrounding bilingual education, particularly Proposition 227 in California. However, xenophobia, either internal or external, did not fuel his sentiments, but rather he presents a thoughtful analysis and interpretation of his life experiences in his memoir. In a recent commentary on NPR, Rodriguez expresses his gratitude toward undocumented immigrants for all they have sacrificed for the benefit of Americans, including him. Rodriguez's and my words, experiences, and viewpoints, however "un-Xicano" they may be considered, are patches of the same quilt, or cobija in this case. Our atypical experiences and perspectives broaden the discourse of Chicana/o identity.

In *The Archaeology of Knowledge*, Michel Foucault posits that a text is a reference point to other texts:

> The frontiers of a book are never clear-cut: beyond the title, the first lines, and the last full stop, beyond its internal configuration and its autonomous form, it is caught up in a system of references to other books, other texts, other sentences: it is a node within a network. (23)

Therefore, as Foucault suggests, Rodriguez's and my own narrative interconnect to a broader and larger framework. The experiences from which we derive our narratives are our individual hermeneutic lenses, subjectively inscribing meaning upon certain life events. Both Rodriguez and I are nodes within Foucault's network.

Initially, a writer is motivated to write in order to make sense of her/his respective reality. The product, a synthesis of the writer's life experiences and readings, affect the reader's thoughts, ideas, and perhaps actions. Reading alters a person's consciousness forever and can serve as an impetus for a transformative process.[2] Ultimately, I wish to create an intimate bond with my reader, an unmasked and unsheathed dialogue.[3]

Furthermore, I draw inspiration from multiple types of texts and cite them throughout this work. Academic readings, novels, dreams, the laughs with friends as we dance the night away, popular culture, my grandmother's cuentos, the gestural communications with anonymous sex partners, music lyrics—particularly those from songs from the post punk or "alternative" era of the eighties and the house music of the early nineties—are material drawing me to the page in order to entice the reader into my world and help her/him make sense of it. Essentially, I am mapping my journey toward a destination of mutual understanding with my reader.

---

2   See bell hooks's documentary *Cultural Criticism and Transformation* for her comments regarding the agency granted to people once they acquire the skills of critical thinking plus literacy.

3   A character in the film *V for Vendetta* remarks regarding the dangers of masking one's identities, "We wear a mask for so long that we forget who we are underneath them." Conversely, the film illustrates the benefits of concealing one's identity to form a collective consciousness of an oppressed populace. The anonymity of the mask, therefore, provides strength in order to resist a tyrannical force. In essence, the masks allow people to lose their fear. See also Gracia Limon's novel *Erased Faces* for an example of masking one's identity in order for a marginalized community to organize against its oppressor, in this case the EZLN against the Mexican government. The Zapatistas proclaim, "We had to put on masks in order to be seen." In *V for Vendetta* and *Erased Faces*, their present movements link to historical struggles, thus crossing a temporal threshold in order to provide a context for the audience. Moreover, sheaths "protect" one person from the horror of exchanging fluids yet also prevent the parties from making an instinctual connection with each other during sexual intercourse.

Similarly, an ancient map foretells the ultimate destiny of the Tigua. The destiny of the indigenous tribe of Ysleta del Sur, Texas, also known as the "People of the Sun," is symbolized pictorially by a half-sun creeping over the horizon, while a snake-like arrow, resembling the non-linear course of the Rio Grande, meanders north towards its ancestral home into a kiva-like structure. The Tigua legend says that when only one Tigua survives in Ysleta del Sur, she/he will return to our ancestral home in New Mexico, to rejoin the clan. This is my ultimate endeavor in this work—to find *my* way home amidst a torrent of shadows while focusing on the rare glimpses of sunlight.

Moreover, after years of struggle, both internal and external, I currently occupy a transitory space of physiological, emotional, mental, and spiritual clarity. Because this type of intersection is rare and fleeting, I have chosen to document my ubiquitously changing interpretation of life events by applying Geertz's methodology of "thick description" in order to provide the necessary context for the reader. Geertz applies the analogy of an involuntary eye twitch and a conscious wink in order to illustrate this concept:

> The two movements are, as movements, identical; from an I-am-a-camera, "phenomenalistic" observation of them alone, one could not tell which was twitch and which was wink, or indeed whether both or either was twitch or wink. Yet the difference, however unphotographable, between a twitch and a wink is vast; as anyone unfortunate enough to have had the first taken for the second knows. The winker is communicating, and indeed communicating in a quite precise and special way: (1) deliberately, (2) to someone in particular, (3) to impart a particular message, (4) according to a socially established code, and (5) without cognizance of the rest of the company. As Ryle points out, the winker has done two things, contracted his eyelids and winked, while the twitcher has done only one, contracting his eyelids.

> Contracting your eyelids on purpose when there exists a public code in which so doing counts as a conspiratorial signal *is* winking. That's all there is to it: a speck of behavior, a fleck of culture, and—*voilà!*—a gesture. [Furthermore,] the point is that between what Ryle calls the "thin description" of what the rehearser (parodist, winker, twitcher ...) is doing ("rapidly contracting his right eyelids") and the "thick description" of what he is doing ("practicing a burlesque of a friend faking a wink to deceive an innocent into thinking a conspiracy is in motion") lies the object of ethnography: a stratified hierarchy of meaningful structures in terms of twitches, winks, fake-winks, parodies, rehearsals of parodies are produced, perceived, and interpreted, and without which they would not ... in fact exist, no matter what anyone did or didn't do with his eyelids. (6–7)

Geertz's example of the wink versus a twitch illustrates the importance of providing several layers of context to a seemingly innocuous phenomenon. Therefore, it is imperative that I provide a cultural, spiritual, and historical context for my description and interpretation of the events that continue to shape my worldview. Additionally, Geertz's essay speaks to the creative license a writer must take with language if she/he intends on keeping the reader's attention. In the preceding quote, Geertz paints a colorful image in the mind of the reader with his linguistic playfulness. To illustrate his point, he takes a commonplace behavior and injects humor and meaning by continuously providing the context for such simple actions as a wink or a twitch.

Conversely, a wink can lead to devastating outcomes, as Rodriguez comments on the brutal murder of Matthew Shephard: "What does it tell us about heterosexual insecurity that a gay wink in a bar would unleash such murderous rage?" (par. 3). Although no one except for the murdered victim and the two perpetrators will ever know exactly what transpired that cold night in the Wyoming wasteland, the contexts of

queer identity/sexual desire collided tragically with that of heterosexual insecurity/(homo)sexual desire—all with the sign of a simple
wink.

Tragically, Matthew Shepard has had to rely on other people's interpretations of his life and the tragedy that ended it so abruptly and
cruelly. Therefore, I take the opportunity that he did not have. I write in
order to have some semblance of peace, to heal myself, and although
the pain and torment may reside in me always, perhaps my story will
help someone negotiating similar trauma.[4] Applying the methodology
of "thick description" allows me to construct an intimately vivid context
for the reader, one where my memory relinquishes its metaphorical
mask. As the reader cloaks her/himself with my identity, "thick description" provides a prism through which s/he views my world. The tool of
"thick description" allows me to lay each fragment of my life history
upon these pages as if constructing a living discursive ofrenda of my
memory.

In her book *Chicana Art: The Politics of Spiritual and Aesthetic
Altarities*, Laura Pérez regards the work of numerous Chicana artists as:

> sacrificial *ofrenda*, as transmutation of social or personal
> suffering into penetrating visions of the present and brave
> sightings of hopeful, better futures ... [The title] refers to
> these works as offerings on the altar where the material and

---

4   In an interview with María Henríquez Betancor, Gloria Anzaldúa responds to
     the question, "Is writing a need for you? Es una necesidad?" "Yes. It's the only
     way I could survive emotionally and intellectually in this society because
     this society can destroy your concept of yourself as a woman, as a Chicana. I
     survived all the racism and oppression by processing it through the writing.
     It's a way of healing. I put all the positive and negative feelings, emotions,
     and experiences into the writing, and I try to make sense of them ... Writing
     is partly cathartic. In talking about certain experiences I have to go back
     into the wound, and it hurts! But every time I do it, it hurts less; the wound
     starts to heal because I've exposed it. So for me writing is a way of making
     sense of my realities. It's also a way of healing my wounds and helping others
     heal theirs" (248–249). Thus, Santa Gloria decrees the potentially restorative
     powers of writing. Moreover, writing may never make us whole, yet it may lay
     the colorful shards of our shattered realities into a uniquely beautiful mosaic.

the still disembodied are invoked, and where the embodied is reminded of its ultimate identity with the socially or culturally disincarnate that it would "other" or relegate to the realm of seeming nonexistence. (6)

Similarly, I offer my memory as ofrenda, as I describe the physical and metaphysical steps of constructing an altar at the inception of each chapter for both personal and sociopolitical reasons. I do so in order to invoke and commune with the spirit ancestors, yet also to call attention to the corporal pleasure/pain of life as a sexually active queer Indo-Xicano living with AIDS. My memory as ofrenda is an homage to the queer ancestors, the brave souls who risked and gave their lives for future generations of joteria, daring to imagine the time when the otherness of non-heterosexuality will no longer mean the ostracism by family and friends and when HIV/AIDS will not claim another life.

Additionally, Perez cites Lourdes Portillo's 1992 documentary, *La Ofrenda: Days of the Dead*, in which a gay Latino constructs an altar for his lover and others who succumbed to AIDS. Perez cites the hybrid nature of the spirituality of said Chicana artists, which is also reflected in my syncretization of the indigenous Catholic practices of my childhood (including the practice of curanderismo) with my adoption of the belief system Santería and, finally, with my personal practice of the veneration of the butch lesbian of color. Furthermore, Luis Leon's application of "religious poetics" to John Rechy's novel *The Miraculous Day of Amalia Gomez* examines this type of unorthodox practice of spiritualities, thus allowing Chicanas/os "to manage the harsh realities that characterize significant dimensions of everyday life in barrios throughout the Mexican Americas and beyond" (206). Chicana/o spirituality, therefore, is adaptable and malleable in order to negotiate an existence littered with oppression. After centuries of adhering to strict dogma, some Chicanas/os now are subjugating the Church's doctrines. In effect, it is a sort of spiritual reconquista.

I begin each section by describing the steps in my ofrenda's creation as both an epigraph and epitaph. Some may consider the events I have chosen to "formally" document as troubling, tragic, and comical, yet I feel it is imperative to come to terms with my reality and the interpretation the tool of "thick description" allows me to provide. I invite my reader to become active in this process. Take my hand. Trust me. Let us engage in unprotected inter(dis)course.

The concept of unprotected inter(dis)course is the framework in which I will endeavor to create a discursive middle space for the reader and me. Considering the taboo subject matter this work will be broaching—indeed, it has taken years of therapy, several limpias, and many drunken nights at the bar to come to terms with much of it—I wish to connect to my reader on a cerebral, academic level as well as on a primal, visceral one. I strip myself bare of as many defenses as I possibly can in order to reveal the jagged remnant of soul, a flickering life force. As I construct my ofrenda, I ask the reader to take pause in order to examine her/his own attitudes toward the LGBT communities, particularly those of color, and the HIV/AIDS epidemic, remembering those who have passed so that their spirits will avoid the third death of the ancient Mesoamerican belief system.

A further objective is to weave all facets of my identity—Xicano, Indio, Queer, Poz, Frontero, working-class, alcoholic, sexual addict—into a dialectical trenza. I often dress up my trenza with ribbons, unafraid to show it off and swing it in people's faces if need be, thereby letting my greñas blow in the wind. I willingly expose the drag queen, the jota loca within. Other times, I tuck my trenza away and wait for the appropriate moment to confront people's racist, heterosexist, and classist notions of what a gay Xicano living—no, *thriving*—with AIDS should be. Parts of a trenza remain hidden, much like the personal and familial memories I will excavate throughout this testimony, yet I *will* bring them to light. I *will* take a bite of the forbidden fruit; I will *not* avert my gaze. However uncomfortable my words may make some people feel, I have come to the conclusion that my life experiences will serve as an allegory for some, an educational tome for others, and, for a few, a tragic reality. This is a tale of one person wandering through the desert, crossing his internal liminal states, transgressing the acceptable social and moral conduct of our Judeo-Christian society, coming to consciousness—this is my quinceañera.

Ofrenda of Context/Queer History as Recovered Memory

The antepasados heed my call. Their energies envelop me and instruct me to take pause in my endeavor. In order for them to bless my efforts, they request a sacrifice. Additionally, they tell me to rest and listen to their stories.

"As a gay man, I didn't know I had a history."
    —a student in Dr. Nancy Unger's survey course of US history at San Francisco State University in 1986

"Homosexuals are the only minority born into the opposing camp; call it the 'enemy camp.'"
    —John Rechy, interview with Debra Castillo

"Do not ask who I am and do not ask me to remain the same: leave it to our bureaucrats and our police to see that our papers are in order. At least spare us their morality when we write."
    —Michel Foucault, The Archaeology of Knowledge

The excavation of hidden histories brings to light further lines of inquiry. Will further visibility of queer communities truly advance our cause, or will there always be a segment of the heterosexual population that refuses to grant us a seat at the table? Will we always have to be "accepted" by our families and friends? Will queer sexuality and transgressive gender identity ever just *be*? If HIV/AIDS had only stayed within the confines of the gay male and IV drug-using communities, would more than a handful of heterosexuals have cared about the epidemic? If I had been an adult in 1950, would the Mattachine Society have accepted a Xicano into their ranks? Will a complete chronicle of queer Chicana/o history ever be written? These are all questions that I will continue to ponder and explore through writing. Previous pioneers of excavating hidden histories, such as Foucault, Emma Pérez, David Dorado Romo, and John D'Emilio have granted me that license.[5]

Moreover, as a queer Xicano living with AIDS, I am equally proud and ashamed of all the greñas of the trenza of my identity. Heterosexual Chicanas/os can be violently homophobic, and queer White and Black people can be shockingly racist and xenophobic. Even after having come out over twenty years ago, I sometimes feel that I am standing at a crossroads between the seemingly incongruent fragments of my identity. However, the recovered collective memory of my queer forebears, my heterosexual Chicana/o ancestors, and my beloved queer Chicana/o antepasados seeps through the cracks and crevices of my soul, to the sites of resistance and opposition where Perez's decolonial imaginary allows me to venture.

The interstitial spaces of the current queer Chicana/o historiography demand for my autoethnography to be told, thereby adding to the mosaic of both queer and Chicana/o identity. My life has been the source of familial shame and gossip and personal disappointment, and a testament to the inner strength and resilience of which I was unaware. I have written my most personally damaging moments in order to come to some semblance of resolution, dare I even imagine some sort of peace of mind and soul. Writing my memories into this work releases them into a public sphere and will hopefully foster a

---

5   See Pérez's *The Decolonial Imaginary: Writing Chicanas into History*, Dorado Romo's *Ringside Seat to a Revolution: An Underground Cultural History of El Paso and Juárez, 1893–1923*, and D'Emilio's *Sexual Politics, Sexual Communities: The Making of a Homosexual Minority in the United States, 1940–1970* for three examples of excavated histories.

dialogue regarding the complex issues my story addresses. I write my story with the memory of a close friend having recently passed away from complications of AIDS and my thoughts of another who recently seroconverted. This epidemic will never end, and the naïve notions of a cure have long since been purged from my psyche. The lives of gay men suffering and perishing from AIDS are reflections of the heterosexual apathy and revulsion towards our community, concerned only when the threat of HIV threatens to invade their lives. However, we also thrive and live remarkable lives in spite of our physiological ailments. These lives, however outrageous and precarious, must be documented. Regrettably, heterosexual women of color are being decimated by the disease in large numbers as well. It is frighteningly upsetting to think of the thousands of hidden histories that will never be discovered due to the lingering stigma of HIV. Hopefully, the opportunity of writing my life into the fabric of queer, HIV, and Chicana/o history will inspire others to write their hidden histories and begin a collective healing process. Are you ready? This might hurt a bit ...

Ofrenda of Love/Mama A/The Desert

The *antepasados*, the *eggun*, allow me to proceed. I present their requested offering of tequila, mangoes, *pan dulce*, and blood.

It is a sweltering July day in the metropolitan abscess of Los Angeles. The air is thick with the decay of the multitudinous inhabitants and concrete structures; their proximity breeds a virulent strain of toughness and street savvy. I dodge the cacophony of vehicles and strange tongues. I am treading on unknown, foreign soil; I am unsure of my own survival. I would not have been surprised had the city swallowed me whole. I wish to lose myself in an orgy of sensory unfamiliarity, for the sexual ache of the streets beckons. Home is distant.

Trepidly, I walk into the botánica near the corner of Beverly and Vermont with the feelings of peculiarity threatening to send me into a catatonic state. As I enter, a lush yet distressed-looking Chicana leaves the store and ponders my face quizzically. We pause on the proprietor's threshold. Her made-up face softens with a maternal longing and *cariño* that I have not experienced since that time when ... I do not allow that jagged memory to invade this transformative moment. We are both searching for something that can never again be ours. For a brief moment, our damaged souls join kinetically, yet we instinctively know that we must persevere in our quest for our unique substitutes for salvation. Our brief connection is broken, and she leaves abruptly in order to resume her urban venture. I, on the other hand, am about to meet with a santero, a spiritual leader, a priest of the belief system commonly referred to as "Santería." I nervously chat with his wife, a santera, a priestess, until he is ready for me.

I take solace in the familiar saints—*El Niño de Atocha* and Santa Barbara, even *La Muerte*—and stare curiously at the idols with whom I am unfamiliar, particularly a large African woman in a blue gingham dress. I walk towards her as if in a trance. Standing in front of her, I happily recall my all time favorite vocalist, Ella Fitzgerald, and the divas of house music, for the vast majority of them are large, Black women. Their slave wails set to the frenetic and frantic rhythms of house music continue to comfort thousands of gay men, particularly me. This one figure in particular expresses a natural gaiety; her pose suggests a rhythmic twirling or gyration. I smile at the possibility. A house diva santo? I am overcome by feelings of elation and joy (*The house diva, Kim English, belts out her words to the thumping beats (of the Tigua ceremonial drum or that of the* santero?), *"JOY! UNSPEAKABLE JOY! 'Cause they did not give it, and cannot take it away ..." REMIX into Vernessa Mitchell, "This joy has liberated, this joy has liberated, this joy has liberated this joy has liberated ... ME!" REMIX into Loleatta Holloway, "Let me tell you what you are doing to me! You're such a HOT sensation ...*). Suddenly, my reverie is shattered.

The santero calls my name, and I step furtively into a small back room. As soon as I walk into that sacred space, the santero gasps. He tells me to stop. He immediately asks me in Spanish, "What was your maternal grandmother's name?" I respond, "Elisa Mendoza Villanueva." He asks, "How long has she been dead?" I answer, "Two years." He claims, "Her presence around you is so strong, I can almost see her behind you." He then begins to commune with her to assure her that he will do me no harm. Eleggua, the impish and mischievous santo of the crossroads, looks over his shoulder and whispers into the santero's ear, thus allowing a healthy dialogue between the orishas and the interpreter. Through his reading of the caracoles, the santero claims that I do not have any use for God—my grandmother's spirit is all the protection I will ever need. As I wonder what the santero could possibly have divined upon the woman with whom I crossed paths just minutes earlier to upset her so, the santero continues to inform me of my destiny.

> *"But it should begin in El Paso, that journey through the cities of night. Should begin in El Paso, in Texas. And it begins in the Wind ..."*

> —*John Rechy*
> City of Night

"Mama A," I called her. Her name was rooted in my first sense of loss. My first beloved toy was a chalkboard and a set of magnetic letters and numbers. The idea of arranging and rearranging magnetic pieces of plastic to form different sounds was dizzyingly wondrous, and I faithfully mimicked the characters on my favorite program, *Sesame Street*. After much use, I eventually lost the letter "A" and was traumatized. I constantly lamented to my grandmother in broken utterances, "Mama," then "A." Eventually, I contracted the basic vocal sounds into, "Mama A." Many people would come to call her this, and its simplicity belied the strength and complexity of this extraordinary woman. My maternal grandmother. My protector. My hero.

I remember the weathered, calloused hands of my grandmother—a Chicana born into abject poverty and exploitation. My memory recalls her stories of oppression while working different crops throughout the Southwest, told in a tone that was matter-of-fact. I would later absorb the bitterness and rage. Her sun-scorched face, the color of a charred cinnamon stick, would readily recall the nights her family of thirteen would have to spend in a packed chicken coop and her fleeting moments of agency. Often, she would vocalize, in nearly flawless English (she would correct anyone who assumed she was Mexican—*con permiso*, I was born in Ysleta), seemingly random thoughts: "The ranchers would build a new chicken coop—we would have to live in the old one. My mother would hang cloth to make walls, and I would have to clean out all the *mierda* from the chickens. My brothers and sisters would make sure to kill all the bugs, especially the *pulgas*. We all slept on the floor. Sometimes in the rain, in the snow, in the dirt … During school, I had two dresses and one pair of shoes. Every day, I had to wash my other dress … My brother, Isidro, had a glass eye. One day, he was walking home along the *canal* when *la migra* stopped him and asked to see his green card. He took out a handkerchief to clean the dirt from his glass eye. When he tried to explain that he was born here in Ysleta, *la migra* shot and killed him. He was only twenty years old. [After I asked if the migra was ever held accountable:] Nothing happened to *la migra* … I loved to go downtown to see the *luchas*. If we had extra money, your grandfather would take me to downtown on a Saturday. After the fights, we would go dancing. We always had a good time … I beat up your Tia Julia once. When we were little, I always had to wash the dishes. One night, *se tardo a comer*. I washed the dishes and went outside to play before it got dark. *Pinche Julia* wanted to get me in trouble with our father. She put her greasy plate on top of the clean ones. She told our father that I had just wiped them clean without washing them. My father whipped me. The next day, I chased and tackled her with a bunch of jalapeños from our garden in my hand. I tore the jalapeños into pieces and rubbed her eyes, nose, and mouth with the seeds and juice. [Eyes twinkling, laughing.] *Se hincho la cara grandisima.* Her face was so swollen that she couldn't even open her eyes, and she got a rash all over her face. My father whipped me again, but it was worth it ... We were poor. When I was thirteen, my parents married me to a rancher. He owned land in Socorro. We were poor. I divorced him when I was fifteen *porque siempre andaba de plumo*, he had other girlfriends ... Picking cotton is hard work, *m'ijo.* Your back hurts; your knees ache and you get scratched and bleed. Then, you get blisters. *Tu mamá* would get paid fifty cents a day. Your grandpa and me would get paid two dollars. *Estudie.* I skipped the third grade, *pero* I had to drop out of school in the fourth grade to work more. We were poor ... Your grandfather was a highly respected man among the Tiguas. [Her eyes mist; she pauses to reswallow her grief.] When he died, they danced around the fire in front of *la iglesia.* This was a great honor." The humility in her voice, her creased face, the love in her eyes, her toughened persona, the look of peace (or was it joy?) on her face when her spirit wriggled loose of the dry shell of a body—I am here for her, because of her.

I was her first grandchild and the replacement to my grandfather, whom she had lost two years earlier. His death transported her into a hellish existence of isolation. She loved my mother, but the affection for her seemed to dissipate as though it were a mirage, merely a semblance of true emotion. My entrance into this dimension altered Mama A's journey. I became her *raison d'etre* and ontological purpose. At her funeral, several people commented to me that if I hadn't have come along, my grandmother would probably have died of a broken heart. Ironically, it was only after her death that I ignited the spark of my own life.

The bleak landscape of my birth—the El Paso/Juárez border—foretold my future. My orientation in space *era un bocacalle*, an intersection between different worlds in several aspects: industrialized/third-world, supernatural/tangible, queer/normal, transgressive/lawful. One sunny but cold and blustery day in Ysleta, *Tejas*, I became extremely ill in my infancy and the contradictions began. Those who are familiar with the West Texas dust storms know that the wind exposes your flesh to the harsh elements of the desert and cuts to your very soul. Upon her realization of my health, my mother rushed me to the hospital. The diagnosis was shocking—leukemia. The doctors were antiseptically cold with my mother: "There's nothing we can do. Make him comfortable until he dies."

My mother returned me to my grandmother's home, a small, comfortable adobe house built in the traditional style of the Pueblo tribe by my grandfather several decades earlier and situated a mile north of "the border." I was to spend my final few hours in the warm womb of my grandmother's hearth. My mother explained the situation to Mama A and cried herself to sleep. My grandmother, however, was not about to relinquish her first grandchild to *La Muerte* or God. My grandmother was skilled in the practice of *curanderismo*, as were her numerous sisters. While my mother slept, my grandmother "cured" me. As is the mystery of faith, so too are her actions of that day. My mother awoke to find me sleeping peacefully in my crib after Mama A prodded her to check on me. She thought I had slipped into the next phase of existence, but my grandmother assured her that I was going to be fine. Silently skeptical but hopeful (no one ever dared to vocalize any doubt of my grandmother's will), she rushed me to the hospital again. The doctors were flabbergasted. They could not believe I was the same child who had lain on the porch of Death's door earlier that day. There was no sign of the disease, and I have had no reoccurrence of the affliction.

In order to strengthen the magic that surrounded my miraculous recovery, Mama A took me to be blessed the following day, not by a priest but by a most unusual person. We went to a small house near the church where I had been recently baptized, *la Misión de Corpus Christi de San Antonio de la Ysleta del Sur* or Our Lady of Mt. Carmel.

The church had been established three centuries earlier and had managed to survive Pueblo resistance to Spanish Catholic tyranny. The church's roots run deep as those of the oldest yucca plants of the El Paso desert landscape and transcend any notion of arbitrary borders or nation-states. The person whom we were visiting lived in a small adobe house near the church. The woman was an elderly indigenous woman named *Doña* Margarita, Mama A's wet nurse. My grandmother had been *Doña* Margarita's last baby to whom she had provided suckle. I later learned that they had maintained a close, almost familial, relationship. She was in the care of her sister, as she was very old and in poor health. After their greetings, Mama A instructed my mother to hand me to *Doña* Margarita. My mother hesitated, for the woman could barely stand on her own volition. My grandmother glared at my mother—it was dangerous to make her repeat herself. *Doña* Margarita took me into her arms with all the strength she could muster. She held me close to her chest and whispered into my infant ear. Suddenly, she held me up to the ceiling and began chanting in her native indigenous tongue, but in a booming voice alien to her decrepit frame. Her eyes grew large, and she seemed to be possessed by some unseen entity. The three onlookers stood there transfixed. After a few minutes, *Doña* Margarita returned to her body, and she gently handed me over to my grandmother. Short of breath, her sister assisted her to a chair in the sparsely furnished kitchen. My grandmother and mother said their good-byes. The next week, *Doña* Margarita died. My mother never told me this story until after Mama A passed away, and she never knew what exactly had transpired. However, Mama A knew. I know. She died in order to strengthen my weakened body, for Mama A knew that she had stolen me from the clutches of *La Muerte*.

I am grateful for the actions of Mama A and *Doña* Margarita. I believe she gave her life at the behest of my grandmother. However, these stolen years have come at a high price. *La Muerte* and God are still vying for my soul, but Mama A, even in Death, refuses to surrender my corporeal essence from this realm.

"Unnatural desire is a contradiction in terms; downright nonsense. Desire is an amatory impulse of the inmost human parts."

> —*Thomas Cannon,* Ancient and Modern Pederasty Investigated and Exemplified, *published in 1749 and considered to "be the first substantial treatment of homosexuality ever in English," http://www.sitecenter.dk/zauritsbureau/copenhagengaylife/*

El Paso, Tejas, 1978. I am a five-year-old Xicano boy. I walk into an empty living room. The television is on, and the program catches my attention. It is a documentary about the burgeoning gay community in San Francisco. I am riveted to the television. I don't know exactly what it is I am looking at, but I can relate to it somehow. I see two men with their arms around each other, and I instinctually realize that this is my fate.

I didn't even know what sex was until I was twelve, but I knew I was not destined for a heteronormative existence. Did this television program "make" me gay? The possibility of this is laughable, but the images of that program remain with me today.

I remember those early years of my life as happy. Mama A lived with us, and I seemed to have loving parents. My sister, two years younger, was a happy child as well. We lived in a comfortable, working-class neighborhood very close to the border and to the area where my parents and grandparents were raised. I was friends with all of the local children my age, but there was one in particular to whom I was particularly close. Juan was a twin, but he and I spent many afternoons alone together. He was a year older, and one lazy, hot summer afternoon we were watching television in his home. He grabbed my hand and held it. It felt natural, and I didn't know I was doing anything sinful. Other days, we hugged and kissed each other. I felt as alive as a seven-year-old could feel, and I thought I wanted to spend the rest of my life with him. My life was comfortable, but that's when my family began to fall apart.

My parents' screaming matches, those times when my sister and I would cower in Mama A's bosom, resulted in an ugly divorce. My father left to marry a woman with whom he worked, and I overheard him tell my mother that he was tired of his fatherly responsibilities. I remember my mother forcing me to help her pack his clothes. There was a moment when, after throwing a pair of his shoes into a box, he turned to glare at me, as if *I* was the one who had asked him to leave. He left and became a shadow of a father; rarely did he make much more than a cursory attempt to remain in our lives. Subsequently, my mother suffered a nervous breakdown, and she often went to a nurse in the neighborhood who would administer tranquilizers to her. The nurse was a kind woman, and she had a son my age, Salvador. I spent many nights at their home, and my sister would spend the night with cousins. I remember the same curious exploration of bodies in the shower and in bed. Again, I had no idea that I was doing anything wrong. In the midst of this upheaval, my mother put Mama A into an apartment complex for senior citizens. My protector was gone, and I felt lost. I hated my mother for taking her away from me. Little did I know from what else Mama A would have to protect me.

"Just as Jews are asked to never forget their Holocaust I implore all gay people never to forget our holocaust and who caused it and why. Ronald Reagan did not even say the word 'AIDS' out loud for the first seven years of his reign."

—AIDS activist Larry Kramer

I "came out" when I was fourteen, amidst the queer death chambers of the 1980s, commonly known as the Reagan era, when the HIV/AIDS crisis was decimating the gay community. This "coming out" was internalized; I merely recognized the fact that all of my nocturnal emissions were centered on men. I didn't relate what I had done with

Harvey, my mother's second husband, to my same-gender erotic desires. I was in the eighth grade and enrolled in a Catholic confirmation class. During one class, I scrounged up the courage to question the Catholic Church's rigid stance towards the gay community. Naturally, my confirmation teacher instructed the class to open their bibles to the Old Testament—Leviticus, to be exact. She ordered me to read the passage stating that a man who lies with another man as he would with a woman was an abomination. Of course, she did not contextualize this verse. She said any gay person who acted upon their "unnatural" desires would be condemned to Hell. Her gaze never left mine when she said this. After class, I questioned her privately. I came out to her indirectly, and she reiterated my fate if I ever acted upon my sinful yearnings.

Foucault posits the modern "coming out" story as a secular continuation of the Catholic confessional, a baring of one's sins and misdeeds. It is a cleansing of the soul. Coming out, in this context, parallels homosexuality with moral crimes. The contemporary language surrounding lesbian, gay, and bisexual individuals supports this assertion. Queer people "admit" that they are sexually attracted to people of the same gender; people are "suspected" of possessing transgressive feelings. This language should be reserved for criminals. However, queer sex has always been a source of mystery, loathing, and fear—the motivation for our criminalization. In the previous chapter, I discussed the landmark case *Lawrence & Garner v. State of Texas* of 2003, which overturned the remaining sodomy laws in the United States. This is the equivalent of a queer *Mendez v. Westminster* and *Brown v. Board of Education*, the cases that integrated the public schools of California and the United States, respectively.[6] *Lawrence* decriminalized queer sexual practices—namely

---

6   The excavation of history often leads to wonderful discoveries, such as the examination of the precursor to the universally known *Brown* case, *Mendez v. Westminster*. This case desegregated California schools and eventually became a precedent for *Brown*. Few people, outside academia and legal studies, know about the segregation of Chicanas and Chicanos in the Southwest, let alone the deplorable educational inequities under which they suffered. The fact that so few people know about this historic case illustrates the further dichotomization of race in this country. For a thorough treatment of the *Mendez* case, see Philippa

the dreaded sodomy. Although this ruling declared that gay men could *legally* express their sexual desires, I did not feel any less transgressive after the ruling then I did before. Interestingly, it never crossed my mind—before or after the ruling. Heterosexual society's codified moralities cannot and will never regulate or govern queer desire. The archaic sodomy laws did not prevent anal sex any more than its repeal encouraged this Biblical practice. Why would the book of Leviticus ban sodomy if it was not occurring?

Every night for a week, I cursed God for instilling this torturous, burning desire within me. All I could think about was having more intimate contact with another male after my stepfather left. I hated my mother for taking Mama A, my familiar neighborhood, and Harvey away from me. A few years earlier, my mother had moved the three of us from a home she owned into a rundown duplex in a middle-class (White) neighborhood. This was the moment when I first noticed my otherness as a Xicano. I still shudder at the times when my White classmates would laugh at me for bringing bean burritos for lunch. They yelled, "Beaner! Beaner! You dirty Mexicans can only afford to eat beans!" I began to loathe myself for what I was—a working-class Xicano. Why couldn't I be rich and White like my classmates? Nor could I stop dwelling on my eternal damnation. With all of this disruption in my life, I made a momentous decision. The night before my next confirmation class, I attempted to take my own life. *The Smiths wail in the background, "... and if a double decker bus crashes into us, to die by your side is such a heavenly way to die, and if a ten ton truck kills the both of us, to die by your side, well, the pleasure and the privilege is mine ..."* After I had swallowed nearly a full month's supply of Xanax that I had stolen from my mother, clarity began to sink in. My will to live compelled my body to vomit the potentially lethal narcotic. I was alone, lying in my own vomit and shame. I become the tragic boy figure of *City*

Strum's *Mendez v. Westminster: School Desegreation and Mexican-American Rights.*

of Night when he witnesses the body of his beloved dog, Winnie, rotting in the *caliche*-filled earth:

> So he dug up the body, and I stand by him as he shovels the dirt in our backyard (littered with papers and bottles covering the weeds which occasionally we pulled, trying several times to grow grass—but it never grew). Finally the body appeared. I turned away. I had seen the decaying face of death. My mother was right. Soon Winnie will blend into the dirt. There was no soul, the body would rot, and there would be Nothing left of Winnie. (Rechy 11–12)

Fury takes form, and memories wash over my body. I relived the scene from two years prior; my axons, synapses, and neurons began to play on some infinite psychological loop, mimicking a BASIC command I had just learned in my Computer Literacy class. I would carry that rage for years to come, and I exacted retribution on undeserving recipients. When I recovered from my spasms of vomiting and tears, I damned God again (I aimed my imaginary rifle at Him and open fire, just like Johnny Rio from *Numbers*) and my confirmation teacher. The next morning I refused to attend another class. I did not give my mother the reason, and I made the decision to cast off my self-imposed shame. This was the second act of existential agency I exerted over Him.

The first had occurred two years prior. My sister and I had come home from a night of Christmas Eve festivities with my father and stepmother's families. The constant changes that our parents thrust upon us extremely damaged my sister and me, but I tried to make her happy. I spent much of my free time taking care of her. Except for the times that my stepfather would … (*No, not now, I mean, yes, I love you, I want you. But it hurts. I won't tell. I promise. I know it's my fault. It's my fault. I am weak. I am going to Hell. Please, Harvey. I know. Again? I guess so. No, please don't tell Mom. I do like it. Just be slow. Last time it hurt a lot, and I had an accident. Mom yelled at me. Do I have to? I don't like the neighbors. I don't want them to do what you do to me. Only you. I love you. Promise you'll never leave us. I'll do whatever you want. Okay. I promise to go to the neighbors' house. Promise you'll stay? Okay, just put some more Vaseline, maybe that'll make it easier. Promise you'll do it slow? Okay. I'm ready. Ow, Ow, Slower! Okay, that's better. Yes, I love you. Do you love me, too? Yes, I want some more. Yes, I am your boy. I love you! Harder, harder, Daddy …)* …make me spend time with him alone.

Until the following morning—the events which irrevocably damaged our pre-adolescent psyches. The house is dark, still. The only warmth comes from our own beloved dog, Dusty, a dirty blonde Chow Chow. Our stepfather's car is nowhere to be seen. Where could he be at 1:00 a.m. on Christmas morning? Has something happened? Our mother is sound asleep, and her diminutive body gives no sign that she is awake. It is odd that she does not greet us at such a late hour, as she usually does. I tuck in my sister, assuring her that everything is all right. I distract her with the thoughts of a bountiful Christmas Day. But I know something is very wrong. She falls asleep, and I go to bed wondering where Harvey could be. I have long nurtured my sister as a parental figure because our mother sought refuge in the arms of countless men in between and after her two marriages.

I was relieved when she married Harvey. I thought: Maybe she'll be happy now. Maybe we'll be a happy family. I'll do my best to stay out of trouble. I'll study, get good grades, and take care of my sister. I'll be good. But why do I have these feelings? What did I do wrong? I can't stop looking at Harvey. Why does he look at me that way? Why is he only nice to me when we're alone? Please, God, make these thoughts and feelings go away. I can't be a *maricón*. I'm only twelve. Make it stop. I'll be good.

My sister and I wake up to screaming and the crashing of plates. I run to her room, and she is understandably confused and frightened. We call out to our mother, and she screams at us to come to the living room. My mother, possessed, is breaking everything that can be broken. She yells that she and Harvey are getting a divorce. "*NO! He can't leave!*

He lied to me!" I shout in my mind. She screams that we are all going to die today. My sister starts crying and screaming uncontrollably. I don't know what to do. I'm only twelve. What do I do? She comes at me with a fury and a strength that is foreign to her. She attempts to strangle me. I can't get her hands off me! Please, Mama, stop! I love you! Why are you doing this? We don't want to die! No, no, no! Somebody, please help us! I can only gasp these words. My sister, only nine years old, is running around unsure of what to do. Where is Dusty? I finally shake her off, and I fall, dizzy and disoriented. I suck in as much air as possible. While I am on the ground, my mother is forcing sleeping pills into my sister's mouth. I gain my composure and push my mother off my sister. I yell for her to spit out every pill. She does, and she clutches my waist. My mother yells at me and comes after me again. I tell my sister to go to her room and to lock the door. My mother and I physically struggle. I am motivated mostly by the fact that Harvey and I will no longer spend the intimate moments that we had enjoyed the previous year. I manage to pry her thin hands off my neck and slap her. She crumbles before me and starts to sob. I run to my sister's room and coax her to open the door. We spend the remainder of the morning in my sister's room. We hear our mother leave. Alone, we venture out into the house. I make us some breakfast, and we collect the few Christmas presents that my mother did not break into my sister's room, just in case my mother returns. My mother destroyed all of my presents, but there are two that I bought for my sister that she missed—a doll and a book. My sister hugs me and enjoys the presents that I bought her with my allowance. My mother put our dog in the freezing garage, but we quickly rescue her. This is Christmas Day.

The three of us spend the remainder of the day in my sister's room. The next morning, we awaken to an eerie stillness. The living room is clean, but neither my mother nor Harvey is home. To this day, we have never spoken of this incident, yet my mother has attempted to take her own life on five other occasions. But every Christmas thereafter would continue to be a loathsome and depressing occasion. A few weeks later,

Harvey moves out, and I am devastated. He takes our dog, *my* dog, my beloved Dusty. Later, I find out that Harvey could not care for her, but instead of returning her to us, he had her put to sleep. Did I need any other reason to fire my imaginary assault rifle at God?

"Prefiero morir en pie, que vivir en rodillas."

—Emiliano Zapata

I circle the building for the fifth time. I have just turned eighteen, and my sexual curiosity has overtaken any semblance of Catholicism I still harbor. This time I park a block away. The area is a scene of urban blight. Abandoned warehouses and obsolete railroad tracks dot the urban landscape; the owners of the few remaining small businesses hurriedly roll down their chain-linked protection as the sun sets. Lawyers and other professionals leave the confines of their offices to escape to their suburban prisons. For the freaks and faggots will soon encroach upon the area. The sexual *chupacabras* are ready to emerge from their heterosexual shadows into the light of pure carnality.

The border beckons one mile to the south. Mexico's poverty invades the southern areas of El Paso like an incurable viral infection. El Paso's orientation in an industrialized nation is betrayed by its proximity to the Third World. The largest international border community lies in rot, a carcass in the vast desert that has long since been devoured by neo-liberal trade policies. The rise of the maquiladoras in Juarez represents an economic erection for bell hooks's "White supremacist capitalist patriarchy," a system which successfully keeps generations of Chicanas/os in perpetual poverty (118). To illustrate this point, my mother, a fifth-generation Chicana, toiled as a farm worker early in her life and was the first from her extended family to graduate from high school. Meanwhile, the financial prospects for the inhabitants of the once unified cities remain limp and flaccid.

I deftly move among the shadows, careful to avoid the filthy light secreted by the few working lampposts on the dilapidated street. My heart is pounding in my ears, I begin to perspire, and I am on the verge of hyperventilating. I want to vomit, to expel the apprehension, the anxiety, the fear, and the shame. I am about to enter the mouth of the serpent and transform, morph into something wild and carnal, something that my family would reject and revile. The last song playing in my car resonates with the transformative experience I am about to undertake. The Smiths' distinctive grinding moan of a guitar enters my head, with Morrissey's equally haunting lyrics pulsating in my mind: *"There's a club, if you'd like to go, You could meet someone who really loves you, So you go, and you stand on your own, And you leave on your own, And you go home, and you cry, and you want to die ..."* I am about to enter my first gay bar. At last, I will release the sexual and emotional frustration of my adolescence. All the images and stereotypes of gay bars flash in my head, and I am petrified. What will become of me?

Young Chicanas have quinceañeras; Jewish boys have bar mitzvahs; the initial experience in a gay bar for a queer is one of our rites of passage. As I approach the faded and decrepit two-story building, I see young and older men enter. Some are laughing and smiling in groups as they enter. Others are nervously quiet and alone, keeping their heads down, as if entering a confessional after a weekend of vice. Others who enter alone possess stoic expressions as if they have been chiseled into stone. Two teen-aged boys catch my eye, and I pause. They are standing on the side of the building. Waiting. They appear to be my age, and they look at me. Their jeans are torn, and there is a disheveled, desperate look about them. As I approach the entrance, I stop before them. A temporal disruption occurs on that spot behind the largest of El Paso's gay bars—The Old Plantation, or the O.P., as the locals refer to it. One knows something and a subtle, pitiable smile crosses his young brown face. I want to swallow him whole, for our bodies to fuse in an emotional and sexual convergence. Maybe that will keep what he knows from happening to me. I realize I am looking into a mirror, but the image is distorted, fragmented. What do they know? Why haven't they entered the structure? Our mutual gaze is broken by a car that pulls up to them. I walk away feeling even more unsettled. Were they some sort of omen? If they were, what were they warning me of? I resume my quest to attempt to cross yet another threshold into an alternate reality, one from which I will never return. I enter. The door and the world I formerly knew permanently close behind me.

The doorman asks for my ID. His face is a blur. I stand in an alcove before the actual bar. I am standing at the edge of my purgatory, clinging to the chain-link fence, just like I had seen immigrants peering into *el norte*, gazing into Heaven with St. Peter standing before me. I hand him the sweat-lathered piece of laminate. He scrutinizes my age and grunts approval towards the cashier. I hand the heavily made-up, middle-aged man a few crumpled bills. His appearance startles me. I was granted entrance. I walk into the dimly lit space, with the lights momentarily illuminating the faces of the patrons. The foreign music invades my being. I have never heard this type of music. Later, I will discover this genre of gay music—house. Its throbbing beats mimic the frenzied rhythm of mansex, the kind I had experienced several years earlier. I deport those memories from my psyche because I am overcome by the sensory overload. I find an empty spot against a wall, and I remain there, frozen in a catatonic state. My spirit is free, but my fear is too strong to liberate my body. I will remain frozen against the wall for an unknown amount of time, somehow warding off the men who will later become my sole source of sustenance. I leave feeling exhilarated and terrified.

Before my transformative experience at the "O.P.," I existed in the shadows and internalized my sexual angst throughout high school. Amidst the constant taunts and occasional physical attacks from classmates and the domestic terrorism of my mother's depression and nymphomania, I somehow achieved fairly high grades, graduating in the top 5% of my class. Thus, I earned a partial scholarship to a prestigious university in another part of Texas, far away from my mother.

I fled El Paso as a sexual refugee, much like Rechy's protagonist in *City of Night*. Like him, I could never find what I was looking for in that windswept terrain. But I knew I would return. I quickly immersed myself into the queer activism on campus. I felt liberated in a strange manner. I wondered if I would have to keep my life separate from my family. After a short time in my new home, I decided that this would not be the case. During this tumultuous time, I confronted my mother with the issues regarding my sexuality during a routine call home. The tension between us resurfaced when I forced her to accept my *jotería*; returning to a life of sexual silence was not an option. Either I lived my life on my own terms, or I would have no life at all. Her response to my ultimatum, as predicted, was that I would no longer be her son or a part of her life. Her venomous words slashed the last vestiges of maternal bonds with a sharpness comparable only to the jagged thorns of a maguey.

Soon thereafter, I dropped out of school and returned to El Paso. When I remained adamant in my newfound pride, she reiterated her decision to cut me out of her life. Her third husband, a devout Christian, would not permit me to live in the house. I had nowhere to go, and with extremely limited funds, I was set loose upon the streets of El Paso, ready to be devoured. At that moment, I became the guy from my first night at the "O.P." Was I doomed to repeat a cycle of desperate longing, the kind I saw in his eyes?

In order to survive, I began to prostitute myself for both tangible and intangible sustenance. The money and sex I received from countless strangers were a cheap substitute for the love and acceptance I craved from my family. The time I spent sleeping in alleyways, on park benches, and in sleazy motels was a living hell. However, I am proud that I did not retreat back into the closet, although my sexual freedom would come at an extremely high price. The face of the young man outside the "O.P." haunted my memory as I began to inhabit his existence. Interestingly, I never ran into him.

Sometimes, I would take a bus back to my ancestral neighborhood. Those nights that I wandered the desolate streets of El Paso, I considered sacrificing myself to La Llorona by jumping into one of the city's numerous canals. The Rio Grande was a more appropriate site of my self-destruction, though, as its whirlpools, which have claimed the lives of many immigrants attempting to cross, would also claim me. My family was a whirlpool of derisive shame, and the streets were just as cruel. Yet, the many men whom I attracted offered me some comfort, didn't they? Didn't all those men make my mother happy? Her Saturday night sexmoans carried the same rhythmic elation as the church bells alerting the pious to Sunday mass. My mother was always the first one on our block to receive the Holy Spirit every early Sunday morning. On those occasions, I would try to distract my sister by letting her listen to my Walkman. If I didn't recognize the man's car in the driveway, I would be sure to keep her in her room until the faceless man left the next morning. Once he would leave, my mother would spend the remainder of the morning in bed, hungover and lonely. She called these episodes her "headaches." Occasionally, she would call me into her bedroom to lie in the damp spot where the man had been. She would stare at me curiously and longingly, and I would try hard not to notice her nearly nude body, her pale blue robe failing to cover her reddish brown skin completely. She would stroke my hair and face and sometimes hold me tight into her bosom. I detached myself from these actions by inhaling the ghost that had recently occupied that same spot. I smelled him, and this aroma was intoxicating to me. Every time it would be a different smell and each possessed its own unique brand of masculinity. I would be reminded of Harvey's smell. My young body reacted unconsciously to the mix of memory and odor. No matter how much I tried to hide my erections, she always noticed. The smell of man mixed with the alcohol emanating from my mother's pores became our Sunday ritual after Harvey left. I knew never to bother my mother when she had company and made sure to keep my sister quiet. I was too old to make the mistake that the little boy made when his mother was entertaining Johnny Rio:

> The glass door slides open. The little boy who loitered outside stands there watching them. Nervously, hurriedly, he says, "I thought you were through, momma." Desire smashes inside Johnny like glass on tile. He raises his trunks, his cock quickly limp. Adjusting her clothes, Tina yells at the child: "Get the screw out of here, you little bastard! Haven't I told you— ...? Haven't I?" (Rechy 52)

I wasn't as young or naïve as the young boy had been; I knew that once they left they were through with her. Sometimes, I would open my bedroom door slightly and peek at the men to see if there was any resemblance to Harvey. How I wished that one of the men would come into my room and undress me, caress me, kiss me, and ravage me. Once, one man did pause at my door and consumed me with his eyes. I stood there, naked, except for my briefs, and I could see his erection bulging through his jeans. He motioned for me to rub his crotch, and he grabbed mine and started stroking me. He brought me close to him in a tight embrace, and I smelled my mother's perfume on his shirt. I started to unzip his jeans, just as I had done with Harvey. But we heard a noise coming from my sister's room, and he quickly left. I never saw him again. Eventually, the men's faces became a blur of masculinity, and my burgeoning sexuality craved their bodies and their hot wet breaths on my body.

Whatever sympathy I felt for my mother, though, was extinguished by the damage that she had inflicted upon my body and heart. Because of this, I looked toward the maternal figure who would surely accept me. *La Llorona* would be my new patron saint—the one of freaks, faggots, dykes, and other outcasts. Since my own mother had cast out her only son into the cold night, *La Llorona* would wrap me in her rebozo, comfort me, stroke my hair, and sing me a lullaby as I cried in anguish.

She would never expel me for a few extra precious moments with a lover.

Was it she who was howling in the wind the day I was supposed to die as an infant?

As *La Llorona* is doomed to walk the earth each night searching for her children to construct a new familia, would I be destined to a similar fate? She roams the Southwest attempting to reconstruct her *familia*, as did I. *Familia* is one of the major tenets of *Chicanismo*, one upon which we base our identities. When my *familia* rejected me because of my *jotería*, I wandered through a liminal state in an attempt to reconstruct my identity. Many years later, I came to an epiphanic moment and concluded that the concept of *familia* does *not* necessarily revolve around blood; this was the first step in my identity reconstruction. *Is this how Juan Diego felt when he witnessed the apparition of la Virgen de Guadalupe?* Not coincidentally, the slang term for a gay or lesbian person is "family." The word is both singular and plural. They're family=they're queer. He's family=he's queer. While our biological families can be a site of safety and comfort for some, it is also one of pain and silence for others. As a queer Xicano living on the streets of El Paso, I began to construct my new *familia*—drag queens, crackheads, and other lost young men who were forced to imitate hustlers.

I thrived in a subculture within a subculture—a world of sexual semiotics. One night, I befriended an older man who turned out to be a hustler from the seventies, a survivor of the previous era of sexual hedonism. I became his mentee, and he taught me the system of the handkerchief code (a dead form of communication in El Paso by that time) and the correct body language of hustlers. I was fascinated by the historical meaning of the code. Although gay men in El Paso had long since abandoned the use of handkerchiefs, he was teaching me *our* queer history. He was my Herodotus, passing on the rituals and stories of queer people, just as is done in other marginalized communities. It did not matter that he was White, for "there is the queer ... in all races" (Anzaldúa 102).

He warned me of the guys who were into heavy S/M. There weren't that many, but he cautioned me to never involve myself in that scene. A portent poured forth from his lips: "Once you get sucked into that scene, you never get out. Don't ever let yourself get fisted. Don't fist anybody. Your soul dies." He became a nurturing paternal figure to me when my biological father and Harvey had abandoned me. Although there was a mutual attraction, we never acted upon it.

In *City of Night*, the protagonist and a fellow hustler share an intimate moment, but their code precludes them from becoming emotionally involved. My mentor and I followed this code except one night ... One night the frigid wind and sleeting rain kept most men at home. There was no one who would provide me with a warm bed and a few dollars in exchange for an hour's worth of sexual pleasure. I began to wonder where I could spend the night without freezing to death. As I was leaving the bar, I ran into my mentor. My desperation was obvious. He snuck me into his seedy motel room in downtown El Paso, the type of place that charged by the hour and by the person. He undressed me and gazed longingly at my still-forming adolescent body. The text of my body was one that he lovingly archived. He undressed himself and took me into his arms. I had never recounted my family situation to him, but he could read my pain and isolation. He kissed me tenderly, softly. I began to release my rage through a torrent of tears, only the storm outside able to match the severity. He stroked my hair, not saying a word. I buried my face into the fur on his broad chest as I slowly regained my composure. He looked at me and broke the unwritten rule of hustlers. He knew that I wasn't really a hustler, just a young kid in an unfortunate situation. He had always urged me to stop turning tricks. Lying on the musty mattress, our clothing strewn upon the discolored, worn carpet, we devoured each other's rage and pain with an intense passion. Not a word was spoken throughout the exchange. Time stopped. The intensity of our actions drowned out the world outside. I could no longer hear the rain pelting against the tiny window because of our soft yet intense moans and gasps.

We exacted our fury upon each other's bodies and psyches until daybreak. Sunlight crept into the room between the yellowed blinds, thereby alerting us to slip into our consciousness. Nothing. Silence. I waited for some acknowledgement, although I knew none would be forthcoming. To him, I was a text that was to be permanently archived. He looked at me with a guilty expression and muttered a few incoherent words. His body language and emotional distance precluded any type of verbal expression. But I did not need words to understand; the message was implicit. I left after a quick and awkward embrace. The storm had subsided to produce a sunny but crisp desert day. I walked to a bus stop with my belongings. Eventually, I saw less and less of him until one day I stopped seeing him at the local dives. He often told me he never stayed in one place for very long. My memory can no longer recall his name, but I still appreciate his paternal guidance.

Many times, my "clients" did not want to use condoms, and I could only comply. Most of them dehumanized me—I was their "night laborer." I was rarely asked about my life; most did not want to know my name. Just as they exploited other laborers to clean their homes and mow their lawns, I was nothing more than a cock, a mouth, an ass, prepubescent-looking eye candy. They disassociated my labor from my body. A few years later, I read articles about the ongoing clashes in California regarding Proposition 187. At that time, I realized I was no different from the undocumented immigrants who clamored for basic human recognition. My struggles on the barren southwestern cityscape were similar to those that my grandmother experienced as a migrant farm worker many decades earlier. Both our gender and labor were exploited by a system of commoditization where anything and anyone could be bought and sold.[7] Those drunken nights of sex are now a distorted blur. I often awoke in a stranger's bed with no memory of the

7   One needs only to look across the border to Juárez to bear witness to the innumerable murders of the young women employed to work in any one of the hundreds of maquiladoras. None of the murders has been solved. See Diana Washington Valdez's work *The Killing Fields: Harvest Women* for an eye-opening expose of the crimes.

previous night's activities. Several older, well-to-do men wanted me to be their "houseboy," but this is code for sexual slave. Now that my alcoholism is under control, my mind is often flooded with details of that painful year. Even without these memories, however, the virus that is slowly overtaking my body is a constant reminder of that time.

I seroconverted later that year—1993. From that point on, I would forever carry the faggot scarlet letter, "A," (for AIDS) as part of my identity. I responded to the news with little, if any, emotion. I didn't seek treatment, for at that point in the epidemic, only AZT was available, and it carried toxic side effects while extending the lives of the afflicted for only a few months. Also, I did not have any health insurance, so I wouldn't have had access to treatment anyway. I moved back to Austin after a year in El Paso with a man fifteen years older than me who was battling a crack addiction and had fathered three children. This abusive relationship lasted for a few years; I desperately wanted to "save" him so we could live happily ever after. Not surprisingly, this abusive relationship did not survive.

Afterwards, I descended into an orgiastic underworld of drunken nights and anonymous trysts. I frequented bathhouses and adult bookstores; this subculture simultaneously became my church and my opiate. On a nightly basis, I conducted my own dark ritual mass, and the mysterious power of transubstantiation ran through my veins. I willingly offered my communion, and my congregants piously and enthusiastically accepted it. As much physical pleasure as I experienced, I was also motivated by vengeance. I never warned any of my sexual partners of my health status, but I easily rationalized it. I figured that anybody willing to engage in unprotected sex in such places would be doing so at their own risk. Bathhouses and sex clubs became my sanctuary from the rejection of my family and my future health complications. I did not know how much time I had left, and I released my rage through active, unprotected sex. I've had sexual encounters with countless men, but if my partners had been women, would anyone question my behavior?

More likely, I would be labeled as a stud, *un macho*. But because I desire men, my sexual acts are categorized as unnatural and deviant.

Before I left El Paso, I had been rescued by an angel. A drag queen eventually sheltered me from the harsh elements when my own mother would not. She became the human manifestation of La Llorona. My initiation into the El Paso gay community began with my experience with a Chicana drag queen named Moella Bowie. She is (in)famous in the gay subculture of El Paso, Texas. Although she is a high school dropout, she is fluent in the language of deconstructing the racist, iconic images of Texas history. Her parents named her after another infamous Texan, Jim Bowie, one of the so-called "heroes" of the Battle of Alamo. In her male identity, she worked as a bartender and went by the nickname "Moe." When performing at one of the few gay bars in El Paso, she used the stage name Moella Bowie and held the coveted title of Miss Old Plantation—the Miss Universe title of El Paso drag queens. It is a hilarious thought that a 300-pound Chicana drag queen (imagine a brown version of the actor Divine) appropriated the name of an imperialist racist to lip-synch songs by such artists as Peggy Lee (*you give me fever*), Tina Turner (*big wheel keeps on turning, proud mary keeps on burning*), Paquita la del Barrio (*tres veces te engañe*), and Etta James (*at laaaaast, my love has come along*).

Evidenced by her preference for female singers, Moella Bowie truly is all genders and all races. She is the embodiment of the praxis of Anzaldúa's theory of mestiza consciousness. Moella Bowie is the kind soul who took me into her home when she realized that I was turning tricks in her bar. Although she battled a severe substance abuse problem and suffered a series of relationships with abusive men, Moella Bowie is a fun-loving, gregarious, and benevolent person. I have lost contact with Moella Bowie, but in my memory she will always be performing in front of a packed house wearing a sequined brassiere full of dollar bills. Subsequently, I discovered that Moella Bowie was a surrogate mother to other ostracized and lost gay male youths. I became part of her clan, and I was able to stop turning tricks.

Moella often threw festive parties, similar to those thrown by "Miss Destiny," the red-headed, Southern belle drag queen of *City of Night*. These parties showcased the freaks and faggots of the El Paso gay drug scene. On more than one occasion, I often wondered why and how the person who bore me could discard me onto the cruel, unforgiving streets, while a gender-bending substance abusing stranger would shelter and comfort me. I realized that my blood family had done nothing more than tolerate me. This "half-in, half-out" status was not much better than the closet. The homophobia of my family harmed me through silence and emotional distance.

> *"[Cardinal Alfonso Lopez] Trujillo, President of the Vatican's Pontifical Council for the Family, called on governments to urge people not to use condoms."*
>
> *— Chioma Obinna, "HIV/AIDS: Catholic Church in Condom Palaver." http://www.actupny.org/reports/vatican_nyc. html*

I was also motivated by vengeance against the Catholic Church. The incident with my confirmation teacher left an indelible mark of shame and rage upon me, but I had started out like almost every other working-class Xicano in El Paso. I was an obedient Catholic boy, and I wholeheartedly believed in the Trinity, La Virgen de Guadalupe, and the powers of the saints. Conversely, I was also curious about the rituals of the curanderismo practiced in my family. However, like sexuality, these ancient indigenous practices were the fodder of gossip and whispers. Mama A, her sisters, and other older females of the community were highly respected, and their mysterious powers carried on a legacy that is still revered in Ysleta to this day. Curandersimo is the conduit through which Mama A defied La Muerte so many years ago, but amazingly, I had never been told about that incident until after her spirit escaped into the next realm.

My family was cleaning out her home the day after her funeral. My mother, sister, aunts, and I worked in silence. Every paper, photo, olla, and piece of furniture evoked some memory. I was emotionally overwhelmed. The woman who shook her fist in La Muerte's face, whom *I* had redeemed through the simple act of my birth, was gone. She had been in the midst of recovering from quadruple bypass surgery. She was a lifelong smoker and drinker and in her later years developed clogged arteries from a lifetime of cooking with manteca. She refused to cook with vegetable oil, and, consequently, everyone flocked to Mama A's for her famous costillas de puerco en chile colorado y tortillas de harina hecho a mano. My favorite culinary time of the year was definitely Cuaresma. Mama A's Lenten food was outstanding. Tortas de camaron en chile colorado, nopales, lentejas, calabasas, verdolagas, and her piece de resistance—homemade capirotada. Finally, every Easter Sunday we would dine on crispy tacos de tripas with grilled onions and fiery chile de molcajete. The enjoyment of the food served to strengthen my faith in the Church. The food was a celebration of my piety. At that young age, I could never have imagined how the Church would turn its back on me. I had always thought I was the failed person for renouncing my Catholicism, yet I know now that my early faith has simply morphed into a bocacalle of ancient belief systems.

As expected, Mama A was quickly recovering from her open-heart surgery. I am sure she was anxious to return to her home, where she could claim agency over her life, just as she had always done. She was always referred to as a renegada, an Adelita. She frequently disobeyed her parents because they favored her lighter-skinned sisters. Because of this, Mama A had always been the least favorite of her parents. My great-grandparents adhered to an internalized color caste system. Mama A, the prieta of her siblings, was treated as the house negra. She was saddled with the vast majority of the chores—this was an extreme punishment as they were a family of migrant farm workers. However, she did manage to resist the sexism and racism of her reality on a few occasions.

Although I continue to harbor resentment and suspicion against the Church because of the situation with my confirmation teacher, there are two churches which I visit periodically: the Corpus Christi Mission of Ysleta and the San Elizario Mission in Texas. Both were founded hundreds of years ago, and their raices run deep into the southwestern desert. The Mission of Ysleta is where I attended Catechism at the age of five. An eager Catechism student, I never failed to impress my teacher with my memorization skills or my faith. Every Sunday, I looked forward to learning an additional prayer and attending Mass.

Even as an ex-Catholic, I expect to be overcome by feelings of warmth and security from entering locales such as the Corpus Christi and San Elizario missions. On those occasions, I want to turn back the clock. My five senses demand to be stimulated by our memories in such a place: the smell of flour tortillas hecho a mano coming off the comal (on a gas stove), the heat of the tortilla on my hands that I grab from the top of the pile, the taste of the tortilla (with a little butter and salt added for taste) dancing on my taste buds, the sight of my beautiful grandmother wiping sweat off her brow while smiling as I grab a second tortilla, and hearing the most beautiful contraction of words as I finish my snack and resume my activity, "M'ijo." I want to return to that simplest and most cherished of places within myself—the one that existed before the world began to leave its indelible marks of pain and rage upon my body and soul. To return to such a safe space on occasion is a much needed respite from the cruelty exacted by my reality.

A social worker visited my mother in the ICU where Mama A was recovering. She informed my mother that Mama A would have to be admitted to a nursing home or would have to live with my mother. Although Mama A had not regained consciousness, I knew that she did not like the idea of having to depend on either my mother or an unfamiliar nursing staff. Early the next morning, Mama A's health worsened, and we raced to the hospital. I held her rough, calloused hand and whispered her name. I want to believe that she was reacting to my voice, as her eyelids appeared to be making the effort to open. But it was not to be. Instead, she weakly whispered my name three times, "Omar, Omar, Omar." She sighed, and the EKG machine alerted us that her body was vacant. No convulsions, no protestation, only acceptance, peace. There appeared to be a slight smile on her face, and I was happy that she claimed agency in her last act on this world. She had given me twenty-five years of life, stealing them from *La Muerte*, but I knew it would soon be my time to join her. I couldn't wait.

After Mama A's departure, I resumed my activities in the gay underground. Every time I engaged in anonymous sex in the back of an adult bookstore or in a bathhouse, I felt liberated but also empty. The only thing that pushed this feeling aside was more alcohol and more sex. I would meet friends at a gay bar and medicate myself. If I didn't meet anyone to go home with, I would frequent one of the adult bookstores, the sole bathhouse, or the wooded trails behind the city's leather bar. The anonymity and abundance of men were exactly what I craved. Occasionally, I would practice safe sex, but most often, I would inseminate the willing orifices of the men that I encountered. One feature of bathhouses that I especially enjoyed was the fact that most of the patrons searched the interstitial spaces for their next sexual tryst in either a towel or completely nude. I reveled at the profusion of reckless men who would be willing to be penetrated without a condom. Another feature of bathhouses I took pleasure in was the "maze" or "dark room." You literally enter at your own risk. You walk through a pitch-black room, and hands, tongues, and other body parts envelop you in a sensory overload. In these moments, I began to commune with my new God—the one of sheer hedonistic pleasure. I continued to mask my pain with alcohol and meaningless sex. I thought nothing of myself or of other people. I abused myself in this manner for an unknown length of time.

Amidst my worship of my hedonistic lifestyle, my T-cells began to drop dramatically and my viral load exploded. Soon thereafter, I developed pneumocystis carinii, the deadly AIDS-relate pneumonia. This type of pneumonia is caused by a bacterium that has lived in our lungs since our evolutionary past, but a compromised immune system allows it to multiply to the point where the person drowns in their own fluids. Usually this diagnosis means hospitalization, but I didn't want to reenact the scenes from that horrible film, *Philadelphia*. Instead, I did everything to speed the course of the disease along. I continued to work, taking insane amounts of Tylenol in order to control my fevers to remain somewhat functional, and I would collapse into my bed at night. I filled glasses with phlegm every night, but every morning I awoke to another day of physical pain and emotional emptiness.

After three weeks of this subsistence, I had another transformative experience. I crawled into bed with a fever of 104°. I downed the remainder of my Nyquil and attempted to fall asleep. As I lay there shivering in a pool of sweat, with the effects of the Nyquil setting in, I open my eyes to something, an apparition? A miracle? A portal to Hell? "*The Blessed Mother, with her arms outstretched to her*" (Rechy 206). Mama A is standing before me, weeping uncontrollably. She turns to look at me, then kneels before my bed. She wraps her arms around and me presses my head into her bosom. I also begin to sob. She gains her composure and begins to scold me. *What are you doing, m'ijo? Why are you giving up? I sold my soul for you!! I know what you have gone through. You are stronger than that. You can get well and have a good life and be happy again. Remember? I know it was very long ago, but I remember when you were a happy little boy. You were a happy little boy. I know you came to me because your grandfather left too soon. I couldn't let you die as a baby. You made me so happy, m'ijo. You and your grandfather were the most important people in my life. I can't be with him because of what I did to save you. Please, m'ijo. Only you can save me. Aliviate. If you get better and do what you're supposed to do with your life, then your grandfather and I can be together. I am always with you, and I am very strong where I am. Use my strength. I love you, m'ijo. Andale, toma tus medicinas y aliviate. Remember, you are strong. Don't listen to your mother. I love you.* "Amalia held her breath and closed her eyes in awe. [I weep and close my eyes in a feverish delirium.] The Miraculous Mother *was* there ... [Mama A *was* there.] Triumphant, she stood up. 'Yes!' she said exultantly, 'I am sure!'" (Rechy 206). I crumble in my bed and mumble, "Yes ... I am sure." This was another step of my cumulative epiphany.

Silence=Death. Action=Life.

—ACT UP! Slogan

My biological family, especially my mother, has been expecting my death for years now. Yet I have obstinately denied her the starring role as *la madre sufrida*. In my darker moments, I imagine my funeral. I envision an elaborate set in the *camposanto* of Ysleta where the majority of my *antepasados* rejoice. Surrounded by my entire family, my mother is in black; hours of incessant weeping and smeared makeup distort her beautifully brown indigenous face. She plays the martyr as no Hollywood actor can. When it is time for me to return to my original mother, my hysterical mother demands that she be lowered into the grave with her only son and assaults my casket. *Look at me! Look at me! Yo soy la madre sufrida! He sufrido tanto por m'ijo! Llevame a mi Dios!* Mama A and I chuckle at her histrionics (she did the same at her funeral) and Yemaya—the Yoruba goddess of the ocean who the santero divined as my protector orisha years before—provides an unexpected ocean-like, cool breeze for my other mourners, a respite from the scorching desert heat. I look back and whisper into my mother's ear, "Ya no llores, Mom. I am home." Her tears begin to subside. La Llorona releases me from the fabric of her rebozo, kisses me goodbye, and continues the Sisyphean search for her children. I am enveloped by the energy of my protector goddesses, Yemaya, Coatlicue, Tonantzin, La Virgen, and, of course, Mama A. I then take one final look back at my familia—biological and otherwise—before I dissipate into the unknown, into nothing, into the next(?) cycle of existence.

ALLGO seeks to empower our community through political, educational, cultural, health & social programming & services. We recognize that our struggle is linked to the struggle of all oppressed peoples & agree to always be in the forefront in the struggle against all forms of discrimination & oppression in order to transform the World. Our efforts are rooted in the belief that critical consciousness along with self & community empowerment are essential to our gente's survival & well-being.—Former Mission Statement of ALLGO, the Austin Latina/o Lesbian, Gay, Bisexual, and Transgender Organization

Soon after my bout with pneumonia, I sought help. I called ALLGO, for I had heard many positive things about their social services. I had attended several social events that ALLGO had sponsored, including their "Baile de Amor," a queer Latina/o Valentine's dance, but I didn't know how vital this organization was to the LGBT community in Austin. I made an appointment with a social worker, and we met for lunch. A Chicana close to my age, her care and concern for me were immediately apparent. I began to become more involved with ALLGO, and I made a radical life change. I resigned from my job, and I applied for and was offered a position as a health educator at ALLGO. I went from working in a large office with mostly heterosexual, White people to being part of a small staff of ten, the majority being queer people of color. I found my home.

My intellectual awakening began at ALLGO. This revolutionary organization exposed me to radical new ways of thinking, and I had the privilege of meeting amazing writers and other artists. The most important aspect of ALLGO was the creation of a new familia. I created lifelong bonds with a core group of people who understood my drama, some of whom had lived it; they never judged me and accepted me with their open arms, particularly the butch lesbians.

My butch lesbian saviors descended from on high and simultaneously offered me their strength and compassion. One in particular, Priscilla, helped me begin my journey towards self-worth and self-acceptance. Just as I served as a replacement to ease my grandmother's suffering, Priscilla became the source of maternal fortitude that had been missing from my life. She continues to be my touchstone, and she is as important to my survival as my grandmother is.

Although I seemed to be forging a positive new life path, emotionally, I was still suffering on my cross. Every night, after I would talk to people at gay bars and other locales about ALLGO and safer sex practices, I would stay and inebriate myself. I was constantly on the prowl, and I never lacked for eager, willing men to partake of my gift. Although I preached safer sex, I rarely practiced it. Again, my powers of rationalization superseded my impaired judgment. Once, I contracted gonorrhea, but this did not stop me. I picked up a guy at the clinic who was in for the same thing. We had sex a week later, once we were both finished with our antibiotics. My gift was seemingly endless.

After a year and a half at ALLGO, I decided to leave. I had met someone from Los Angeles, and I convinced myself I was in love. However, my damaged soul would never allow me to love another man. I decided I would drink and fuck myself to death in the relative obscurity of the City of Angels. I was tired of this life and this existence. Mama A's visit had not yet convinced me of the value of my life.

The night I left Austin was yet another transformative moment, another landmark on my spiritual map. The executive director of ALLGO threw a going away party for me, and it was a festive evening of food, drink, and music. I put on a brave face, but internally, I considered this event to be my wake. After hours of reveling, it came time to take my leave. At one point during the night, I realized all of my male friends had left—most likely to the bar. "Pinches putas borrachas," I thought. Nevertheless, I couldn't blame them; the Night is a powerful mistress who does not relinquish her slaves willingly. My lesbians were the ones who stayed to send me off into my Night. One by one, each embraced me through the torrent of my tears and blessed my journey. It was the next step of my cumulative epiphany, the one I thought would lead to my death in the following year. I couldn't bear the thought of deteriorating in front of my new family; I longed for an anonymous demise among strangers. I had just turned twenty-eight and didn't think I would live to see thirty.

My first few months in Los Angeles were a whirlwind of alcohol and men. I was delighted that the L.A. area housed many sex clubs and bathhouses. They became my new addiction; on only one occasion can I recall my sex partner wanting to use a condom. Sometimes, I would offer to use one, yet they all refused—the phenomenon of "barebacking" was growing as a result of AIDS "fatigue"—the notion that gay men were growing weary of having to fellate the ideological phallus of safer sex. I pushed my body to greater and greater limits. I lost myself in count-less men, connecting with each on a primal, visceral level. Tongues and penises darted in and out of mouths and asses in a twisted dance of desire and rage. Each time the communion was released within the supplicant, I would bring his body close to mine in a tense yet tender embrace and we'd kiss deeply and profoundly. He would soon begin his own transformation, carrying my essence forever. After a minute of comfortable turned awkward silence, I would leave to shower whatever residue of his body was left behind and prepare myself for the next eager supplicant. Each trip to the bathhouse brought Death closer, and I relished the thought of my body being discovered in one of the dirty, sleazy rooms that were quickly becoming my second home.

After one particularly active evening, I emerge from the bowels of the bathhouse on Kohler, near the East L.A. Bridge, into the putrid early sunlight of downtown Los Angeles, physically exhausted and emotionally numb. I vaguely remember where I parked and collapse in my car over the steering wheel. I drive aimlessly, past skid row, and reminisce about my existence on the streets. I drive away from downtown, and I end up on Beverly at Slammer, a hardcore S/M club. Perhaps this will be the night when I cross the line into another world, one where heretofore I have only been an eager voyeur. I yearn for my own Christ-figure to reveal himself to me. The club doesn't open until 9:00 p.m., and I wonder what to do with my day until it opens. I drive in the opposite direction on Beverly and notice a sign for a botánica, "Botánica Obatala." I recognize the name as one of the most potent orishas in the pantheon of the belief system commonly referred to as Santería. Out of curiosity, I park and approach the establishment cautiously yet stridently. My emotional wounds begin to crave more of their particular salve—alcohol and sex. However, something draws me to this sacred site. I open the door and upon crossing the threshold, a lush Chicana confronts me and our gazes meet ...

Ofrenda of Continuation/The task is never complete ...

I continue building the multidimensional structure. Coyolxauhqui, the dismembered Mexica moon goddess, remains hidden in the shadow of the universe and does not aid me in my task, emblematic of my birth mother. The candles provide the only source of light and, like my diminishing life force, flicker against the indeterminable starless Night. The queer rainbow-colored papel picado hangs ethereally from the sky, dancing in the ocean breeze. I mark the boundaries of the site with the HIV meds I will no longer take, the poison that prolonged my life just long enough for my memory to remain relatively intact. The pungent smell of the cempoalxochitl mixes with the brine of the sea to form an intoxicatingly aromatic sensation. My breathing and heartbeat synchronize themselves with the rhythm of the crashing waves. I am ready. I commune with my ofrenda for an immeasurable length of time. As my body weakens, my spirit strengthens. In the distance, the sacred drum of the

Tigua beats increasingly faster. Louder. They are the same rhythm and beats which ushered my grandfather's spirit into the next cycle. His weathered, calloused hand extends to mine and coerces my spirit out of its tired, broken, disfigured shell. After the pre-determined amount of time passes, the antepasados place my picture on the altar. My grandfather smiles.

On a sweltering summer's day in the San Fernando Valley, I walked into the Chicana/o Studies Department office at California State University at Northridge not knowing what to expect. I had made the difficult decision to change my major from Accounting to Chicana/o Studies, and I was confident that I was on the right path. What transpired during my appointment was nothing short of Fate stroking my cheek in acknowledgement of my perseverant and resilient nature. She placed a surrogate maternal figure in my path who would guide me along my academic and intellectual journey. Indeed, Fate has placed several supporting female figures in my path to help stimulate the gray matter that I had abused for far too long. I have come to consider them my surrogate lesbians. It does not matter that they carry the tragic deficiency of heterosexuality. My queer family at ALLGO planted the seeds of intellectual awakening, but my mentors in the Chicana/o Studies Department cultivated them. This work is the bloom.

"I will entertain you recounting the story of my life ... They call me La Agrado, because I have always tried to make everyone's life more pleasant ... Aside from being pleasant I am also very authentic: almond shaped eyes, 80 thousand; silicone in lips, forehead, cheeks, hips and ass, the liter costs sixty thousand pesetas ... you add it up because I stopped counting. Tits? Two, I'm no monster. Seventy each, but these have been fully depreciated. It cost me a lot to be authentic, but we must not be cheap in

regards to the way we look. Because a woman is more authentic the more she looks like what she has dreamed for herself."

—*Speech given by the character,* "*La Agrado,*" *in Pedro Almodóvar's film* Todo Sobre Mi Madre

"I'm just a sweet transvestite from Transsexual, Transylvania."

—*Dr. Frank-N-Furter's self-identification in* The Rocky Horror Picture Show

Pure joy. Amid all their personal peccadilloes and dramas, La Agrado and Dr. Frank-N-Furter exude joy and revel in the moment. They both painstakingly constructed their identities to the images in their heads. Nothing, not biology, financial constraints, social acceptance, or even originating in this plane of existence, can stop them from achieving their ultimate goals of self-creation, all the while laughing and dancing along the way.

This is the feeling of elation that I have experienced on many occasions in gay bars. Even amidst my personal dramas, I simply enjoyed myself, surrounded by my friends and dancing the night away. On those nights, our problems ceased to exist. We were there to celebrate that time together, regardless of our family's or society's disapproval. Most gay clubs, except for ones like Rechy's Rushes, are accepting of heterosexuals, and I know several straight women who prefer them over straight bars. They are overcome by the sense of freedom and liberation that envelops them when they step out onto the dance floor. That is what I see at a gay club. Granted, many may be under the influence of some type of narcotic, but we, the LGBT communities, claim the dance floor as our space of identity, and we openly welcome non-queer people to revel in the festive atmosphere. The moment on the dance floor is all we have. Off the dance floor, we must deal with our cruel realities, struggling in order to shout one more time, "Let's do the time warp again!"

> *"I learned something about family tonight. They're not always the ones that love you the most. Sometimes, it's the family that you make for yourself."*
>
> —Betty Suarez to Mark, whose mother had just realized his son is gay and rejected him, from Ugly_ Betty

In order to construct a healthy, positive identity, I have had to cast off any lingering shame; this scenario, unfortunately, does not include my biological family. The lovable Agrado creates family with the people that her circumstances put her around. I have followed her lead and continue to realize that the person that *I* have dreamed of becoming cannot emerge from his cocoon with his family's scornful eyes glaring at him. My desires, my loves, my sexual acts, my memories, my life should never again be a source of shame or silence. Cognizant of this dilemma, I nevertheless continue to intricately negotiate my identities in order to entwine my Chicanismo, my *jotería*, and my seropositive status into a beautifully woven *trenza*, one worthy of the fiercest drag queen's wig. Snap!

> *"Death and I have been on familiar speaking terms for a long time; death plays with me without hurting me."*
>
> —*Jose Ruben Romero*, La vida inútil de Pito Pérez

My story will continue with or without its corporal shell, and I recognize the privilege of having told my story. But how many stories of countless queer Xicano men will never be heard because of the HIV/AIDS epidemic? Last summer, I went out with an old friend of mine to a popular gay Latino club in Hollywood. Just as I had done on count-less occasions in my twenties, I lost myself in the hypnotic rhythms of the house music. At one moment during the night, however, I looked around the massive establishment and wondered how many more of those brown lives would be sacrificed at the altar of the HIV epidemic. I wondered how many of them were poz, yet did not know it. Did the poz guys take their meds according to their doctor's recommendations? Did they struggle with the headaches, nausea, diarrhea, dizziness, night terrors, the rage, and the shame that I struggled with? How are they treated by their families? Are they hopeful for their futures? Who will remember them?

The prospect of hundreds more, if not thousands, of extinguished voices is truly frightening and saddening. Just like the Mexican govern-ment smothered the voices of hundreds, if not thousands, of its citizens in 1968, the Chicana/o community has lost and continues to lose an innumerable amount of lives. This is lost history, akin to the wealth of knowledge inscribed in the amoxtli destroyed by the Spanish friars during the conquest of Mesoamerica, one that will never be regained if the stigmatic silence from the heterosexual Chicana/o community persists.

Conversely, I am somewhat hopeful of my ability to illuminate the attitudes of some heterosexual Chicanas/os. Because of their contact with me, a few of my brethren changed their opinions regarding queer men. One openly admitted that he was once defiantly homophobic. I can only smile when I hear that I have been the impetus for such a change of heart. While it would be safer for me to sequester myself into a world of LGBT homogeny, like I did at ALLGO, I believe I can still educate many more heterosexual Chicanas/os. If the majority of them only realized that Cesar Chavez and Dolores Huerta, two of the co-founders of the United Farm Workers, both overtly advocated for LGBT rights and worked to destroy *all* oppression. In fact, Cesar Chavez, a devout Catholic, spoke at the 1987 Gay and Lesbian March on Washington; he certainly understood the complexity of overlapping oppressions.[8]

Conversely, I challenge the LGBT communities to confront the racism, classism, sexism, and xenophobia currently running rampant throughout our society. The LGBT communities must continue to shout from the forefront of *all* movements for social justice. Only when oppression against all people is eradicated will queer Chicanas/os truly be free. As I continue to tell my story and other queer Chicanas/os tell theirs, thereby confronting and transforming heteronormative attitudes, we will openly and proudly flaunt our *trenzas* of identity and liberation—while embracing our friends and lovers.

> *Are flowers carried to the kingdom of death?*
> *It is true that we go,*
> *it is true that we go!*
> *Where do we go?*
> *Where do we go?*
> *Are we dead there or do we still live?*
> *Do we exist there again?*
>
> *—Lines from a Nahuatl poem, author unknown*

> *"I change myself, I change the world."*
>
> *—Gloria Anzaldúa,* Borderlands/La Frontera: The New Mestiza

My story is one of survival, yet it is also a celebration of the people I choose to surround myself with. You may pity, scorn, or admire me,

---

8   What is not commonly known about Cesar Chavez is that he spoke on behalf of gay and lesbian rights well before the Stonewall Rebellion, yet this dimension of his activism remains unearthed under layers of ahistorical rubble.

but do not let my story end when you put down this manuscript. I urge everyone to first look inward and name your own prejudices, and begin to heal yourself. Most of us are damaged in some way, yet it is easier to lash out at others than to truly work on our own personal dramas. It isn't easy. Also, let's foster a frank discussion of sexuality and urge everyone in our respective communities to get tested for HIV and other sexually transmitted infections. Silent ignorance is no longer a viable option for the Chicana/o community regarding HIV, or it will literally be the death of us. AIDS may be the bullet that kills many in our community, yet silence is what pulls the trigger.

Currently, AIDS is no longer an automatic death sentence. I have met some individuals who have survived with the virus since the onset of the epidemic. Sometimes, I can envision myself as a wrinkled and crotchety old fag living well into my fifties and even sixties, but I am not that hopeful. A recent study declared that HIV+ people usually survive twenty-four years with the disease; I have lived with this virus for eighteen years now. However, I will not leave my quinceañera without a titanic struggle. I do feel guilty, however. I feel guilty because I have had access to the life-saving meds that millions in other parts of the country and the world are desperate for. I am worried about the fact that the seroconversion rate for gay Xicanos and Latinos and heterosexual Xicanas and Latinas keeps increasing. I mourn, and more importantly remember, the generation of gay Xicanos whom I could not take counsel from because of this epidemic. Indeed, we should all mourn and remember these lost lives.

However, I no longer fear *La Muerte*. Her shadow has been cast over my soul since my birth, but, occasionally, I have managed to steal glimpses of sunlight. Inevitably, I know my body will tire of our dance, but I will not be sad or regretful. Part of my cumulative epiphany has been the acceptance of *La Muerte*'s impending and eventual arrival. She lives within me, having transformed from a cancer of the blood to the form of a mutating virus that is ready to devour and ravage my body, as my body was devoured and ravaged by my mother, my stepfather, and the countless, faceless men. At this precise moment, she is sleeping, dormant because of the poison I ingest twice a day and Mama A's magic. Yet, as she slumbers, she waits for her opportunity to consume me. I only pray that when the time comes, I will dance my way into oblivion to the fiercest house beats that echo the drums of Yemaya's tribal chants. Cue La India's house classic, "Love and Happiness":

> Universal Mother Yemaya
> I'm singing to you
> I wanna let, wanna let the world know
> That you represent all the richness of the world
> Oh yes you do
> Oh yes you do
> Yes you do
> Oh and I wanna let the whole world know
> Goddess of sweetness is Ochun
> Oh yes it is
> Oh she'll ask you
> Ask you to pray to her
> When you're out of reach
> When you aint got no love
> She'll be there for you
> All you gotta do
> Is pray to Ochun
> She is love and sweetness too
> You've just got to believe there is Love and Happiness ...

Recently, one of my constructed *familia* members told me that when my spirit does cut loose from the bondage of its bodily restraints, she and my other *familia* will build an altar in my honor for *Día de los Muertos*. On that occasion, as my spirit is being nourished and communes with my loved ones, I will smile, take Mama A's hand, and prepare for the long, arduous journey back into the unknown.

Ofrenda of Transition/Epilogue

I take my reserved place among the eggun, the ancestors, with simultaneous orientations in the bosom of the maternal energy of the universe and my lover's embrace. My bodily remains, ashes of memories, are magically blown towards the haunting desert landscape of my childhood in order to germinate the endless mesquite shrubs, yucca plants, and, perhaps, the memory and soul of another young queer Xicano boy.

Section V

Men of Heart

New Man

Raúl al-qaraz Ochoa

man of stone
man of heart
man of fire

I don't neatly fit into the meaning of manhood. I feel powerless, suffocating, experiencing things beyond my control. How can I question the expectations of manhood I have been taught all my life? How many people will I disappoint? How much longer will I continue hurting? Life would be so much easier if I fit neatly into that box. I've tried coiling inside, but the box always bursts open. Reality rises, unfortunately—I can't escape my own truth. It's haunting. These thoughts and frustrations turn into tears streaming down my burning face.

My stomach aches, my head spins, my spirit hurts. Bury my body next to my wounded soul because I do not belong. I feel inadequate, in need of comfort and protection. I want to be accepted for who I am, not for who I am expected to be. Sometimes I wish I could disown this struggle. I don't want to deal with queer identity. It's painful and revolutionary, revolutionary because society is so backwards ... The world is broken and so am I. I am wind. My feet do not belong on this earth. My spirit is tired of roaming through chaos and confusion. I belong to the air, floating through the universe. I want to be free. Drums beat to a liberation song as I ride through the winds of history.

I cannot allow my dreams to fade into the obscurity of my deepest insecurities.

I just want to be me—loved, liberated, embracing myself without borders, discomfort, guilt, or shame. Am I strong enough to withstand this monumental challenge? The creator made me this way. I should feel blessed.

I am not a traditional,
conventional Xicano man.

What does it mean
to be a Xicano-Indigenous man?

man of stone
man of heart
man of fire

I am a New Man, emerging like the wind:
phoenix rising: liberated, empowered
flying towards the beginning of a new sun!

Coming Out

Yosimar Reyes

 I came out to myself in a poem. I was sixteen when I realized how broken I was.

"Sometimes I wish I were nothing
Invisible Like Breath
Like Wind,

No Body, No Head.
Sometimes I wish I were nothing ...
Nothing But Voice"

B rown boys don't come out of a closet like other boys do. Fuck, we got no closets to come out of. We jump borders, break chains, break systems; we escape jails, we run, we hide. We don't come of closets. It's a constant battle of walls and borders. It is our life to not get trapped in these traditions. We are always running and constantly hiding.

The first time I realized how beautiful I was, I was seventeen, when young boys my age would hug me and tell me that my poems spoke truth to them. It was the fact that so many of them would ask me to keep on doing what I was doing that helped me understand that what we carry is a message. I remember crying because these battered souls were my brothers my sisters and this hurt we have inside, this pain we carry in the center of our whole is much too common. At seventeen was when I realized that for every tear I had shed there had been millions, that for every poem I had written, hundreds of lives had been lost.

There is something you get from another brother or sister like you when they hug you that makes you realize the beauty of our resilience. As if the embrace we share reminds us that we must carry each other now. When the sky has fallen and walls have been built to keep us contained, we remind one another that we are still breathing.

I was sixteen when I came out to myself in a poem. I remember crying then, but now all I can do is

Smile

La Vida Loca

An apolitical in-your-face odyssey of a Mexican immigrant

Carlos Manuel

LA VIDA LOCA, although written as a series of long stories, is a very theatrical piece. The actor is the storyteller, so he controls the theatricality, the pace, and the "magic" of the play. It is a very physical theatre piece, allowing the actor to run, jump up and down, lie on the floor, and hide behind platforms or cubes, or whatever has been designed as a set.

The actor also controls the lights and the music, using "finger snaps" or specific gestures to indicate a change of rhythm or mood, or time and space. For example, after each "level" mentioned in the script, the actor should snap his fingers to change mood, time, or rhythm. Or for each "Spanish lesson," the actor should gesture or do something that will bring the audience out of the "storytelling" and into a more direct and personal relationship with the actor—lights could come up on the audience to establish a "teacher–student" relationship.

A note about announcing each level: the actor should use a "gringo" accent to say each level. Once the actor reaches "level número nueve," the actor should no longer use a gringo accent.

The play requires the aid of many images. There are many instances where what is being said is enhance by a picture. This will not only make the play more theatrical and more vivid, but also will give the audience a better understanding of what is going on in the narrator's head. For example, when the actor talks about specific Mexican artists, such pictures should project on stage to help the audience understand what the actor is talking about. In one of the lessons, when the actor talks about bisexuality, the actor doesn't translate from Spanish to English, but rather says, "You broke Ellen's heart, bitch!" referring to a picture of Anne Heche, thus creating a joke, and also emphasizing the issue of bisexuality and the issue of bilingualism.

I have decided to include the images in the script in order to help in the visualization while reading the play. However, the director and production team are free to decide whether to use such images or not. In short, communication with the playwright about the artistic vision of the play is highly encouraged.

1. La Vida Loca

(In the dark, the English version of Ricky Martin's "Livin' La Vida Loca" is heard. Slowly, lights come up on stage. We see an actor, dancing to the rhythm. At an appropriate time, the actor starts speaking over the music.)

Me encanta esa canción *(sings)* "Livin' la vida loca ..." You may or may not know this, but that song has two different meanings, one in Spanish, one in English. ¡Sí, en serio! In English, the song is about a girl who's into superstitions, black cats and voodoo dolls, a girl that makes you take your clothes off and go dancing in the rain ... And that's good ... I guess ... Whatever! Honestly, the only thing I like about the English version is the beat. Porque déjenme decirles que in Spanish the song has nothing to do with a girl. And that's very good ... at least for me ... and for Ricky Martin, if you know what I mean. And now that he's come out of the closet, you *really* know what I mean.

In Spanish, the song is about "life being crazy." And how life will give you everything you want, as if you were the Son of God. But just like Jesus, life will drop you into the world and then crucify you for your sins. Oh, y eso no es todo. "Livin' La Vida Loca" has a double meaning. One, you already know, the other—I'm still waiting for Ricky's reply to all my emails. And since his coming out, I have a feeling he will soon answer them.

Time for a lesson in Mexican Spanish:

In Spanish, "loca" means crazy. "Loca" also refers to a homosexual man. Example: "Esa persona está loca," which means, *[image of W Bush]* "that person is crazy."

Another example: "Esa persona es una loca," which means, *[image of Elton John]* "that person is a fag." End of lesson.

When people ask me, "how you doing?" I always say "Fine! Living la vida loca, and ju?" Some people go into a state of shock, some turn around and leave, and some join in the fun. Either way, I'm living la vida loca!

But I need to clear a few things up. Porque no quiero que empiezen a levantar altares con veladoras y merjunges caseros en mi nombre. I don't want to find out that someone has a shrine with my name on it or that somewhere in cyberland there's a webpage titled: "www.carlos-the-loca.com." That would be weird. It would be a boost to my ego, but it would be weird. I'm living la vida loca, all right, but it wasn't always like this. You see, I'm ... I'm Mexican. As if you couldn't tell by the golden brown of my beautiful and well-treated skin tone and by the mystical and, how do you people put it ...? Oh, yes! The "exotic intonation of your voice"—commonly known as an accent. As if you couldn't tell by the dark brown in my eyes, which have been going bad thanks to the many years I used colored contact lenses so I could believe I was another "americano" in Gringoland ... But more about that later.

I lived in Mexico City for fifteen years, three months, and two days before my mamá decided to bring my two brothers, my sister, and me to this country. So (*A la "EL Pachuco"*) sit back, relax, and enjoy the pretence. ¡Orale!

2. The Immigrant

[Image of modern Mexico City] Welcome to Méjico, where people do make "a run for the border." *[Image of Tijuana, Mexico]* This is Tijuana—virtual reality TJ, upgraded version 2010. Only available for your PC, your Personal Cerebro. The video game of life begins.

Level número uno.

It is dark. It is cold. It is scary. It is like being forced to watch an entire day of "Barney & Friends" episodes. I am lying down on the ground. My two brothers, my sister, my mamá, my tía, my three cousins, my two uncles, and a couple of friends, they are all lying down on the ground just like me, pressing our chests against the mud and trying to disappear under the matorrales. Our "tour guide," commonly known as "el coyote," the guy who's helping us cross the border, gave us instructions not to talk, not to move, not to breathe, and above all, not to look up. We can't look up because in the deep valleys of la frontera, the Immigration and Naturalization Service's airplanes circle the sky with beam lights. And we, humanos imperfectos, like to look up at the sound of an airplane. And it's exactly at that moment that your eyes shine like a cat's eyes under the airplane's beam light. And sometimes you close your eyes right away, and other times you keep them open 'cause you've been hypnotized as if that light were the light at the end of the tunnel and as if the sound of the airplane were the sound of a mosquito.

And before I realize it and even faster than I can say "chingao," a two-headed monster stands besides me. (*Gringo accent*) "Livante! la te descubremos, ia tus amigos también. Get up, pronto."

And because I'm still a child, because I'm scared, and because I'm wondering how the hell a two-headed monster can ruin my language, I get up. One by one, my two brothers, my sister, my mamá, my tía, my three cousins, my two uncles, and the couple of friends come out of their own hideouts. It is then I realize the two-headed monster is nothing else but an ugly man in uniform sitting on a horse bigger than himself. It is then I realize we have been captured by the INS officers, commonly known as "la migra." And it is then I realize I have been looking up and keeping my eyes open. And it's all my fault … ¡Chingao!

But I don't feel guilty about that. At least we spent the rest of the night under a roof. It was a cold jail but it was dry. Early the next morning we are sent back to Tijuana in a bus full of people who also didn't reach the beginning of the "American Dream," a bus so full, it reminds me of Mexico City's transportation system. And I smile; that is a good feeling. Things are looking up.

Back to Level número uno.

That same day, at night, we made our second attempt to cross the border. This time, I don't open my eyes. This time, I run as fast as I can. This time, I help my brothers climb the so many wired fences we encounter. This time, we all spend part of the night in a wet, dark, cold, and stinky sewer tunnel. And this time, I am able to have my first view of the United States of America: *[image of a freeway at night]* In the dark, a never-ending stream of golden lights, steadily moving far, far away. "¿Tío, qué's eso?"

"¿Eso? 'Pos that mijo, that is the pinche freeway."

Yes, it is true. That never-ending stream of golden lights steadily moving far away in the distance commonly known as "the pinche freeway" is my first view of the good old USA. And yes, it is true. If we want to succeed, we need to reach that freeway before daybreak. And yes, it is also true: the coyote is my uncle. Hey, what can I say? Importation is a family tradition; it "runs" in the family.

Level número dos.

We reach our destination before daybreak and we spend the entire day hiding in an avocado tree field, eating dry bologna sandwiches and drinking warm water.

Late in the afternoon two cars arrive. And for the first time in our family trip, our group is separated. We are on our way to Los Angeles but before we get there, we must cross the last and most difficult migra check point. We are separated for obvious reasons.

Level número tres.

I am lucky enough to be in the back seat of one of the cars. One of my brothers is stuck in the trunk of another. Mi mamá is sweating and breathing heavily. She is all curled up and lying down by my feet, in the space between the front and back seat of the car. I look down at my mamá and see her eyes shut tight, her lips moving fast in prayer. Now I do feel guilty and I feel sad. She should be the one sitting up, not me. But another relative is driving and she decides that one of my girl cousins and I look like her children, in case la migra asks any questions.

But nobody does. The check point at San Clemente is closed. There are no officers on duty. Once we pass the migra checkpoint, my mamá is able to sit next to me. And that way, but still with one of my brothers hiding in the trunk of one the cars, we arrive at the City of Angels.

Level número cuatro.

It is then that I taste American freedom. We drive around the city. The streets are congested with traffic. People are running all over the place. All around us the sound of laughter is mixed with the sounds of fireworks. Music blasts from people's houses and car stereos as the foreign language is being spoken all around us.

For a moment I feel like Jesus when he arrived in Jerusalem, except that instead of on a donkey, I arrive in a two door, light blue Chevy. My tía parks the car, and we walk among the multitudes. I notice something strange: I understand them; they speak my language. I ask: "Tío, ¿dónde están los güeros? Where are all the gringos?" My tío, the coyote, looks at me and with a proud smile says: "Mijo, welcome to East L.A., cabrón."

We arrive at a relative's house, a wolf's hideout no doubt, and we are welcomed by happy brown faces:

"¡Bienvenidos! Pasen, Pasen, Por favor."

"Gracias, gracias." *[image of fireworks]* "Tía, tía, que están celebrando?" "Ay mijo, tan bonito y chulo mi Carlitos. We are celebrating la Independencia Americana."

And I smile. Her answer to my question is a very good sign. I knew then I had arrived in the "land of the free." And what better date to do it than on July 4th, 1985, Independence Day, an independence day I will never forget, an independence day that marks when I started "living la vida loca."

3. High School

We only stayed in East LA for a couple of days. After that, the entire familia hopped in the car and my uncle drove us up north, to Stockton, California where, at the time, my mamá was living with her brand new French-American husband.

Level número cinco.

[*Image of Stockton*] Ah, Stockton, California, the city of ... the city of ...

So I started school in the fall of eighty-five at Franklin High. Out of the two years I was there, I only remember three things: my drama teacher, Mrs. Rosselli, "Walk like an Egyptian" by the Bangles, and Danny Sánchez, no, González. I mean, Rodríguez. Fine! I don't remember his whole name, okay? Sue me! It doesn't matter what his real name was. He wasn't a great lover, anyway. Oops!!!

(Voice over)
Danny Sánchez González Rodríguez was never Carlos' lover. In Carlos' mind Danny Sánchez González Rodríguez was "all that and a bag of chips." But in real life, Danny Sánchez González Rodríguez was not even worth the bag the chips come in.

Okay, okay, I confess, Danny Pérez was not even my friend. He was just a kid whom I secretly admired because of his light blond hair, beautiful fair skin, and deep green eyes. And his real name wasn't even Danny Pérez, so don't waste your time trying to find him in the high school yearbook. You won't find it.

[*"Walk like an Egyptian" is heard in the background.*]

Ah, but what was real was the Bangles and their number one hit, "Walk like an Egyptian." Oh yes, I may not have understood what the hell the song was all about but I sure knew how to walk like an Egyptian.

I remember wearing my favorite baggy white pants, nicely rolled up and carefully tight at the ankle. I remember my oversized bright colored, long sleeve shirts, a la MC Hammer. My hair was all curly and fluffy, very much a la Kirk Cameron from "Growing Pains." And for those who are too young to know who Kirk Cameron from "Growing Pains" is, I have two things to tell you: a) I hate you, b) *[image of Kirk]* Kirk Cameron from "Growing Pains" is to my generation what *[image of Guarini]* Justin Guarini from "American Idol" is to your generation. The three of us had the same fluffy curly hair, except that Kirk and I wore it back in the eighties. I also wore many of those hand-made bracelets. Remember those?

What the hell was I thinking? The eighties were the Great Depression of the fashion industry. Some of us looked like *[image of Janet Jackson]* we were the dancers from Janet Jackson's "Nasty Boys" video, others tried to imitate *[image of the Jon Bon Jovi Band]* Jon Bon Jovi's "Slippery When Wet" look, and the rest, well, the rest were secretly following *[image of George Michael]* George Michael's career as a member of the musical group "Wham" and waiting for him to come out of the closet or to be found in a public restroom doing nasty things with another man, whichever came first. We know the answer to that one, don't we?

But please, don't hate me 'cause I was beautiful back in the eighties. I was just trying to fit in. I was just trying to become part of the "in-crowd." I was just following the examples set by the other kids at school, which only meant: I looked stupid, acted stupid, and believed I was right ... a perfect example of the Reagan era.

What I loved the most about my high school years was my drama teacher, Mrs. Rosselli. When I first walked into her classroom, she welcomed me with her arms open, and I walked right in with my mouth open. I couldn't believe that her classroom was an actual theatre.

Mrs. Rosselli treated everyone the same. It didn't matter if you spoke English or not. In her classroom, I was as good, as bad, and as stupid as everyone else.

"All right kids! We're going to do improvisations. Are you ready, honey?"

"¿Qué?"

"Are you ... oh never mind! Carlos, be a soldier."

"¿Qué?"

"A soldier."

"¿Qué?"

"You know ... a soldier."

Mrs. Rosselli gave me a part in almost every show she directed. I was always part of the ensemble, and I was always placed in the back row ... way, way, way in the back row.

But that didn't matter to me. Even if I was town person number twenty-seven in a show of twenty-seven people, I was happy; I was on stage; I was alive! Alive! Alive I tell ya! I was town person number twenty-seven: the good-hearted mute actor, the one that, very much a la Mexican soap operas, could always make big facial expressions and become one with the leading actress, communicating my thoughts, my feelings, my desires, just like that bitch of a dog named Lassie.

I figured if a dog could communicate with an entire family, so could I. And besides, Mrs. Rosselli always told me, "There are no small parts, just small actors." And I sure in hell wasn't going to be one of them.

I do love Mrs. Rosselli, for I did learn a lot from her, especially about the endless struggle of cultural identification. I once played a practical joke on one of my fellow actors. Everyone was amused, but not Mrs. Rosselli:

"Carlos! What do you think you're doing? What-Are-You-Doing? This is not the circus, young man. This is a school and this is MY theatre. And you're here to learn how to become a big Hollywood movie star, like Patrick Swayze or Jason Priestly, not just some overworked and underpaid high school drama teacher. How do you explain yourself?"

"¿Qué?"

"Don't you 'que' me, young man. I know you hear good and understand me even better. And look at me when I am talking to you!"

"Pero ..."

How could I look up? How could I look at Mrs. Rosselli? How could I fix my eyes on an adult that was reprimanding me? Toda la vida I had been taught never to look at an adult when being reprimanded and reminded what a piece of worthless caca I was.

(Voice over)

"Carlos, never look up, always bow your head as a sign of humility and acceptance of your errors, even if is not your fault."

And there she was, Mrs. Rosselli, asking me to look at her as she reprimanded me and reminded me what a piece of worthless caca I was. I was so confused.

A few months later I had a confrontation with my mamá. She was mad because I had slapped my sister, if you can believe that. And although my mamá is a very short person, she's as tough as they come.

"Carlos, ¿que le pegaste a tu hermana? ¿Porqué le pegaste a tu hermana? ¿Cuántas veces te he dicho que no le pegues a tus hermanos? Si no hacen lo que les dices, deja que yo llegue y yo les pego. ¡Y no me mires así, Carlos Manuel!"

"But, mom ..."

I suddenly found myself caught between two cultures. From Mrs. Rosselli I learned to look up when being reprimanded and reminded of what a piece of worthless caca I was. And now my mamá was slapping me for looking up while being reprimanded and reminded what a piece of worthless caca I was. I was so confused ... and suddenly full of rage. I didn't know what to do. The one thing I knew was that no matter what culture I was in, I was always a piece of worthless caca.

It got worse. The clashes between my Mexican culture and the American culture I was beginning to understand became increasingly confusing. Here people order "burritos" for lunch. ¿Qué, qué? In my country [image of a burrito] a burrito is [image of a donkey] a donkey. Do you people eat donkey? And some of you get grossed out because we eat "menudo." You know, tripe. Cow's guts. *[image of a plate of menudo]* Hmmmm!

And what about "Chicken quesadillas." Excuse me? There's no such thing as a "chicken quesadilla" in my country.

Time for a lesson in Mexican Spanish: In Spanish, the word "quesadilla" comes from two Spanish words: "queso," which means cheese, and (Mexican pronunciation) "tortilla," which means (Americanized pronunciation) tortilla. You put the "queso" in the "tortilla" and you get a "quesadilla." But chicken is "pollo" in Spanish. If you put "pollo" in a tortilla, do you get a "pollodilla"? ¡No! We call that tacos de pollo, and if we put cheese in them, we call them "tacos de pollo con queso." End of lesson.

Trying to understand American manners between teenagers and adults as well as trying to comprehend the names of all the "new" Mexican foods was very frustrating. So I became very confused and full of rage! And then I realized no one was to blame for it, not Mrs. Rosselli, not my mamá, and not even me. So I became really confused and full of rage. Even today, sometimes I'm very confused and most of the time I'm full of rage. Even right now, I am so confused and full of rage that I don't even know how to end this pinche monologue. I am confused and full of rage! ¡Chingao!

4. A Chorus Line

(The song "One," from A Chorus Line *is heard.)*

A Chorus Line, one of the longest running Broadway shows ever, is one of my three favorite musicals. My other two are *[image of West Side Story] West Side Story* and *[image of Zoot Suit] Zoot Suit. Zoot Suit,* by Luis Valdez, is the first Chicano musical that ever made it to Broadway. Unfortunately, New Yorkers didn't understand its Chicano roots, so it bombed. But in L.A. *Zoot Suit* was an incredible success. Oh, and when the movie came out, it made *[image of James Olmos as "El Pachuco"]* Edward James Olmos, as "El Pachucho," a household name.

I've been in *West Side Story* twice even though the show is not very realistic. Let's face it, a white dude goes to Spanish Harlem in the middle of the night and calls for Maria, and only one girl comes out? Please, you go to my barrio and yell "Maria" and the entire street will be filled with women, young and old, and a few guys too.

A Chorus Line, well, that was the first American musical I saw in this country. But I have to confess that at first, I didn't want to see it. To me the word "chorus" meant choir. And after being in Catholic schools all my life, the last thing I wanted to hear was another rendition of *(mockingly singing)* "Ave Maria." But somehow I ended up sitting in the audience … in the back row … way, way, way in the back row. And as a magical world was displayed in front of me, I was hypnotized, I was mesmerized, I was transformed!

Aside from all the good singing and incredible dancing, three factors in the play gave me a new look at reality. One: the show is about people who want to be successful in theatre (read: me) Two: in the show there is a homosexual character. Well, there are a few homosexual characters, but this character is not flamboyant and doesn't wear a dress. Up to that moment, I thought all homosexuals were very flamboyant, had high-pitched voices, wore dresses, and worked in beauty parlors. And three: one of the lead characters in the show is an actual Latina by the name of Morales. Not Johnson, not Smith, but *(in Spanish)* "M-o-r-a-l-e-s, Morales."

Now, you may think that these factors aren't a big deal. But allow me to remind you that I come from a country where acting is only possible for the children of movie and television stars, where homosexuality is a disease, a sin, and an unspeakable truth.

Level número seis.

I used to spend my summer vacations with my grandparents in the state of Michoacán, five hours north of Mexico City and two hours east of Guadalajara City, in a small town called Cojumatlán. One summer I was kicking it with my cousin Pepe and his friends. We were doing what everyone in that little town does best on a Sunday morning: nothing! We were just sitting on a street corner, talking about who had taken a "run for the border" in search of a better life in "el Norte," and about who was dating the most beautiful girl in town, when suddenly and without warning, walking towards us came Tito, better known to every one else as "el jotito."

Footnote: In Spanish, "Jotito" means fag.

Tito was two years older than me. He wore ripped blue jeans with dirty long-sleeved shirts at all times. At first sight, he looked like everyone else in town, but once he walked down the streets or once he opened his mouth, he was far from being like everyone else in town. As he walked, his hips went from side to side in a way that not even Salma Hayeck could match. Every time he talked, his voice reached a high-pitched level that only deaf dogs could hear. And that wasn't all. His mannerisms were big and graceful, as if he were conducting the symphony.

Oh, and we "real men" listened to macho music by Los Tigres del Norte, Ramón Ayala, o *[image of Vicente Fernandez]* Vicente Fernández, songs like: *(singing) "Salieron de San Ysidro/ procedentes desde Tijuana/ traían las llantas del carro/ repletas de yerba mala/ era Emilio Barrera/ y Camelia la tejana."* He listened to music by Menudo, Timbiriche, *[image of Juan Gabriel]* o Juan Gabriel, songs like *(signing and moving very much like Juan Gabriel) "Ay mariposa/ tienes una mirada/ de los refinada/ y misteriosa/. Ay mariposa/ porque siempre caminas/ como las bailarinas/ mira que cosa."* Every time Tito walked down the street and passed a group of high-testosterone-immature-sexless-horny-insecure-pendejo-mocosos-pretending-to-be-macho guys like us, Tito was a victim.

"¿Qué honda, a dónde vas, jotito?"

"Psst … Psst … ¡Maricón! Mira lo que tengo para tí, ¡cabrón!"

"¿Qué prisa llevas, puto?"

"Excuse me? No, no, no, no, no, no, no. En primer lugar: Mi nombre es TITO y no JOtito. En segundo lugar: Si soy un puto, es mi decisión y mi culo, por lo menos tengo los 'güevos' para admitirlo. Y tercero: Tú. Sí, te estoy hablando a tí, gringo wannabe. You have nothing to offer me 'cause the last time you went to see my cousin Cecilia you paid me a little visit. And I really do mean little, 'cause let me tell you that this … doesn't even satisfy the pigs you like to fuck."

"Hey, man, what the hell is this joto talking about?"

"Yeah, Pepe, are you gonna let him talk to you like that?"

"Déjenlo. Don't worry. Es un puto. I'll get him later."

Next summer I heard that Tito had been found dead. He had been beaten up, tied to a tree trunk, his face half smashed with a big rock, and worse, lo habían capado, his penis stuffed in his own mouth. No one ever knew who did it, and no one ever cared to investigate, not even the town authorities. Even some of my family members said, "that's what he deserved for playing for the other team." Not satisfied with the explanations, I asked my cousin Pepe if he knew anything about it.

"I don't want to talk about it. Not tomorrow. No le busques cuatro patas al gato, Carlos."

Which basically is saying "the cat has four legs, don't look for more."

"¿Me entiendes? Or what, are you a pinche fag too?"

My cousin and I have not spoken since.

So you see, *A Chorus Line* was my first step towards a different reality in life. The show gave me the opportunity to think about actually becoming seriously involved in theatre. The show also gave me a new way of thinking about my homosexual feelings. Maybe I was not the only homosexual person in the world; maybe being a homosexual did not mean I needed to be flamboyant, and maybe having homosexual feelings was as natural as the color of my skin, and not a sin I had been born with, or disease I had acquired. And they say "the arts" are not educational. Shit!

5. Dramatic Irony

It was dark. It was cold. But it wasn't scary. It was, in fact, a very beautiful night, with a dark, clear sky and millions of shiny stars over my head. And even though it was three in the morning, there was a pleasant, warm feeling about the place. And even though it was dark, there were no valleys to cross, no INS airplanes to hide from, no freeways to reach.

Instead, there were beautiful, green gardens to walk on, small fountains and tall statues to admire, and elegant roses to smell. Instead of migra officers wondering around, two or three couples walked hand in hand, strolling under the clear sky and whispering sweet nothings to each other. Era todo un paraíso, hermoso, pacífico, inolvidable. A paradise where nothing bad could happen, only the magical moment of a loving kiss, the extraordinary sound of laughter, the unforgettable time spent with friends.

That particular night I walked alone across campus, on my way to my dorm room after a night full of video games, pizza, and friendship. I reached the adobe wall, which reminds every student that our university was once a small, humble mission, and I knew I was almost half way home.

Pasé por la estatua de Jesucristo, the statue of Jesus with the inscription saying, "come to me, venid a mi, venite edme." And as I passed it, someone suddenly approached me.

"Hey, do you have a light?"

"Sorry, I don't smoke."

"It's too bad, man."

Suddenly and without warning, a fist lands on me. I cover my face right away and make an attempt to defend myself, but a third person jumps out of nowhere and suddenly I am being hit from all directions.

"Hold him!" A fourth voice suddenly orders.

"So, you like it up the ass, eh? You fucking faggot!"

"Anthony?"

I met Anthony during my first quarter, in Japanese 101. He was a Japanese-American student who was now trying to learn the language he avoided during his childhood. He and I became good friends, attending college games and parties, helping each other with our homework, working out together, going out to the movies, making fun of other people, and even cracking the politically incorrect joke once in a while.

We were good friends. One day lo inevitable pasó. At one of those wild parties someone told him I was gay. The next day he didn't talk to me, and the day after he avoided me. My mission: to confront him.

"Why are you mad?"

"You know why. You lied to me!"

"About what?"

"Is it true? Are you only my friend 'cause you wanna get me into bed?"

"What? NO!"

"But you're gay, right?"

"Uh ... yes ... but ..."

"You and I made fun of fags all the time. We were friends. You saw me in my underwear!!!"

"We 'were' friends?"

And without another word, Anthony closed the door in my face and left me standing in the hallway. I was so shocked. I felt so stupid; I felt so hurt. All I needed at that moment was an elegant gown and a long staircase leading to my bedroom where I could run and throw myself on the bed as the credits rolled on.

Two weeks passed. Anthony suddenly called me and invited me to dinner. I happily accepted. And his friends were there, just like before. After dinner he invited me to play video games, and I happily accepted. And his friends were there too, just like before. We ordered pizza and we played until very late. And his friends were there, just like before.

But now my body is on the ground. Hit by hit and blow by blow, my body feels the strong dry impacts from the four strangers. The first blow to my face is so strong that I feel warm liquid running down my face, sangre en mi cara, blood on my hands, pain all over me. I am suddenly being attacked by four strangers who, without a doubt, know me well, but who I can't recognize yet.

(Drumming music is heard. The Beat Up Dance is performed.)

I don't know how long I was on the ground. I don't know who found me. I don't even know how I ended up in the hospital. But there I was, in a strange, cold room, white walls and colorless curtains. I knew it wasn't heaven 'cause, let me tell you, my heaven has a touch of lavender and overall a sense of style.

I had a strong headache, and my body burned with pain. I tried to open my eyes but it wasn't easy.

(Voice over)
"Ah, you're finally awake. I'm Dr. White, Carlos. Do you know what happened to you? Well, it looks like you were attacked by a gang. Do you do drugs? Well, no matter. Whoever beat you up broke your nose and gave you two deep cuts on the right side of your face. Hey, don't touch it. You have a deep cut above your eyebrow and one below your eye. You're pretty lucky. Half an inch more and you would have been blind in your right eye. But you'll be okay. I gave you thirty-seven stitches."

Thirty-seven stitches! Thirty-seven stitches! It took Thirty-seven stitches to fix the damage! Thirty-seven stitches! One day in the hospital. Two weeks in bed, and a bill for almost $2,500.00, which I still refuse to pay.

When I crossed the border, I ran in the dark valleys of la frontera. I hid from migra officers, and I risked my life along with my familia so we could live in this country. I was in a strange land, a scary land, a land where people shoot to kill, a land where people are robbed and left in the desert to die, a land where people drown crossing rivers. And yet, nothing happened to me or any of my relatives. *[Image of Santa Clara University]* And here I was, in a "safe place," a land full of palm trees, rose bushes, and water fountains, a private Catholic university where I was spending my days and nights receiving an education. A place I considered home. A place my familia considered my best chance for a better future. And yet, I, Carlos, was severely beaten. And not because I was a foreigner, or an "illegal" immigrant, or a minority who was ruining the country's economy, no! I was beaten because I am gay. And that is the irony of the situation, that in the place where I felt most safe, most happy, and most protected, I am constantly reminded that I am not entirely welcome in the "land of the free." Sometimes your friends can become your worst enemies.

And that, my friends, is called "dramatic irony," used by the best playwrights because, well … It is ironic. Isn't it?

6. Puro Católico

(Mozart's Laudate Dominum is heard. Image of La Virgen de Guadalupe.)
(As a chant) 95% of the Mexican population is born Catholic;
the other five per cent is going to hell. Amen.

At least that is what, abuelita, my grandmother told me when I was a little mocoso. She also told me that if I wanted to go to heaven, believing in God was not enough. She said that in order to go to heaven, I also needed to believe in the Virgen of Guadalupe, for she was the mother of God, and I also needed to obey what His Holiness the Pope commanded. Otherwise, I was going to burn in the eternal fires of hell. Oh yeah, my abuelita's words were always sweet and very effective.

Level número siete.

"Carlitos, mijo, ven aquí, mi niño. Sabes, si te quieres ir al cielo, creer en Dios no es suficiente. No mijo. Si te quieres ir al cielo, también tienes que creer en la Virgen de Guadalupe porque ella es la madre de Dios. Si mijo, y también tienes que obedecer *[image of John VI]* lo que Su Santidad el Papa diga, sino, pues te condenarás en los fuegos infernales ... ales ... ales ... ales..."

Needless to say, I peed in my pants. Every member of my familia is a true believer: Católico, Apostólico, y Guadalupano.

Just to make sure we all understood the importance of our Catholic religion, mi abuelita gathered us every evening to recite the rosary. And because, thanks to Adam and Eve and Catholic dogma, we were all born in sin, my abuelita made all of us recite the entire Rosary on our knees. It was a form of sacrifice and redemption, a "two for one" special.

She believed the rosary needed to be done right at sunset. Unfortunately, that was the time when all the kids from the barrio came out of their casas to play games. She never quite understood that taking us away from our games was sacrifice enough. Or maybe she knew it and she was only sharing her good Catholic guilt. She was so good at Catholic guilt and sacrifices that if for some reason any of my cousins or my brothers or I were involved in a fight or were disobedient at rosary time, she would place a small brick on our hands. And we had to hold those two bricks while kneeling and reciting the entire rosary, which usually lasted thirty to forty minutes, depending on which version she was using that particular evening. Come to think of it, every time I had to hold the bricks, my abuelita used the "uncut" version of the rosary because those prayers were long. According to my abuelita, a true descendent of the Aztecas, being physically punished by an elder was not enough. If I ever doubted I was a descendent of the Moctezuma, believe me, she would remind me of it.

Pero no me mal interpreten. Mi abuelita fué una persona muy buena. She was the sweetest lady in my entire family. Her devotion to the Catholic Church was nothing else but her own beliefs, which she inherited from her mother, who inherited them from her mother, who inherited from her mother, and so on. If I seem to have problems with any religious beliefs, it is not because of my grandma. No, mi abuelita taught me the good things about her Catholic faith. My disagreements are rooted in my own personal experiences. After all, I went to catholic school all my life, from kindergarten all the way until I came to this country. And even when I went to college, I chose to go to a Catholic university, for God's sake! I tell ya, the rumors about how most Mexicans like to become martyrs are true. And if you don't believe me, just watch a Mexican telenovela.

Time for a lesson in Mexican Spanish:

In Spanish, "Telenovela" means "soap opera." But unlike American soaps, Mexican novelas have a beginning, a middle, and an end. Example: Man and Woman meet. Man and Woman fall in love. Man and Woman get married and live happily. Two weeks after that, Man goes out for cigarettes. He meets New Woman and has an affair. Wife finds out and goes into the already expected and obligatory "crying and suffering" period while Man continues to have not one, but two or three different affairs, because the more affairs he has, the more macho he becomes. In the mean time, Wife continues to cry and to suffer, waiting for her lover to return, not daring to even look at the picture of another man 'cause if she does, she's a total whore.

Another example:

[Interactive video montage, recorded: the male part. Live: the female part played by the actor. Or the actor can play the two roles live.]

"Pero José Raúl, ¿Cómo me puedes hacerme esto? ¿Cómo te puedes acostar con María Consuelo, con mi propia hermana? ¿Cómo? Tú ... tú ... bastardo, ingrato."

"Así es la vida, Maria Ignacia. C'est la vie! Y eso no es todo, María Ignacia, I was going to save this melodramatic news for another episode, but I might as well tell you now."

"¿Qué? ¿Qué tienes que decirme, desgraciado?"

"Your sister María Consuelo and I got married the day after you and I came back from our honeymoon."

"No, no, no es verdad."

"Sí, it is true. And that's not all, está embarazada, with my child."

"No! No! Nooo!"

"Sí! Sí! Siii! Well, I'm off to the office. María Lourdes called me. She says she has something very important to show me."

"Pero María Lourdes es tu secretary."

"I know. Oh, don't forget. Today is Tuesday and on Tuesdays I like to eat Pollo en mole for dinner. Don't forge,t woman! Hasta la vista, baby."

"NOOOOO! I hate you José Raúl. I hate you! I hate you! I hate you! But I love you too. I swear José Raúl, I, Maria Ignacia Guadalupe Consuelo Socorro del Llanto y Llanto y Chiquita Banana will seek revenge on you and everyone in your house. And as God is my witness, I will never go hungry again!" End of lesson.

We Mexicans eat that shit, man. We watch too many of those damn novelas, and we start to believe that our lives are a novela. If a relationship is going well, we find a way to sabotage it. And all so we can have some excitement in our lives because, somehow, in this messed up mind of ours, we think that if everything is good, if everything is well, and if everything smells like roses, we must step on fire and burn our feet, just like the conquistadores did to Cuahutémoc—yet another clear example that we are truly descendents of the Aztecas.

As you can see, the combination of being a novela watcher and a Catholic schoolboy, as well as my desire to explore other religions, has made me into the person I am today. I have many religion stories, stories such as the one when I was "born again" and the Holy Ghost descended upon me.

"And the Lord said ... and Jesus said ... and the Angels of the Lord came upon ... Incoming message from the 'big giant head.' In three, two, one."

(Voice over)
"One of you has a secret that must be confessed. Oh, Carlos, you must confess your darkest, deepest secret."

I knew what the Holy Ghost was talking about, so I confessed.

"Forgive me, Lord, for I have sinned. I masturbate three times a day ... seven days a week ... three hundred sixty-five days a year. Oh, and I'm gay too."

(Sound of an explosion and also an image of the atomic bomb.)

Suddenly, the entire congregation was quiet. So quiet, in fact that I felt like grabbing the pastor's microphone and announcing: "Your attention blue light shoppers. The Holy Ghost has left the building."

I don't know what I was expecting. All I know is that most of my "Christian" brothers started to avoid me, and soon I found myself sitting solo. I took that as a sign and never went back. I have many other religious stories. But I'm not going to bore you with the details, okay?

All you need to know is that I'm still a believer. I believe in God, but I don't have to go to church to prove it, and I don't feel guilty about it. I pray whenever I feel the desire to do so, and the best part is that I don't impose my spiritual beliefs onto anyone.

I believe in God.

[Image of Huitzilopochtli and Coyoloxhaqui]

I believe in Huitzilopochtli and Coyoloxhaqui, the Sun God and the Moon Goddess of my ancestors. I believe in the Four Hundred Gods of the South, which are the stars. *[Image of Coatlicue]* I believe in Cóatlicue, Mother Earth. And I know that my abuelita, now that she has gone away, understands why I'm not a true católico, apostólico, y Guadalupano. She understands my beliefs, and as part of the Four Hundred Gods of the South, she guides my way and contributes to my protection. That makes me very happy, and that's good enough for me.

7. Pendejo

(The English version of Ricky Martin's "Livin' La Vida Loca" is heard.)

I love that song. *(sings)* "Livin' la Vida Loca ..." You may or may not know this, but in this country that song reached the number one spot on two different music charts at the same time. ¡Sí en serio! The English version reached the number one spot in Billboard Top One Hundred. The Spanish version reached the number one spot in Billboard's Latino charts. Y eso no es todo; "Livin' la Vida Loca" became the number one song in Mexico, in Puerto Rico, in Latin America, in parts of Europe, in parts of Asia, and in many places I can't even pronounce. And that, my friends, is one of the benefits of being a "bicicleta."

Time for a lesson in Mexican Spanish: In Spanish, bicicleta means bicycle. Bicicleta also refers to someone who is bilingual, or bisexual, or both. Example: Hey, me gusta tu bicicleta, which translates to *[image of a bicycle]* "Hey, I like your bike." Another example: No me gustas por bicicleta, which basically means *[image of Anne Heche]* (*Very angry*) "You broke Ellen's heart, bitch!" (*To the audience*) Oh, sorry. I'm a friend of Ellen and ...

Some people say that being a "bicicleta" is a good thing because "you get the best of both worlds, man." But as I always say, he or she who serves two masters, sooner or later, is going to end up screwing with one of them. I mean, "screwing up with one of them." Sorry, mi English no good, me foreign country. Me poor immigrant. End of lesson.

Level número ocho.

My college years were the best years of my life despite the fact I was beaten up. Despite the fact that the Oklahoma City bombing happened around that time and two of my closest friends lost their parents in that unfortunate incident. Despite the fact that Selena, the Tex-Mex diva, was shot, and we Latino people lost a rising music star. Despite the fact that Hollywood turned my favorite video game, "Mortal Combat," into a bad movie. And despite the fact that Mariah Carey recorded two albums during my college years. Despite all of that, the most important thing I discovered was the fact that I am Mexican. No, really, it might sound funny or even strange, or even unbelievable, but the fact is that for a couple of years before I went to college, I started to deny my Mexican heritage. I became the ultimate "pendejo."

Time for a lesson in Mexican Spanish: Pendejo describes someone who is stupid or does something stupid. It is a common everyday word, and it's probably the least offensive Mexican curse. The Dictionary of the Royal Academy of the Spanish Language defines pendejo as a "pubic hair." The second definition of a pendejo is a coward. And then there are definitions according to country: In Argentina, a pendejo is a boy who is trying to act like an adult. In Colombia, El Salvador, and Chile, a pendejo is a fool or a drug dealer, in Cuba a pendejo is a coward, and in Mexico a pendejo is an idiot. End of lesson.

Most of us come to this country seeking the American Dream, and soon we find ourselves in the middle of a cultural battleground, facing racism, discrimination, and misunderstandings. So, soon many of us try to find ways to hide our backgrounds. For example, we might change our names from Alberto to Albert, from Jesús to Jesse, from Carlos to Charlie, from Enrique José Martín Morales to Ricky Martin. At the same time, some of us deny we are from México; we become Hawaiians or Europeans. I did. I told people I was born in España, de la región de Andalusia. As if that isn't enough, many of us try to change the color of our eyes, from black or brown to green, blue, or hazel. I mean, why not? For only $69.99 and a two-hour visit to Lenscrafters you can chose from a variety of colors, styles, and brand names. And I did! I wore colored contact lenses so I could make myself believe I was another "Americano" in Gringoland. It didn't matter if my eyes glowed in the dark. I had blue colored contact lenses 'cause I was a gringo and I was determined to let everyone else know my newborn identity. Man, my contact lenses were heavy in their coloration 'cause soon I believed I was fooling everyone when in reality I was blinded by my own pendejismo.

I was so blinded that in my first year of college, I met my public enemy number one: Movimiento Estudiantil Chicano de Aztlán—MEChA—a national Chicano student organization. They were so radical, so political, so angry, and so loud, that they immediately reminded me of one thing: Me!!! So we immediately clashed. MEChA became the number one guerilla group against me, and I became their number one vendido.

Time for a lesson in Mexican Spanish: Vendido refers to something that has been sold. Vendido also refers to a Mexican person, male or female, who decides to deny her own culture, heritage, and roots in order to pass for gringo, Hawaiian, or European. Example: He vendido mi bicicleta, which means, I have sold my bike. Another example: ¡Carlos, eres un vendido! Which means, Carlos, you're a sell-out-white-wash-Michael

Bolton-macaroni and cheese-peanut butter-and-jelly-sandwich-no rhythm-and-an-ultimate-white boy wannabe pendejo. End of lesson.

[*Image of Santa Clara University*] And so there I was, starting college at Santa Clara University. Everyday I found myself fighting against anything that could identify me as Mexican. There was no Mexican music in my collection. My favorite drink became seltzer water. I only ate Mexican food on special occasions and only at Taco Bell, the pinnacle of Mexican cuisine. I found myself arguing with MEChA because they were ... well ... racist. And my accent ... what accent? I didn't have an accent. In short, I was "Legally Blond" before Reese Witherspoon.

But then, he came into my life. He saw me as the lost sheep that I was and took me in his arms. He looked into my eyes and found the last hint of hope behind my plastic blue eyes. He rescued me; he saved me from my own self. He took my hand and guided me in the right direction. He healed my troubled soul with a simple smile, a simple touch, and a few words full of wisdom.

"Carlos, no seas pendejo. You're Mexican. No matter how long and how far you run, you can't escape who you are. You are what you are because God made you that way. And you should be proud to belong to a civilization full of Gods and Goddesses whose towns are made of stone and whose crowns are made of feathers. You are part of a world that died fighting for its own survival, a world which now cries to be remembered by its children. The sun, the moon, the earth, and the stars are your gods and the gods of your ancestors. En tí runs Aztec blood. Don't let it be discolored by anyone or anything. Tus abuelos worked in the fields, your mother still works in the fields, you yourself worked in the fields. Why run from who you are? Be out, be proud, be brown."

It was so easy and so simple. Just like that his words cleared my mind and gave me a sense of worthiness. That's what "El Pachuco" did to me the day he visited SCU. Except that [*image of EL Pachuco*] "El Pachuco" had no zoot suit and no calco shoes. Instead, he wore jeans and tennis shoes, and his name was [*image of James Olmos*] Edward James Olmos. That night I went to my room and threw away my year's supply of colored contact lenses. I wept, and fell asleep, remembering his black shiny eyes, his voice, and his wise words: "Carlos, no seas pendejo."

I knew I needed to go back to my Mexican roots, my Tenochtitlan. And so the cleansing began, and with it many problems. How to tell my family that I wasn't straight but gay. How to tell MEChA that blond wasn't my natural color. How to replace my Michael Bolton collection. No, wait, that was very easy. What wasn't easy was to truly accept myself.

I attended a workshop on personal identification and self-worth, and I was asked to choose an animal that would help me identify myself. Instead I chose *[Actor removes his shirt. Underneath he's wearing a cut off T-shirt of Marvin the Martian.]* "Marvin the Martian." He is an alien. I am an alien. He's from another planet. Most of the time, people look at me as if I am from another planet. I assure them that I'm just from another country. "Marvin the Martian" is always trying to take over the world, and although that's not my ultimate goal, it is a good motivation to keep on going. "Marvin the Martian" is always trying to force Bugs Bunny to take him to his leader. With the way things are today, I wish Bugs Bunny could take me to his leaders too. I have a few things I would like to say to them.

Now, if you wonder why I'm telling you about all this, it is for one single reason: Edward James Olmos, "El Pachuco," and Marvin the Martian became my holy trinity, the ones that helped me to be born again: A Chicano actor, a Chicano legend, and a Loony Toon. Crazy!!!

8. La Vestida

(The Spanish version of Patsy Cline's "Crazy," sang by Marisela is heard. It continues throughout.)

The first time I went to a gay nightclub, I was excited and scared all at the same time. However, nothing compares to the moment when, among all the people in the club, I was pointed out by a vestida who was singing on stage.

Time for a lesson in Mexican Spanish: In Spanish, Vestida means "to be dressed up." It also refers to a man who likes to dress up like a woman, in other words, a drag queen. Example: "Ay mi niña se ve tan bonita vestida así," which means, *[image of a young lady celebrating her Quinciañera]* "My little girl looks so pretty dressed up like that." Another example: "Ay niña, pero si eres toda una vestida," which basically means, *[image of the actor in drag]* "Girl, you are such a drag queen."

(If done right, the actor finishes speaking as the first music bridge starts. During the bridge, the actor becomes La Vestida, mimicking putting on makeup, a wig, and false breasts. Once the musical bridge is over, the actor joins the song, lip-synching till the end, then "she" addresses the audience.)

"Gracias, gracias y buenas noches tengan ustedes damas y caballeros! Yo soy su anfitriona 'La Condonera.' Bienvenidos a 'El Chile Relleno' donde todo es barato, incluyendo los hombres. Se siente tan bonito ver a tanta gente hermosa esta noche que me dan ganas de derramar una lágrima. Pero no lo voy hacer; se me arruina el maquillaje. Oh my God! ¿Y qué tenemos aquí? ¡Carne fresca, fresh meat, señores!! ¿Y cómo te llamas cariño? Ay, cálmate, niña no te estoy hablando a tí. A tí todo mundo te conoce, tú ya estás más corrida que un freeway. I'm talking to him! A tí, dhaling, ¿como te llamas? ¿Qué? Carlos? Carlos, Carlos, Carlos. Que nombre tan común es ese. No eres de aquí, ¿verdad? Es tu primera vez que vienes a este congal. Oh, honey, trust me. I know. Yo lo sé todo, todo, todo, todo, todo, todo. Oh, pero papi, no te pongas nervioso. I don't bite, not in this outfit. No te voy a morder … ahorita. Ay, pero sabes qué, mijo. Me caes bien y te voy a invitar una copa cuando termine con el show. Así que no te vayas a ir o a esconder. Porque te busco y te encuentro. Y entonces, no me hago responsable. Bueno, diviértanse. Y que Dios me los bendiga a todos. Hoy, mañana, y siempre. Y que reciban de mí siempre paz, mucha paz, pero sobretodo, mucho, pero mucho ¡Amor!" End of lesson.

And that's how I was welcomed into the gay nightlife. And no, nothing happened between la vestida and me. We simply became very good friends. La Vestida became a very strong influence in my life. She taught me how to walk in heels, how to hide certain parts of my body if I wanted to wear a dress. She taught me what it meant to be a diva like La Lupe, Selena, Barbra Streisand, Gloria Gaynor, Marisela, and Sir Elton John. But even though she taught me many things, "La Vestida" is not the only female influence in my life. I have plenty of female influences: my mamá, my abuelita, Mrs. Rosselli, Auntie Mame, Anzaldúa, and "La Llorona."

9. La Llorona

Time for a lesson in Mexican Spanish: In Spanish, La Llorona means "the weeping woman." And it is said that La Llorona, enraged by her husband's cheating, drowned her children in a river. Since then, La Llorona weeps for her children, walking the streets of every town, howling and looking for them: "ay mis hijos ... ay mis hijos." The story of La Llorona is so popular that poems, short stories, novels, songs, movies, and a TV series have been done with La Llorona in mind. Among parents and grandparents, the story of La Llorona has become the most important children's bedtime story. She even has her own song.

(We hear pre-recorded "corrido" music for La Llorona.)

"I want to thank the academy. I would like to dedicate this song to those drag queens, who spent hours every weekend trying to look like

La Lupe, Barbra Streisand, or Marisela, but most of them end up looking more like 'La Llorona' than anything else."

Salías del templo un día, Llorona cuando al pasar yo te vi.
Salías del templo un día, Llorona cuando al pasar yo te vi.
Hermoso Huipil llevabas, Llorona que La Virgen te creí.
Hermoso Huipil llevabas, Llorona que La Virgen te creí.

Ay, de mi, Llorona, Llorona, Llorona llévame al río.
Ay, de mi, Llorona, Llorona, Llorona llévame al río.
Tápame con tu rebozo, Llorona porque me muero de frío.
Tápame con tu rebozo, Llorona porque me muero de frío.

Dos besos llevo en el alma, Llorona, que no se apartan de mí.
Dos besos llevo en el alma, Llorona, que no se apartan de mí.
El último de mi madre, Llorona, y el primero que te dí.
El último de mi madre, Llorona, y el primero que te dí.

Ay, de mi, Llorona, Llorona de azul celeste.
Ay, de mi Llorona, Llorona de azul celeste.
No dejaré de quererte, Llorona, aunque la vida me cueste.
No dejaré de quererte, Llorona, aunque la vida me cueste ...

Thank you. Thank you. This song has way too many verses. And if I tried to sing all of them, we'd be here for a long time. Besides, this is not a PBS special or a Cinco de Mayo celebration, so moving on.

10. Mexnifesto

Enough of making a fool of myself and getting in trouble with my two brothers, my sister, my mamá, my tía, my three cousins, my two uncles, and a couple of friends.

Level número nueve.

I came to this country illegally, and I did not speak any English. Today I am a US citizen, a writer, a college teacher, an actor, a playwright, a theatre director, and whatever else I feel like being depending on the mood. I realized that if I ever get bored, I can always demand a "state government recall" and run for governor. Why not? If the "The Terminator" did it, why not "Marvin the Martian?" I assure you, I could become the first openly gay immigrant homosexual, with a very colorful political platform, and my advising team would be referred to as "the faggets."

Every day I hear that we immigrants come here to take away the jobs of "American People." Some people say we come here in search of the American Dream. Some people say that we are fugitives from our own country and we come here to hide. Some people say we are terrorists. As an immigrant, one day I'm one thing, the next day something else.

So who are we, anyway? Does it matter? Of course it does. In the forties we were Pachucos, in the seventies we became a "Frito Bandido in your house." By the eighties we turned into revolutionaries, in the nineties we became a "Yo Quiero Taco Bell" Chihuahua, and today, today we are your modern Mexican helper.

I've been trying to convince myself that I'm just another human being in this crazy world, full of crazy contradictions. But if I do that, I'll be fooling myself. We are not just another person in the world. WE ARE US!!! The undocumented immigrants walking in the downtown streets. We are the Campesinos, working the country's fields, picking pesticide-coated grapes and vegetables. We are the guys who clean your table at a restaurant, the ones that washes dishes in the back, and the ones who, most of the time, cook your meals when you go out to eat. We are the teachers struggling to keep our language alive. The citizens who refuse to accept proposition 187, who refuse to accept the Knight Initiative, and today we stand against proposition 8. We are the office employees who try not to be classified as "Hispanics." We are the actors who refuse to play the drug dealer or the gang member one more time. The critics who know we lack representation in the theatre, in the movies, and on TV. We are the neighbors who listen to Mariachi music, not because it is Cinco de Mayo but because it is our birthdays. We are the Latino people who dance to salsa, meringue, and cumbia music; the gay and lesbian Chicanos who dresse like Frida Khalo and Pachucos and go to gay clubs. We are the immigrants who come to this country, running away from revolutions, the Mexicans who come to live here for many reasons, but mostly to let you know that Taco Bell is NOT Mexican food, even if you think outside the bun.

We are that voice you hear day in and day out; that voice that reminds you WE ARE US, WE ARE HERE! And we are NOT going away.

[Image of the actor as a child]

My life is a video game with a background song playing over, and over, and over. In this game of life there are so many different levels to achieve, so many obstacles to pass, so many enemies to defeat, so much energy to gain. As the years go by, the game gets more complicated and more sophisticated. But I keep playing because I want to be able to write my name in the number one spot. And what do I call this game of life? The game of "la vida loca," of course! But don't ask me how the game ends because I don't know. I just keep playing, knowing that sooner or later the game will be over. By the time it ends, even if my name is not in the number one spot, at least I can say that I "played a good game." I know that the game of life has no guarantees. The only certain thing is that sooner or later the game will be over for each and every one of us. But hey, at least we can say that we played a good game. "La Vida Loca." What a great name for a cool video game. Don't you think?

Level número diez.

[Image of the actor in the present]

To be Continued ... Con safos!

END OF PLAY

Little Brown Heart

Gibrán Güido

In my room, cold and wet
I find myself thinking of you.

How the perversities that satisfy-ied
me will be the ones you'll be doing
With others.

How my feet turn cold and my heart begins to protest.
Thinking to myself, how could that be? ...
My heart in its jealous rage, not wanting to let you go ...
But my half-filled heart is in protest
because it's given so much to you.

Given so that this little brown heart of mine
wants to
beat to your desires.

This little brown heart of mine
has loved you so —
and it's known only you,

It's beat to
the love of your being
and placed your demands above its own —
knowing that its own will be half met.

Beat to
The scorn of not letting it into
your small circles of unity.

Beat to
The jealousy that it won't be
your object of devotion.
That another little heart—
will have its place.

But more than anything ...
little brown heart
At least we know
We weren't enough.

On Reclaiming Machismo

Xuan Carlos Espinoza-Cuellar

Brothers need to cry too
Let their anguish out through their eyes
Instead of living skin
Instead of wounded flesh

. . ..

I've seen my father's fists
Cry on my mama's face
I know
I've felt his tears
As they tore through my skin
I know
I heard his tears
Chocking me like a rope
Surrounding my neck
Incrusted in my soul
Provoking me to sleep ...
Sleep
Sleep
Sleep

. . ..

'cause only in my sleep
Could I dream, and dream on
I dreamed of smiling tears
That never slammed my door

. . ..

Brothers need to cry
Let their tears drop from their eyes
Instead of sending them traveling
Through smokes and silent plants

. . ..

I've seen my brother cry
I smelled his tears afar
Making his visions blurry
Making his voice more rough
(Like real men should talk)

. . ..

I've felt my brother's tears
And disenchanted dreams
My head bleeding and sore
His tears were nevermore
His hands crafted in me
A reminder of what can be
When tears are not let go

Section VI

Marifesto: The Black and
the Red of Jotería Studies

Out in the Field

Mariposas and Chicana/o Studies

Daniel Enrique Pérez

As is the case for all mariposas, crossing borders is a way of life. Continually traveling from one side to the other and back, never standing still, never feeling quite as if we truly belong anywhere, while trying to learn the skills to survive and shine in all of the various spaces we inhabit. We are chameleons of sorts—adapting to our environment while maintaining our own identity. Our wings mark us as the most beautiful among our species, yet we have been silenced, abused, and made to feel ashamed of what we are.

Rich in Texan blood and dark skin, I was born in abject poverty. My parents were also Tejanos and migrant farmworkers—always on the go, searching for fields that were ready to be harvested. Their migrations led them to Phoenix, a place where farmworkers could usually find work year round. My parents divorced when I was nine, and I was raised in the onion fields outside of the Phoenix area by my mother. With hands too small to wear gloves, I reeked of onions at school and often became the target of cruel classmates who teased me for being poor, an onion picker, and on welfare. I learned at an early age how to fight, but it was not until years later that I learned how to be proud of all the things that make me who I am.

In school, my first love was math; it was a beautiful subject. Perhaps learning how to count green onion manojos by the dozen paid off. Math was one of the few subjects in high school that was somewhat free of cultural biases. I enjoyed getting lost in numbers, equations, and geometric figures. I began to see math as a universal language where it didn't matter that I didn't speak English or Spanish very well. It mesmerized me to think that everyone in the world spoke this language, and so I was eager to learn it well.

I was lucky to have a high school teacher, Ms. Shirley Filliator, recognize my math aptitude. I was in her pre-calculus course my last year in high school, and when I graduated, she gave me a fifty-dollar scholarship—perhaps one of the most significant investments anyone other than my parents has made in me. If Ms. Filliator believed in my math aptitude enough to give me fifty whole dollars, then I must be good at math, I believed. During my undergraduate studies, every time I was on the verge of quitting, I thought of Ms. Filliator and the fifty-dollar scholarship. I was filled with doubt about my presence at Arizona State University, especially when I was often the only Chicano in so many of my math classes, not to mention the only queer as far as I knew.

While I completed my B.A. in Mathematics, I also did a minor in Spanish, where I was introduced to my first courses in Chicana and Chicano Studies. For once in my life I was learning about my own history and culture and reading literature written by my own people. Chicana and Chicano texts validated my existence as a queer Chicano. They provided visibility and a voice to an identity within me that was struggling to materialize. They described a space that I was anxious to explore and that felt like home. The first Chicano novel I read was José Antonio Villarreal's *Pocho*. To this date, when I see the novel, I see myself on the front cover—the resemblance to me as a child is startling. I connected with Richard Rubio in a very intimate way. After years of reading and rereading the novel, I finally understand why—Richard Rubio is queer, like me. He is one of several characters I claim as queer in my book *Rethinking Chicana and Chicano Popular Culture*, where I conduct queer analyses of a number of our cultural texts to expand the breadth of queer visibility in Chicana and Chicano Studies.

Discovering Gloria Anzaldúa and Cherríe Moraga was a way to explore other aspects of my history and my identity. They provided me with the tools I needed to revisit my childhood and understand my family and my culture. I devoured all the books I could get my hands on that confirmed that there were others who shared a history and an identity with me. The experience was so transformative that I decided to dedicate the rest of my life to the field. I had to continue to explore these spaces, these voices. I also felt a strong desire—perhaps even an obligation—to share this experience with others in order to advance our people and our communities.

Besides teaching me about myself and my gente, Chicana and Chicano authors taught me how to love myself and how to accept every aspect of my identity. As is the case with many maricones, I too hated myself and was suicidal for most of my youth. I could not look at myself in the mirror without wanting to run my fist through it, take a piece of glass, and hurt myself. I could not hold a sharp object of any sort without contemplating stabbing myself. I constantly reminded myself how fat, ugly, poor, and abnormal I was. I wrote the letters and made the plans that many of us make to end our lives early. The person who kept me from following through with any such plans was my mother— not because she ever knew what I was going through, but because she loved me so much and depended on me so much that I knew she would not survive my death. I could kill myself; however, I could not kill my mother.

The only queer role models I had in my family were a great uncle and a second cousin—both lived in Fortworth, Texas, and rarely visited us in Phoenix. Elías, my mother's tío, was an alcoholic. I did not get to know him very well because we were never to be left alone with him. Although they seldom called him names when he was present, when he was not present he was a pinche maricón, puto, joto, and chupa verga. When he visited Phoenix he would occasionally go out at night on his own, but I never knew where or with whom. The chisme that spread while he was out that evening or throughout the next day made it clear that he was out puteando, which I did not fully comprehend as a child. I never saw him as anything other than the distant uncle who was single, an alcoholic, dangerous, and the target of endless homophobic jokes.

When I was thirteen, I met my second cousin, Esteban, through a picture in my grandmother's house; he was approximately my age. He was dressed in a crisp white shirt with a red sash draped over his shoulders, and he held a saxophone to his chest. From the moment I saw his picture, I fell in love with him. I fantasized about meeting Esteban in person, but he rarely visited Phoenix. On the other hand, Dominga, his mother, visited often and always talked about him. I hung on to her every word, waiting for any bit of information she might divulge.

When we were both in our early twenties, Esteban was finally on his way to Phoenix. By this time, my family knew that Esteban was gay. Although Dominga still never discussed her son's sexuality openly, the rumors had spread. It was also rumored that he was sick, and that that was the reason why he and his mother were moving to Phoenix.

Once again, my family was eager to protect me. When he arrived, I was shocked to discover that the handsome young man I had fallen in love with in the picture was not the young man who now lived in my neighborhood. He had also become an alcoholic and was not in good health. My mother and my aunts refused to leave us alone together. Any time Esteban was around, they would cling to me as if to protect me from a monster. They would strategize to keep us apart, and we never had a private moment together. I wanted to talk to him about being gay, but my tías and my mother made sure I never had the opportunity to have such an intimate conversation with him.

The closest I ever got to Esteban was on his deathbed at Good Samaritan Hospital in Phoenix; we were approximately twenty-two years old. According to Dominga, Esteban had una enfermedad de los pulmones, but we all knew it was AIDS. This was during the late eighties, when being diagnosed with the disease was basically a death sentence. I can still see his sunken face and big eyes. I can still feel the bones in his hands, the only time I touched him. I can also hear his gasps for breath, his cries for help. When I think about Esteban, I try to focus on the picture of him at thirteen, a young Adonis, but I will never forget the last time I saw his face in that hospital. His life as a gay man was ending at twenty-two, while mine was just beginning.

I told my mother I was gay approximately one year after Esteban's death. I was twenty-three and still at ASU. For the first time, I was living with a "friend" and "roommate"—Jesús Barrón. My mother had met Jesús, and they were getting along very well. I was under the impression that she knew that Jesús was my lover because by this time most of my family had stopped asking the "When are you going to get married?" question. In retrospect, I rarely really shared intimate aspects of my life with my mother. I could not tell her when I was head over heels in love or upset because Jesús and I had had an argument. However, my mother and I had developed a very good relationship; she was sharing things with me that I never imagined had happened to her, and I wanted to be as open and honest with her as I could about my life. When I finally worked up the strength to say, "Ma, I'm gay," she began to cry. When she could finally speak, she began asking the standard questions: "How?" and "What did I do wrong?" I tried to explain that it was not her fault, that I didn't choose to be gay, and that there were enough studies to prove that it was genetic. Nevertheless, she continued to cry. I'm sure she immediately thought about Esteban and associated being gay with AIDS and death. I assured her that I was healthy and happy.

I never feared that my mother would disown me or that her love for me would diminish. I think the greatest fear was that she would be disappointed and that she would worry about me. Overall, having that conversation with her was a positive experience. Within a year she came to terms with her son being gay, and our relationship was stronger than ever. All of the silences that prevented us from knowing one another fully were shattered, and the most important person in my life knew who and what I really was. At one point, she told me that she was proud of me and that she wanted to tell everyone—meaning her entire side of the family—that I was gay. I told her that if she wanted to, she should feel free to tell anyone but that it didn't matter to me. The most important thing to me at that time was that she knew.

After completing my B.A., I knew I had to continue with my education, but I had little knowledge of what graduate school involved, much less where I could do a graduate degree in Chicana/o literature. At the time, there was not a graduate program specifically in Chicano Studies as far as I knew, but I did know Chicano Studies courses were offered in both English and Spanish programs in their respective departments. I decided to apply to M.A. programs in both areas.

The Spanish program at ASU in the Department of Languages and Literatures (now the School of International Letters and Cultures) offered me a teaching assistantship along with a tuition waiver; naturally, that is where I decided to go. Somehow, I got it into my head that I would do comparative literature. I had no clue what it was or what it involved, I just knew that I did not want to be limited to a Spanish program or an English program. This was my way to remain in the liminal space that I had become so accustomed to inhabiting. This is how I straddled both worlds and created my own queer Chicano space in academia.

After completing my M.A., I decided to do the Ph.D. in Spanish at ASU because, again, it was the best offer—teaching assistantship, tuition, etc. However, I also wanted to develop my creative writing skills, so I decided to do a subspecialization in creative writing. I was lucky to have advisors who never told me I couldn't do something. They always trusted my judgment and allowed me to virtually develop my own program. They supported me in my research and my chosen coursework. In many ways, I was spoiled by my mentors. They protected me and created a safe space for me. They encouraged me to do the research I was interested in doing no matter how escandaloso I was, and I was ecstatic to finally be given such an opportunity. I intentionally placed faculty from other departments on my committees so that I could continue to develop my queer Chicano space. All along, my research leaned towards the intersections of Chicana/o Studies, Latin American Studies, Queer Theory, and Feminist Theory.

In graduate school, I learned the importance of networking and being "present." As a graduate student I very much wanted to become a part of the department culture. In retrospect, I understand that many of the opportunities that I was given for advancing as a graduate student and getting scholarships, fellowships, and teaching gigs happened because I just happened to be around the department a whole lot. When you are hanging around the department so much and a faculty member gets information about a scholarship or fellowship, they are much more likely to share it with you or encourage you to apply for it. I truly did not have access to any magical database, Internet sites, or one person who informed me about the many opportunities for securing funding for my graduate education. Like many, I often had no idea how I would get by the next semester. What I did have was a good working relationship with my mentors so that they kept me in mind when these opportunities arose.

An important lesson I learned from my participation in the Preparing Future Faculty program at ASU was how to start visualizing myself as a faculty member. Many of us tend to have this impression that there is a monumental barrier that stands between graduate students and faculty. For many years I had allowed myself to accept that I was "only a graduate student" until I got that Ph.D. In some departments an "us–them" culture may be the norm; however, I can't say that it was the culture at ASU. I can see now that for the most part I created it myself. As professionals, we should always be treated as such. It was not until I began visualizing myself as a faculty member that I began being treated as a faculty member. It required a "de-linking" or "de-programming" of sorts. After all, the people I had chosen to work with throughout my program of study always treated me with respect and always valued what I had to contribute. I'm certain I chose faculty members who recognized the potential in me to be my mentors because they treated me as a colleague and not always as a student. I wanted to learn from them, but they also made it clear that they wanted to learn from me. It is this sort of exchange with these types of people that one needs to cultivate and maintain.

When I was ready to conduct the job search, I knew, above all, that I had to be true to myself. I had to be open and up front about my queer Chicano/Latino research agenda and identity. I was not willing to go to an institution that had a homophobic or racist environment. I was prepared not to take a job anywhere and do something outside of academia with my Ph.D. My CV might have best been described as hyperqueer, with the terms *queer, joto,* and *homosexual* scattered throughout the titles of various publications, research projects, and presentations I had done at conferences. At the risk of limiting my job prospects, I hid nothing.

When I was ready to get on the job market in search of a tenure-track job, I applied to over thirty schools; I got four interviews. I noticed a pattern among those schools that granted me an interview. In each, there was at least one member of the search committee who was gay. It became obvious to me that I got those interviews because those gay members advocated on my behalf. In an unusual rejection letter that I received after an interview at MLA, the committee chair confessed that my application was very strong and that I was an outstanding candidate. He also named two faculty members (not including himself) who admired my work and who advocated strongly on my behalf. It was absolutely no surprise to me that they were both openly gay.

I began a tenure-track position at the University of Nevada, Reno in the fall of 2004. It has been a veritable rollercoaster ride. As a faculty member of color in a predominantly white institution, I get asked to do a slew of things that the majority of faculty members do not. If there is an event, committee, or research project related to diversity, I am often contacted and asked to participate. I am asked to speak on many occasions, serve on committees, or attend functions that center on tino, queer, feminist, gender, or several other diversity issues. I get calls during any holiday that has to do with Latino culture or any issue in the news that has to do with Latinos: immigration, Cinco de Mayo, the 300 millionth American, racial profiling, latino voters, ICE raids, how to pronounce "Nevada," etc. As a feminist and queer faculty member, I get an equal number of invitations from all the queer and feminist groups and events in my community: panels for National Coming Out Day, Brown Bag discussions on sexuality, protests to demand domestic partners benefits, Women Without Borders events, and vigils for fallen warriors.

One of the most difficult lessons I have had to learn is how to say no to protect myself from the double workload that exists for faculty of color—a workload that is even greater for queer faculty of color, especially those of us who have a commitment to social justice and social transformation. One of the biggest challenges has been setting aside time to do my research. Somewhere in the midst of developing new courses and programs, serving on multiple committees, giving talks, and mentoring and teaching countless students, I try to focus on my research. I understand the importance of doing Queer Chicano Studies. There are so many areas in the field that remain to be explored and explained. We have gaps in our theory and in our history that must be filled. And so I continue to write, produce, and contribute to these dialogues in order to advance this causa, mi gente.

Having mentors along this journey has been one of the most important aspects of my success in the field. We all need mentors, no matter how far along we may have advanced in the system. We all need to interact with others, especially our own people, in order to truly flourish. We need to create strong networks of people who will help us and support us in various ways. I depend highly on the advice of senior scholars in my field, and I have been able to create a community of friends and colleagues who help me survive at UNR, where I am the only Chicano faculty member in the entire university. As such, I feel a tremendous responsibility to a large number of students, faculty, staff, and communities. I'm a mentor to many but I also still need to be mentored.

In Austin, on March 21, 2008, I read the poem below, which I wrote to honor the madrinas and padrinos who have been key allies through-out the history of the National Association for Chicana and Chicano Studies (NACCS) Joto Caucus. We were celebrating the fifteenth an-niversary of the caucus, and we decided to have a quinceañera during the NACCS annual conference. I dedicate this poem to all the madrinas and padrinos who have ever mentored jotos.

Poema a las Madrinas y a los Padrinos

Madrinas, Padrinos,
Thank you
for showing us
the true meaning
of a Queer Aztlán
where jotería,
veteranos
y todos los atravesados walk
hand in hand
mano a mano.

Thank you
for sheltering us
detrás de la falda
when we needed
to retreat.

For protecting us
from El Cucuy
El Chupa Cabras
El Diablo, La Religión.

Madrina, Padrino,
Thank you
for showing me
that I too
had a history
a culture
a home.

For introducing me
to mi Mamá
La Mera Mera
y toda la bonche
de jotería
mi familia
mi gente preciosa
my queer raza.

Thank you
for letting me
be me
no matter
how escandaloso
i was.

For accepting
me y toda mi
mariconada
como si nada
importara más
que el amor.

Thank you
for teaching me
how to tirar chingazos

when it was necessary
and how to love my enemies
to death
in order to cultivar
peace
justicia
y cambio social.

Thank you
for teaching me
how to stand
tall and say
con todo orgullo:
Soy
Marica
Joto
Maricón
Puto
Desvergonzado
Mariposa
Mamón
Torcido
Chupa Verga
Atravesado
¿Y Qué?
¿Y Qué?

Madrinas, Padrinos,
Thank you
for showing us
that God
is not a man
but a beautiful human being
in each of us

And that we
are the chosen ones:
Los Descolonizados
Los Iluminados
Los Bautizados
Creadores
Of a Xueer Aztlán.

When I am near my madrinas or padrinos, or with other maricones, I feel bold and empowered, as in this poem. At NACCS, when the Joto Caucus members get together, we flourish. We are also probably much louder and more visible than we typically are in our respective communities. At NACCS in New Brunswick in April of 2009, I recall the Saturday evening I went out with a few Joto Caucus members to a gay bar to celebrate the end of the conference. We had made much progress getting ourselves organized, mentoring our newest members, relishing in each other's company, and planning research projects and events. When we arrived at the Hyatt via taxi late in the evening, there was a group of Indian-American men smoking in front of the hotel. I arrived in the first taxi along with Jaime García and Carlos Manuel Chavarría; the three of us entered the hotel lobby. The second taxi was carrying Eddy Alvarez and two other NACCS members. When the second group walked in, Eddy was upset because the men in front of the hotel were intentionally making homophobic remarks when he and the others were exiting the cab and entering the hotel. While we were all discussing the incident, the men walked into the hotel, and we eventually walked by them when we were ready to turn in for the evening. I happened to be at the very end of our group, and after we passed them, one of them exclaimed, "Hello, gay people!" I think I was the only one who heard him. I turned around immediately, smiled at him, and winked—my silent but daring act of resistance. I felt empowered enough in our group of jotos to commit such an act; I doubt I would have done such a thing if I were alone. I didn't tell the rest of the group what the guy said nor what I did, but later, restless in bed, I pondered all of the other things I could have said and done; I also imagined our confrontation turning into a bloody melee—the jotos against the homophobes. It was a disheartening way to end such a wonderful and empowering conference, but it was also a very real reminder of the amount of homophobia we still face, no matter how empowered or safe we may feel.

I recently submitted my tenure file for review, and I feel confident that I will be granted tenure. Nevertheless, as I know is the case for most mariposas, I often think about quitting academia. All along I have wondered if this space is really for me. In my conversations with other Chicanas and Chicanos at various levels in the pipeline, I now understand that it is natural and very common to do this. During those times when I want to give up, I think about all of the young jotitos who are going through all of the challenges I have faced. I think about my current students—the Chicanas and Chicanos who need me to be there for them so that they can have the privilege of discovering themselves. I think about my undergraduate student, David Torres, who submitted a short story in one of my courses, which he titled "Stage Two Fag"; in it, he describes his transition from a Stage One Fag, "when you first start dating and you're not slutty because you hope to find another boy who isn't slutty and you boys want to live together in your non-slutty world" to a Stage Two Fag, which is about "getting over the fear of touching another body," "letting go and accepting yourself," and "putting yourself out there and taking a risk." I feel honored to have created a space for him, for us, to express our true selves in all of our mariconadas.

There is no singular experience for queer Chicanos. There's never one way to do some of the difficult things that we must do to affirm our identities in the various spaces we inhabit throughout our lives. We will inevitably have doubts along the way about our own skills and our participation in various academic spaces. I hear it all the time: "Am I in the right program? Do I really want to do this? Is it worth it?" I can honestly say that nine times out of ten the answer is "Yes!" Certainly, the workload can be taxing, the responsibilities are enormous, and the stress can be even greater as you ascend the academic ladder; however, you learn how to manage the stress better, you learn how to be at home and in your element, you learn how to create safe and fruitful spaces for yourself and for others to soar in all their glory.

Being Chicano and being queer means you are transgressive no matter where you go. As queer Chicanos, we fit in nowhere and we fit in everywhere. Flourishing in the academy is not something that anyone can do alone. We need a supportive, safe, and friendly community to be the mariposas we have the potential to be. We must continue to cultivate the Queer Aztlán that Cherríe Moraga called for in 1993—a space free from homophobia, racism, and misogyny. We need to feel free to spread our wings and fly wherever we must go, and we need to know that we can land safely in unchartered territories so that we can continue to build our homeland.

Gil Cuadros' Azt-Land

Documenting a Queer Chicano Literary Heritage

Pablo Alvarez

W hen I first discovered, at sixteen years of age, that the local bookstore had a section of gay and lesbian authors, I immediately made it a ritual every third Monday of the month to look for my queer Chicano brother writers and share in their passion for storytelling. I had just passed my driver's test, and the California State Department of Motor Vehicles had given me the opportunity to explore the city's bookstores on my own. The bookstores were my home away from home. They were the places where I would escape in search of peace, comfort, and knowledge.

In the "Hispanic" section I came across such classics as *Y No Se Lo Trago La Tierra* by Tomas Rivera and Rodolfo Anaya's *Bless Me Ultima*. From the "Hispanic" section I would locate the Women's Studies section, where I read through the pages of bell hooks's *Ain't I a Woman* or *Talking Back*. After gaining awareness and determination from hooks, I could move on to the gay and lesbian section. At the gay and lesbian section I would scan the titles in search of any word that would spark a Mexican sentiment. Switching strategies, I would glide my index finger across the author's names, searching for familiar Mexican last names. Unfortunately, this strategy let me miss John Rechy's classic novels, as I was limiting my awareness by judging a book by its author's last name.

"Will I ever find a queer Chicano writer?" I asked myself after disappointed departures from late evenings of searching books that spoke to my queer Chicano experiences. Then the day finally came when my index finger stopped at the last name of Cuadros. I slid the book out of its slot, read the title *City of God,* and felt a familiarity with the front cover of the book design. The image of an upside down city landscape (presumably Los Angeles) filled the top half of the cover, and the bottom half detailed rows of lit candles inside tall glass containers displaying the image of the Sacred Heart of Jesus, like the kind of candles my mother always brought home from the local *carnecería* and kept lit every evening on the kitchen table. The entire backdrop of the cover constituted a late evening in the city. At the center was the writer's full name, Gil Cuadros. And on the first page, first paragraph, I read the word Mexico.

I drove home that night captivated by the pages I read while waiting at red lights. Cuadros's short stories and poetry reflected a reality that I understood. The language and the imagery, with each sentence and stanza, inspired nostalgia. Simultaneously, I read the pages in secret. Certain stories were difficult for me to read because they spoke to my own desires and fears. My reading of *City of God* became a ceremonious act. As the reader, I became engaged in the creation of Cuadros's narrative. Every range of emotion was triggered with each turning of a page. My reading of *City of God* was composed of dreams and deceptions that merged with notions of hopes and awakenings. Cuadros's work also allowed me to question how identity had been distorted in my previous academic reading of Chicano sexuality. The objectification and eroticization of the queer Chicano had been erased from Cuadros's *City of God.* I began a dialectical relationship between the reading and the writing that fueled my search for other queer Chicano artists, specifically, other queer Chicano writers who incorporated the sacredness of their sexuality with their spirituality.

When I started researching queer Chicano writers through the McNair Scholars Program at California State University, Long Beach in 1998, about ninety percent of the time the work came to me in the form of disease and sexual positioning. The literature I read replicated the works of social scientists that embarked on understanding queer Chicano sexuality through a Euro-American lens insensitive to languages and cultures. Social scientists borrowed from critical theories that reflected the privileging of an American gay movement. These social scientists did not allow for the sacredness in sexuality to exist within a queer Chicano experience. The elements that Cuadros utilizes in his writing expand the notion of queer Chicano identity and reject previous attempts that misrepresent the realities of queer Chicano men. Cuadros's writing encompasses a spiritual and sacred world of sexuality and creativity that is not found in most literature presenting queer Chicano experiences and identity. Cuadros utilizes literary tools such as social realism to highlight Chicano identity during a critical time for men living with HIV in Los Angeles in the 1990s. His work encompasses the elements of border identity, traditional family life, and the complexities of a queer Chicano identity within an Anglo gay landscape. His writing promotes Gloria Anzaldua's idea of translating theories into *teorias,* making theories that complement Chicana and Chicano reality in an accessible, creative, and strategic manner.

Cuadros's writing on queer Chicano sexuality and AIDS is a crossing of borders between his Mexican family and white culture. Spiritually and politically, Cuadros tells the story of a Queer Chicano growing up in the cities surrounding Los Angeles while living with AIDS on the battlegrounds of his Aztlán. In an interview documented in the 1994 April issue of *Positive Living,* before the publishing of *City of God,* Cuadros reflects,

> One of my favorite of my own stories, one not yet published, is called "My Aztlán." I chose the title because it had a kind of Chicano-studies feel to it, like a school essay, and in it is an essay about my life. Even though it's been fictionalized, it's very much about who I am and how I grew up and the city I live in—with AIDS. There's also a kind of an in-joke, because in the language of the people native to this region Aztlán

means "white place," but I also see it as "AZT-Land." It's the story of a gay Chicano male who lives in a white city that has literally been built above the one he's native to, with freeways laid over the neighborhood where he was born. The freeways are part of the interconnectedness of the city, and also the structure of the story. (3 &11)

For many Chicano/as Aztlán continues to be a place of reflection, meditation, and resistance. For Cuadros, it is a place where AIDS (AZT-Land) is also present, which complicates the romanticized notion of Aztlán and simultaneously contradicts the constructs of a Chicano identity. As a writer, he incorporates the roots of his resistance with the political awareness of location and the spaces he occupies. In addition, Cuadros utilizes the structure of his city and the connectedness of its freeways to serve as departures for his writing. He places his Aztlán buried underneath the 710 Freeway, and built upon it is a white world, one that sometimes is in conflict with his Mexican upbringing. Simultaneously, Cuadros confronts identity and race instantly and challenges not only the white world built above his but challenges the Mexican family buried underneath it. The mythical, magical, and material spaces of his location enable Cuadros to demonstrate how limitless writing can be in both the material and spirituality realms. While tracing historical changes, Cuadros incorporates his ancestry into his writing to reinforce his identity as a Chicano artist who reclaims his family: "... this is my Aztlán, a glimpse of my ancient home, my family ... Like the house, these words spiral in on themselves, stab into the moist earth ..." (55).

Cuadros's narrative voice returns to Aztlán with truth about his sexuality and HIV. From the blurred vision of West Hollywood bars where "Their fingers are pale compared to my darker skin. They run them down my neck, under my lapel. They ask where I'm from, Disappointed at my answer, as if *they*, are the natives" (53) to the street lights reflecting off the City Terrace Drive freeway exit to his neighborhood, where

"I imagine the house still intact, buried under dirt and asphalt, dust and neglect. Hidden under a modern city ..." (55).

In 1994 I met my queer community at the Silver Lake Junction festival in Los Angeles. It was the summer of my senior year, and I was invited by my cousin to volunteer and register people for the APLA Walk-A-Thon. I hadn't known about gay pride festivals, and my only identification with gay men was by watching them on TV talk shows like Geraldo and Donahue. Typically, these men were white with a terrible sense of fashion and a traumatic past; I didn't believe that I was just like them. So when I walked into the Silver Lake Junction, as an APLA volunteer, I clearly knew I had found other members of my queer community of color. Up until this point I didn't realize the LGBT community existed outside of the exploitation and misrepresentations of mainstream media. I quickly and lovingly created distance between my cousin and me. I took my clipboard with registration forms to another location at the festival and explored the community I was searching for. On our way home, my cousin seemed surprised but not apologetic, saying she had no idea we were going to a gay event. That might have been both of our first times at a pride festival. I went back the following day and the following year.

When I came out to my *familia*, my mother's first and greatest concern was, and is today, her fear that I will one day test positive. Her fear is real, and each time she senses that I have caught a cold or some virus impairing my health she looks at me, deep into me, asking, "*Que tienes, estas enfermo? Dime, Pablo.*" I talk her down with silliness, but my mother will always have this real fear inspired mostly by the way we have been conditioned to view AIDS. David Roman is one writer who addresses these failings by referencing AIDS cultural critic Douglas Crimp in *Acts Of Intervention: Performance, Gay Culture, and AIDS*:

> Douglas Crimp discusses the ramifications of this conflation of AIDS and gay men when he states that [w]hat is far more significant than the real *facts* of HIV transmission in

> various populations throughout the world, however, is the initial conceptualization of AIDS as a syndrome affecting gay men ... The idea of AIDS as a gay disease occasioned two *interconnected* conditions in the U.S.: that AIDS would be an epidemic of stigmatization rooted in homophobia, and that the response to AIDS would depend in very large measure on the ... gay movement .... (xxiii)

AIDS activism initially opened the doors for me to explore and be close to the gay and lesbian community. Being an APLA volunteer allowed me to be in or near the queer community without having to "officially" out myself as a queer Chicano. I took that activism into the classroom, and later that year, now a junior in high school, I made a class presentation on AIDS in my US history course. It was obvious that the majority of students hardly knew anything about AIDS, nor did my history teacher, and mostly what they knew was in reference to gay men and Africa, a clear indication of the prevailing racist and homophobic ideologies delegated by the powers that be.

My first HIV test took place at a free clinic in the city of Norwalk, California, in 1995. I went with my oldest brother, who wanted to be tested. Because he knew I was doing AIDS volunteer work, he trusted that I would understand. We went through the process together, and we both waited together for the results without knowing exactly the complexities of AIDS and how we would be understood. My initial understanding and activism regarding AIDS had also brought me closer to my brother. At the same time, however, we never spoke about our experience. It was like a matter of fact; we went in, gave blood, waited a week, tested negative, and never spoke about it again, and it is this type of silence that continues to disrupt our understanding and reinforces the silences regarding HIV/AIDS.

Cuadros's writing illustrates how creativity informs identity. He incorporates the sacredness of sexuality into his writing. Cuadros's short stories and poetry reflect how the creative act of writing promotes social and cultural survival in a time of great loss. The sacredness in sexuality and spirituality is manifested between the writer and the reader. The act of reading as ceremonious is vital to the writer's creation and illuminates my own identity as a queer Chicano on a spiritual journey.

Being in a ceremonious relation to the act of reading is familiar to my Mexican ancestry. When I opened up Gil Cuadros's Book *City of God* I took on the responsibility to work in collaboration with the writer in his creation. I gave my trust to Cuadros's writing, and as the reader of his creation I gave in to the freedom of his expression. With this trust and freedom, working in collaboration with the writer, I was guided back to my understanding of the written word as a tool for our survival and proof of our creative heritage. In conjunction with my own Catholic upbringing, Cuadros gives me permission to explore the sacredness of my sexuality through the creative act of writing.

References

Aguilar, Laura. Personal Interview. 11 May 2008 & 15 May 2008.

Alarcon, Francisco X. "Reclaiming Ourselves, Reclaiming America." *The Colors of Nature: Culture, Identity, and the Natural World.* Ed. Alison H. Deming and Lauret E.Savoy. Minneapolis: Milkweed Editions, 2002. 28–48.

Alfaro, Luis. "Heroes and Saints." *O Solo Homo: The New Queer Performance.* Ed. Holly Hughes and David Roman. New York: Grove Press, 1998. 326–331.

Almaguer, Tomás. "Chicano Men: A Cartography of Homosexual Identity and Behavior." *The Lesbian and Gay Reader.* Ed. Henry Abelove, Michèle Aina Barale, and David M. Helperin. New York: Routledge, 1993. 255–273.

Anaya, Rudolfo A. *Bless Me, Ultima.* New York: Warner Books, 1999.

Anzaldua, Gloria. *Making Face, Making Soul/Haceindo Caras: Creative and Critical Perspectives by Women of Color.* Ed. Gloria Anzaldua. San Francisco: Aunt Lute, 1990.

Cady, Joseph. "AIDS Literature." *GLBTQ: An Encyclopedia of Gay, Lesbian, Bisexual, Transgender, and Queer Culture*. 2002. Web. 18 May 2008. <http://glbt.com/literature/latino_lit>

Cantú, Lionel, Jr. "Entre Hombres/Between Men: Latino Masculinities and Homosexualities." *Gay Masculinities*. Ed. Peter Nardi. Thousand Oaks, CA: Sage Press, 2000. 224–246.

--------. *The Sexuality of Migration*. Ed. Nancy A. Naples and Salvador Vidal-Ortiz. New York: New York University Press, 2009.

Carrier, Joseph. "Miguel: Sexual Life History of a Gay Mexican American." *Gay Culture In America: Essays from the Field*. Ed. Gilbert H. Herdt. Boston: Beacon Press, 1992. 202–224.

Cuadros, Gil. *City of God*. San Francisco: City Lights, 1994.

--------. "4AM." 133–134.

--------. "911." 125–126.

--------. "At Risk." 120–123.

--------. "Baptism". 77–89.

--------. "DOA." 135–136.

--------. "Holy." 71–75.

--------. "ICU." 127–128.

--------. "Indulgence." 2–14.

--------. "My Aztlán: White Place." 53–58.

--------. "RM#." 131–132.

--------. "Sight." 95–99.

--------. "Unprotected." 59–70.

--------. "The Emigrants." *Frontiers Magazine*. 19 June 1992: 89

--------. "THERE ARE PLACES YOU DON'T WALK AT NIGHT, ALONE." Special Issue of *High Performance: A Quarterly Magazine for the New Arts*. Summer 1992. T. Track 5. CD.

--------. "Birth." TS. Pasadena, CA. 19 June 1991.

--------. "Hands." TS. West Hollywood, CA. Oct. 1995.

--------. "Last Supper." TS. Pasadena, CA. 6 June 1991.

Faderman, Lillian and Stuart Timmons. *Gay L.A.: A History of Sexual Outlaws, Power Politics, and Lipstick Lesbians*. Berkeley and Los Angeles: University of California Press, 2009.

Feinberg, Leslie. "Death of Trans Immigrant In Detention Forges United Protest." 2007. Web. 27 April 2008. <http://portland.indymedia.org/en/2007/09/364859.html>

Fernandez, Charles. "Undocumented Aliens in the Queer Nation." *Outlook*. Spring 1991.

Freud, Sigmund. *Three Essays on the Theory of Sexuality*. New York: Basic Books, 2000.

González, Omar. "Constructing an Ofrenda of My Memory: An Autoethnography of a Gay Chicano." *MS Thesis*. U. of California, Northridge, 2008.

Hanh, Thich Nhat. *Touching Peace: Practicing the Art of Mindful Living*. Berkeley: Parallax Press, 1992.

hooks, bell. *Ain't I A Woman: Black Women and Feminism*. Boston: South End Press, 1981.

---------. *Talking Back: Thinking Feminist, Thinking Black*. Boston: South End Press, 1989.

Iser, Wolfgang. "The Reading Process: A Phenomenological Approach." *Reader-Response Criticism: From Formalism to Post-Structuralism*. Ed. Jane P. Tompkins. Baltimore: The John Hopkins University Press, 1980. 50–69.

Martin, Kevin. "Writer Gil Cuadros: Creating in the Face of AIDS." *Positive Living*. April 1994. Vol. 3 No. 4: 3.

Monette, Paul. *Borrowed Time: An AIDS Memoir*. San Diego, CA: Harcourt Inc., 1988.

Office of Minority Health and Bureau of Primary Health Care. "Hispanics/Latinos HIV/AIDS." 4 March 2009. Web. <http:/erc.msc.org/provider/information/HL_HIV-AIDS_Overview.pdf>

Peabody, Barbara. *The Screaming Room: A Mother's Journey of Her Son's Struggle with AIDS—A True Struggle of Love, Dedication, and Courage*. New York: Avon Books, 1986.

Ramon, David. *ACTS of Intervention: Performance, Gay Culture, and AIDS*. Bloomington and Indianapolis: Indiana University Press, 1998.

--------. "Latino Literature." *GLBTQ: An Encyclopedia of Gay, Lesbian, Bisexual, Transgender, and Queer Culture*. 2002. 4 Oct. 2008. Web. <www.glbt. com/literature/latino_lit.html>

Rivera, Tomas. *Y No Se Lo Tragó La Tierra*. Texas: Arte Público Press, 1992.

Rodriguez, Richard. *Hunger Of Memory: The Education of Richard Rodriguez*. New York: The Dial Press, 2005.

Sartre, Jean Paul. "Why Write." *The Critical Tradition: Classic Texts and Contemporary Trends*. 2nd ed. Ed. David H. Richter. Boston: Bedford, 1998. 624–634.

Selden, Raman, Peter Widdowson, and Peter Brooker. *A Reader's Guide to Contemporary Literary Theory*. 4th ed. New York: Prentice Hall/Harvester Wheatsheaf, 1997.

"The Day of the Dead in Aztlán: Chicano Variations on the Theme of Life, Death and Self Preservation." 4 April 2009. Web. <http://www.chicanoart.org/dia01.html>

Wolverton, Terry. Personal Interview. 30 May 2007.

--------. *Indivisible: New Short Fiction by West Coast Gay & Lesbian Writers*. Ed. Terry Wolverton and Robert Drake. New York: Plume, 1991.

In Search of My Queer Aztlán

Luis H. Román Garcia

This has been a long time cum-ing. A misguided sense of who I am: son, brother, hijo, friend, lover, puto, joto, y Chicano. Forced, I would argue, to strategically enforce, deconstruct, reinforce, and juggle all these pinchi identities. Some may say this may be a personal prerogative—for my mother refuses to see herself in the mirror; but I have had the opportunity to free myself of el dolor, the burden inherited for being just that: a queer Chicano.

As I try to situate myself within the context of the larger global social spectrum, I find it difficult to map my own identity. How can I write about who I am, where I come from, and where I want to go, when I have no place, either physical or metaphysical, that I can call home? A home where I can feel comfortable sharing with you, or anyone else, my experiences as a queer Chicano immigrant. My coming out story has been a story of looking for a home, a reflection of my values, my experiences, and my identity.

In order to understand what to look for in a home, I have had to first define what home is. My initial bewilderment and difficulty in defining home is a result of the alienation and uncertainty that patriarchal, capitalistic nationalism begets.

Defining Home: Not the Place but the State of Mind

Capitalistic nationalism has curtailed what I can call home because it limits where I can look for a home. Transnational feminist Chandra Telpade Mohanty questions this notion of home: "What is home? The place I was born? Where I grew up? ... How one understands and defines home—is profoundly political" (487). Mohanty suggests that a home can be a metaphysical place, a state of mind. Thus, my now queer Chicano identity continues to be theoretically validated, because even though I am not on a quest to take back the nationalistic romanticized nation of Aztlán (although not opposed to the idea), nor trying to force my sexual identity onto others, I carry the spirit of who I am everywhere I go. Home can therefore be "an imaginative, politically charged space in which the familiarity and sense of affection and commitment lay in shared collective analysis of social injustice, as well as a vision of radical transformation" (Mohanty 491). Mohanty allows me to explore my own politicized identity, which is epitomized by my conscious decision to reject a heteronormative Hispanicization and identify as a queer Chicano. By defining myself as a queer Chicano, I am rejecting the subjugation imposed because of my ethnicity, immigration status, or sexuality. Instead, I am reclaiming my agency and power to assert my politicized racial, sexual, and immigrant identification in situations that would otherwise try to curtail it.

However, this process of agency and consciousness has been a difficult one for one who is afflicted by *un dolor del alma*, a heartache and a broken sense of love. I have come to learn that queer men of color love differently. Home, the traditional site of love, is also the place of rejection. Thus, colored queerness becomes a rejected love, a broken heart. How do you recover from a broken heart? Can you? What do you do? You feed it love. What type of love, when the love that you knew of before was the one that has provoked this heartache? Perhaps a new type of love that is embedded in the genetic memory of your family, the type of love only you can provide yourself. A type of love full of resistance and honesty. A type of love that is so beautiful people will envy you. But you will return that envy with more love. Because love, real honest love, never hurts. This is my struggle to come out, to find a loving home.

Home: *Mi primera traición*

The word family originally meant "servants of a household;" it was not until 1667 that the contemporary concept of family, between blood-related individuals, was widely accepted in Euro-Anglo cultural communities. In this heteropatriarchal Euro-Anglo "American" society, the social construction and privatization of the family makes it difficult for me, as a writer and lover of my family, to openly criticize and try to explicate the difficulties of being in a family that has continually rejected my existence as a queer Chicano.

I have felt like I have always had to flee from my own family. Although I was born in Mexico, I grew up in the United States. I was taught to abide by Eurocentric ideologies and practice a feckless Anglo-American culture. As a consequence, for a very long time I wanted to be White, because I was embarrassed by my Mexican parents. I was ashamed of the fact that they could not speak English (they still cannot), humiliated by the cars they drove and the small room we rented in a stranger's family apartment. I never asked for this "lifestyle," and I blamed my parents for it. Had we stayed in Mexico, although we would have been in a worse financial situation, there would have been no higher standard to compare us to, because everyone in the rural area of Mexico we knew was the same.

My mother justified our move to the United States by explaining that the family would finally be reunited. My father immigrated to the United States when he was fifteen years old. He came looking for a job that would pay. He would often visit his family back in Mexico, and in one of those trips, he met my mother. Like the traditional romanticized stories of love, they met, dated, and fell in love, and he asked her parents for their permission to marry. My mom says she married virginal; I never bothered to ask my father. But nine months after their marriage, my older brother was born. My father went back to the United States, and on his next trip, in the cold winter of December 1988, I was conceived (I assume the sex was used to keep warm), and nine months after, in September, I was born. Of course, as soon as I was born, my father left back to the United States. The next time I saw him was two years later, when he came back and impregnated my mother with my younger-also-gay brother.

I hated my father for not being in Mexico with us. But this was common among many of the young children in the *ranchito* I grew up in. Everyone had a father or an older brother who was *en el otro lado* (in the United States), and yet no one seemed to discuss the political and emotional consequences of that. I had to learn what no one discussed because it was all part of surviving. Everyone seemed to acknowledge, and almost accepted, that the transnational family and single parenthood was the only option.

Coming to the United States meant that I would have my father closer to me. Even though I now had my father physically close to my life, his presence was never obvious. He got up at nine in the morning every day and would not return until two the following morning. Admitting that my father was a dishwasher was very difficult for me. Many to this day do not know what type of labor my dad had to endure daily. Before, I had to constantly compare myself to a neighborhood that, although it was not middle class, was definitely not in the slums. Now, a student at UCLA, not only do I have to compare myself to the White students whose parents very likely did not have to perform menial labor, but to middle class Latinos. I cannot but feel guilty for being selfish and hating him for never being at home. To deal with my father's absence, I constructed a pseudo *machista* father in my imagination. I developed this character by encompassing various images and traits of what I considered a father should be. This pseudo-father had expectations of me, and I desired nothing more but to meet them.

School: *El lugar de mis lágrmias*

In my culture, there is an expectation for boys to be masculine, athletic, and heterosexual. Schools perpetuate and encourage these expectations at a young age. I always found this country's feckless capitalistic values for individualism to be ironic, because at the same time this society cannot abide without social groupings and categories. In the fifth grade, they would often divide us by gender. Such heterosexist division always made me uncomfortable. I knew we were going to talk about girls, sex, and puberty, but I felt like I could not relate. One time, as the girls were stepping outside the classroom, a fellow male student, who I thought was a friend, shouted, "Hey *Louis*, don't you belong outside with them?" While everyone laughed, I felt like I was shrinking, slowly melting in my chair. I knew that my face probably resembled a tomato's red skin. My teacher's immediate response was to defend my dignity. He demanded the bullying cease because, he reasoned, one day I would be the bullies' boss. The teacher told the class that my intelligence would accomplish much more than their undignified statements. His words ameliorated the public humiliation I felt, but they did not end the taunts outside the classroom. Although the bullying continued, I began to internalize the positive comments of the teacher: *was I really smart?*

The anger I had towards the kid who embarrassed me in front of the entire class was justified, but so was his ignorance. None of my classes ever mentioned anything about queerness. In fact, my only knowledge of sexuality stemmed from ignorant or hateful sources such as religion, the family, and the media. All I knew was that I was attracted to the male body—that I could not help but stare at boys. I befriended young girls and was scared of the boys. I did not want to be like the rest of the boys, but I wanted to be with them, physically. I wanted them to embrace me with their growing broad arms; I wanted to ask them if they wore boxers or white underwear. As much as I was uninformed about my own feelings, my cretinous classmate was too uninformed of a lot things. I blamed this on the little I knew of Catholic dogma, because it preached that homosexuality should be feared and curtailed. In addition, the media's feminized queer addendum suggested that being a feminine male meant that I was gay. Assuming that that was all my classmate knew, it did not surprise me that he chose to discriminate and humiliate me about my supposed sacrilegious persona and sexuality.

Through the early years of my life, the only correlation between homosexuality and me was my effeminate characteristics. While my "straight" (but really they were just masculine—I never knew for a fact that they were straight) peers lived their lives without the fear of being physically hurt in school or having to check their gestures, I consciously chose to sit on the sidelines and read books. I did not want to confront my peers about why I acted the way I did and repeat yet another provocative flustered moment. Being a smart boy was safe; I never had to challenge authority because they fed me this idea of smartness.

I could not go home and tell my mom that the boys pushed me into going to the girl's restroom, or that I was kicked for playing baseball "like a girl" (whatever that truly meant), or that boys spit in my free food for speaking funny (now I understand that I spoke with a stereotypical gay lisp). There was no possible way that I could tell my mom that the boys were confusing me with a girl; how could she possibly understand that? I could also not tell my pseudo-father that I was not meeting his expectations—I could not disappoint him that way.

Coming Out: El Closet

I knew of my queerness long before I knew of my Chicano identity. It was hard for me to admit, mostly because I did not know the language to use. The age of technology allowed me to engage in homosocial, homoerotic bonds. Daily, I would run home from school and head straight to the computer, where I had access to a world beyond me. I would engage in conversations with older men, talk about life, schools, relationships, and sex. I felt comfortable with these men because I would never actually meet them in person. They were cyber crushes: safe and fun.

Every night after my mom went to sleep, I would google the word "gay." The results varied from pornographic websites to nonprofit organizations and chat rooms. After I got over chatting with random guys, I enjoyed the thrill of watching porn. Seeing men kiss, suck, eat, and fuck each other turned me on. Their hands spanking as they rode one another, the dick covered in saliva. I couldn't contain my erection as I stared at the Virgen de Gudalupe's image hanging on the living room wall. I begged her for forgiveness as I rubbed on my hard penis. Just as penises erupt with cum, I knew that if I continued to bubble all of my confused feelings, they would eventually erupt. Sure enough, they did.

Coming out of the closet meant risking my family's acceptance; it also meant engaging in Gloria Anzaldúa's conocimiento, the rupture in my life. When I finally had the courage to come out, I cried for my mother's acceptance. Instead, I found rejection and solitude.

I was forced to come out to my parents. It was one of the teenage nightmare evenings at home when I was questioned about my lack of investment in the household. We got into an argument because I was fed up with my mother's micromanagement of my life. At the age of sixteen, I just wanted to live my own life at the time without parental patrolling. After an awful academic junior year in high school, my family felt completely disrespected. All they ever asked of me was to do well in school. However, I was unable to focus on my academics because I could not even have a grasp of my own changing identity and sexual desires. I blamed my family for my poor academic endeavors, stating that they were responsible due to their lack of support. Blaming them was easier than actually admitting the truth.

I stormed out of the house after screaming at my mother, calling her a witch (she hated that word more than the B word). My mom chased me down the driveway and told me to return. I ran to my bed and hid under the covers, crying. Later that night, when my dad arrived from his daily shift of washing dishes, my mom woke me up so we could have a talk. She wanted to know what I mean when I said, "lack of support." I was unable to utter the words "soy gay," so I wrote it on a piece of paper. I first gave it to my mom, and when she read it she screamed and started calling me a hypocrite. She gave the note to my dad, to which he responded, "it was about time you came out." My dramatic mother ran out of the house and sat on the porch, crying. My dad, I could hear, tried to console her, telling her that I needed them the most now.

My mother was unable to love me because all she knew of queerness was the same thing that the boy in my fifth grade class knew—nothing but stereotypes. I was told to leave the house until I knew for a fact that I was not really gay. For a few days, I lived with a friend, and I spent another week in a homeless shelter. Trying to stay sane and alive without the support of those that I love the most (my family) has become a daily struggle. Not being able to have my mother proud of the activism work that I do, or not being able to share the work that I am learning at school is a wounding experience. But at the same time, I knew at sixteen that I could not live in the streets. I decided to go home and lie about my sexuality. As I swallowed the inexhaustible pain of living in a lie about myself, I became a hermit and continued to allow my imagination to live my life through books. I used books to fill the void left when my family could not provide the comfort I was already missing from school. I could use books as the foundation for an imaginative family—a caring, loving, accepting, family—a White family.

To this day I am unable to tell my extended family that I am queer. During most holidays, I have to endure the "y tu novia" question. "Where is your girlfriend?" my uncles always ask. But I am grateful that I have the full support of my siblings (one of whom recently also came out). My father has been the only parental figure in my life who has been able to discuss this issue directly with me. He constantly reminds me to be safe and protect myself. My mother, on the other hand, refuses to talk to me about my "cochinadas," as she has come to call my identity.

As soon as I came out to her, I wrote her this letter, which remains unedited:

Mommy,

I just want you to know that I love you. As time passes by, I see you age. Your grace is so blissful, so calm, and so beautiful. Yet I know that you are in pain. That your body aches, that your mind is scared. You are worried for us, your children, your loves. I know that you did not always support me in everything I did. But it was because you were afraid. Afraid of what they may say, but worse—of what they may do. I now realize that you did not hate me for being gay, you hated that this world is so cruel and would do without my existence. You worried that they would talk behind your back, make you a failing mother. But mommy, look at me—do I look like I failed you? I hope not. You have given me the voice you never had. The power you held in secrecy. Mommy, my grandma told me. Told me about your childhood. Told me how you were robbed. How she selfishly dragged you in. she told me of your grandmother. My grandma told me she was scared, and she fucked it up for you. Mommy, please don't be afraid—it will all be okay. I wont let anyone harm you. mommy, please know that I love you.

Mommy, you no longer have to hide in the darkness. You are free to blossom into that beautiful flower you were meant to be. Mommy, please come and say hello. Tell me you love me. You never did. Can't you tell that I need to hear that from you. I need to believe that you do love me. I think you do, you have proven it to me, but you never told me you did. Oh mommy, these people with skin as light as yours, they are always happy and smiling. I've never seen you that happy. I've seen you stressed, depressed, in pain. mommy, it's okay now. No one will harm you for show- ing tears. She is no longer here. She will no longer harm you. can't you see that you've been hurting us too? All the pain you have inside, its affecting us.

Mommy, I know you disagree but you are a feminist, a fighter, a revolutionary. Mommy, you are strong, independent, and smart. I know you hid behind those books, just like I did. I know you could have been that nurse you've always wanted to be. But mommy, they took your life away. They sucked your spirit. Mommy, are you there? Listening to me?

Mommy, I cried every night for an entire year. Did you hear? I was really calling for you. I needed you to hug me. To tell me it would be okay. Tell me that there is nothing wrong with me. Oh mommy! You never woke up. You kept sleeping like everything was okay. But I knew it was not okay. Its okay mommy. You know why? Because I knew you were tired. I knew you were sick. I knew you were dying. And mommy, I know you are still tired, still sick, and still dying. Mommy, listen to me! I know you are dying. I know that you are not getting any stronger, you are getting weaker. But it is not because of age, it is not because of time, it is because you are dying. You are dying right in front of my eyes, and I cant do anything about it.

Mommy, you lied to me! You told me you will take care of my own kids, yes mommy I am still going to have kids. But I know you wont be here. Mommy, I cant believe you are leaving me. Please don't. I promise I will behave. Promise I will visit you more frequently. But please don't leave me. I need you to chase the monsters away. I need you to tell me it will be okay. I need you mommy. Please don't leave me.

You said you will last at least three more years. That you will try. it is not fair. You cant try to live, you need to live mommy. You started aging way before you were supposed to. Its not fair. They took advantage of you. they used you. they got what they wanted. All I want is a mommy to last me forever. That is all I want. But you've said you wont give me what I want. Am I not your son? Your gay son? Your brown son? Your prince? Your product? Your baby? Your child? Am I not that? How can you not grant me my only wish, mommy.

Fuck them if they don't want to pay for your medical bills, you need to find a way! Fuck them if they want to stop treating you! Fuck them if they want you dead! Fuck them! it is not about them, mommy! It is about you, me, dad, and everyone else! Fuck them! stay with me and live forever. Forever in our liberation. Forever in our freedom. Forever in our love. Forever in our foreverness.

Mommy before you leave, just know one thing: I love you. and that mommy, is not a lie.

She will probably never be able to read this letter. It will kill her, as much as it has killed me.

How To Break a Joto Corazon

Confused, I replaced the act of sex for love—unprotected, wild sex, defying my dad's wishes for me to be safe.

No one ever touched me as you did, with that tender embrace, that genuine affection, and your most sincere love. I will for sure miss the sex, our bodies next to each other, the passion steaming with radiating heat, our hearts beating at an indescribable rate, the pulse of the thrust, the moans yielding to intimacy, the screams demanding more.

There was more to him. There was that smile hidden in his face, the rough spots in his soft hands, the warmth of his body, and his eyes always stealing a glimpse of me. That was when I knew of love.

Around here, they know me for my services. *For a mere buck, I'll blow your cock.* Someone once suggested I use that as my business card's tagline.

I have had my share of free fucks. Some I met in bus stops, a few over the Internet, many others at the park. That was before I became a professional. Now they pay me to fuck. Before, I would fuck for dinner or a place to stay. The routine rarely changed: suck, fuck, sticky warm cum all over my face. They usually asked me to smoke weed with them before we fucked, or cocaine even. To them, this made the fucking more pleasurable. To me, it eased the pain. It was a growing sting, resentment, an act of *rebeldia* against my parents, against my *cultura*. I sold my body to a white man.

When I was younger, I searched for that physical touch any prepubescent *joto* strongly desired. I got what my naïve capitalist-oriented mind needed. He bought me whatever I wanted. The first time he asked me to give him oral sex, I did not want to, but I consented. My shaking lips wrapped the head of his cut penis. As I circled my tongue around the corona, I began to breathe warm air on it. The air got hotter; my face got warmer. I did not want to continue. I kissed his belly button, hoping he would assume that it was all part of this magic-making process. While I groped his hard *pre-cumming* penis with my hand, I lay on the bed, deliberating my life. In disgust, I began to replay the actions I was engaging in. I had that white man shoot his warm sticky cum all over my face. That was not the first time, and certainly not the last.

With such beauty came hardships. Stubborn by nature, I was not able to defy the values I established before I laid eyes on you. I could not let go of the thorn that was pricking at your heart, so you chose to walk the other direction. I can't blame you for thinking with your head, but that jealousy that erupted was untamed like a wild beast at the local zoo. In spite of what I did, who I did, when I did it, it was you who I whispered sweet things to. You were the one I missed at night; you were the one I wanted. But it was you who I was hurting. The same jealousy that drove me to love you drove you to hate me. It was that type of love that shines brighter than lust and jealousy, and dimmer than reality—but my reality is no longer you.

My desire for the male body has gotten me into a lot of trouble—from alleys in Downtown to elevators at Union Station and cruising zones at Elysian Park. My tongue wrapped around the penis head was something I desired the most. His lukewarm lips creating a warm sensation around the most sensitive part of my penis was what I craved. It was in those spaces that I was able to engage with my sexual needs and desires using my mother's tongue. I was revolting against La Raza, for gay erotic sex was no longer just in English, but in my own Brown mother's tongue. Talking to those men with the same words I used to talk to my mother—oh how blasphemous! But it was raunchier, it was exotic, it fulfilled every sexual desire that my body was yielding for.

Knowing that I could easily get sex from people in more common places, I could not rebel against my mother there. Instead, I craved for the same people who exploited me. See, it was Brown men, not white men, who fucked with my life every day while I was growing up. Brown men like my father, my brother, my uncle, brown like me. It was the men who look like me that fucked with me every day. Now, I can seduce them, I have the power to fuck with them back.

The room was cold, my skin scaly, and my bones shivering. I was an amateur, he a professional. I knew it was wrong but had no other alternative; like a twister progressing in our direction, not by chance but by force. I stood there, hesitant. What was I losing and what was I gaining? Perhaps there is no answer.

Now that I turn back to see it, my virtuousness was mugged. The intimacy was not there, the anger was intensely present, the love was long lost. As soon as I saw myself fly away, I knew it was all long gone. Inch by inch, feet by feet, my life was soon vanishing right in front of my eyes. You said you were everlasting, that you would never die off. You made me believe that you would be next to me until the day the sun never rose. And I plunked there in trepidation as your words crumbled out of your sweet lips. As your eyes glared through the midst of confusion, I believed your every word.

I am coerced into admitting that my love life, for a brown queer man, has been a failed attempt. Maybe I have not found the one, the few, the many. But I met one. He cheated, of course—using heteronormative practices to hurt the ones we love the most. Brown queer bodies, I have come to learn, are re-learning the meaning of love. A joto type of love.

Politicization: A Big Fuck You!

What I did with men, white men particularly, I did because they were the only ones who embraced me. My mother chose to deny me; my father left me to wash dishes every day, all day; and Brown people, well they were the ones who were kicking my ass every day after school for no reason other than being feminine. White gays, as I have come to learn, take you in, but once you are done fucking or getting fucked by them, they do not want you. Being a queer person of color means not fitting in; being a queer Chicano, a *pinchi joto*, means being a threat. *La joteria* challenges everything about society—who you have sex with, why you have sex, when you have sex (yes I am insinuating that life is sex, because life comes from sex).

Nonetheless, it is a fallacy to presume that racial minorities, who already recognize the essence of oppression, are more welcoming and affirming of other oppressed identities. The Combahee River Collective beautifully recognizes how the Black community (and, I would add, other communities of color) prioritized a patriarchal way of thinking that benefited men of color. Nationalist movements like the 1960s–70s Chicano Movement (emphasis on the Chicano) were very patriarchal, and if women disobeyed they were ridiculed and called Malinches (traitors). This is a multi-faceted and complex way of thinking because it essentializes manhood and suggests that all men are the same.

Oppressions are multi-layered, and even those who are already oppressed further marginalize "politically weaker" members of their community. For instance, Chicano/as come from an extremely hetero-sexist patriarchal culture, just like everyone else. Because Chicano/as are oppressed in this White Supremacist society, they resort to a socialized competitive nature and try to attack anyone or anything that may be inferior or weaker; queers of color are politically weaker. However, queer men, and in this case queer Chicanos, were denied access to (heterosexual) male privilege and were pushed outside of the movement by the heterosexual men. In addition, queer men of color had, and still do have access to, male privilege within the larger queer (white) community. While it may seem obvious for Chicana lesbian and gay Chicanos to unite, the truth is that gay Chicanos resorted to using their male privilege by collaboration with white gay men to advance themselves, leaving their lesbian sisters behind. After reading Cherríe Moraga's "Queer Aztlán," I was reminded of my own privilege among queer brownness. Through my own research I have found that sex has been used as a foundation to negotiate identities. Sex with White men has been used as a form of assimilation and resistance among queer Chicanos.

The desire to fit in somewhere drives queer people of color to find some type of sanctuary within the majority gay community; but, as stated earlier, even the gay community is hesitant to engage queer people of color. Queer people of color start to act and feel inferior to everyone else because they have nowhere to turn. Because of heterosexist patriarchy, I cannot live at home in my beloved East Los Angles. Similarly, gay-affirming West Hollywood denies me access to its racist capitalist spaces. Instead, queer people of color are stuck in this *Nepantla* metaphysical place. According to Anzaldúa, the nepantla state is "exposed, open to other perspectives, more readily able to access knowledge derived from inner feelings, imaginal states, and outer events, and to 'see through' them with a mindful, holistic awareness" (167). This idea of mapping oppressed identities is found in Kimberle Williams Crenshaw's "Mapping the Margins: Intersectionality, Identity Politics, and Violence Against Women of Color," in which we are encouraged to situate ourselves in order to develop our political identity. Therefore, mapping my complex, multi-faceted, and differently powered identity, I stand in solidarity with all those who are oppressed, but in particular I stand with other queer people of color who are looking for a home.

(Re)Finding a New Home—Que viva la Jotería!

Through a long period of self-discovery, and using Anzaldúa's conocimiento process, I have accepted a new identity—that of a *joto*, a proud *joto*! However, a joto needs a home. Having a solid foundation of what a home is, it is vital to decolonize myself and help those around me. In *This Bridge Called My Back: Writings by Radical Women of Color*, Moraga and Anzaldúa proclaim that "the revolution begins at home." I want to help in creating a new Aztlán, one that reaches a true egalitarian, borderless, feminist-conscious, and queer-affirming utopia. Finding my passion for social justice was simultaneous to finding my voice in the midst of much uncertainty. To this day my love for him, the unknown brown man, remains the center of my nameless home.

Mapping New Directions for a Radical Jotería Agenda

Omar O. González

I would like to begin by invoking the saints for a queer Xicana/o community.[1] I choose to do this as a community, to make this ritual communal, as a way for us to connect to one another and as a method for queering spiritualities that heretofore have been co-opted by conservative Catholics and fundamentalists. As we make intellectual connections in the discursive spaces and feel the warmth and cariño of each other's embrace, it is crucial that we bond on a spiritual level as well. If we are truly going to build a queer Xicana/o community, then we must establish one that interweaves the corporal energy of the living with the mysterious power of the dead. The first two saints I wish to invoke are two beloved authors, Arturo Islas and Gil Cuadros. These two talented souls escaped to the other realm in the time that I call the pre-cocktail meds era of the HIV/AIDS epidemic, 1981–1996 (or 1959, if you choose to view HIV/AIDS from a non-Western perspective. One of the first documented cases of an HIV/AIDS-like death occurred in Africa in 1959.) An entire generation of queer brothers was lost in that long night. I would like to take a moment for each of us to pause and reflect and say the name of a person who has succumbed to the scourge. I do this because the

---

1   I choose to write "Xicana/o" with an "X" to further cast off the shackles of my colonial masters, those who imposed the moniker "Gonzalez" on my ancestors and forced us to forget our true names.

silence around HIV/AIDS is almost as cruel as the death itself. And how many times have Queer Latino males died and even in death been left in the closet? As a queer Xicano who has lived with this virus for nearly two decades and has borne the scarlet letter of an AIDS diagnosis for twelve years, I wish to renounce all feelings of shame and self-loathing that I and every single person whose name was called out had to suffer. I choose to invoke writers as queer Xicano saints because the written word is one conduit through which we not only work through our traumas but also name them. We negotiate our realities and claim self-agency through writing. Although writing is a solitary act, I believe sharing our words creates a discursive founda-tion for the writer as well as the reader. The reader becomes affected by the written word forever; from that point on our perspectives are altered by reading. Additionally, in an op-ed piece entitled "The Lost Art of Reading," David Ulin of the *Los Angeles Times* extols the action's virtues and reinforces Foucault's idea of the interconnectedness of texts, thus creating a rhetorical third space:

> I find myself driven by the idea that in their intimacy, the one-to-one attention they require, books are not tools to retreat from but rather to understand and interact with the world ... [T]he ability to still my mind long enough to inhabit someone else's world, and to let that someone else inhabit mine. Reading is an act of contemplation, perhaps the only act in which we allow ourselves to merge with the conscious-ness of another human being. We possess the books we read, animating the waiting stillness of their language, but they possess us also, filling us with thoughts and observations, asking us to make them part of ourselves.

Ulin speaks of a dialectic constructed between the writer and the reader; the collision between the intentions of the author and the ex-periences of the reader creates a discursive mestizaje. This theoretical perspective stresses the importance of literacy and those who create art in the written form who forever change our intellectual and emotional landscapes. I think of all the texts that have transformed my life upon me reading them: *Borderlands* by Gloria Anzaldúa, *City of Night* by John Rechy, and *Occupied America* by Rudy Acuña, among others. I take this ritual of popular religiosity from my own indigenous Mexican Catholic upbringing yet strip it of the confining dogma of the Church. The Vatican and its patriarchy play no part in my faith, as I have shaped my spiritual beliefs to accommodate my experiential reality, as we all have the power to do, thus creating another strategy of resistance. Not only can we as queer Xicanas/os connect to each other through this form of ritual, but we can also heal ourselves. I now name my third queer Xicana/o saint, my maternal grandmother, Elisa Mendoza Villanueva. I name her as my personal queer Xicana/o saint because of this one fact. When I came out to her twenty years ago, she continued to love me unconditionally from the moment that I uttered those magical words. These are the people in our lives who should be our personal queer Xicana/o saints—the people who did not have to "get over it" or learn to "accept" our identities, as if we must be grateful for our presence to be "tolerated." This is why we must begin to reject the concept of "tolerance" and "acceptance," as they are rooted in a deficit perspective. These words begin with the supposition that queer people are lesser than and grants the power to the person doing the "tolerating" and the "accepting." Queer people do not need anybody's tolerance or acceptance. We deserve the same respect as human beings as heterosexuals. As a progressive community, we "tolerate" the corporate servitude of the Democrats and Obama's penchant for compromise. We "accept" the fact that the few depictions of gay Xicano males in the media will have them invariably fall for a white man (*Quinceanera, La Mission, Ugly Betty*). Similarly, we must examine the language of coming out. I often hear the phrases, "He admitted that he was gay," or "I suspected that she was a lesbian." This reinscribes the criminality of homosexuality, as only seven years have passed since the landmark decision of

Lawrence v. Texas gave queer people some agency over their bodies. Similarly, the use of terms such as "admit" and "suspect" parallel the use of the terms "illegal" and "alien" for undocumented immigrants. Therefore, it is time that as queer Xicanas/os we claim power over our own well-being. Not only is there power in the written word, but in the spoken word as well. Speaking our truths liberates us from the shackles of silence; this act frees us from hiding from the pain instilled by family members, friends, and ourselves. We then can confront our traumas and begin the journey of healing. This was evident in a recent episode of *Project Runway*. I realize that the fashion industry is guilty of the subjugation of thousands, if not millions of women, mostly women of color, working in slave-like conditions in sweat shops all over the world. This is the effect of rampant, unchecked global capitalism, which I assert has done more to enslave people of color around the world than organized religion (although one can argue that these two systems of oppression go hand in hand). Moreover, the fashion industry does promote and perpetuate our society's culture of consumption, especially in the mainstream upper-class gay male community. This culture of consumption is evident whenever I glance through any mainstream gay magazine. Gay has become a brand—our identities have become commodified, from clothing to home furnishings and vacations to our very bodies. We are commodities to be packaged, marketed, and consumed. The "gay" identity, once an identity of subversion and protest, has been hijacked by the machinery of capitalism via such multinational corporate propaganda as *Queer Eye for the Straight Guy*.[2] Moreover, the fashion industry reflects the class caste system of the US (clearly evidenced by the designer labels one flaunts). Finally, reality competition shows like *Project Runway* represent the mythical "American Dream," where fame and riches are ensured to those who simply work hard enough and who are willing to cut another's throat to get there, and somehow,

---

2   For an excellent analysis on this subject, please refer to the text, *A Queer Eye for Capitalism: The Commodification of Sexuality in US Television* by Yarma Velazquez-Vargas.

creativity is ranked and measured, all for the glory of television ratings. However, *Project Runway* is one of the few television programs where the men are queer, mostly, and sometimes they include queer men of color. Thus, this brings me to my fourth queer Xicana/o saint, a living saint, Mondo Guerra, a current contestant on this season's *Project Runway*. Having grown up in a conservative Catholic family, Mondo recounted his coming out story in a recent episode. He came out to his mother, who instructed him not to tell anybody else in the family. By doing so, Mondo's mother reinforced the culture of sexual silence that haunts so many of us in the Xicana/o and Latina/o communities—not just gay men but also women. This is one lesson that is painful to learn—that our flesh and blood can be our worst enemies. Another glaring example of this is evident in Rafael Diaz's groundbreaking work, *Latino Gay Men and HIV*, where he posits this familial silence as one of the factors that contribute to the disconnect between our knowledge of safer sex practices and persistent engagement in higher risk sexual practices. One of Diaz's research participants mentioned one of his father's sayings in an interview: "Mi hijo, mejor muerto que maricon" (My son, better dead than queer). How do we recognize the damage that our families inflict upon us yet still negotiate their presence in our lives? Rechy, my literary hero, declares that homosexuals are "the only minority born in the opposing camp; call it the enemy camp." As difficult as it may be to consider our families as "enemies," a strategy of survival may be to isolate ourselves from those who claim to love us unconditionally yet still inflict harm upon us. Furthermore, disclosure of one's HIV positive status is perhaps an even more daring act than coming out as queer, for there remains an incredible stigma against poz people, even in the gay community. This act not only takes incredible courage but is also inspirational in a country where poz people are subject to criminal penalties, not to mention the lingering social derision. Thirty years into the epidemic, HIV+ people negotiate a social environment where HIV+ people are still considered "dirty" and are infested with "bugs." Isn't this the same paranoid rationale that propelled the US Border Patrol to force Mexican immigrants (both men and women) to be strip searched, inspected for lice, shaved from head to toe, and doused with kerosene upon entering the US? This was a common practice in the early twentieth century on the El Paso/Juárez border, as documented by David Dorado Romo in *Ringside Seat to a Revolution: An Underground Cultural History of El Paso and Juárez: 1893–1923*. Nevertheless, Mondo Guerra's display of courage and bravery inspires me to name him as a queer Xicana/o saint, as he disclosed his status as a person who has lived with HIV for ten years. His revelations evoked my memories of Pedro Zamora, the young gay HIV+ Cubano on MTV's *The Real World: San Francisco*. For those of you who may not be familiar with him, Pedro Zamora is a former member of MTV's *The Real World: San Francisco* (circa 1994) who educated its viewers about LGBT and HIV/AIDS issues. Without trepidation, he broadcast to the world his message of love and let us into his world, one where only one AIDS medication existed at the time.[3] His corporal presence left the world in 1994, the day after the season finale's episode aired. He is one of my role models, and I continue to be in awe of his bravery to be not only an out person of color on television, but also an out person of color living with AIDS. I remember watching a reunion show for *The Real World* and crying after a clip montage of Pedro. Because of the extra dimension of HIV/AIDS to Zamora's queer identity, I believe he is as impactful a person to the LGBT community as Harvey Milk is. Even if you are not a fan of *Project Runway*, I encourage you to watch the episode of Mondo's disclosure of his HIV+ status.

Finally, I would like to invoke the gente who founded ALLGO, originally named the Austin Latina/o Lesbian & Gay Organization. As a response to the inaction of the federal government and the racism of the White gay community, a group of concerned Xicana/o lesbians

---

3   Prior to 1996, only AZT existed as a temporary remedy to quell the HIV virus. In 1996, pharmaceutical companies introduced the AIDS "cocktails," a combination of different medications, which have successfully suppressed the virus in the fortunate populations that have access to the expensive drugs (a month's regimen can cost upwards of $4000).

and gay men in central Texas founded ALLGO in 1985. The founders wished to provide HIV services in a culturally sensitive environment to the working-class Black and Latina/o communities of Austin, Texas, and the surrounding areas. ALLGO's commitment to social justice is unparalleled, and it has branched out to work on other causes affecting marginalized populations, such as strengthening the bridges between communities of color, the plight of undocumented immigrants, breast cancer among lesbians, and mitigating the effects of the government's war on terror.

ALLGO, the longest-surviving Latina/o LGBT organization in the US, continues to thrive after a quarter century of activism and challenges the ultra-nationalist sensibilities of the original Xicano movement; patriarchy was not to be challenged in the original vision of Aztlán. Women were secondary and queer men were invisible. The women who did dare raise issues of gender equality were quickly labeled as "vendidas," often by other women. Fortunately, they continued to challenge the cultural nationalists and the racism of the mainstream feminist movement to create the vibrant Xicana feminism that is alive in the works of such authors as Gloria Anzaldúa, Cherríe Moraga, Ana Castillo, Sonia Saldivar-Hull, Adelaida Del Castillo, Aida Hurtado, Mary Pardo, Marta Menchaca, Shirlene Soto, Vicki Ruiz, Alicia Gaspar de Alba, and others. Furthermore, the Xicana lesbians opened another world of research for Xicana/o queer scholars. Because the works of these scholars represent radical and revolutionary ideas, I believe its roots come from a community negotiating multiple oppressions, similar to ALLGO's founders. Many of the founders had been members of an LGBT group that focused on state electoral politics. One ALLGO founder, Saúl González, stated in 2002:

As Latinos, we would advocate for ALGPC [Austin Lesbian and Gay Political Caucus] to get involved and be visible in activities important to Latinos in Austin such as supporting

the United Farm Worker's Movement.[4] The steering committee of ALGPC would decline participation in such activities
stating these were not gay issues. However, from our perspective, all issues of liberation were related. Being Latino
and gay were very much related, and we felt that ALGPC was
not meeting our needs. Around the same time, a couple of
guys from Houston, who were involved in that city's Gay &
Lesbian Hispanics Unidos (GLHU), told us they would be interested in starting a similar organization in Austin. We met
to discuss how we would launch such a group and decided
that a social/cultural event on Día de la Raza (Oct. 12, 1985)
would be ideal ... To our amazement, more than 200 people
attended that first event. Needless to say, we organizers
were elated ... We felt we were responding to racism in the
gay community. We also knew that there was a significant
amount of homophobia in the Latino and mainstream communities. We had our hands full in combating ignorance at
many levels. Just the act of organizing ALLGO caused an up-
roar. Many accused us of dividing the gay community along
racial lines. Our response was that the gay community was
never really united to begin with. Most of the gay events and
functions in Austin at the time were overwhelmingly white.
Simple things like the food and music never reflected Latino
culture. By forming ALLGO, what we were actually doing was
building a new community that did not previously exist ...
[ALLGO is still necessary because we] still live in a world
where race and sexual orientation are an issue. Although
much has changed in the last 17 years, many opportunities

---

4   How myopic of the ALGPC to not join forces with Cesar Chavez and the UFW,
     for there is much evidence of his support for LGBT rights, even before the
     Stonewall Rebellion of 1969. In fact, Cesar Chavez was one of the keynote
     speakers at the 1987 Gay and Lesbian March on Washington. The UFW and
     Dolores Huerta continue to be outspoken leaders on behalf of the LGBT
     communities.

for our community have developed. For better or worse, there will always be a need for ALLGO. Ideally, no racism or homophobia would exist. However, even if that were to happen, the need to celebrate our unique culture, our strength and endurance will always exist. (¡ALLGO PASA! 14)

González and the other visionaries who founded ALLGO possessed the foresight to not isolate oppressions and realized that all movements of social justice are inextricably linked. Additionally, the founders of ALLGO realized that the queer Xicana/o community was unique unto itself—they neither were anomalous byproducts of Xicanas/os nor were they "exotic" queer people. They were brave in confronting both the homophobia of their homes and the racism of the mainstream queer community, thereby necessitating the creation of a space for queer people of color in Austin. An example of this racial division in the LGBT community can be found in an edition of the now defunct queer publication *The Texas Triangle*. A cartoon depicting a group of queer White people held a banner proclaiming, "It's not our fault there aren't more people of color involved in the gay movement. We invited them." This is the kind of racialized thinking that ALLGO was responding to in the mid-eighties. Powerfully, González states, "... from our perspective, all issues of liberation were related," which illustrates the progressive thinking of the founders, especially in the midst of the Reagan era *(¡ALLGO PASA!* 14). ALLGO represents the praxis that the field of Xicana/o Studies laments has been lost—the connection to community. Although ALLGO was able to negotiate and secure government funding for several years, it never forsook its community roots in order to become a cumbersomely large social service agency. Unfortunately, ALLGO has had to rely solely on private grants and donations since its loss of all government funding. Although this financing was a major source of its operating budget, ALLGO then practiced the ancient art of *rasquachismo*, Mexican/Xicana/o resourcefulness, and restructured. ALLGO is thriving well into its third decade of operation due to its reorganization as a node within a state network of Texan queer people of color agencies and its dedication to the cultural arts. The following text is taken from its website:

> In 2005 *allgo* presented the challenge to itself of stepping further into fully embodying its vision toward a just and equitable society that celebrates and nurtures vibrant people of color queer cultures. During this process, significant gaps were identified in the social justice organizing taking place in Texas in terms of queer people of color activists, groups and organizations working often in isolation or with little contact with similar organizers. In addition, the disconnection between people of color and the greater LGBT movement was rather evident, with LGBT voices silenced in the larger dialogue. As these needs were identified ALLGO was renamed *allgo*, taking the organization's old acronym as its name to honor the organization's history while acknowledging the inclusion of all queer people of color. The newly expanded organization made the monumental decision to honor its vision by returning to its initial mission and moving entirely as a social justice organization. *allgo* also thought it important to put the lessons it had learned over twenty years to work throughout the state of Texas. In addition to continuing our <u>Wellness Program</u> (Health Education and Advocacy) our <u>Cultural Arts Program</u>, and our <u>Multi-Issue Action Teams</u>, *allgo* now works with a network of LGBT activists of color across Texas. The network seeks to identify LGBT people of color priorities and strategies as they relate to Reproductive Justice, Sexual Freedom, Anti-Violence and Immigrant and Refugee Rights. Once a year *allgo* brings these activists together for an annual summit to design strategies for the coming year and celebrate our accomplishments. (www. allgo.org)

Moreover, ALLGO is a site of memory and history for queer Xicanas/os and other people of color due to its documentation of the unique stories of negotiating and thriving among the lower rungs of domination. ALLGO's newsletter, *¡ALLGO PASA!*, published since its inception, therefore, is as vitally important to the annals of Xicana/o history as Acuña's *Occupied America: A History of Xicanos*. Both represent texts of marginalized peoples. Acuña's tome continues to breathe life into a community whose history is rarely taught or discussed. Furthermore, *¡ALLGO PASA!* brings an even more alienated community out of the shadows to bond and celebrate our lives without shame and to mourn those who have crossed the final material barrier. González's statements and the activism of *allgo* regarding the interconnection of oppressions belie the narrow-minded assumptions of the cultural nationalists of the Xicana/o Movement. Therefore, I invoke the founders of *allgo* as queer Xicana/o saints.

Mapping New Directions for Radical Queer Xicanas/os

The first action for a progressive queer Xicana/o agenda is to break the tenuous link with the mainstream LGBT rights movement. Similar to the first wave of feminism, the mainstream LGBT rights movement does not address issues of race, class, or global military imperialism in a meaningful or progressive fashion. It is essential that queer progressive Xicanas and Xicanos build a movement that includes a serious analysis and activist movements that work toward a just and equitable society for all people, animals, and the earth.

Firstly, we cannot support the current "Don't Ask, Don't Tell" movement, although it is the current cause *célèbre* of organizations such as the Human Rights Campaign. Even the progressive pinnacle of journalism *Democracy Now!* with Amy Goodman presents the plight of ejected gay and lesbian soldiers without any critical analysis of their desire to join the armed forces. The US military is the tool of the largest imperialist power in the history of humankind.[5] The hundreds of military bases represent the chains of global slavery. They exist to extract natural resources, to import and export merchandise, and to ensure that global markets remain open for business, thus reaping billions for multinational corporations. Joining the military only serves the purposes of the empire, one that continues to enslave non-white populations in a never-ending cycle of poverty, exploitation, and forced migration. Thus, progressive queer Xicanas and Xicanos should not support an institution that has killed hundreds of thousands of working-class people in Iraq and Afghanistan and threatens military actions in Iran and North Korea. How can we demand our civil rights when the military that represents us is slaughtering people who pose no threat to us? Shouldn't we as a citizenry be held accountable for our government's actions? Our hands are as bloodstained as those who led us into these illegal wars. Therefore, we must organize to broaden educational opportunities for our young people, so that they do not consider military enlistment (or any other branch of law enforcement for that matter) as their only viable option in an uncertain economy. The same vigor that the mainstream LGBT rights movement applies to "Don't Ask, Don't Tell" should be directed towards ending the wars, closing all military bases around the world, and providing more access to institutions of higher learning, thus creating more spaces to critically discuss LGBT issues.

The next issue that a progressive Xicana and Xicano movement should address is the current debate surrounding same-gender marriage. Yes, I agree that if heterosexual people have the right to marry and enjoy all the privileges and undertake the responsibilities, then queer people should partake in the same freedom. However, I do not view the current debate surrounding same-gender marriage as a civil rights issue—the movement is clearly driven by middle-class economic

---

5   See Joel Andreas's *Addicted to War: Why the U.S. Can't Kick Militarism* for an excellent historical analysis of our country's military imperialism in comic book form that is appropriate for audiences from middle-school to adulthood.

motives. I understand that people have not been allowed in hospital rooms and families of lovers have taken over assets, and people who have built a life together need to be afforded the same legal protections. Nonetheless, I view the demand for same-gender marriage as a demand for equal tax deductions. Although I wholeheartedly believe that marriage rights should be enjoyed by LGBT partnerships, I cannot devote any time to this cause until the following issue of social justice is addressed and rectified—immigration.

In 2009, the Obama administration deported nearly 400,000 immigrants, many more than any year under his predecessor. Obama won key battleground states with the overwhelming support of the Latina/o communities. However, what does it say that Bush was more progressive on the issue of immigration than Obama? As progressive queer Xicanas and Xicanos, it is imperative that we organize to defend the rights of our undocumented brothers and sisters and not allow Immigration and Customs Enforcement (ICE), the Tea Party, or right-wing commentators like Lou Dobbs to further demonize the most vulnerable population in this country. Why haven't any mainstream LGBT organizations rallied around the cause for immigrant rights or the recent protests against the passage of the xenophobic Arizona legislation? Hasn't one person from these organizations realized that people flee their homelands for a myriad of reasons, sexual persecution being one of them? We, as US citizens, strip the labor from undocumented workers as they toil in the fields, providing our sustenance; in our homes and office buildings, keeping them clean; caring for the children of the middle-class and the wealthy; and performing any number of services we deem too lowly to perform ourselves.

For example, one of the young persons who barricaded himself in the office of Senator John McCain to protest the inaction of the federal legislature on the Dream Act is a young gay undocumented Iranian. What an act of bravery to endanger himself in such a way. Not only could he be deported but the current climate in Iran toward its LGBT community is extremely perilous, as two young gay teens were lynched recently. Without the passage of the Dream Act, thousands of students are stuck in a limbo in what the ancient Mesoamericans called "nepantla," a state of limbo where they await transformation. Because the current political discourse surrounding immigration is being shaped by xenophobic societal contingents and because of our current administration's penchant for compromise, it is unrealistic to believe that the Dream Act and a meaningful comprehensive immigration bill will become law in the near future. That being said, progressive queer Xicanas and Xicanos who enjoy the privilege of citizenship must stand in solidarity with the undocumented until they are granted full amnesty and we no longer exploit laborers in the fields and sweat shops, in this country or in any other.

Finally, the issue that frames the preceding ones that a progressive queer Xicana/o agenda should address is the dismantling of capitalism in order to transform into an equitable and horizontal economy. Multinational corporations have co-opted the mainstream LGBT movement (mostly the "G") and have created an identity based on material goods and an exorbitant rate of consumption. Glance through any magazine targeted towards gay men, and you will see page after page of advertisements for high-end clothing, home products, and extravagant vacations. It is as if one must consume excessively in order to participate in queer culture. This is what passes for growing acceptance of the LGBT community—a wide range of corporate marketing campaigns that simply photoshop a gay or lesbian couple in for a heterosexual one as they purchase a luxury vehicle or go on a decadent cruise. Freedom, in both the heterosexual and queer worlds, has devolved from the ability to organize for causes of social justice into a rote transaction of consumption.

Moreover, capitalism is a cruel hierarchy of the increasingly shrinking group of haves enslaving the increasing population of have-nots, yet the American economy is tied inextricably to the act of consumption. Therefore, we must act to create meaningful change in our society. How many more bailouts of the rich will the bottom 98% tolerate until we organize to overthrow those who run this plantation called the United States? When will the masses wake up from their dreams of joining the exclusive club of the obscenely wealthy? When will we value the contributions people make to society rather than the emblems on their automobiles, bags, and shoes? When will we overcome our fears of "socialized medicine" and demand a universal health care system? Capitalism is the underlying cause of our society's ills, one that must be permanently destroyed if we are to free ourselves from the chains of our present-day hierarchy. Our society is ready for a fundamental change. We must demand a more equitable, horizontal economy, preferably based on organizations such as the Ejército Zapatista de Liberación Nacional (EZLN). We can no longer wait. The time to act is now.

Ofrenda of Communion/Memory

Finally, I would like to honor ACT-UP! and all other organizations that rallied a vibrant response to our government's inaction to the HIV/AIDS epidemic. As a person who has lived with HIV for nearly two decades, I owe Larry Kramer (another unsung hero of the LGBT rights movement) and his colleagues my life for the bravery of executing such tactics as disrupting Mass at St. Patrick's Cathedral and the iconic Rose Bowl Parade in order to bring awareness to the disease. Though the major pharmaceutical companies have reaped billions of dollars of profit since the advent of the first anti-retroviral drug, the medications have managed to prolong the lives of millions of HIV+ people around the world. However, we must follow Brazil's lead and demand that these drugs be made available as cheap generics, not a regimen that is cost prohibitive. Furthermore, we must demand that more funding be made available in the efforts to create a vaccine to prevent further seroconversions. As I offer my communion of ingesting my own regimen in memory of those like Kramer who forced our government into action, I offer the memory of my own life to those who have recently seroconverted, to hope and dream of a cure and for a world without HIV.

Section VII

International Print Sources

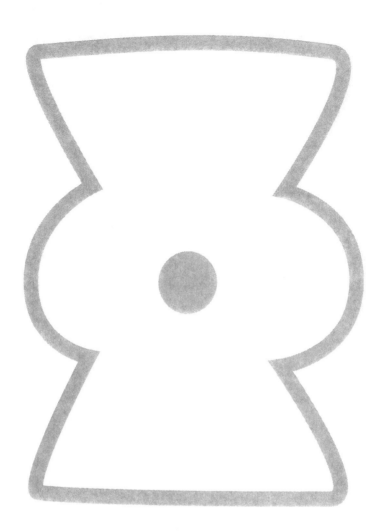

Queer Chicano/Mexicano Bibliography

Adelaida R. Del Castillo and Gibrán Güido

 This preliminary collection (created by the editors) of print sources gives emphasis to themes on or by queer Chicano and Mexicano authors on male sexuality, homoerotic writing, literary criticism, fiction, plays, poetry, performance art, HIV/AIDS, biography, and autobiography.

Acereda, Alberto. "Nuestro más profundo y humilde secreto: Los amores transgresores entre Rubén Darío y Amado Nervo." *Bulletin of Spanish Studies: Hispanic Studies and Researches on Spain, Portugal and Latin America* 89.6 (2012): 895–924. Print.

---. "Testimonios sobre la injuria homofóbica en el Modernismo hispánico." *Siglo Diecinueve: Literatura Hispánica* 18 (2012): 7–27. Print.

Acero, Rosa María. *Novo ante Novo: Un novísimo personaje homosexual.* Madrid: Pliegos, 2003. Print.

Acosta, Oscar Z. *Autobiography of a Brown Buffalo.* New York: Vintage, 1989. Print.

---. *Revolt of the Cockroach People.* New York: Vintage, 1989. Print.

Aguilar, Pedro Bustos. "Nueva Flor de Canela." *Virgins, Guerrillas, and Locas: Gay Latinos Writing about Love.* San Francisco: Cleis, 1999. 183–93. Print.

Alarcón, Francisco X. *Body in Flames. Cuerpo en llamas.* Trans. Francisco Aragón. San Francisco: Chronicle, 1990. Print.

---. *De amor oscuro/Of Dark Love: Poems*. Trans. Francisco Aragón. Santa Cruz, CA: Moving Parts, 1992. Print.

---. "Dialectics of Love." *Virgins, Guerrillas, and Locas: Gay Latinos Writing about Love*. Ed. Jaime Cortez. San Francisco: Cleis, 1999. 105–17. Print.

---. *From the Other Side of Night/Del otro lado de la noche: New and Selected Poems*. Tucson: U of Arizona P, 2002. Print.

---. *No Golden Gate for Us: Poems by Francisco X. Alarcón*. Introd. Juan Felipe Herrera. Santa Fe: Pennywhistle, 1993. Print.

---. *Poemas zurdos*. Naucalpan de Juárez, México: Factor, 1992. Print.

---. "Reclaiming Ourselves, Reclaiming America." *The Colors of Nature: Culture, Identity, and the Natural World*. Ed. Alison H. Deming and Lauret E. Savoy. Minneapolis: Milkweed, 2002. 28–48. Print.

---. Rev. of "Reunion: Asalto a un Tabu Sexual." *Revista Literaria de El Tecolote* 2.3–4 (1981): 11. Print.

---. *Snake Poems: An Aztec Invocation*. San Francisco: Chronicle, 1992. Print.

Alarcón, Francisco X., and Lorna Dee Cervantes. "Chicanas y Chicanos en Diálogo." *Quarry West* 26. Santa Cruz, CA: Porter College, U of California, 1989. Print.

Alarcon, Norma. "Tropology of Hunger: The 'Miseducation' of Richard Rodriguez." *The Ethnic Canon: Histories, Institutions, and Interventions*. Ed. David Palumbo-Liu. Minneapolis: U of Minnesota P, 1995. 140-52. Print.

Aldama, Frederick Luis, ed. *Arturo Islas: The Uncollected Works*. Houston: Arte Público, 2003. Print.

---. *Brown on Brown: Chicana/o Representations of Gender, Sexuality and Ethnicity*. Austin: U of Texas P, 2005. Print.

---, ed. *Critical Mappings of Arturo Islas's Fictions*. Tempe, AZ: Bilingual Press/ Editorial Bilingüe, 2008. Print.

---. *Dancing with Ghosts: A Critical Biography of Arturo Islas*. Berkeley: U of California P, 2005. Print.

---. "Penalizing Chicana/o Bodies in Edward J. Olmos's *American Me*." In *Decolonial Voices: Chicana and Chicano Cultural Studies in the 21st Century*,"

Ed. Arturo J. Aldama and Naomi H. Quiñóez, Bloomington: Indiana UP, 2002. 78–97. Print.

---. *Spilling the Beans in Chicanolandia: Conversations with Writers and Artists.* Austin: U of Texas P, 2006. Print.

Alfaro, Luis. "Cuerpo Politizado." *Uncontrollable Bodies: Testimonies of Art and Culture.* Ed. Rodney Sappington and Tyler Stallings. Seattle: Bay, 1994. 216–41. Print.

---. "Downtown." *O Solo Homo: The New Queer Performance.* Ed. Holly Hughes and David Román. New York: Grove, 1998. 313–48. Print.

---. " 'Electricidad': A Chicano Take on the Tragedy of 'Electra.' " *American Theatre*, 23.2 (2006): 63–85. Print.

---. "Excerpt from 'Downtown,' A Solo Performance Work." *Blood Whispers: L.A. Writers on AIDS.* Ed. Terry Wolverton. Los Angeles: Silverton Books, 1991. 13–16. Print.

---. "Nicholas." *Blood Whispers. Vol. 2: L.A. Writers on AIDS.* Ed. Terry Wolverton. Los Angeles: Silverton Books, 1994. 87–92. Print.

---. "Pico-Union." *Men on Men 4: Best New Gay Fiction.* Ed. George Stambolian. New York: Plume, 1992. 268–83. Print.

---. "Straight as a Line." *Out of the Fringe: Contemporary Latina/Latino Theatre and Performance.* Ed. Caridad Svich and María Teresa Marrero. New York: Theatre Communications Group, 2000. 1–42. Print.

Algarín, Miguel. *Love is Hard Work: Memorias de Loisaida.* New York: Simon and Schuster, 1997. Print.

Allatson, Paul. " 'My Bones Shine in the Dark': AIDS and the De-scription of Chicano Queer in the Work of Gil Cuadros." *Aztlán: A Journal of Chicano Studies* 32.1 (2007): 23–52. Print.

---. " 'Siempre feliz en mi falda': Luis Alfaro's Simulative Challenge." *GLQ: A Journal of Lesbian and Gay Studies* 5.2 (1999): 199–230. Print.

Almaguer, Tomás. "Chicano Men: A Cartography of Homosexual Identity and Behavior." *Differences: A Journal of Feminist Cultural Studies* 3.2 (1991): 75–100. Print.

Alonso, Ana Maria, and Maria Teresa Koreck. "Silences: Hispanics, AIDS, and Sexual Practices." *Differences: A Journal of Feminist Cultural Studies* 1.1 (Winter 1989): 101–24. Print.

Alurista, and Rigoberto González. *Xicano Duende: A Select Anthology*. Tempe, AZ: Bilingual Press/Editorial Bilingüe, 2011. Print.

Alvarez, Pablo. "Gil Cuadros' AZT-Land: A Queer Chicano Literary Heritage." MA thesis California State U, 2009. Print.

Amuchástegui, Ana y Ivonne Szasz, Coordinadoras. *Sucede que me canso de ser hombre: Relatos y reflexiones sobre hombres y masculinidades en México*. México, D.F.: El Colegio de México, 2007. Print.

Anderson, Danny J. "Difficult Relations, Compromising Positions: Telling Involvement in Recent Mexican Narrative." *Chasqui* 24.1 (1995): 16–28. Print.

Anguiano, Sergio. *Hermanos. Hermanos! Hermanos?* Senior thesis U of California, 1993. Print.

Anthony, Adelina, Dino Fozz, and Lorenzo Herrera y Lozano. *Tragic Bitches: An Experiment in Queer Xicana & Xicano Performance Poetry*. San Francisco, Kórima, 2011. Print.

Anzaldúa, Gloria. *Borderlands/La Frontera: The New Mestiza*. San Francisco: Aunt Lute, 1987. Print.

Aponte-Parés, Luis. "*Outside/*In: Crossing Queer and Latino Boundaries." *Mambo Montage: The Latinization of New York*. Ed. Agustín Laó-Montes and Arlene Dávila, New York: Columbia UP, 2001. 363–85. Print.

Arévalo, Sandra, and Hortensia Amaro. "Sexual Health of Latina/o Populations in the United States." *Latina/o Sexualities: Probing Powers, Passions, Practices, and Policies*. Ed. Marysol Asencio. New Brunswick, NJ: Rutgers UP, 2010. 75–89. Print.

Arguelles, Lourdes, and Anne Rivero. "Working with Gay/Homosexual Latinos with HIV Disease: Spiritual Emergencies and Culturally Based Psycho-Therapeutic Treatments." *Culture and Difference: Critical Perspectives on the Bicultural Experience in the United States*. Ed. Antonia Darder. Westport: Bergin & Garvey, 1995. 155–68. Print.

Arreola, Sonya Grant. "Latina/o Childhood Sexuality." *Latina/o Sexualities: Probing Powers, Passions, Practices, and Policies*. Ed. Marysol Asencio. New Brunswick, NJ: Rutgers UP, 2010. 48–61. Print.

Arteaga, Arturo. *Chicano Poetics: Heterotexts and Hybridities*. New York: Cambridge UP, 1997. Print.

Austin Latino Lesbian and Gay Organization, ed. *Queer Codex: Chile Love*. Austin: ALLGO, 2004. Print.

Ayala, George. "Homophobia, Racism, Financial Hardship and AIDS: Unpacking the Effects of Social Discrimination on the Sexual Risk for HIV among Latino Gay Men." *HIV Prevention with Latinos: Theory, Research, and Practice*. Ed. Kurt C. Organista. New York: Oxford UP, 2012. Print.

---. "Retiring Behavioral Risk, Disease, and Deficit Models: Sexual Health Frameworks for Latino Gay Men and Other Men Who Enjoy Sex with Men." *Latina/o Sexualities: Probing Powers, Passions, Practices, and Policies*. Ed. Marysol Asencio. New Brunswick, NJ: Rutgers UP, 2010. 274–78. Print.

Ayala, George, Jaime Cortez, and Patrick "Pato" Hebert. "Where There's Querer: Knowledge Production and the Praxis of HIV Prevention." *Latina/o Sexualities: Probing Powers, Passions, Practices, and Policies*. Ed. Marysol Asencio. New Brunswick, NJ: Rutgers UP, 2010. 150-72. Print.

Baca Zinn, Maxine. "Chicano Men and Masculinity." *The Sociology of Gender: A Text-Reader*. Ed. Laura Kramer. New York: St. Martin's, 1991. 221–32. Print.

Balderston, Daniel. "Poetry, Revolution, Homophobia: Polemics from the Mexican Revolution." *Hispanisms and Homosexualities*. Ed. Sylvia Molloy and Robert McKee Irwin. Durham, NC: Duke UP, 1998. 57–75. Print.

Balderston, Daniel, and Donna Guy, eds. *Sex and Sexuality in Latin America*. New York: New York UP, 1997. Print.

Bañuelos Enriquez, Ernesto. "La Mía y la Historia de Algunos Amigos en Estos Trozos de Amores Cotidianos [The Story of Myself and Some Friends in These Fragments of Daily Loves]." *Gay Sunshine: A Journal of Gay Liberation*. 26/27.4 (1975): 10-13. Print.

Barbachano Ponce, Miguel. *El diario de José Toledo*. México, D.F.: Era, 1964. Print.

Barrera, Reyna. Salvador Novo. Navaja de La Inteligencia. México, D.F.: Plaza y Valdes, 1999. Print.

Bautista, Juan Carlos. *Bestial*. México, D.F.: El Tucán de Virginia, 1993. Print.

Bell, David, and Gill Valentine, eds. *Mapping Desire: Geographies of Sexuality*. London: Routledge, 1995. Print.

Bellatín, Mario. *Beauty Salon*. Trans. Kurt Hollander. San Francisco: City Lights, 2009. Print.

---. *Jacobo el mutante*. México, D.F.: Alfaguara, 2002. Print.

---. *Shiki Nagaoka: Una nariz de ficción*. Buenos Aires: Sudamericana, 2001. Print.

Benavidez, Max. "Chicano Art: Culture, Myth, and Sensibility." *Chicano Visions: American Painters on the Verge*. Ed. Cheech Marin, Max Benavidez, Constance Cortez, and Terecita Romo. Boston: Little, Brown and Co., 2002. 11–21. Print.

---. *Gronk*. Minneapolis: U of Minnesota P, 2007. Print.

---. "Gronk: Master of Urban Absurdity." Exh. cat. San Francisco: Mexican Museum, 1994. Print.

---. *Cantar del Marrakech*. Mexico, D.F.: Consejo Nacional para la Cultura y las Artes, 2003. Print.

Blanco, José Joaquín. *Calles como incendios*. México, D.F.: Océano, 1985. Print.

---. *Función de mediodía: Ensayos de literatura cotidiana*. México, D.F.: Era, 1981. Print.

---. *Mátame y verás*. México, D.F.: Era, 1994. Print.

---. "Ojos que da pánico soñar." *Función de mediodía: Ensayos de literatura cotidiana*. México, D.F.: Era, 1981. Print.

---. *Las púberes canéforas*. México, D.F.: Océano, 1983. Print.

Blanco, José Joaquín, José Dimayuga, y Luis Zapata. *Triple función*. México, D.F.: Quimera, 2007. Print.

Blanco, José Joaquín y Luis Zapata. "¿Cuál literatura gay?" Sábado: Suplemento de *Unomásuno* 310 (1983): 11. Print.

Bonfil, Carlos. "Los 41." Enrique Florescano, Coord. *Mitos Mexicanos*. México, D.F.: Aguilar, 1995. 219–24. Print.

Bracho, Ricardo A. *A to B*. Alexandria, VA: Alexander Street, 2005. Print.

---. "Daddy." *Virgins, Guerrillas, and Locas: Gay Latinos Writing about Love*. San Francisco: Cleis, 1999. 157–63. Print.

---. "Huevos de Oro: On Passion and Privilege" *Cast Out: Queer Lives in Theater*. Ann Arbor: U of Michigan P, 2006. 191–94. Print.

---. "*The Sweetest Hangover (and Other STDs)*." Alexandria, VA: Alexander Street, 2005. Print.

Brandes, Stanley. "Drink, Abstinence, and Male Identity in Mexico City." *Changing Men and Masculinities in Latin America*. Ed. Matthew Gutmann. Durham, NC: Duke UP, 2003. 153–76. Print.

Brito, Alejandro. Prólogo. *Que se abra esa puerta: Crónicas y ensayos sobre la diversidad sexual*. México, D.F.: Paidós, 2010. Print.

Bronfman, Mario and Sergio Lopez Moreno. "Perspectives on HIV/AIDS Prevention Among Immigrants on the U.S.-Mexico Border." *AIDS Crossing Borders: The Spread of HIV Among Migrant Latinos*. Ed. Mishra, Connner, and Magaña. Boulder, CO: Westview, 1996. 49–76. Print.

Brouwer, Daniel C. "Counterpublicity and Corporeality in HIV/AIDS 'Zines.'" *Critical Studies in Mass Communication* 22.5 (2005): 351–71. Print.

Bruce-Novoa, Juan. "Homosexuality and the Chicano Novel." *Confluencia: Revista Hispanica de Cultura y Literatura* 2.1 (1986): 69–77. Print.

---. "In Search of the Honest Outlaw, John Rechy." *Minority Voices* 3.1 (1979): 37–45. Print.

Buffington, Robert. "Homophobia and the Mexican Working Class, 1900-1910." *The Famous 41: Sexuality and Social Control in Mexico, 1901*. Ed. Irwin, McCaughan, and Nassar. New York: Palgrave Macmillan, 2003. 193–225. Print.

Bustos-Aguilar, Pedro. "Mister Don't Touch the Banana: Notes on the Popularity of the Ethnosexed Body South of the Border." *Critique of Anthropology* 15.2 (1995): 149–70. Print.

Byers, James, Michael Nava, and David E. Owen. *Three Poets: James Byers, Michael Nava, David Owen.* Colorado Springs, CO: Bon, 1975. Print.

Cabrera, Jorge Mario. "En el labertino de la universalidad: Una charla con Francisco X. Alarcón." *De ambiente: la revista bisexual, lésbica, y gay latina de Los Ángeles* 5 (1994): 24–25, 41–42. Print.

Calva, José Rafael. *El jinete azul.* México, D.F.: Katún, 1985. Print.

---. *Utopía gay,* México, D.F.: Oasis, 1983. Print.

Campo, Rafael. *Diva.* Durham, NC: Duke UP, 1999. Print.

Cantú, Lionel, Jr. "*De Ambiente:* Queer Tourism and the Shifting Boundaries of Mexican Male Sexualities." *GLQ: A Journal of Lesian and Gay Studies* 8.1–2 (2002): 139–66. Print.

---. "Entre Hombres/Between Men: Latino Masculinities and Homosexualities." *Gay Masculinities.* Ed. Peter Nardi. Thousand Oaks, CA: Sage, 2000. 224–46. Print.

---. "A Place Called Home: A Queer Political Economy of Mexican Immigrant Men's Family Experiences." *Queer Families, Queer Politics: Challenging Culture and the State.* Ed. Mary Bernstein and Renate Reimann. New York: Columbia UP, 2001. 112–36. Print.

---. *The Sexuality of Migration: Border Crossings and Mexican Immigrant Men.* Ed. Nancy A. Naples and Salvador Vidal-Ortiz. New York: New York UP, 2009. Print.

Cantu, Robert. "Arturo Islas," *Dictionary of Literary Biography.* Vol. 122. *Chicano Writers Second Series.* Ed. Francisco Lomeli and Carl Shirley. Detroit: Gale Research, 1992. 146–54. Print.

Carballido, Emilio. *El Norte.* Xalapa, Ver.: Universidad Veracruzana, 1958. Print.

Carrier, Joseph. "Cultural Factors Affecting Urban Mexican Male Homosexual Behavior." *Archives of Sexual Behavior* 5 (1976): 103–24. Print.

---. *De los otros: Intimacy and Homosexuality Among Mexican Men.* New York: Columbia UP, 1995. Print.

---. "Family Attitudes and Mexican Male Homosexuality." *Urban Life: A Journal of Ethnographic Research* 5.3 (1976): 359–76. Print.

---. "Gay Liberation and Coming-Out in Mexico." *Journal of Homosexuality* 17.3–4 (1989): 225–52. Print.

---. "Mexican Male Bisexuality." *Journal of Homosexuality* 11.1–2 (1985): 75–86. Print.

---. "Miguel: Sexual Life History of a Gay Mexican American." *Gay Culture in America: Essays from the Field*. Ed. Gilbert Herdt. Boston: Beacon, 1992. 202–24. Print.

---. "Participants in Urban Mexican Male Homosexual Encounters." *Archives of Sexual Behavior* 1 (1971): 279–91. Print.

---. "Reflections on Ethical Problems Encountered in Field Research on Mexican Male Homosexuality: 1968 to Present." *Culture, Health and Sexuality* 1.3 (1999): 207–21. Print.

---. "Sexual Behavior and Spread of AIDS in Mexico." *Medical Anthropology* 10 (1989): 129–42. Print.

---. "Urban Mexican Male Homosexual Encounters: An Analysis of Participants and Coping Strategies." Diss. U of California, 1972. Print.

Carrier, Joseph, and J. Raul Magaña. "Use of Ethnosexual Data on Men of Mexican Origin for HIV/AIDS Prevention Programs." *The Journal of Sex Research* 28.2 (1991): 189–202. Print.

Carrillo, H.G. *Loosing My Espanish*. New York: Random, 2005. Print.

Carrillo, Héctor G. "Another Crack in the Mirror: The Politics of AIDS Prevention in Mexico." *International Quarterly of Community Health Education* 14.2 (1993): 129–52. Print.

---. "Cultural Change, Hybridity and Male Homosexuality in Mexico." *Culture, Health and Sexuality* 1.3 (1999): 223–38. Print.

---. "Imagining Modernity: Sexuality, Policy, and Social Change in Mexico." *Sexuality Research and Social Policy* 5.3 (2007): 74–91. Print.

---. "Neither *Machos* nor *Maricones*: Masculinity and Emerging Male Homosexual Identities in Mexico." *Changing Men and Masculinities in Latin America*. Ed. Matthew Gutmann. Durham, NC: Duke UP, 2003. 351–69. Print.

---. *The Night is Young: Sexuality in Mexico in the Time of AIDS*. Chicago: U of Chicago P, 2002. Print.

---. "Sexual Culture, Structure, and Change: A Transnational Framework for Studies of Latino Migration and HIV." *HIV Prevention with Latinos: Theory, Research, and Practice.* Ed. Kurt C. Organista. New York: Oxford UP, 2012. Print.

---. "Sexual Migration, Cross-Cultural Sexual Encounters, and Sexual Health." *Sexuality Research & Social Policy* 1.3 (2004): 58–70. Print.

Carrillo, Héctor, and Jorge Fontdevila. "Rethinking Sexual Initiation: Pathways to Identity Formation Among Gay and Bisexual Mexican Male Youth."

Archives of Sexual Behavior 40.6 (2011): 1241–1254. Print.

Case, Sue Ellen, Philip Bret, and Susan Leigh Foster, eds. *Cruising the Performative: Interventions into the Representation of Ethnicity, Nationality, and Sexuality.* Bloomington: Indiana UP, 1995. Print.

Casillo, Charles. *Outlaw: John Rechy.* Los Angeles: Alyson, 2002. Print.

Castillo, Alberto. *Letargo de bahía.* México, D.F.: CONACULTA, 1992. Print.

Castillo, Debra. "Interview: John Rechy." *Diacritics* 25.1 (1995): 113–25. Print.

Castrejón, Eduardo A. *Los cuarenta y uno: Novela crítico-social.* México, D.F.: Tipografía popular, 1906. Print.

Ceballos-Capitaine, Alicia, Jose Szapocznik, Nancy T. Blaney, Robert O. Morgan, Carrie Millon, and Carl Eisdorfer. "Ethnicity, Emotional Distress, Stress-related Disruption, and Coping Among HIV Seropositive Gay Males." *Hispanic Journal of Behavioral Sciences* 12.2 (1990): 135–52. Print.

Ceballos Maldonado, José. *Después de todo.* México, D.F.: Premiá, 1986. Print.

Cerdeño, A.F., A.P. Martínez-Donate, J.A. Zellner, F. Sañudo, H. Carrillo, M. Engelberg, C. Sipan, and M. Hovell. "Marketing HIV Prevention for Heterosexually Identified Latino Men Who Have Sex with Men and Women: The Hombres Sanos Campaign." *Journal of Health Communication* 17.6 (2012): 641–58. Print.

Cervantes-Gutierrez, Jose Jesse. *Sexual Attitudes and Behaviors of the Latino Gay Male.* Diss. Graduate School of Psychology, Wright Institute, 1981. Print.

Chabram-Dernersesian, Angie, ed. *The Chicana/o Cultural Studies Forum: Critical and Ethnographic Practices.* New York: New York UP, 2007. Print.

---, ed. *The Chicana/o Cultural Studies Reader.* London: Routledge, 2006. Print.

---, ed. Special Issue: Chicana/o Latina/o Cultural Studies, *Cultural Studies,* 12.2 (1999). Print.

Chaves, José Ricardo. "Afeminados, hombrecitos y lagartijos: Narrativa mexicana del siglo XIX." *México se escribe con J: Una historia de la cultura gay.* México, D.F.: Planeta, 2010. Print.

Chávez-Silverman, Susana. "Tropicolada: Inside the U.S. Latino/a Gender B(l)ender." *Tropicalizations: Transcultural Representations of Latinidad (Re-encounters with Colonialism: New Perspectives on the Americas).* Ed. Frances R. Aparicio and Susana Chávez-Silverman. Hanover, NH: U of New England P, 1997. 101–18. Print.

Chavoya, C. Ondine. "Internal Exiles: The Interventionist Public and Performance Art of Asco." *Space, Site and Intervention: Situating Installation Art.* Ed. Erika Suderburg. Minneapolis: U of Minnesota P, 2000. 189–208. Print.

---. "Pseudographic Cinema: Asco's No-Movies." *Performance Research* 3.1 (1998): 1–14. Print.

Christian, Karen. "Will the 'Real Chicano' Please Stand Up? The Challenge of John Rechy and Sheila Ortiz Taylor to Chicano Essentialism." *The Americas Review* 20.2 (1989): 89–104. Print.

Cole, Dana. "A Linguistic Journey to the Border." *Apples: Journal of Applied Language Studies.* 5.1 (2011): 77–92. Print.

Collado, Fernando del. *Homofobia. Odio, crimen y justicia, 1995–2005.* México, D.F: Tusquets, 2007. Print.

Colon, Edgar. "An Ethnographic Study of Six Latino Gay and Bisexual Men." *Journal of Gay & Lesbian Social Services.* 12.3–4. (2001): 77–92. Print.

Comfort, Megan, Carmen Albizu-García, Timoteo Rodriguez, and Carlos Molina III. "HIV Risk and Prevention for Latinos in Jails and Prisons." *HIV Prevention with Latinos: Theory, Research, and Practice.* Ed. Kurt C. Organista. New York: Oxford UP, 2012. Print.

Conner, Ross F., Shiraz I. Mishra, and J. Raul Magaña. "HIV Prevention Policies and Programs: Perspectives from Researchers, Migrant Workers and Policymakers." *AIDS Crossing Borders: The Spread of HIV Among Migrant Latinos.* Ed. Mishra, Conner, and Magaña. Boulder, CO: Westview Press, 1996. 185–214. Print.

Contreras, Daniel T. *Unrequited Love and Gay Latino Culture: What Have You Done to My Heart?* New York: Palgrave Macmillan, 2005. Print.

Cook, Stephen. "Containing a Contagion: Crime and Homosexuality in Post-revolutionary Mexico City." MA thesis U of California, 2008. Print.

Córdova Plaza, Rocío. "The Realm Outside the Law: Transvestite Sex Work in Xalapa, Veracruz." *Decoding Gender: Law and Practice in Contemporary Mexico.* Ed. Baitenmann, Chenaut, and Varley. New Brunswick, NJ: Rutgers UP, 2007. 124–48. Print.

Coronado, Raúl. "Bringing it Back Home: Desire, Jotos, Men, and the Sexual/ Gender Politics of Chicana and Chicano Studies." *The Chicana/o Cultural Studies Reader.* Ed. Angie Chabram-Dernersesian. New York: Routledge, 2006. 233–40. Print.

---. "Unthinkable Bodies (Un) Made: Notes Towards a Historicizing of Chicana/o Sexuality." *Expanding Raza World Views: Sexuality and Regionalism: Selected Proceedings from the 22nd NACCS Conference.* Ed. Adalijiza Sosa-Riddell and National Association for Chicana and Chicano Studies Conference. National Association for Chicana and Chicano Studies, 1999. 65–80. Print.

Cortazar, Alejandro. "Implicaciones subalternas de un proliferado discurso coloquial en la obra narrativa de Luis Zapata." *Hispanófila* 129.3 (2000): 59–74. Print.

Cortez, Jaime, ed. "Introduction." *Virgins, Guerrillas, and Locas: Gay Latinos Writing about Love.* San Francisco: Cleis, 1999. xiii-xv. Print.

---. "The Nasty Book Wars." *Bésame Mucho.* Ed. Jaime Manrique and Jesse Dorris. New York: Painted Leaf, 1999. 213–24. Print.

---. *Sexile = Sexilio.* Los Angeles: Institute for Gay Men's Health, 2004. Print.

---. *Turnover: A Collection of HIV Prevention Comics.* Los Angeles: Institute for Gay Men's Health, 2005. Print.

---, ed. *Virgins, Guerrillas, and Locas: Gay Latinos Writing about Love.* San Francisco: Cleis, 1999. Print.

Cota, Albert E. "Down Below." *Bésame Mucho.* Ed. Jaime Manrique and Jesse Dorris. New York: Painted Leaf, 1999. 51–59. Print.

Crisman, Robert. "History Made: First Lesbians/Gays of Color Conference." *Freedom Socialist* 5.4 (1979–80): 7. Print.

Cruz-Malavé, Arnaldo, and Martin F. Manalansan IV, eds. *Queer Globalizations: Citizenship and the Afterlife of Colonialism.* New York: New York UP, 2002. Print.

Cuadros, Gil. "At Risk." *Blood Whispers: L.A. Writers on AIDS.* Ed. Terry Wolverton. Los Angeles: Silverton Books, 1991. 58–60. Print.

---. "Birth." *His2: Brilliant New Fiction by Gay Writers.* Ed. Robert Drake and Terry Wolverton. Boston: Faber. 120-22. Print.

---. "The Breath of God That Brings Life," "There Are Places You Don't Walk at Night, Alone," and "To the First Time." *Persistent Voices: Poetry by Writers Lost to AIDS.* Ed. David Groff and Philip Clark. New York: Alyson, 2009. 60-66. Print.

---. "Chivalry." *Gay American Autobiography: Writings from Whitman to Sedaris.* Ed. David Bergman. Madison: U of Wisconsin P, 2009. 381–89. Print.

---. *City of God.* San Francisco: City Light, 1994. Print.

---. "Hands: A Story by Gil Cuadros." *Transcend AIDS: Work by Los Angeles Artists with HIV/AIDS.* Ed. Arseneault, Moore, Eggan, and Cuadros. Los Angeles: Estate Project for Artists with AIDS, 1995. 16–19. Print.

---. "Indulgences" *High Risk 2: Writings on Sex, Death, and Subversion.* Ed. Amy Scholder and Ira Silverberg. New York: Plume, 1994. 146–53. Print.

---. "RM#." *Blood Whispers: L.A. Writers on AIDS.* Ed. Terry Wolverton. Los Angeles: Silverton Books, 1991. 23–24. Print.

---. "Sight." *Blood Whispers. Vol. 2: L.A. Writers on AIDS.* Ed. Terry Wolverton. Los Angeles: Silverton Books, 1994. 58–60. Print.

---. "Unprotected." *Indivisible: New Short Fiction by Gay and Lesbian West Coast Writers.* Ed. Terry Wolverton and Robert Drake. New York: Plume, 1991. 25–32. Print.

Cuéllar, José Tomás de. *Historia de Chucho el Ninfo.* 1871, 1890. Estudio Preliminar de Belem Clark de Lara. México, D.F.: UNAM, 2011. Print.

Cunningham, John C. "' 'Hey, Mr. Liberace, Will You Vote for Zeta?' Looking for the Joto in Chicano Men's Autobiographical Writing." *Race-ing Masculinity: Identity in Contemporary U.S. Men's Writing.* New York: Routledge, 2002. 69–94. Print.

Curtis, Wayne. "Gay Latino Lawyer Mystery Writer: Michael Nava." Rev of *How Town,* by Michael Nava. *Gay Community News* 15 July 1990: 8–9,11. Print.

Cutler, John Alba. "Prothesis, Surrogation, and Relation in Arturo Islas's *The Rain God.*" *The Chicano Studies Reader: An Anthology of Aztlán, 1970-2000.* Ed. Noriega, Avila, Davalos, Sandoval, and Pérez-Torres. Los Angeles: UCLA Chicano Studies Research Center Publications, 2001. 647–72. Print.

Dallal, Alberto. *Mocambo.* Barcelona: Grijalbo, 1976. Print.

Danahay, Martin A. "Richard Rodriguez's Poetics of Manhood." *Fictions of Manhood: Crossing Cultures, Crossing Sexualities.* Ed. Peter Murphy. New York: New York UP, 1994. 290-307. Print.

Dauster, Frank N. *Xavier Villaurrutia.* New York: Twayne, 1971. Print.

Decena, Carlos. "Epilogue: Rethinking the Maps Where 'Latina/o' and 'Sexuality' Meet." *Latina/o Sexualities: Probing Powers, Passions, Practices, and Policies.* Ed. Marysol Asencio. New Brunswick, NJ: Rutgers UP, 2010. 279–86. Print.

Decker, Jeffrey Louis. "Mr. Secrets: Richard Rodriguez Flees the House of Memory." *Transition* 61 (1993): 124–32. Print.

de la Garza, Luis Alberto, and Horacio N. Roque Ramírez." Queer Community History and the Evidence of Desire: The Archivo Rodrigo Reyes, a Gay and Lesbian Latino Archive." *The Power of Language: Selected Papers from the Second REFORMA National Conference.* Ed. Lillian Castillo-Speed and the REFORMA National Conference Publications Committee. Englewood, CO: Libraries Unlimited, 2000. 181–98. Print.

de la Mora, Sergio. *Cinemachismo: Masculinities and Sexuality in Mexican Film.* Austin: U of Texas P, 2006. Print.

---. "Fascinating Machismo: Toward an Unmasking of Heterosexual Masculinity in Arturo Ripstein's *El lugar sin límites.*" *Journal of Film and Video* 44.3–4 (1992–3): 83–105. Print.

Del Castillo, Adelaida R., and Gibran Guido, eds. *Queer in Aztlán: Chicano Male Recollections of Consciousness and Coming Out.* San Diego: Cognella, 2014. Print.

Días y Morales, Magda, coord. *Juan García Ponce y la Generación del Medio Siglo.* Xalapa, Ver.: Instituto de Investigaciones Lingüístico-Literarias, Universidad Veracruzana, 1998. Print.

Díaz, Rafael M. *Gay Latino Men and HIV: Culture, Sexuality, and Risk Behavior.* New York: Routledge, 1998. Print.

Díaz, Rafael M., Jorge Sánchez, and Kurt Schroeder. "Inequality, Discrimination and HIV Risk: A Review of Research on Latino Gay Men." *HIV Prevention with Latinos: Theory, Research, and Practice.* Ed. Kurt C. Organista. New York: Oxford UP, 2012. Print.

Díaz Barriga, Miguel. "*Vergüenza* and Changing Chicana and Chicano Narratives." *Men and Masculinties* 3.3 (2001): 278–98. Rpt. in *Changing Men and Masculinities in Latin America.* Ed. Matthew Gutmann. Durham, NC: Duke UP, 2003. 256–80. Print.

Díaz-Sánchez, Micaela. "Impossible Patriots: The Exiled Queer Citizen in Cherríe Moraga's *The Hungry Woman: A Mexican Medea.*" *Signatures of the Past: Cultural Memory in Contemporary Anglophone North American Drama.* Ed. Marc Maufort and Caroline De Wagter. New York: Peter Lang, 2008. 141–150. Print.

Domínguez-Ruvalcaba, Héctor. "From Fags to Gays: Political Adaptations and Cultural Translations in the Mexican Gay Liberation Movement." *Mexico Reading the United States.* Ed. Linda Egan and Mary K. Long. Nashville, TN: Vanderbilt UP, 2009. 116–34. Print.

---. *La modernidad abyecta: Formación del Discurso Homosexual en Hispanoamérica.* Xalapa, Ver.: Universidad Veracruzana, 2001. Print.

---. *Modernity and the Nation in Mexican Representations of Masculinity: From Sensuality to Bloodshed.* New York: Palgrave Macmillan, 2007. Print.

Doty, Alexander. *Making Things Perfectly Queer: Interpreting Mass Culture.* Minneapolis: U of Minnesota P, 1993. Print.

Drake, Robert, and Terry Wolverton, eds. *His2: Brilliant New Fiction by Gay Writers.* Boston: Faber and Faber, 1997. Print.

"El Sexo en México." Special dossier. *Nexos* 12.139 (1989): 29–80. Print.

Escobar Latapí, Agustín. "Men and Their Histories: Restructuring, Gender Inequality, and Life Transitions in Urban Mexico." *Changing Men and Masculinities in Latin America.* Ed. Matthew Gutmann. Durham, NC: Duke UP, 2003. 84–114. Print.

Espinoza, Alex. *The Five Acts of Diego Leon: A Novel.* New York: Random, 2013. Print.

---. *Still Water Saints: A Novel.* New York: Random, 2008. Print.

Espinoza-Cuellar, Xuan Carlos. "De Leche y Galletas de Animalitos," "I Like It When You Cum," "Chamo," "Sex in Texas," "La Campesina," "Tu Maldición Toda," "Wetback." *Mariposas: A Modern Anthology of Queer Latino Poetry.* Ed. Emanuel Xavier. Mountain View, CA: Floricanto Press, 2008. 142–50. Print.

Estrada, Gabriel S. "The 'Macho' Body as Social Malinche." *Velvet Barrios: Popular Culture & Chicana/o Sexualities.* Ed. Alicia Gaspar de Alba. New York: Palgrave Macmillan, 2003. 41–60. Print.

Fernandez, Charles. "Undocumented Aliens in the Queer Nation." *Out/Look* 12 (1991): 20-23. Print.

Ferretis, Jorge. *El coronel que asesinó a un palomo y otros cuentos.* México, D.F.: FCE-Tezontle, 1952. Print.

Flores, Lauro. "Chicano Autobiography: Culture, Ideology and the Self." *Americas Review* 18.2 (1990): 80-91. Print.

Forster, Merlin H. *Fire and Ice: The Poetry of Xavier Villaurrutia.* Chapel Hill: U of North Carolina P, 1976. Print.

Foster, David William. *El Ambiente Nuestro: Chicano/Latino Homoerotic Writing.* Tempe, AZ: Bilingual Press/Editorial Bilingüe, 2006. Print.

---. *Chicano/Latino Homoerotic Identities.* New York: Routledge, 1999. Print.

---. *Gay and Lesbian Themes in Latin American Writing.* Austin: U of Texas P, 1991. Print.

---. "Homoerotic Writing and Chicano Authors." *The Bilingual Review/ La Revista Bilingüe* 21.1 (1996): 42–51. Print.

---. Review of *Adonis García: A Picaresque Novel,* by Luis Zapata. Trans. E. A. Lacey. Ed. Winston Leyland. *My Deep Dark Pain Is Love: A Collection of Latin American Gay Fiction. Chasqui* 13.1 (1983): 90-92. Print.

---. *Sexual Textualities: Essays on Queer/Ing Latin American Writing.* Austin: U of Texas P, 1997. Print.

---. *Spanish Writers on Gay and Lesbian Themes: A Bio-Critical Sourcebook.* Westport, CT: Greenwood, 1999. Print.

Foxx, Dino. "Día de los Muertos," "Early Hours of a Sunday," "Thin Line," "Four Seasons, "An American Tale," "Broken Spanish." *Mariposas: A Modern Anthology of Queer Latino Poetry.* Ed. Emanuel Xavier. Mountain View, CA: Floricanto Press, 2008. 44–54. Print.

Frati, Gina. *La Homosexualidad: El Mundo y el Drama del Tercer Sexo.* Colección *Duda Seminal.* México, D.F.: Lito Offset Victoria, 1973. Print.

García, Bernardo. *The Development of a Latino Gay Identity.* New York: Garland, 1998. Print.

García, Ramón. "Against Rasquache: Chicano Identity and the Politics of Popular Culture in Los Angeles." *Critica: A Journal of Critical Essays* 3 (1998): 1–26. Rpt. in *The Chicana/o Cultural Studies Reader.* Ed. Angie Chabram-Dernersesian. New York: Routledge, 2006. 211–23. Print.

---. "Amor Indio: Juan Diego de San Diego." *Virgins, Guerrillas, and Locas: Gay Latinos Writing about Love.* San Francisco: Cleis, 1999. 141–46. Print.

---. "Miss Primavera Contest." *The Floating Borderlands: Twenty-five Years of U.S. Hispanic Literature.* Ed. Lauro Flores. U of Washington P, 1998. 397–98. Print.

Garza Carvajal, Federico. *Butterflies will Burn: Prosecuting Sodomites in Early Modern Spain and Mexico*. Austin: U of Texas P, 2003. Print.

Getlin, Josh. "200,000 Call for More AIDS Research Funds: Gays, Lesbians and Backers March in Capital, Demand Federal Law Against Discrimination." *Los Angeles Times* 12 Oct. 1987. Print.

Giles, James R., and Wanda Giles. "An Interview with John Rechy." *Chicago Review* 25.1 (1973): 19–31. Print.

Girman, Chris. "Familiar, Familial Voices: Latino Men Speak Out." *Mucho Macho: Seduction, Desire, and the Homoerotic Lives of Latin Men*. New York: Harrington Park, 2004. 293–327. Print.

---. "The Final Act: Why it All Matters." *Mucho Macho: Seduction, Desire, and the Homoerotic Lives of Latin Men*. New York: Harrington Park, 2004. 375–82. Print.

---. "Head, Hands, Balls, and Ass." *Mucho Macho: Seduction, Desire, and the Homoerotic Lives of Latin Men*. New York: Harrington Park, 2004. 89–140. Print.

---. "Introduction." *Mucho Macho: Seduction, Desire, and the Homoerotic Lives of Latin Men*. New York: Harrington Park, 2004. 1–19. Print.

---. "Machismo and Macho Performance." *Mucho Macho: Seduction, Desire, and the Homoerotic Lives of Latin Men*. New York: Harrington Park, 2004. 21–88. Print.

---. "Performing Matter[s]: Masculinities, the Male Body, and the Evocation of the [Not] Real." *Mucho Macho: Seduction, Desire, and the Homoerotic Lives of Latin Men*. New York: Harrington Park, 2004. 329–74. Print.

Gómez-Peña, Guillermo. "Border Brujo: A Performance Poem (From the Series 'Documented/Undocumented')." *TRD: The Drama Review* 35.3 (1991): 48–66. Print.

Gómez-Peña, Guillermo. "The Multicultural Paradigm: An Open Letter to the National Arts Community." *Negotiating Performance: Gender, Sexuality, and Theatricality in Latina/o America*. Ed. Diana Taylor and Juan Villegas. Durham, NC: Duke UP, 1994. 7–29. Rpt. in *Beyond the Fantastic: Contemporary Art Criticism from Latin America*. Ed. Gerardo Mosquera.

London: The Institute of International Visual Arts; Cambridge, MA: The MIT P, 1996. 183–93. Print.

---. *The New World Border: Prophecies, Poems, and Loqueras for the End of the Century.* San Francisco: City Light Books, 1996. Print.

---. *Warrior for Gringostroika: Essays, Performance Texts, and Poetry.* Intro. Roger Bartra. St. Paul, MN: Graywolf Press, 1993. Print.

Gonzales-Berry, Erlinda. "Sensuality, Repression, and Death in Arturo Islas's *The Rain God*." *The Bilingual Review/La Revista Bilingue* 12.3 (1985): 258–61. Print.

González, Omar O. "Construction of an Ofrenda of My Memory: A Queer Poz Indo-Chicano Maps His Way Home." MA thesis California State U, 2008. Print.

González, Rigoberto. *Antonio's Card/La Tarjeta de Anotonio.* Children's Book, 2005. Print.

---. *Autobiography of My Hungers (Living Out: Gay and Lesbian Autobiography).* Madison: U of Wisconsin P, in press. Print.

---. *Black Blossoms.* Four Way, 2011. Print.

---. *Butterfly Boy: Memories of a Chicano Mariposa.* Madison: U of Wisconsin P, 2006. Print.

---. *Camino del Sol: Fifteen Years of Latina and Latino Writing.* Tucson: U of Arizona P, 2010. Print.

---. *Crossing Vines.* Norman: U of Oklahoma P, 2003. Print.

---. "The Flight South of the Monarch Butterfly." *The Floating Borderlands: Twenty-five Years of U.S. Hispanic Literature.* Ed. Lauro Flores. Seattle: Washington UP, 1998. 399–400. Print.

---. "Ghost Story." *The Floating Borderlands: Twenty-five Years of U.S. Hispanic Literature.* Ed. Lauro Flores. Seattle: Washington UP, 1998. 401–02. Print.

---. *The Mariposa Club.* New York: Alyson, 2009. Print.

---. *Mariposa Gown.* Tincture, 2012. Print.

---. *Men Without Bliss.* Norman: U of Oklahoma P, 2008. Print.

---. *The Night Don Pedro Buried His Best Friend the Rooster.* Berkeley: U of California, Chicano Studies Program, 1998. Print.

---. *Other Fugitives and Other Strangers.* Dorset, VT: Tupelo, 2006. Print.

---. "La Quebrada." Bésame Mucho. Ed. Jaime Manrique and Jesse Dorris. New York: Painted Leaf, 1999. 69–77. Print.

---. *Red-Inked Retablos.* Tucson: U of Arizona P, in press. Print.

---. *Skins Preserve Us: Poems.* Davis, CA: Abbey Road, 1999. Print.

---. *Soledad Sigh-Sighs/Soledad Suspiros.* Children's Book, 2003. Print.

---. *So Often the Pitcher Goes to Water Until It Breaks.* Chicago: Illinois UP, 1999. Print.

González, Rigoberto, and Roni Gross. *The Soldier of Mictlán.* New York: Center for Book Arts, 2007. Print.

González de Alba, Luis. *Agapi mu (Amor mío).* México, D.F.: Cal y Arena, 1993. Print.

---. *Los días y los años.* México, D.F.: Planeta, 2008. Print.

---. *La orientación sexual: Reflexiones sobre la bisexualidad originaria y la homosexualidad.* México, D.F.: Paidós, 2003. Print.

---. *El vino de los bravos.* México, D.F.: Katún, 1981. Print.

González-López, Gloria. "Heterosexuality Exposed: Some Feminist Sociogical Reflections on Heterosexual Sex and Romance in U.S. Latina/o Communities." *Latina/o Sexualities: Probing Powers, Passions, Practices, and Policies.* Ed. Marysol Asencio. New Brunswick, NJ: Rutgers UP, 2010. 103–16. Print.

Griego, Adán. "Onions are for Men." *Bésame Mucho.* Ed. Jaime Manrique and Jesse Dorris. New York: Painted Leaf, 1999. 78–99. Print.

Guajardo, Paul. *Chicano Controversy: Oscar Acosta and Richard Rodriguez.* New York: Peter Lang, 2002. Print.

Güereña Burgueño, F., A. S. Benenson, J. Bucardo Amaya, A. Caudillo Carreño, and J. D. Curiel Figueroa. "Sexual Behavior and Drug Abuse in Homosexuals, Prostitutes and Prisoners in Tijuana, Mexico." *Revista latinoamericana de psicología* 24.1–2 (1992): 85–96. Print.

Guerra, Erasmo. *Between Dances: A Novel.* New York: Painted Leaf Press, 2000. Print.

---. "Between Dances." *Bésame Mucho.* Ed. Jaime Manrique and Jesse Dorris. New York: Painted Leaf, 1999. 199–211. Print.

---. "Introduction." *Latin Lovers: True Stories of Latin Men in Love.* New York City: Painted Leaf, 1999. 3–10. Print.

---. *Once More to the River: Family Snapshots of Growing Up, Getting Out and Going Back.* S.l: Createspace Independent, 2012. Print.

---. "SEXMONEYLOVE." *Virgins, Guerrillas, and Locas: Gay Latinos Writing about Love.* San Francisco: Cleis, 1999. 93–98. Print.

Guido, Gibran. "Navigating the Abyss: A Queer Chicano Semiotics of Love and Loss." MA thesis California State U, 2012. Print.

Gutiérrez, Elena R. "Latina/o Sex Policy." *Latina/o Sexualities: Probing Powers, Passions, Practices, and Policies.* Ed. Marysol Asencio. New Brunswick, NJ: Rutgers UP, 2010. 90-102. Print.

Gutiérrez, Eric-Steven. "Latino Issues: Gay and Lesbian Latinos Claiming La Raza." *Positively Gay: New Approaches to Gay and Lesbian Life.* Ed. Betty Berzon. Berkeley, CA: Celestial Arts, 1992. 240-46. Print.

Gutiérrez, León Guillermo. "La ciudad y el cuerpo en la novela mexicana de temática homosexual." *Anales de Literatura Hispanoamericana* 38 (2009): 279–86. Print.

---. "El cuerpo urbano y las calles de la piel en *El diario de José Toledo*: Primera novela mexicana de temática homosexual." *Tema y Variaciones de Literatura* 34 (2010): 165–75. Print.

Gutiérrez, Ramón A. "Community, Patriarchy and Individualism: The Politics of Chicano History and the Dream of Equality." *American Quarterly* 45.1 (1993): 44–72. Print.

---. "The Erotic Zone: Sexual Transgression on the U.S.-Mexican Border." *Mapping Multiculturalism.* Ed. Avery Gordon and Chris Newfield. Minneapolis: U of Minnesota P, 1996. 253–63. Print.

---. "A History of Latina/o Sexualities." *Latina/o Sexualities: Probing Powers, Passions, Practices, and Policies.* Ed. Marysol Asencio. New Brunswick, NJ: Rutgers UP, 2010. 13–37. Print.

---. "Mexican Masculinities." Ed. Víctor M. Macías-González and Anne Rubenstein. Albuquerque: U of New Mexico P, 2012. 262–72. Print.

---. "Mexican Masculinities." Rev. of *Mexican Masculinities,* by Robert McKee Irwin. *Journal of the History of Sexuality* 13.4 (2004): 525–28. Print.

Gutiérrez-Jones, Carl. "Desiring B/order." *Diacritics* 25.1 (1995): 99–112. Print.

Gutmann, Matthew C. *The Meanings of Macho: Being a Man in Mexico City.* Berkeley: U of California P, 1996. Print.

---, ed. *Changing Men and Masculinities in Latin America.* Durham, NC: Duke UP, 2003. Print.

Guzman, Mario. "Los Homosexuales en Mexico." *Contenido* (1971): 44–54. Print.

Haggerty, George E. *Gay Histories and Cultures: An Encyclopedia.* Vol. 2. New York: Garland, 2000. Print.

Halperin, David M., and Valerie Traub, eds. *Gay Shame.* Chicago: U of Chicago P, 2009. Print.

Hames-Garcia, Michael. "Between Repression and Liberation: Sexuality and Socialist Theory." *Toward a New Socialism.* Ed. Anatole Anton and Richard Schmitt. New York: Lexington Books, 2007. 247–65. Print.

---. "Can Queer Theory be Critical Theory?" *New Critical Theory: Essays on Liberation.* Ed. Jeffrey Paris and William S. Wilkerson. New York: Rowman & Littlefield, 2001. 201–22. Print.

---. *Identity Complex: Making the Case for Multiplicity.* Minneapolis: U of Minnesota P, 2011. Print.

---. "What's at Stake in 'Gay' Identities?" *Identity Politics Reconsidered.* Ed. Alcoff, Hames-García, Mohanty, and Moya. New York: Palgrave Macmillan, 2006. 78–95. Print.

Hames-Garcia, Michael, and Ernesto Javier Martínez, eds. *Gay Latino Studies: A Critical Reader.* Durham, NC: Duke UP, 2011. Print.

Hernández, Carlos. "A Gay Life Style (Only if *La Familia* Approves)." *Firme* 1.5 (1981): 18–19. Print.

Hernández, Ellie D. "Denationalizing Chicana/o Queer Representations." *Postnationalism in Chicana/o Literature and Culture.* Austin: U of Texas P, 2009. 155–81. Print.

Hernandez, Robb. "Performing the Archival Body in the Robert 'Cyclona' Legoreta Fire of Life/El Fuego de la Vida Collection." *Aztlán: A Journal of Chicano Studies* 31.2 (2006): 113–25. Print.

Hernández, Tony. *A mi manera--: La vida de un homosexual*. México, D.F.: Costa-Amic, 1988. Print.

Hernández-Gutiérrez, Manuel de Jesús. "Building a Research Agenda on U.S. Latino Lesbigay Literature and Cultural Production: Texts, Writers, Performance, and Critics." Ed. David William Foster. *Chicano/Latino Homoerotic Identities*. New York: Routledge, 1999. 397–449. Print.

---. "Francisco X. Alarcón (United States; 1954)." *Latin American Writers on Gay and Lesbian Themes: A Bio-Critical Sourcebook*. Ed. David William Foster. Westport, CT: Greenwood, 1994. 7–13. Print.

Herrera y Lozano, Lorenzo, ed. *Joto: An Anthology of Queer Xicano & Chicano Poetry*. San Francisco: Korima, in press. Print.

---. "Newfound Religion," "Relicario de Tu Deseo," Psalm 69 (Unmastered)," "Puerta a Mi Infierno," "St. Gabriel of Madden," "Deseos Reciclables." *Mariposas: A Modern Anthology of Queer Latino Poetry*. Ed. Emanuel Xavier. Mountain View, CA: Floricanto Press, 2008. 24–30. Print.

---. "Poetry of the Flesh." *For Colored Boys Who Have Considered Suicide When the Rainbow Is Still Not Enough: Coming of Age, Coming Out, and Coming Home*. Ed. Keith Boykin. New York: Magnus, 2012. 294–300. Print.

---, ed. *Queer Codex: Rooted!* Vol. 2. Austin: ALLGO; New York: Evelyn Street, 2008. Print.

---. *Santo de la Pata Alzada: Poems from the Queer/ Xicano/ Positive Pen*. New York: Evelyn Street, 2005. Print.

Herrero-Olaizola, Alejandro. "Homosexuales en escena: Identidad y *perfor-mance* en la narrativa de Luis Zapata." *Antípodas* 11–12 (1999–2000): 249–62. Print.

Hirsch, Jennifer S., and Emily Vasquez. "Mexico-US Migration, Social Exclusion, and HIV Risk: Multi-sectoral Approaches to Understanding and Preventing Infection." *HIV Prevention with Latinos: Theory, Research, and Practice*. Ed. Kurt C. Organista. New York: Oxford UP, 2012. Print.

Hoffman, Stanton. "The Cities of Night: John Rechy's *City of Night* and the American Literature of Homosexuality." *Chicago Review* 17.2–3 (1964): 195–206. Print.

Howard, Phil. "La Tierra, Nuestra Madre: Land, Burial, Memory and Chicanidad in the Dramaturgies of Alfaro, Moraga, and Sanchez-Scott." *Signatures of the Past: Cultural Memory in Contemporary Anglophone North American Drama*. Ed. Marc Maufort and Caroline De Wagter. New York: Peter Lang, 2008. 129–40. Print.

Huerta, Dolores. "Our Fight is Your Fight: Dolores Huerta and Julian Bond Speak Out Loud and Clear for GLBT Equality." *The Dolores Huerta Reader*. Ed. Mario T. Garcia. Albuquerque: U of New Mexico P, 2008. Print.

Huerta, Jorge. "*Cherríe Moraga's Heroes and Saints: Chicano Theatre for the '90s.*" *Theatre Forum* 1 (1992): 49–52. Print.

---. *Chicano Drama: Performance, Society and Myth*. New York: Cambridge UP, 2000. Print.

---. "Looking for the Magic: Chicanos in the Mainstream." *Negotiating Performance: Gender, Sexuality, and Theatricality in Latina/o America*. Ed. Diana Taylor and Juan Villegas. Durham, NC: Duke UP, 1994. 37–48. Print.

---. "An Overview of Chicana/o Theatre in the 1990s." *Latin American Theatre Review* (2000): 217–28. Print.

Instituto Familiar de la Raza/Latino AIDS Project. *Eyes that Fail to See, A Story of Our Times ... About Our Lives and the Reality of AIDS: A Complete Fotonovela*. San Francisco: Instituto Familiar de la Raza, 1990. Print.

Irwin, Robert McKee. "As Invisible as He Is: The Queer Enigma of Xavier Villaurrutia." *Reading and Writing the Ambiente: Queer Sexualities in Latino, Latin American, and Spanish Culture*. Ed. Susana Chávez-Silverman and Librada Hernández. Madison: U of Wisconsin P, 2000. 114–46. Print.

---. "The Famous 41: The Scandalous Birth of Modern Mexican Homosexuality." *GLQ: A Journal of Lesbian and Gay Studies* 6.3 (2000): 353–76. Print.

---. *Mexican Masculinities*. Minneapolis: U of Minnesota P, 2003. Print.

Irwin, Robert McKee, Edward J. McCaughan, and Michelle Rocío Nassar, eds. *The Famous 41: Sexuality and Social Control in Mexico, 1901*. New York: Palgrave Macmillan, 2003. Print.

Islas, Arturo. "Algol/Algolagnia," "Moonshine," and "Video Songs." *Persistent Voices: Poetry by Writers Lost to AIDS*. Ed. David Groff and Philip Clark. New York: Alyson, 2009. 151–55. Print.

---. *Migrant Souls: A Novel*. New York: Morrow, 1990. Print.

---. *La Mollie and the King of Tears*. Albuquerque: U of New Mexico P, 1996. Print.

---. *The Rain God: A Desert Tale*. 1984. New York: Harper Perennial, 2003. Print.

Jaén, Didier T. "La Neo-Picaresca en México: Elena Poniatowska y Luis Zapata." *Tinta* 1.5 (1987): 23–29. Print.

---. "Rechy, John (United States; 1934)." *Latin American Writers on Gay and Lesbian Themes: A Bio-Critical Sourcebook*. Ed. David William Foster. Westport, CT: Greenwood, 1994. 349–56. Print.

Jagose, Annamarie. *Queer Theory: An Introduction*. New York: New York UP, 1996. Print.

Jenness, Morgan. "Introduction to Luis Alfaro." *Extreme Exposure*. Ed. Jo Bonnie. New York: Theatre Communications Group, 2000. Print.

Jones, Ryan. "'Estamos en todas partes': Male Homosexuality, Nation, and Modernity in Twentieth Century Mexico." Diss. U of Illinois, 2012. Print.

Kaminsky, Silvia, William Kurtines, Olga O. Hervis, Nancy T. Blaney, Carrie Millon, and Jose Szapocznik. "Life Enhancement Counseling with HIV-infected Hispanic Gay Males." *Hispanic Journal of Behavioral Sciences* 12.2 (1990): 177–95. Print.

Katsulis, Yasmina. *Sex Work and the City: The Social Geography of Health and Safety in Tijuana, Mexico*. Austin: U of Texas P, 2008. Print.

Kissinger, Patricia, and Michele G. Shedlin. "HIV/STI Risk among Latino Migrant Men in New Receiving Communities: A Case Study of Post-disaster New Orleans." *HIV Prevention with Latinos: Theory, Research, and Practice*. Ed. Kurt C. Organista. New York: Oxford UP, 2012. Print.

Klawitter, George. "Nava, Michael (United States; 1954)." *Latin American Writers on Gay and Lesbian Themes: A Bio-Critical Sourcebook*. Ed. David William Foster. Westport, CT: Greenwood, 1994. 311–13. Print.

Laguarda, Rodrigo. *La Calle de Amberes: Gay street de la Ciudad de México.* México, D.F.: Universidad Nacional Autónoma de México, 2011. Print.

---. *Ser gay en la ciudad de México: Lucha de representaciones y apropiación de una identidad, 1968–1982.* México, D.F.: CIESAS, 2010. Print.

León, Jesús de. *Los pavorreales y otros cuentos gay para llevar.* México, D.F.: La Terquedad, 2003. Print.

Levi, Heather. "Lean Mean Fighting Queens: Drag in the World of Mexican Professional Wrestling." *Sexualities* 1.3 (1998): 275–85. Print.

Levin, James. *The Gay Novel: The Male Homosexual Image in America.* New York: Irvington, 1983. Print.

Lewis, Vek. *Crossing Sex and Gender in Latin America.* New York: Palgrave Macmillan, 2010. Print.

Leyland, Winston, ed. *My Deep Dark Pain Is Love: A Collection of Latin American Gay Fiction.* Trans. E. A. Lacey. San Francisco: Gay Sunshine, 1983. Print.

---, ed. "John Rechy." *Gay Sunshine Interviews.* Vol. 2. San Francisco: Gay Sunshine, 1978. 251–68. Print.

Limón, José E. *American Encounters. Greater Mexico, the United States, and the Erotics of Culture.* Boston: Beacon, 1998. Print.

---. "Carne, Carnales, and the Carnivalesque: Bakhtinian Batos, Disorder, and Narrative Discourses." *American Ethnologist* 16.3 (1989): 471–86. Print.

---. *Dancing with the Devil: Society and Cultural Poetics in Mexican-American South Texas.* Madison: U of Wisconsin P, 1994. Print.

---. "Editor's Notes on Richard Rodriguez." *Texas Studies in Language and Literature* 40.4 (1998): 389–95. Print.

List Reyes, Mauricio. *Hablo por mi diferencia: De la identidad gay al reconocimiento de lo queer.* México, D.F.: Ediciones Eón, 2009. Print.

---. *Jóvenes corazones gay en la ciudad de México: Género, identidad y socialidad en hombres gay.* Puebla: Benemérita Universidad Autónoma de Puebla, 2005. Print.

López, Enrique G. "The Intersection of Ethnicity and Sexuality in the Narrative Fiction of Three Chicano Authors: Oscar Zeta Acosta, Arturo Islas, and Michael Nava." Diss. Ohio State U, 1998. Print.

López Páez, Jorge. "El viaje de Berenice." *Los invitados de piedra.* Xalapa, México: Universidad Veracruzana, 1962. Print.

Lujan, Albert. "Strong Arms." *Virgins, Guerrillas, and Locas: Gay Latinos Writing about Love.* San Francisco: Cleis, 1999. 147–53. Print.

---. "Ruby Díaz." *Bésame Mucho.* Ed. Jaime Manrique and Jesse Dorris. New York: Painted Leaf, 1999. 227–38. Print.

Lumsden, Ian. *Homosexualidad: Sociedad y estado en México.* México, D.F.: Solediciones; Toronto: Canadian Gay Archives, 1991. Print.

Macías-González, Víctor M. "The Bathhouse and Male Homosexuality in Porfirian Mexico." *Masculinity and Sexuality in Modern Mexico.* Ed. Víctor M. Macías-González and Anne Rubenstein. Albuquerque: U of New Mexico P, 2012. 25–52. Print.

---. "The *Largartijo* at *The High Life*: Notes on Masculine Consumption: Race, Nation, and Homosexuality in Porfirian Mexico." *The Famous 41: Sexuality and Social Control in Mexico, 1901.* Ed. Irwin, McCaughan, and Nassar. New York: Palgrave Macmillan, 2003. 227–49. Print.

Macías-González, Víctor M., and Anne Rubenstein, eds. *Masculinity and Sexuality in Modern Mexico.* Albuquerque: U of New Mexico P, 2012. Print.

Magaña, J. Raul, Olivia de la Rocha, and Jaime L. Amsel. "Sexual History and Behavior of Mexican Migrant Workers in Orange County, California." *AIDS Crossing Borders: The Spread of HIV Among Migrant Latinos.* Ed. Mishra, Connner, and Magaña. Boulder, CO: Westview, 1996. 77–93. Print.

Marcos, Sylvia. *Taken from the Lips: Gender and Eros in Mesoamerican Religions.* Leiden, Netherlands: Brill, 2006. Print.

Marquet, Antonio. *El crepúsculo de heterolandia: Mester de jotería: Ensayos sobre cultura de las exhuberantes tierras de la nación queer.* México, D.F.: Universidad Autónoma Metropolitana, Azcapotzalco, 2006. Print.

---. *Que se quede el infinito sin estrellas!: la cultura gay a fin de milenio.* México, D.F.: Universidad Autónoma Metropolitana, Azcapotzalco, 2001. Print.

Márquez, Antonio C. "Richard Rodriguez's *Hunger of Memory* and New Perspectives on Ethnic Autobiography." *Teaching American Ethnic Literatures; Nineteen Essays.* Ed. John R. Maitino and David R. Peck. Albuquerque: U of New Mexico P, 1996. 237–54. Print.

---. "Richard Rodriguez's *Hunger of Memory* and the Poetics of Experience." *Arizona Quarterly* 40.2 (1984): 130-41. Print.

Marrero, M. Teresa. "Out of the Fringe: Desire and Homosexuality in the 1990s Latino Theater." *Velvet Barrios: Popular Culture & Chicana/o Sexualities.* Ed. Alicia Gaspar de Alba. New York: Palgrave Macmillan, 2003. 283–94. Print.

---. "Public Art, Performance Art, and the Politics of Site." *Negotiating Performance: Gender, Sexuality, and Theatricality in Latina/o America.* Ed. Diana Taylor and Juan Villegas. Durham, NC: Duke UP, 1994. 102–20. Print.

Martin, Kevin. "Writer Gil Cuadros: Creating in the Face of AIDS." *Positive Living* 3.4 (1994): 3. Print.

Maufort, Marc, and Caroline De Wagter, eds. *Signatures of the Past: Cultural Memory in Contemporary Anglophone North American Drama.* New York: Peter Lang, 2008. Print.

Mayer, Oliver. *Blade to the Heat.* Rev. ed. New York: Dramatists Play Service, 1996. Print.

McCaughan, Edward J. "Gender, Sexuality, and Nation in the Art of Mexican Social Movements." *Nepantla: View from South* 3.1 (2002): 99–143. Print.

McKenna, Teresa. *Migrant Song: Politics and Process in Contemporary Chicano Literature.* Austin: U of Texas P, 1997. Print.

Melo, Juan Vicente. "Los amigos." *Los muros enemigos.* Xalapa, Ver.: Universidad Veracruzana, 1962. 59–76. Print.

Miano Borruso, Marinella, compilador. *Caminos inciertos de las mascu-linidades*. México, D.F: Instituto Nacional de Antropología e Historia, Escuela Nacional de Antropología e Historia, 2003. Print.

---. *Hombre, Mujer y Muxe' en el Istmo de Tehuantepec*. México, D.F.: Plaza y Valdes, 2002. Print.

Miller, John. "Acosta, Oscar Zeta (United States; 1934–1974?)." *Latin American Writers on Gay and Lesbian Themes: A Bio-Critical Sourcebook*. Ed. David William Foster. Westport, CT: Greenwood, 1994. 1–3. Print.

Mirandé, Alfredo. *Hombres y Machos: Masculinity and Latino Culture*. Boulder, CO: Westview, 1997. Print.

Mishra, Shiraz I., and Ross F. Conner. "Evaluation of an HIV Prevention Program Among Latino Farmworkers." *AIDS Crossing Borders: The Spread of HIV Among Migrant Latinos*. Ed. Mishra, Connner, and Magaña. Boulder, CO: Westview, 1996. 157–82. Print.

Mishra, Shiraz I., Ross F. Connner, and J. Raul Magaña, eds. *AIDS Crossing Borders: The Spread of HIV Among Migrant Latinos*. Ed. Mishra, Connner, and Magaña. Boulder, CO: Westview, 1996. Print.

Mitchell, Pablo. "Making Sex Matter: Histories of Latina/o Sexualities, 1898 to 1965." *Latina/o Sexualities: Probing Powers, Passions, Practices, and Policies*. Ed. Marysol Asencio. New Brunswick, NJ: Rutgers UP, 2010. 38–47. Print.

Molloy, Sylvia. "The Politics of Posing: Translating Decadence in Fin-de-Siècle Latin America." Perennial Decay: On the Aesthetics and Politics of Decadence. Ed. Liz Constable. Philadelphia: U of Pennsylvania P, 1999. 183–97. Print.

---. "Sentimental Excess and Gender Disruption: The Case of Amado Nervo." *The Famous 41: Sexuality and Social Control in Mexico, 1901*. Ed. Irwin, McCaughan, and Nassar. New York: Palgrave Macmillan, 2003. 291–306. Print.

---. "Too Wild for Comfort: Desire and Ideology in Fin-de-Siècle Spanish America." *Social Text* 31/32 (1992): 187–201. Print.

Molloy, Sylvia, and Robert McKee Irwin, eds. *Hispanisms and Homosexualities*. Durham, NC: Duke UP, 1998. Print.

Monsiváis, Carlos. "The 41 and the Gran Redada." Trans. Aaron Walker. *The Famous 41: Sexuality and Social Control in Mexico, 1901.* Ed. Irwin, McCaughan, and Nassar. New York: Palgrave Macmillan, 2003. 139–68. Print.

---. *Amor Perdido.* México, D.F: Era, [1976], 2005. Print.

---. *Carlos Pellicer: Iconografía.* México, D.F: Fondo de Cultura Económica, 2003. Print.

---. *Entrada libre, crónicas de la sociedad que se organiza.* México, D.F: Era, 1987. Print.

---. *Esenas de Pudor y Liviandad.* México, D.F: Grijalbo, 1988. Print.

---. "Los iguales, los semejantes, los (hasta hace un minuto) perfectos desconocidos. A cien años de la redada de los 41." México, D.F.: CONACULTA-INBA, 2001. Print.

---. "Mexican Cinema: Of Myths and Demystifications." *Mediating Two Worlds: Cinematic Encounters in the Americas.* London: British Film Institute, 1993. 140-46. Print.

---. *Mexican Postcards.* New York: Verso, 1997. Print.

---. "El mundo soslayado." *La estatua de sal.* Ed. Salvador Novo. México, D.F.: Fondo de Cultura Económica, 1998. 13–14. Print.

---. "Ortodoxia y heterodoxia en las alcobas." *Debate Feminista* 6.11 (1995): 183–210. Print.

---. *Pedro Infante: Las leyes del querer.* México, D.F: Aguilar, 2008. Print.

---. "Prólogo." *Jacinto de Jesús.* México, D.F.: Fontamara, 2001. Print.

---. *Que se abra esa puerta: Crónicas y ensayos sobre la diversidad sexual.* México. D.F.: Paidós, 2010. Print.

---. *Salvador Novo: Lo marginal en el centro.* México, D.F: Era, 2000. Print.

Monsiváis, Carlos, y Carlos Bonfíl. *A través del espejo: El cine mexicano y su público.* México, D.F.: El Milagro, 1994. Print.

Montagner, Eduardo. *Toda esa gran verdad.* México, D.F.: Alfaguara, 2006. Print.

Monteagudo, José. Review of *City of God,* by Gil Cuadros. *Lamda Book Report* 4.8 (1995): 34. Print.

Moraga, Cherríe. *Heroes and Saints and Other Plays.* Albuquerque, NM: West End Press, 1994. Print.

---. "Queer Aztlán: The Re-formation of the Chicano Tribe." *The Last Generation: Poems and Essays.* Boston: South End, 1993. 145–74. Print.

Morales, Edward S. "HIV Infection and Hispanic Gay and Bisexual Men." *Hispanic Journal of Behavioral Sciences* 12.2 (May 1990): 212–22. Print.

Mulholland, Mary-Lee. "Mariachis Machos and Charros Gays: Masculinities in Guadalajara. *Masculinity and Sexuality in Modern Mexico.* Ed. Víctor M. Macías-González and Anne Rubenstein. Albuquerque: U of New Mexico P, 2012. 234–61. Print.

Muñoz, José Esteban. *Disidentifications: Queers Of Color and the Performance of Politics.* Minniapolis: U of Minnesota P, 1999. Print.

---. "Feeling Brown: Ethnicity and Affect in Ricardo Bracho's *The Sweetest Hangover (and Other STDs)." Theatre Journal* 52.1 (2000): 67–79. Print.

Muñoz, Mario. "El cuento mexicano de tema homosexual." *Revista de literatura Mexicana contemporánea* 2.6 (1997): 16–22. Print.

---. *De amores marginales. 16 cuentos mexicanos.* Xalapa, Ver.: Universidad Veracruzana, 1996. Print.

---. "En torno a la narrative mexicana del homosexual." *La Palabra y el Hombre* 84 (1992): 21–37. Print.

---. "La generación de la *Revista Mexicana de Literatura*: Esbozo mínimo de una aproximación." *La Palabra y el Hombre,* enero-marzo. 113 (2000): 83–89. Print.

---. "Juan Vicente Melo en el contexto de su generación." *Contigo, cuento y cebolla.* Ed. Mario Muñoz and Alfredo Pavón. Tlax.: Universidad Autónoma de Tlaxcala (Serie Destino Arbitrario,18), 2000. 1–12. Print.

---. "Sexismo en la literatura Mexicana." *Imagen y realidad de la mujer.* Ed. Elena Urrutia. México, D.F: Sep-Setentas-Diana, 1979. Print.

Murphy, Peter F., ed. *Fictions of Masculinity: Crossing Cultures, Crossing Sexualities.* New York: New York UP, 1994. Print.

Murray, Stephen O. *Latin American Male Homosexualities*. Albuquerque: U of New Mexico P, 1995. Print.

Nandino, Elías. *Juntando mis pasos*. México, D.F.: Aldus, 2000. Print.

Nava, Michael. "Abuelo: My Grandfather, Raymond Acuña." *A Member of the Family: Gay Men Write about Their Families*. Ed. John Preston. New York: Dutton, 1992. 15–20. Print.

---. *The Burning Plain*. New York: Putnam, 1997. Print.

---. *The Death of Friends*. New York: Putnam, 1996. Print.

---, ed. *Finale: Short Stories of Mystery and Suspense*. Boston: Alyson, 1989. Print.

---. *Goldenboy*. Boston: Alyson, 1988. Print.

---. *The Hidden Law*. New York: HarperCollins, 1992. Print.

---. *How Town*. New York: Ballantine, 1991. Print.

---. *The Little Death*. Los Angeles: Alyson, 1986. Print.

---. *Rag and Bone*. New York: Putnam, 2001. Print.

Nava, Michael, and Robert Dawidoff. *Created Equal: Why Gay Rights Matter to America*. New York: St. Martin's, 1994. Print.

Navarro, Ray. "Eso me está pasando." *Chicanos and Film: Essays on Chicano Representation and Resistance*. Ed. Chon A. Noriega. Minneapolis: U of Minnesota P, 1992. 312–16. Print.

Nelson, Emmanuel S. "John Rechy, James Baldwin, and the American Double Minority Literature." *Journal of American Culture* 6.2 (1983): 70-74. Print.

Nelson, Emmanuel Sampath, ed. *Contemporary Gay American Novelists: A Bio-Bibliographical Critical Sourcebook*. Westport, CT: Greenwood, 1993. Print.

Nericcio, William Anthony. *The Hurt Business: Oliver Mayer's Early Works [+] PLUS*. San Diego: Hyperbole Books, 2008. Print.

---. "Tex[t]-Mex: Seductive Hallucinations of the 'Mexican' in America." Austin: U of Texas P, 2007. Print.

Novo, Salvador. *La estatua de sal*. México, D.F.: CONACULTA, 1998. Print.

---. *Las locas, el sexo y los burdeles y otros ensayos*. México, D.F.: Diana, 1979. Print.

---. *Sátira, el libro cabrón.* (*Satyre, the F*** Book*). Diana. 1970. Print.

Núñez Noriega, Guillermo. "Hombres indígenas, diversidad sexual y vulnerabilidad al VIH-Sida: Una exploración sobre las dificultades académicas para estudiar un tema emergente en la antropología." *Desacatos: Revista de Antropología Social* 35 (2011): 13–28. Print.

---. *Masculinidad e intimidad: Identidad, sexualidad y sida.* México, D.F.: PUEG-UNAM, Miguel A. Porrúa, El Colegio de Sonora, 2007. Print.

---. *¿Qué es la diversidad sexual? Reflexiones desde la academia y el movimiento ciudadano.* Quito: Abya Ayala-Universidad Politécnica Salesiana y CIAD, A.C., 2011. Print.

---. "Reconociendo los placeres, desconstruyendo las identidades. Antropología, patriarcado y homoerotismos en México." *Desacatos: Revista de Antropología Social* 6 (2001): 15–34. Print.

---. *Sexo entre varones: poder y resistencis en el campo sexual.* Hermosillo, Sonora, México: El Colegio de Sonora, 1994. Print.

---. *Vidas vulnerables: Hombres indígenas, diversidad sexual y VIH.* México, D.F: CIAD, A.C. y EDAMEX, 2009. Print.

Ocasio, Rafael. "Salas, Floyd (United States; 1931)." *Latin American Writers on Gay and Lesbian Themes: A Bio-Critical Sourcebook.* Ed. David William Foster. Westport, CT: Greenwood, 1994. 394–96. Print.

Ochoa, Juan D. "Finding Familia at UCLA: Joteando in the 1990's--Charting Gay Chicano Political Activism." MA thesis California State U, 2012. Print.

Ochoa, Marcia. "Latina/o Transpopulations." *Latina/o Sexualities: Probing Powers, Passions, Practices, and Policies.* Ed. Marysol Asencio. New Brunswick, NJ: Rutgers UP, 2010. 230-42. Print.

Ojeda, Jorge Arturo. *Muchacho solo.* México, D.F.: Grijalbo, 1976. Print.

---. *Octavio.* México, D.F.: Premiá, 1987. Print.

---. *Personas fatales.* México, D.F.: Mester, 1975. Print.

---. *Piedra caliente.* México, D.F.: Fontamara, 1995. Print.

Olvera, Joe. "Gay Ghetto District." *Flor y Canto IV and V: An Anthology of Chicano Literature from the Festivals held in Albuquerque, New Mexico,*

1977, and Tempe, Arizona, 1978. Eds. Jose Armas and Justo Alarcon. Albuquerque, NM: Pajarito, 1980. Print.

Organista, Kurt C., ed. *HIV Prevention with Latinos: Theory, Research, and Practice.* New York: Oxford UP, 2012. Print.

Organista, Kurt C., Héctor Carrillo, and George Ayala. "HIV Prevention with Mexican Migrants: Review, Critique, and Recommendations." *Journal of Acquired Immune Deficiency Syndromes* 37.S4 (2004): S227–S239. Print.

Organista, Kurt C., Paula Worby, Jim Quesada, Alex Kral, Rafael Diaz, Torsten Neilands, and Sonya Arreola. "The Urgent Need for Structural Environmental Models of HIV Risk and Prevention in US Latino Populations: The Case of Migrant Day Laborers." *HIV Prevention with Latinos: Theory, Research, and Practice.* Ed. Kurt C. Organista. New York: Oxford UP, 2012. Print.

Oropesa, Salvador A. *The Contemporaneos Group: Rewriting Mexico in the Thirties and Forties.* Austin: U of Texas P, 2003. Print.

Ortiz, Christopher. "Hot and Spicy: Representation of Chicano/Latino Men in Gay Pornography." *Jump Cut: A Review of Contemporary Media* 39 (1994): 83–90. Print.

Ortiz, Ricardo L. "John Rechy and the Grammar of Ostentation." *Cruising the Performative: Interventions into the Representation of Ethnicity, Nationality, and Sexuality.* Ed. Case, Brett, and Foster. Bloomington: Indiana UP, 1995. 59–70. Print.

---. "Sexuality Degree Zero: Pleasure and Power in the Novels of John Rechy, Arturo Islas, and Michael Nava." *Journal of Homosexuality* 26.2–3 (1993): 111–26. Print.

Painter, Thomas M., Kurt C. Organista, Scott D. Rhodes, and Fernando M. Sañudo. "Interventions to Prevent HIV and Other Sexually Transmitted Diseases Among Latino Migrants." *HIV Prevention with Latinos: Theory, Research, and Practice.* Ed. Kurt C. Organista. New York: Oxford UP, 2012. Print.

Palacio, Jaime del. *Parejas: Tres narraciones enlazadas.* México, D.F.: M. Casillas, 1982. Print.

Palaversich, Diana. "Apuntes para una lectura de Mario Bellatin." *Chasqui* 32.1 (2003): 25–39. Print.

Paravisini-Gebert, Lizabeth. "Richard Rodriguez's *Hunger of Memory* and the Rejection of the Private Self." *U.S. Latino Literatures: A Critical Guide for Students and Teachers.* Ed. Harold Augenbaum and Margarite Fernández Olmos. Westport, CT: Greenwood, 2000. 81–92. Print.

Paredes, Américo. "Over the Waves is Out." *New Mexican Review* 23.2 (1953): 177–87. Print.

Parra, Eduardo Antonio. "Nomás no me quiten lo poquito que traigo." *Tierra de nadie.* México, D.F.: Era, 1999. 43–52. Print.

Paz, Octavio. *The Labyrinth of Solitude.* Trans. Lysander Kemp. New York: Grove, 1961. Print.

---. *Nostalgia for Death & Hieroglyphs of Desire: A Critical Study of Villaurrutia.* Port Townsend, WA: Copper Canyon, 1992. Print.

Pellicer, Carlos. *Colores en el mar y otros poemas, 1915–20.* 1921. San Diego: Fondo de Cultura Economica USA, 1998. Print.

---. *Piedra de sacrificios.* 1924. México, D.F.: Equilibrista, 1993. Print.

Peña, Susana. "Latina/o Sexualities in Motion: Latina/o Sexualities Research Agenda Project." *Latina/o Sexualities: Probing Powers, Passions, Practices, and Policies.* Ed. Marysol Asencio. New Brunswick, NJ: Rutgers UP, 2010. 188–206. Print.

Peralta, Braulio. *Los nombres del arcoiris: Trazos para redescubrir el movimiento homosexual.* México, D.F.: Nueva Imagen, 2006. Print.

Pérez, Daniel Enrique. "Barrio Bodies: Theorizing Chicana/o Popular Culture as Queer." Diss. Arizona State U, 2004. Print.

---. "Gonzalo (*sic*), Rigoberto. Butterfly Boy: Memories of a Chicano Mariposa." Rev. of "Butterfly Boy: Memories of a Chicano Mariposa" by Rigoberto González. *Chasqui: Revista de Literatura Latinoamericana* 36.1 (2007): 152–55. Print.

---. "Masculinity (Re) Defined: Masculinity, Internalized Homophobia, and the Gay Macho Clone in the Works of John Rechy." *Beginning a New Millennium of Chicana and Chicano Scholarship: Selected Proceedings of the 2001 NACCS Conference: Selected Proceedings of the of the 2001*

NACCS Conference. Ed. Jaime H. García. San Jose, CA: The Association, 2006. Print.

---. "*Mi Familia* Rara: Why Paco Isn't Married." *Studies in Latin American Popular Culture*. 25 (2006): 141–56. Print.

---. "(Re) Examining the Latin Lover: Screening Chicano/Latino Sexualities." *Performing the U.S. Latina and Latino Borderlands*. Ed. Aldama, Sandoval, and García. Indiana: Indiana UP, 2012. 437–56. Print.

---. *Rethinking Chicana/o and Latina/o Popular Culture*. New York: Palgrave Macmillan, 2009. Print.

Pérez, Emma. "Decolonial Border Queers: Case Studies of Chicana/o Lesbians, Gay Men, and Transgender Folks in El Paso/Juárez." Performing the US Latina and Latino Borderlands. Ed. Aldama, Sandoval, and García. Bloomington: Indiana UP, 2012. 192–211. Print.

Pérez, Hiram. "You Can Have My Brown Body and Eat It, Too!" *Social Text* 84–85.3–4 (2005): 171–91. Print.

Perez, Miguel A., and Katherine Fennelly. "Risk Factors for HIV and AIDS Among Latino Farmworkers in Pennsylvania." *AIDS Crossing Borders: The Spread of HIV Among Migrant Latinos*. Ed. Mishra, Connner, and Magaña. Boulder, CO: Westview, 1996. 137–56. Print.

Pérez-Torres, Rafael. "The Ambiguous Outlaw: John Rechy and Complicitous Homotextuality." *Fictions of Masculinity: Crossing Cultures, Crossing Sexualities*. Ed. Peter Murphy. New York: New York UP, 1994. 204–25. Print.

---. *Mestizaje: Critical Uses of Race in Chicano Culture*. Minneapolis: U of Minnesota P, 2006. Print.

Pesqueria, Randy. "Daddycakes." *Virgins, Guerrillas, and Locas: Gay Latinos Writing about Love*. San Francisco: Cleis, 1999. 53–58. Print.

Peterson, John L., and Gerardo Marin. "Issues in the Prevention of AIDS Among Black and Hispanic Men." *American Psychologist* 43.11 (1988): 871–77. Print.

Piccato, Pablo. "Interpretations of Sexuality in Mexico City Prisons: A Critical Version of Roumagnac." *The Famous 41: Sexuality and Social Control in*

Mexico, 1901. Ed. Irwin, McCaughan, and Nassar. New York: Palgrave Macmillan, 2003. 251–66. Print.

---. "'Such a Strong Need': Sexuality and Violence in Belem Prison." *Gender, Sexuality and Power in Latin America since Independence.* Ed. William E. French and Katherine Elaine Bliss. Lanham, MD: Rowman & Littlefield, 2007. 87–108. Print.

Piedra, José. "Nationalizing Sissies." *?Entiendes? Queer Readings, Hispanic Writings.* Ed. Emilie L. Bergmann and Paul J. Smith. Durham, NC: Duke UP, 1995. 371–409. Print.

Pilcher, Jeffrey M. "The Gay Caballero: Machismo, Homosexuality, and the Nation in Golden Age Film. *Masculinity and Sexuality in Modern Mexico.* Ed. Víctor M. Macías-González and Anne Rubenstein. Albuquerque: U of New Mexico P, 2012. 214–33. Print.

Po, Paolo. *41 o el muchacho que soñaba en fantasmas.* México, D.F.: Costa-Amic, 1964. Print.

Poma, Edgar. "Reunion: A Play in Two Acts." Berkeley, CA: Archivos Rodrigo Reyes. Print.

Ponce, Patricia. *Sexualidades costeñas: Un pueblo veracruzano entre el río y la mar.* México, D.F.: Centro de Investigaciones y Estudios Superiores en Antropología Social, 2006. Print.

Ponce, Patricia, y Guillermo Núñez Noriega. "Pueblos indígenas y VIH-Sida." *Desacatos: Revista de Antropología Social* 35 (2011): 7–10. Print.

Postel, Virginia I., and Nick Gillespie. "The New, New World: An Interview with Richard Rodriguez." *Reason* 26.4 (1994): 35–41. Print.

Prieto, Antonio. "Incorporated Identities: The Subversion of Stigma in the Performance Art of Luis Alfaro." *Chicano/Latino Homoerotic Identities.* Ed. David William Foster. New York: Garland, 1999. Print.

---. "La poetica de la frontera." *Lucero: A Journal of Iberian and Latin American Studies* 10 (1999): Spring: 38–43. Print.

---. "Queer/Joto: Performing the Epidermic Cartography of Lesbian and Gay Chicanos." Stanford University. Data Center's Information Services Latin America, 2000. Print.

Prieur, Annick. "Bodily and Symbolic Constructions among Homosexual Men in Mexico." *Sexualities* 1.3 (1998): 287–98. Print.

---. *Mema's House, Mexico City: On Transvestites, Queens, and Machos*. Chicago: U of Chicago P, 1998. Print.

Quintana Hopkins, Robert. *The Glass Closet*. Oakland, CA: AfroChicano, 2009. Print.

Quiroga, José. "Nostalgia for Sex: Xavier Villaurrutia." In *Tropics of Desire: Interventions from Queer Latino America*. New York: New York UP, 2000. 50-75. Print.

---. "Latino Cultures, Imperial Sexualities." In *Tropics of Desire: Interventions from Queer Latino America*. New York: New York UP, 2000. 191–226. Print.

---. "Tears at the Nightclub." In *Tropics of Desire: Interventions from Queer Latino America*. New York: New York UP, 2000. 145–68. Print.

Quiroga, José, and Melanie López Frank. "Cultural Production of Knowledge on Latina/o Sexualities." *Latina/o Sexualities: Probing Powers, Passions, Practices, and Policies*. Ed. Marysol Asencio. New Brunswick, NJ: Rutgers UP, 2010. 137-49. Print.

Ramírez, John. "The Chicano Homosocial Film: Mapping the Discourses of Sex and Gender in *American Me*." *PRE/TEXT: A Journal of Rhetorical Theory* 16.3-4 (1995): 260-74. Print.

Rechy, John. *Beneath the Skin: The Collected Essays of John Rechy*. New York: Carroll & Graf, 2004. Print.

---. *Bodies and Souls: A Novel*. New York: Carroll & Graf, 1983. Print.

---. *City of Night*. New York: Grove, 1963. Print.

---. *The Coming of the Night*. New York: Grove, 1999. Print.

---. *This Day's Death: A Novel*. New York: Grove, 1969. Print.

---. *The Fourth Angel*. New York: Viking, 1973. Print.

---. *The Life and Adventures of Lyle Clemens*. New York: Grove, 2003. Print.

---. "Love in the Backrooms." *Men on Men 4: Best New Gay Fiction*. Ed. George Stombolian. New York: Plume, 1992. 10-18. Print.

---. *Marilyn's Daughter: A Novel*. New York: Carroll & Graf, 1988. Print.

---. *The Miraculous Day of Amalia Gomez*. New York: Arcade, 1991. Print.

---. *Numbers.* New York: Grove, 1994. Print.

---. "On Being a 'Grove Press Author.' " *The Review of Contemporary Fiction* 10.3 (1990): 137–42. Print.

---. *Our Lady of Babylon: A Novel.* New York: Arcade, 1996. Print.

---. "El Paso del Norte." *Evergreen Review* 2.6 (1958): 127–40. Print.

---. *Rushes: A Novel.* New York: Grove, 1979. Print.

---. *The Sexual Outlaw: A Documentary.* New York: Grove, 1977. Print.

---. *The Vampires.* New York: Grove, 1971. Print.

Reinhardt, Karl J. "The image of Gays in Chicano Prose Fiction." *Explorations in Ethnic Studies* 4.2 (1981): 41–55. Print.

Reyes, Alfonso. "Once cartas de Rubén Daréo a Amado Nervo." *La Pluma* I:3 (1920): 132–36. Print.

Reyes, Guillermo. *Deporting the Divas. Gestos* 14 (1999): 109–158. Print.

---. Men on the Verge of a His-panic Breakdown: A Play in Monologues. Woodstock, IL: Dramatic Publishing, 1999. Print.

---. "What I've Discovered." *Ollantay Theater Magazine* 2 (1997): 39. Print.

Reyes, Rodrigo. "Carnal Knowledge." *Ya Vas, Carnal.* San Francisco: Humanizarte, 1985. 8–9. Print.

---. "Latino Gays: Coming Out and Coming Home." *Nuestro* (April 1981): 44–45, 64. Print.

Reyes, Rodrigo, Francisco X. Alarcón, and Juan Pablo Gutiérrez. *Ya Vas, Carnal.* San Francisco: Humanizarte, 1985. Print.

Reyes, Yosimar. *For colored boys who speak softly.* N.p., n.p., 2009. Print.

---. "Silent No Longer," "For colored boys who speak softly," "Queer Aztlan," "R(e)Evolution," "Eres un Río (Un Poema Pa' un Poeta)" *Mariposas: A Modern Anthology of Queer Latino Poetry.* Ed. Emanuel Xavier. Mountain View, CA: Floricanto Press, 2008. 70-78. Print.

Rhodes, Scott. "Demonstrated Effectiveness and Potential of Community-Based Participatory Research for Preventing HIV in Latino Populations." *HIV Prevention with Latinos: Theory, Research, and Practice.* Ed. Kurt C. Organista. New York: Oxford UP, 2012. Print.

Rice, David. "Sinners Among Angels, or Family History and the Ethnic Narrator in Arturo Islas's *The Rain God* and *Migrant Souls*." *Lit: Literature Interpretation Theory* 11.2 (2000): 169–97. Print.

Ridinger, Robert B. Marks, ed. *The Homosexual and Society: An Annotated Bibliography.* Westport, CT: Greenwood, 1990. Print.

Rivera, Nayar. *El deshielo.* México, D.F.: Felou, 2011. Print.

---. *En la casa de la sal. Monografia, crónicas y leyendas de Iztacalco.* México, D.F.: Delegación Iztacalco, 2001. Print.

---. *Reglas de urbanidad.* México, D.F.: Quimera, 2008. Print.

Rivera, Tomas. "Richard Rodriguez' Hunger of Memory as Humanistic Antithesis." *MELUS* 11.4 (1984): 5–13. Print.

Rivera Colón, Edgar, Miguel Muñoz-Laboy, and Diana Hernández. "Clean Sweeps and Social Control in Latino Bisexual Male Sex Markets in New York City." *HIV Prevention with Latinos: Theory, Research, and Practice.* Ed. Kurt C. Organista. New York: Oxford UP, 2012. Print.

Rocha Osornio, Juan Carlos. "El *performance* del insulto en los albores de la novela mexicana de temática homosexual: *41 o el muchacho que soñaba en fantasmas* (1964) de Paolo Po." *Cincinnati Romance Review* 34 (2012): 97–111. Print.

Rodriguez, Antoine. "Homo-resistencias en México (1971–1988): Estrategias para salir de los sótanos clandestinos de la vida social." Paper delivered at the *Cultura y política en México, dos décadas de resistencia (1968–1988).* Université Charles de Gaulle-Lille 3, France, 14 Nov. 2009. Print.

Rodríguez, Oscar Eduardo. *El personaje gay en la obra de Luis Zapata.* México, D.F.: Fontamara, 2006. Print.

Rodríguez, Ralph E. *Brown Gumshoes: Detective Fiction and the Search for Chicana/o Identity.* Austin: U of Texas P, 2005. Print.

---. "A Poverty of Relations: On Not 'Making *Familia* from Scratch,' but Scratching *Familia*." *Velvet Barrios: Popular Culture & Chicana/o Sexualities.* Ed. Alicia Gaspar de Alba. New York: Palgrave Macmillan, 2003. 75–88. Print.

Rodriguez, Randy A. "Richard Rodriguez Reconsidered: Queering the Sissy (Ethnic) Subject." *Texas Studies in Language and Literature* 40.4 (1998): 396–423. Print.

Rodriguez, Richard. "Complexion." *Hunger of Memory: The Education of Richard Rodriguez, An Autobiography.* New York: Bantam, 1982. 113–39. Print.

---. *Days of Obligation: An Argument with My Mexican Father.* New York: Viking, 1992. Print.

---. *Hunger of Memory: The Education of Richard Rodriguez, An Autobiography.* New York: Bantam, 1982. Print.

---. "Late Victorians: San Francisco, AIDS, and the Homosexual Stereotype." *Harper's Magazine* (Oct. 1990): 57–66. Print.

---. "Masculinity, Femininity, and Homosexuality: On the Anthropological Interpretation of Sexual Meanings in Brazil." *Blackwood* (1991): 155–64. Print.

---. "Sodom: Reflections on a Stereotype." *Image* [Sunday Supplement to *San Francisco Examiner*] 10 June 1990: 11–16. Print.

Rodriguez, Richard A. "A Qualitative Study of Identity Development in Gay Chicano Males." Diss. U of Utah, 1991. Print.

Rodríguez, Richard T. "Carnal Knowledge: Chicano Gay Men and the Dialectics of Being." *Gay Latino Studies: A Critical Reader.* Ed. Michael Hames-García and Ernesto J. Martínez. Durham, NC: Duke UP, 2011. 113–40. Print.

---. "Imagine a Brown Queer: Inscribing Sexuality in Chicano/a Latino/a Literary and Cultural Studies." *American Quarterly* 59.2 (2007): 493–501. Print.

---. *Next of Kin: The Family in Chicano/a Cultural Politics.* Durham, NC: Duke UP, 2009. Print.

---. "Queering the Homeboy Aesthetic." *Aztlán: A Journal of Chicano Studies* 31.2 (2006): 127–37. Print.

---. "Serial Kinship: Representing la Familia in Early Chicano Publications." *Aztlán: A Journal of Chicano Studies* 27.1 (2002): 123–38. Print.

---. "The Verse of the Godfather: Signifying Family and Nationalism in Chicano Rap and Hip-Hop Culture." *Velvet Barrios: Popular Culture & Chicana/o Sexualities.* Ed. Alicia Gaspar de Alba. New York: Palgrave Macmillan, 2003. 107–22. Print.

Rodríguez Cetina, Raúl. *El desconocido.* México, D.F.: Plaza y Valdés, 2007. Print.

---. *Flash back.* México, D.F. Premiá, 1982. Print.

Rodriguez Kessler, Elizabeth. "Searching for Sexual Identity in a Homophobic Society: *Hunger of Memory* and *Pocho.*" *Beginning a New Millennium of Chicana and Chicano Scholarship: Selected Proceedings of the 2001 NACCS Conference.* Ed. Jaima H. García. San Jose, CA: The Association, 2006. Print.

Román, David. *Acts of Intervention: Performance, Gay Culture, and AIDS.* Bloomington: Indiana UP, 1998. Print.

---. "Fierce Love and Fierce Response: Intervening in the Cultural Politics of Race, Sexuality, and AIDS." *The Journal of Homosexuality* 26.2–3 (1993): 195–219. Print.

---. "Latino Performance and Identity." *Aztlán: A Journal of Chicano Studies* 22.2 (1997): 151–68. Rpt. in *The Chicano Studies Reader: An Anthology of Aztlán, 1970-2000.* Ed. Noriega, Avila, Davalos, Sandoval, and Pérez-Torres. Los Angeles: UCLA Chicano Studies Research Center Publications, 2001. 386–401. Print.

---. Rev. of "Luis Alfaro's *Electricidad* and Euripides' *Hecuba.*" *Aztlán: A Journal of Chicano Studies* 31.1 (2006): 167–72. Print.

---. "¡Teatro Viva! Latino Performance and the Politics of AIDS in Los Angeles." *¿Entiendes? Queer Readings, Hispanic Writings.* Ed. Emilie L. Bergmann and Paul J. Smith. Durham, NC: Duke UP, 1995. 346–69. Print.

---. "Tropical Fruit." *Tropicalizations: Transcultural Representations of Latinidad (Re-encounters with Colonialism: New Perspectives on the Americas).* Ed. Frances R. Aparicio and Susana Chávez-Silverman. Hanover, NH: U of New England P, 1997. 119–38. Print.

Romo, Laura F., Erum Nadeem, and Claudia Kouyoumdjian. "Latina/o Parent-Adolescent Communication about Sexuality: An Interdisciplinary

Literature Review." *Latina/o Sexualities: Probing Powers, Passions, Practices, and Policies.* Ed. Marysol Asencio. New Brunswick, NJ: Rutgers UP, 2010. 62–74. Print.

Roque Ramírez, Horacio N. "Claiming Queer Cultural Citizenship: Gay Latino (Im)Migrant Acts in San Francisco." *Queer Migrations: Sexuality, U.S. Citizenship, and Border Crossings.* Ed. Eithne Luibhéid and Lionel Cantú, Jr. Minneapolis: U of Minnesota P, 2005. 161–88. Print.

---. "Communities of Desire: Queer Latina/Latino History and Memory, San Francisco Bay Area, 1960s-1990s." Diss. U of California, 2001. Print.

---. "Rodrigo Reyes." *The Encyclopedia of Lesbian, Gay, Bisexual and Transgender History in America.* Vol. 3. Ed. Marc Stein. New York: Charles Scribner's Sons/Thomson/Gale, 2004. Print.

---. "'That's My Place': Negotiating Racial, Sexual, and Gender Politics in San Francisco's Gay Latino Alliance, 1975–1983." *Journal of the History of Sexuality* 12.2 (2003): 224–58. Print.

Rose, Shirley K. "Metaphors of Myths of Cross-Cultural Literacy: Autobiographical Narratives by Maxine Hong Kingston, Richard Rodriguez, and Malcolm X." *Melus* 14.12 (1987): 3–15. Print.

Ruiz, Ariel. "Raza, Sexo y Politica en *Short Eyes* by Miguel Pinero." *Americas Review* 15.2 (1987): 93–102. Print.

Saalfield, Catherine, and Ray Navarro. "Not Just Black and White: AIDS, Media and People of Color." *Centro Bulletin* 2.8 (1990): 70-79. Print.

Salazar, Severino. "También hay inviernos fértiles." *Las aguas derramadas.* Xalapa, Ver.: Universidad Veracruzana, 1986. 31–49. Print.

Saldívar, José David. "Remapping American Cultural Studies." *The Chicana/o Cultural Studies Reader.* Ed. Angie Chabram-Dernersesian. New York: Routledge, 2006. 472–91. Print.

Saldívar, Ramón. *Chicano Narrative: The Dialectics of Difference.* Madison: U of Wisconsin P, 1990. Print.

Sánchez, Marta E. "Arturo Islas' *The Rain God*: An Alternative Tradition." *American Literature* 62.2 (1990): 284–304. Print.

Sanchez, Rosaura. "Calculated Musings: Richard Rodriguez's Metaphysics of Difference." *The Ethnic Canon: Histories, Institutions, and Interventions.*

Ed. David Palumbo-Liu. Minneapolis: U of Minnesota P, 1995. 153–73. Print.

Sandoval, Alberto. "Staging AIDS: What's Latinos Got To Do With It?" *Negotiating Performance: Gender, Sexuality, and Theatricality in Latina/o America.* Ed. Diana Taylor and Juan Villegas. Durham, NC: Duke UPg, 1994. 49–66. Print.

Sandoval, Chela. *Methodology of the Oppressed.* Minneapolis: U of Minnesota P, 2000. Print.

Sandoval, Lito. "I Love You Alto." *Virgins, Guerrillas, and Locas: Gay Latinos Writing about Love.* San Francisco: Cleis, 1999. 27–30. Print.

Sandoval, Trino, Daniel E. Pérez, and Guillermo A. Reyes. *Borders on Stage: Plays Produced by Teatro Bravo.* Phoenix: The Lion & The Seagoat, 2008. Print.

Santiago Ramírez, Enrique Guarner, and Isabel Díaz Portillo. *Un homosexual, sus sueños.* México, D.F.: Universidad Nacional Autónoma de México, Facultad de Psicología, 1983. Print.

Satterfield, Ben. "John Rechy's Tormented World." *Southwest Review* 67.1 (1982): 78–85. Print.

Schaefer-Rodriguez, Claudia. *Danger Zones: Homosexuality, National Identity, and Mexican Culture.* Tucson: U of Arizona P, 1996. Print.

---. "Latin America, Sexualities, and Our Discontents." *Latin American Research Review* 40.3 (Oct. 2005): 230-43. Print.

---. "The Power of Subversive Imagination: Homosexual Utopian Discourse in Contemporary Mexican Literature." *Latin American Literary Review* 33 (1989): 29–41. Print.

Schantz, Eric. "Meretricious Mexicali: Exalted Masculinities and the Crafting of Male Desire in a Border Red-Light District, 1908–1925." *Masculinity and Sexuality in Modern Mexico.* Ed. Victor M. Macías-González and Anne Rubenstein. Albuquerque: U of New Mexico P, 2012. 101–31. Print.

Schlit, Paige. "Anti-Pastoral and Guilty Vision in Richard Rodriguez's *Days of Obligation." Texas Studies in Language and Literature* 40.4 (1998): 424–41. Print.

Schneider, Luis Mario. *La novela mexicana entre el petróleo, la homosexualidad y la política*. México, D.F.: Nueva Imágen, 1997. Print.

---. "El tema homosexual en la nueva narrativa mexicana." *Casa del tiempo* 49–50 (1985): 82–86. Print.

Schuessler, Michael K., y Miguel Capistrán, coordinadores. *México se escribe con J: Una historia de la cultura gay*. México, D.F: Planeta, 2010. Print.

---. "Vestidas, locas, mayates y machos." *México se escribe con J: Una historia de la cultura gay*. México, D.F.: Planeta, 2010. Print.

Schulz-Cruz, Bernard. *Imágenes gay en el cine mexicano. Tres décadas de jotería 1970-1999*. México, D.F.: Fontamara, 2008. Print.

Serna, Enrique. *Amores de segunda mano*. Xalapa, Ver.: Universidad Veracruzana, 1991. Print.

---. "El alimento del artista." *Amores de segunda mano*. Xalapa, Ver.: Universidad Veracruzana, 1991. Print.

---. *Fruta verde*. México, D.F.: Planeta, 2006. Print.

---. "Hombre con minotauro en el pecho." *Amores de segunda mano*. Xalapa, Ver.: Universidad Veracruzana, 1991. 49–73. Print.

Shilts, Randy. "Media Star." *The Mayor of Castro Street: The Life & Times of Harvey Milk*. New York: St. Martin's, 1982. 189–210. Print.

Sigal, Pete. "The *Cuiloni*, the *Patlache*, and the Abominable Sin: Homosexualities in Early Colonial Nahua Society." *Hispanic American Historical Review* 85.4 (2005): 555–93. Print.

---. "Gender, Male Homosexuality, and Power in Colonial Yucatán." *Latin American Perspectives* 29.2 (2002): 24–40. Print.

---. *Infamous Desire: Male Homosexuality in Colonial Latin America*. Chicago: U of Chicago P, 2003. Print.

---. "Queer Nahuatl: Sahagún's Faggots and Sodomites, Lesbians and Hermaphrodites." *Ethnohistory* 54.1 (2007): 9–34. Print.

Skjerdal, Kristi, Shiraz I. Mishra, and Sandra Benavides-Vaello. "A Growing HIV/AIDS Crisis Among Migrant and Seasonal Farmworker Families." *AIDS Crossing Borders: The Spread of HIV Among Migrant Latinos*. Ed. Mishra, Conner, and Magaña. Boulder, CO: Westview, 1996. 27–48. Print.

Solis, Genaro. *La máscara de cristal.* México, D.F.: Costa-Amic, 1973. Print.

Soto, Sandra. "Américo Paredes and the De-Mastery of Desire." *Reading Chican@ Like a Queer.* Austin: U of Texas P, 2010. 87–120. Print.

---. "Fixing Up the House of Race with Richard Rodriguez." *Reading Chican@ Like a Queer.* Austin: U of Texas P, 2010. 39–58. Print.

Staten, Henry. "Ethnic Authenticity, Class, and Autobiography: The Case of *Hunger of Memory.*" *PLMA* 113.1 (1998): 103–16. Print.

Stavans, Ilán. *The Hispanic Condition: Reflections on Culture and Identity in America.* 2nd ed. New York: HarperCollins, 2001. Print.

---. "The Journey of Richard Rodriguez." *Commonweal* 120.6 (26 Mar. 1993): 20-22. Print.

---. "The Latin Phallus." *Muy Macho: Latino Men Confront Their Manhood.* Ed Ray González. New York: Doubleday, 1996. 143–64. Print.

Sternad, Jennifer Flores. "Cyclona and Early Chicano Performance Art: An Interview with Robert Legorreta." *GLQ: A Journal of Lesbian and Gay Studies* 12.3 (2006): 475–90. Print.

Sullivan, Edward J. "Nahum Zenil's Auto-Iconography ('Mexican-ness' in Mexican Painting of the Eighties)." *Arts Magazine,* Nov. 1988, 86–91. Print.

Sullivan, Edward J., Agustín Arteaga, and Cristina Pacheco. *Nahum Zenil: Witness to the Self.* San Francisco: Mexican Museum, 1996. Print.

Tatum, Charles M. "The Sexual Underworld of John Rechy." *Minority Voices* 3.1 (1979): 47–52. Print.

Taylor, Clark. "El Ambiente: Male Homosexual Social Life in Mexico City." Diss. U of California, 1978. Print.

Taylor, Clark L. "How Mexicans Define Male Homosexuality." *The Kroeber Anthropological Society Papers* 53/54 (1976): 106–28. Print.

---. "Mexican Gaylife in Historial Perspective." *Gay Sunshine: A Journal of Gay Liberation* 26/27 (Winter): 1–3. Print.

---. "Mexican Male Homosexual Interaction in Public Contexts." *Journal of Homosexuality* 11.3 (1986): 117–36. Print.

---. Rev. of *Adonis Garcia: A Picaresque Novel,* by Luis Zapata. *Gay Sunshine* 46 (1981–82): 4. Print.

Taylor, Diana, and Juan Villegas, eds. *Negotiating Performance: Gender, Sexuality, and Theatricality in Latina/o America*. Ed. Diana Taylor and Juan Villegas. Durham, NC: Duke UP, 1994. Print.

Teichman, Reinhard. *De la onda en adelante: Conversaciones con 21 novelistas mexicanos*. México, D.F: Posada, 1987. Print.

---. "Entrevista con Luis Zapata." *De la onda en adelante: Conversaciones con 21 novelistas mexicanos*. México, D.F: Posada, 1987. 353–74. Print.

Téllez-Pon, Sergio. *Poesía Homoerótica*. México, D.F.: Alforja, 2006. Print.

Teruel, Alberto X. *Los inestables*. México, D.F.: Costa-Amic, 1968. Print.

Thomas, Raul. "They Say I'm One of Those." *Virgins, Guerrillas, and Locas: Gay Latinos Writing about Love*. San Francisco: Cleis, 1999. 33–46. Print.

Thompson, David. "Outlawed: The Sexual Outlaw." Rev. of *The Sexual Outlaw* by John Rechy. *Gay Left: A Gay Socialist Journal* 8 (1979): 36. Print.

Tilden, Norma. "Word Made Flesh: Richard Rodriguez's 'Late Victorians' as Nativity Story." *Texas Studies in Language and Literature* 40.4 (1998): 442–59. Print.

Torres, Hector A. "'I Don't Think I Exist': Interview with Richard Rodriguez." *MELUS* 28.2 (2003): 165–202. Print.

Torres, Víctor Federico. "Del escarnio a la celebración: Prosa mexicana del siglo XX." *México se escribe con J: Una historia de la cultura gay*. México, D.F.: Planeta, 2010. Print.

Torres-Ortiz, Víctor F. *Transgresión y ruptura en la narrativa de Luis Zapata*. Diss. U of New Mexico, 1997. Print.

Torres-Rosado, Santos. "Canon and Innovation in *Adonis García: A Picaresque Novel*." *Revista monográfica* 7 (1991): 276–83. Print.

Trexler, Richard. *Sex and Conquest: Gendered Violence, Political Order and the European Conquest of the Americas*. Ithaca, NY: Cornell UP, 1995. Print.

The Uniting American Families Act: Addressing Inequality in Federal Immigration Law: Hearing Before the Committee on the Judiciary, United States Senate, One Hundred Eleventh Congress, First Session, 3 June 2009. Washington: U.S. G.P.O., 2010. Print.

Urquijo-Ruiz, Rita E. "Comfortably Queer: The Chicano Gay Subject in Dan Guerrero's ¡Gaytino!" *Ollantay Theatre Magazine* 25.29–30 (2007): 147–67. Print.

---. *Wild Tongues Transnational Mexican Popular Culture*. Austin: U of Texas P, 2012. Print.

Valdemar, Carlos. *Cielo tormentoso*. México, D.F.: Costa-Amic, 1971. Print.

Valdés, Francisco. "Notes on the Conflation of Sex, Gender, and Sexual Orientation: A QueerCrit and LatCrit Perspective." *The Latino Condition: A Critical Reader*. Ed. Richard Delgado and Jean Stefancic. New York: New York UP, 1998. 543–51. Print.

Valenzuela Arce, José Manuel. *A La Brava, Ese*. Tijuana: Colegio de la Frontera Norte, 1988. Print.

Vargas, Deborah R. "Representations of Latina/o Sexuality in Popular Culture." *Latina/o Sexualities: Probing Powers, Passions, Practices, and Policies*. Ed. Marysol Asencio. New Brunswick, NJ: Rutgers UP, 2010.117–36. Print.

Vega, Manuel de Jesús. "Chicano, Gay, and Doomed: AIDS in Arturo Islas' *The Rain God*." *Confluencia: Revista Hispanica de Cultura y Literatura* 11.2 (1996): 112–18. Print.

Vidal-Ortiz, Salvador. "Religion/Spirituality, U.S. Latina/o Communities, and Sexuality Scholarship: A Thread of Current Works." *Latina/o Sexualities: Probing Powers, Passions, Practices, and Policies*. Ed. Marysol Asencio. New Brunswick, NJ: Rutgers UP, 2010. 173–87. Print.

Vidal-Ortiz, Salvador, Carlos Decena, Héctor Carrillo, and Tomás Almaguer. "Revisiting *Activos* and *Pasivos*: Toward New Cartographies of Latino/ Latin American Male Same-Sex Desire." *Latina/o Sexualities: Probing Powers, Passions, Practices, and Policies*. Ed. Marysol Asencio. New Brunswick, NJ: Rutgers UP, 2010. 253–73. Print.

Viego, Antonio. "The Place of Gay Male Chicano Literature in Queer Chicana/o Cultural Work." *Discourse: Journal for Theoretical Studies in Media and Culture* 21.3 (1999): 111–31. Print.

Villalobos, Hugo. *Jacinto de Jesús*. México, D.F.: Fontamara, 2001. Print.

Villalón, Joel Antonio. "Awakened from Their Dreams." *Bésame Mucho.* Ed. Jaime Manrique and Jesse Dorris. New York: Painted Leaf, 1999. 139–45. Print.

---. "Boots." *Virgins, Guerrillas, and Locas: Gay Latinos Writing about Love.* San Francisco: Cleis, 1999. 13–26. Print.

Villanueva-Collado, Alfredo. "Growing Up Hispanic: Discourse and Ideology in *Hunger of Memory* and *Family Installments.*" *Americas Review* 16.3–4 (1988): 75–90. Print.

Villarreal José, Antonio. *Pocho: A Novel.* New York: Doubleday, 1959. Print.

Villarruel, Antonia M., Vincent Guilamo-Ramos, and Jose Bauermeister. "Reducing HIV Sexual Risk for Latino Adolescents: An Ecodevelopmental Perspective." *HIV Prevention with Latinos: Theory, Research, and Practice.* Ed. Kurt C. Organista. New York: Oxford UP, 2012. Print.

Villaurrutia, Xavier. *Antología.* Selección y prólogo de Octavio Paz. México, D.F.: Fondo de Cultura Económica, 1980. Print.

---. *Cartas De Villaurrutia a Novo, 1935–1936.* México, D.F.: Instituto Nacional de Bellas Artes, Departamento de Literatura, 1966. Print.

---. *Homesick for Death: Dead Nocturnes: The Complete Poems of Xavier Villaurrutia.* Trans. Drew McCord Stroud. San Francisco: Saru, 2004. Print.

---. *Nostalgia de la muerte: Poemas y teatro.* México, D.F.: Secretaría de Educación Pública, Cultura SEP, 1984. Print.

---. *Obra Poética/Xavier Villaurrutia.* Edición crítica y estudio introductorio de R. García Gutiérrez. Madrid: Hiperión, 2006. Print.

---. *Obras: Poesía, Teatro, Prosas Varias, Crítica.* México, D.F.: Fondo de Cultura Económica, 1974. Print.

---. *Xavier Villaurrutia, 1903–2003, 100 Años: Homenaje.* Guadalajara, México, D.F.: Paraíso Perdido, 2003. Print.

---. *Xavier Villaurrutia: … Y mi voz que madura.* Roxana Elvridge-Thomas, compiladora. México, D.F: CONACULTA, 2003. Print.

Waugh, Thomas. "The Kiss of the Maricón, or Gay Imagery in Latin American Cinema." *The Fruit Machine: Twenty Years of Writings on Queer Cinema.* Durham, NC: Duke UP, 2000. 172–86. Print.

Wesley, Andrew. "Gay, Lesbian Latinos Hold First Meeting." *The Advocate* Oct. 1981:9. Print.

Westcott, Gloria. "Interview: Francisco X. Alarcón." *Tiempo Latino*. (5 July 1989). Print.

Westmoreland, Maurice. "Camp in the Works of Luis Zapata." *Modern Language Studies* 25.2 (1995): 45–59. Print.

Wolf, Sara. "Luis Alfaro, the Pulse of L.A." *American Theater* 14.9 (1997): 52–54. Print.

Wolford, Lisa. "Introduction to Gómez-Peña." *Extreme Exposure*. Ed. Jo Bonnie. New York: Theatre Communications Group, 2000. 276–77. Print.

Woods, Richard D. "Richard Rodriguez (31 July 1944–)." *Dictionary of Literary Biography*. Vol. 80. *Chicano Writers: First Series*. Ed. Francisco Lomelí and Carl R. Shirley. Detroit: Gale, 1989. 165–77. Print.

Xavier, Emmanuel. *Mariposas: A Modern Anthology of Queer Latino Poetry*. Mountain View, CA: Floricanto, 2008. Print.

"Xochipilli." *Cassell's Encyclopedia of Queer Myth, Symbol, and Spirit: Gay, Lesbian, Bisexual, and Transgender Lore*. Ed. Conner, Sparks, and Sparks. Forward by Gloria Anzaldúa. London: Cassell, 1997. 351. Print.

Ybarra-Frausto, Tomás. "The Chicano Movement and the Emergence of a Chicano Poetic Consciousness." *New Scholar* 6 (1977): 81–109. Print.

———. "Rasquachismo: A Chicano Sensibility." *Chicano Art: Resistance and Affirmation, 1965–85*. Ed. Griswold del Castillo, McKenna, and Yarbro-Bejarano. Los Angeles: Wright Art Gallery, 1991. 155–62. Print.

Zamora, Carlos. "Odysseus in John Rechy's *City of Night*: The Epistemological Journey." *Minority Voices* 3.1 (1979): 53–62. Print.

Zamora, Rodolfo. "The Lost City." *Virgins, Guerrillas, and Locas: Gay Latinos Writing about Love*. San Francisco: Cleis, 1999. 59–64. Print.

Zamostny, Jeffrey S. "Comings Out: Secrecy, Sexuality, and Murder in Michael Nava's *Rag and Bone*." *MELUS* 34.3 (2009): 183–204. Print.

Zapata, Luis. *Adonis García: A Picaresque Novel*. San Francisco: Gay Sunshine, 1981. Print.

———. *Las aventuras, desventuras y sueños de Adonis García: El vampiro de la colonia Roma*. 1979. México, D.F.: Grijalbo, 1996. Print.

---. *De amor es mi negra pena.* México, D.F.: Panfleto y Pantomima, 1983. Print.

---. *De cuerpo entero.* México, D.F.: UNAM, 1990. Print.

---. *De pétalos perennes.* México, D.F.: Katún, 1981. Print.

---. *En jirones.* México, D.F.: Posada, 1985. Print.

---. *Ese amor que hasta ayer nos quemaba.* México, D.F.: Posada, 1989. Print.

---. *Hasta en las mejores familias.* México, D.F.: Novaro, 1975. Print.

---. *La hermana secreta de Angélica María.* México, D.F.: Cal y Arena, 1989. Print.

---. *La historia de siempre.* México, D.F.: Quimera, 2007. Print.

---. *La más fuerte pasión.* México, D.F.: Océano, 1995. Print.

---. *Melodrama.* México, D.F.: Quimera, 1983. Print.

---. *Paisaje con amigos: un viaje al occidente de México.* México, D.F.: CONACULTA, 1995. Print.

---. *¿Por qué mejor no nos vamos?* México, D.F.: Aguilar, Léon y Cal, 1992. Print.

---. *Los postulados del buen golpista.* México, D.F: Cal y Arena, 1995. Print.

---. *Siete noches junto al mar.* México, D.F.: Colibrí. 1999. Print.

---. *The Strongest Passion.* Mountain View, CA: Floricanto, 2006. Print.

Zea, Maria Cecilia, Carol A. Reisen, Fernanda T. Bianchi, and Paul J. Poppen. "Contextual Influences of Sexual Risk among Latino MSM." *HIV Prevention with Latinos: Theory, Research, and Practice.* Ed. Kurt C. Organista. New York: Oxford UP, 2012. Print.

Zimmerman, M.A., J. Ramirez-Valles, E. Suarez, G. de la Rosa, and M.A. Castro. "An HIV/AIDS Prevention Project for Mexican Homosexual Men: An Empowerment Approach." *Health, Education and Behavior.* 24.2 (1997): 177–90. Print.

Contributors

Aarón Aguilar-Ramírez

Aarón is a student in college at the time of this contribution's writing, fascinated by discourses of identity and distressed by those of closets and coming out.

Raúl al-qaraz Ochoa

Raúl is originally born in Jalisco, México 27 years ago to two loving parents. Raúl believes in the power of flower and song (flor y canto). He grew up in Richmond, California where his struggles as a migrant child fueled his passion for social justice and community power. Raúl has organized around educational justice, youth power, queer justice and migrant rights issues. Thanks to those who struggled before him during the Third World Liberation Front strike of 1968 at San Francisco State University, he was able to study in the Raza Studies Department. In 2006, Raúl left life and work in the Bay Area to live in the desert/ borderland of Tucson, Arizona where he currently organizes for community and migrant liberation. He works with migrant families and youth *dedicadandose a la concientización, organización y movilización de nuestro pueblo para algún día llegar a vivir libres*. Evident through his insurgent-style poetry and radical blogging journalism, Raúl imagines a world free of borders and oppression and continuously struggles towards creating "a world where many worlds fit."

Eddy F. Alvarez

Eddy F. Alvarez was raised in North Hollywood, California by his mother Ramona, from Ensenada, Baja California, México and by Eddy Francisco Sr., from Havana, Cuba. He has two sisters Gabriela and Patricia. He received his Bachelor's and Master's degrees in Spanish from California State University, Northridge. He holds a Master's in Chicana and Chicano Studies from the University of California at Santa Barbara where he is currently a doctoral candidate also in Chicana and Chicano Studies with a Feminist Studies emphasis. While in graduate school at UCSB, he was a member of W.O.R.D., Women of Color Revolutionary Dialogues and Yolotl de Papalotl, collectives of women and queer people of color who practiced healing and transformation through writing, dialogue and spoken word. He has taught at CSUN, UCSB, and California, State University, Fullerton. He is a practitioner of SWAPA or Spoken-Word-Art-Performance-As-Activism. He writes to archive, to heal, to love and to leave a legacy for his jotería and for his niece, Gabriela Tatiana, his nephews Julian and Nicolás and his *ahijada* Tatiana Williams.

Pablo Alvarez

Pablo Alvarez is a first generation Chicano from the city of Pico Rivera, California. He holds a BA in English and Human Development from Cal State Long Beach and an MA in Chicana/o Studies from California State University, Northridge. He is a member of Writers at Work, Los Angeles.

Edgar-Arturo Camacho-González

Edgar-Arturo is a Queer Xicano activist and poet originario de Jalisco, México. He is currently a substance abuse counselor. He is grateful to have Guillermina González and Francisco Camacho as parents and the support of his siblings Francisco, Alvaro, Alex, and Claudia. He writes as a form of expression and activism toward deconstructing the inevitability of social tensions. Edgar has utilized his ability to touch others through his art to engage his communities. He is committed to liberation through art, Edgar pens through a de-colonial lens that is fueled by one of his mother's lessons: "Te hice de fierro y no de madera." Edgar was the recipient of the 2009 Mr. Gay Latino title in the San Francisco Bay Area. He resides in Napa, California.

Vincent D. Cervantes

I am a queer Chicano writer, scholar and graduate student at Harvard University, my research and writing have been dedicated to exploring the intersections of religion, gender, and culture. My hope is that through my work and testimony of experiences, I can present a critical witness to incite others to speak proudly and openly about their own brown jotería experiences.

Gil Cuadros

Gil Cuadros (1962–1996) was a Los Angeles writer and activist. He studied at East L.A. College and Pasadena Community College. From 1988 until 1995 he was a participant in Terry Wolverton's writing workshop for people with AIDS at the Los Angeles Gay and Lesbian Center. One of the first Chicanos to document a critical time in Los Angeles during the AIDS pandemic of the 1990s, his poetry and short stories have been published in *His 2, Indivisible, Blood Whispers,* and *Persistent Voices,* and on compact disc, *Verdict and the Violence: Poets' Response to the L.A. Uprising.* A collection of his writing, *City of God,* was published in 1994 by City Lights Books. Among his awards are the 1991 Brody Literature Fellowship and the PEN Center USA/West grant for writers with HIV, of which he was one of the first recipients. "Coming Out" and "Last Supper" are published for the first time with the permission of his estate.

Ernest Doring

I have lived in San Diego with my partner for the past 6 years having previously lived in Alexandria, Virginia. I am deeply honored to write and share my story with those who may come across it. I hope the young man or woman who reads it can gain from it. In light of recent bullying and immigration policies mostly directed toward Latinos, many of us may believe that we are second-class citizens or not worthy enough. Far from it! We were created in God's spirit. Take from my story what you wish and discard the rest. May your lives be full of peace, love, and tolerance ... and yes, "si se puede."

Xuan Carlos Espinoza-Cuellar

Xuan Carlos is a third world xueer/ista, indigenista, mexican@, xingon/a!, activista, izquierdista, radical, proud GORDA! intelectuala, estudiante, poeta y bruja. A xueer who believes in social justice, a pansexual jot@ *que cree* that poetry has the potential to revolutionize the world, *cada palabra* is a spark of consciousness, *cada poema una transformacion profunda.* his performance ranges from cabaret to slam poetry. His vision is one of reclaiming art from and to the margins,

dignifying our forms of expression and use laughter to heal and inter-
rupt/resist oppression and exploitation.

Omar O. González

Omar, a native of El Paso, Texas, earned a B.A. and an M.A. in Chicana and
Chicano Studies at California State University, Northridge. Currently, he
is part of the historic first cohort of the Ph.D. program in Chicana and
Chicano Studies at University of California at Los Angeles and teaches
at California State University, Northridge and East Los Angeles College.
His research interests include examining the intersection of queer and
Chicana/o identity, queer Chicano literature, Chicano masculinities,
Chicana/o literacy, recovering our indigenous memories, and queer
indigenous spiritual practices. A twenty-plus year survivor of HIV, Omar
works toward eradicating the stigma of HIV in the Chicana/o community. Finally, Omar credits the work of John Rechy as his inspiration for
his academic and activist pursuits.

Rigoberto González

Rigoberto is the author of eight books, most recently of the young
adult novel, *The Mariposa Club*, and a story collection, *Men without
Bliss*. The recipient of Guggenheim and NEA fellowships, winner of the
American Book Award, and The Poetry Center Book Award, he writes a
Latino book column for the *El Paso Times* of Texas. He is contributing
editor for *Poets and Writers Magazine*, on the Board of Directors of the
National Book Critics Circle, and is Associate Professor of English at
Rutgers – Newark, State University of New Jersey.

Lorenzo Herrera y Lozano

Lorenzo is a queer Xicano writer of Rarámuri descent born in San José, CA and raised in Estación Adela, Chihuahua. A St. Edward's University Masters of Liberal Arts graduate, he is the author of *Santo de la Pata Alzada: Poems from the Queer/Xicano/Positive Pen* (Evelyn Street Press), editor of Queer Codex: Chile Love and Queer Codex: ROOTED! (both *allgo*/Evelyn Street Press), as well as the forthcoming *Joto: An Anthology of Queer Chicano Poetry* (Kórima Press). A member of the Macondo Writing Workshop, his work also appears in *Mariposas: A Modern Anthology of Queer Latino Poetry* (Floricanto Press), *ZYZZYVA: The Journal of West Coast Writers and Artists,* and *Yellow Medicine Review: A Journal of Indigenous Literature, Art, and Thought.*

Emmanuelle Neza Leal-Santillan

Emmanuelle "Neza" Leal-Santillan is a Queer Xicano-Indígena poet, performer, and organizer. He was born en el pueblo de Villa Union in Durango, Mexico and grew up in Las Vegas, Nevada. Neza's work speaks to the queer, jot@, undocumented, two-spirited, chunti, and immigrant experience. He is a founding member of La MariColectiva, a performance troupe of fierce jotas. Neza counts the works of Gloria Anzaldua, Cherríe Moraga, and Adelina Anthony as his greatest influences. He currently lives in Albuquerque, NM where he writes, organizes and farms to his hearts content.

Carlos Manuel

Carlos Manuel is the Director of the Theatre Program at Bellarmine University in Louisville, KY. As a playwright, Carlos tries to bring strength, awareness, hope, and laughter with his plays. Carlos Manuel has recently published his play *La Vida Loca*. His personal experiences as an immigrant and as a joto are shared in his writings with all Jot@s because their voices matter.

Mario Martinez

Mario Martinez is 24 years old and originally from Los Angeles, California. He is currently enrolled at San Diego Community College. His intended major is in Forensic Psychology where he wishes to pursue a career as a Social Worker or Health Educator. Mario has been in a serodiscordant relationship where he and his partner are very content with their lives.

Michael Nava

Michael Nava is the author of an acclaimed series of seven crime novels featuring a gay Latino criminal defense lawyer named Henry Rios. He is also co-author of the book *Created Equal: Why Gay Rights Matter to America*. Currently he is writing a series of historical novels set in Mexico, the Arizona–Mexican border, and Hollywood between 1895 and 1929. He can be reached via his website: http://michaelnavawriter. com.

Daniel Enrique Pérez

Daniel Enrique is associate professor of Chicana/o-Latina/o studies and a faculty associate of the Gender, Race, and Identity Studies Program at the University of Nevada, Reno. His research focuses on the intersections of gender, ethnicity, and sexuality in Chicana/o and Latina/o cultural production. In addition to his book *Rethinking*

Chicana/o and Latina/o Popular Culture (Palgrave Macmillan, 2009), he has published several essays related to Jotería studies and is the editor of two anthologies of plays.

Yosimar Reyes

Yosimar was born in Guerrero, Mexico, a Two-Spirit Poet/Activist based in San Jose, California. He holds the title for the 2005 and 2006 South Bay Teen Grand SLAM Champion. He has been featured in the Documentary 2nd Verse: The Rebirth of Poetry. His work is included in *Mariposas: A Modern Anthology of Queer Latino Poetry* (Floricanto Press, 2008).

Roberto Rodriguez

Roberto was born and raised in San Francisco. He received his undergraduate training at the University of California, Davis in the fields of Spanish and Economics. After having worked in social services, he wishes to pursue a career in healthcare, as a nurse practitioner and is currently working towards that goal in San Diego. He loves his mama.

Luis H. Román Garcia

Luis Roman is a queer Chicano immigrant from a ranchito in rural Jalisco, Mexico. At the age of four, Luis and his family immigrated to California and lived in Lincoln Heights, an Asian & Latino barrio in Los Angeles. Luis studied Chicana/o Studies & Women's Studies at UCLA. He currently lives in Chicago completing a community integration civic engagement fellowship with Lambda Legal and the Illinois Coalition for Immigrant and Refugee Rights.

Luis Alberto Salazar

Luis was born and raised in the Imperial Valley, El Centro and Calexico respectively. He has been working for the betterment of humanity for the better part of 19 years. He currently calls San Diego home and would like every eligible man to know he is single and welcomes applicants!

Raul Martin Serrano

Raul Martin Serrano is a writer and filmmaker living in New York City.

About the Editors

Adelaida R. Del Castillo

Adelaida received a PhD in anthropology from the University of California at Los Angeles. She is an Associate Professor in the Department of Chicana and Chicano Studies at San Diego State University, which she chaired from 2007-2010 representing its first woman chair since the formation of the department in 1970. A student activist in the Chicana feminist movement of early 70s, she published, while an undergraduate, one of the first historical treatments on La Malinche from a Chicana feminist perspective. Since then she has edited anthologies on Chicana and Mexican women in the United States and published articles on gendered covert cultural norms in Mexico City, social citizenship among unauthorized immigrants in a postnational world, and cultural citizenship within the nation-state.

Gibrán Güido

Gibrán Güido was born in San Diego and raised in San Ysidro, California. He is currently a doctoral student in the Department of Literature with an emphasis in Cultural Studies. He completed his M.A. program in the department of Chicana and Chicano Studies at San Diego State University. His thesis, titled, "Navigating the Abyss: A Queer Chicano Semiotics of Love and Loss," represents spiritual activist and public intellectual work. The thesis is a scholarly exercise to comprehend how the process of writing about pain and loss permitted the recuperation of all aspects of self. Inspired by the work of Anzaldúa and Aztec iconography and philosophy, the thesis explores ways of writing about the queer Chicano subject in the face of despair and heartbreak.

While attending school he also worked in the field of HIV/AIDS prevention and counseling. In 2010 he organized the 5th Annual Queer People of Color Conference in San Diego at San Diego State University and co-organized the National Association for Chicana and Chicano Studies 3rd Jotería Conference held at the University of Oregon in Eugene, Oregon. In 2007, Gibrán graduated from the University of California, Davis with his Bachelor of Arts in Chicana/o Studies; Women and Gender Studies and minored in Sexuality Studies.

Index

A

C

D

G

M

CPSIA information can be obtained
at www.ICGtesting.com
Printed in the USA
LVOW07s1945250817
546396LV00001B/1/P